CURRENT TECHNIQUES IN ARCHITECTURAL PRACTICE

THE AMERICAN INSTITUTE
OF ARCHITECTS

ROBERT ALLAN CLASS, AIA
ROBERT E. KOEHLER, HON. AIA
EDITORS

Published jointly by
The American Institute
of Architects
Washington, D.C., and
Architectural Record Books
New York

Library of Congress Cataloging in Publication Data

Current techniques in architectural practice.

    Bibliography: p.
    Includes index.
    1. Architectural practice—Handbooks, manuals,
etc. I. Class, Robert Allan. II. Koehler,
Robert E.
NA1996.C87   658′.91′720973   76-5887
ISBN 0-07-002324-7

Administrative editors: Carole J. Jacobs and Martin Filler.
Designer: Marilyn Housell.
Jacket and binding designer: Peter Bradford.
Composition: Helvetica, by Monotype Composition Company.
Printing and binding: Halliday Lithographic Corporation.

Published jointly by
The American Institute of Architects
1735 New York Avenue, N.W.
Washington, D.C. 20006 and
Architectural Record,
A McGraw-Hill Publication,
1221 Avenue of the Americas,
New York, New York 10020

Contents

Foreword

The survival and advancement of architecture as an art and a science are dependent in large part on the ability of architects to conduct their practices as soundly run businesses.

The concept of management within an architectural firm is equally applicable to quality control of design solutions and their documentation, to project and office economics, to client satisfaction, and to the administration of the team responsible for producing good architecture. Competent management of a door detail is no less important than management of a firm's cash flow.

Because the overall management of an architectural practice entails the coordination of increasingly complex factors, it is critical that architects understand and use the tools and techniques made possible by advancements in management principles and various areas of technology. *Current Techniques in Architectural Practice* has been developed as a response to these needs. Its contributors have been carefully chosen for a clear mastery of their respective subject areas. This book constitutes the most comprehensive treatise now available on management of the architectural firm and the projects entrusted to architects.

LOUIS DE MOLL, FAIA
President, The American Institute
of Architects

Washington, D.C.
April 15, 1976

Preface

This book is about management. Its interrelated material emphasizes the most important techniques by which an architect may improve efficiency in practice management and communication. Initiated in the Department of Professional Practice of The American Institute of Architects, it is the latest in a planned series of practice-aids publications.

In 1966, The American Institute of Architects published the research report, *Emerging Techniques of Architectural Practice.* It served its purpose of opening new vistas by identifying many innovations developed by architects in their own practices. Two years ago, the AIA's Committee on Office Practice concluded that these techniques had become commonplace and recommended publishing a succeeding volume of more comprehensive and contemporary scope.

A four-month literature search of substantive material published on the pragmatic aspects of architectural practice turned up only scattered bits and pieces. This reinforced the decision to prepare all-new material and put it in one place. Successful practitioners were enlisted as contributing authors to share their firsthand experience. Coupled with further material drawn by the authors from their peers and a bibliography for additional reading, the book is intended to provide a comprehensive but not necessarily detailed knowledge of contemporary architectural practice. It covers today's business and tools of architecture plus something about tomorrow's.

Current Techniques in Architectural Practice has been developed as a cohesive volume, built around the professional organization and the external and internal forces which influence it. Part One examines various approaches to structuring an architectural firm and the methods of project delivery which affect the firm's organization and operation. Part Two is devoted to the firm's business management: basic management principles and the specific concerns of client relations, marketing and financial management as well as insurance management and personnel relations. Part Three deals with the handling of projects within the office: basic principles of project management and the techniques of budgeting and scheduling, programming, construction cost control and coping with building regulations. Part Four discusses many of the tools and processes used in management and production: office machines from copiers to computers, networks for scheduling, techniques for producing drawings and specifications. While the entire book is an information storehouse, the chapter on information resources delves into likely sources for initiating a specific data search and contains suggestions for organizing the data for later retrieval. The closing chapter explores trends in architectural practice to aid readers in planning for their future.

Those in practice or about to enter practice should draw the most benefit from this book. Architectural educators will find its content and arrangement most suitable as a teaching resource for courses in practice management. Engineers and allied professionals can identify many of the techniques as being equally applicable to their practices. And clients who retain architects can gain insight into the architectural process relative to their respective projects.

Duplication of material emanating from the AIA has been avoided for the most part. Although the editors have attempted to employ uniform terminology throughout the book to reduce confusion, some terms used by individual contributors are uniquely their own and do not appear in other chapters.

The editors and the profession are indebted to the contributing authors and other contributors listed on an accompanying page for sharing their extensive knowledge and to those who reviewed and encouraged this work. And special thanks to Lynn Dunning for the initial research and to Melissa Boyle for the word-processing effort.

Robert Allan Class, AIA
Robert E. Koehler, Hon. AIA
Editors

Contributors

ROBERT ALLAN CLASS, AIA. Director, Management Division, and Technical Director, The American Institute of Architects, Washington, D.C. Former principal, Martin, Stewart, Noble & Class, Philadelphia. Former president, Philadelphia Chapter AIA. Editor/contributor, *Compensation Management Guidelines for Architectural Services;* contributor, *Uniform Construction Index.* B. Arch., University of Pennsylvania, 1937.

Co-editor/administrator, *Current Techniques in Architectural Practice;* author, Chapter 1, "The Business and Tools of Architecture," and Chapter 20, "Trends in Architectural Practice"; co-author, Chapter 14, "Information Resources."

ROBERT E. KOEHLER, HON. AIA. Editor/writer, Washington, D.C. Former editor, *AIA Journal* and *Architecture/West.* Charter member and former director, Society of National Association Publications. Architectural contributor, *Parents Magazine Press Yearbook.* B.A., University of Wisconsin, 1948.

Co-editor, *Current Techniques in Architectural Practice.*

DAVID R. DIBNER, FAIA. Principal, The Grad Partnership, Newark; Vice President, Walker-Grad Inc. Former member, AIA Documents Board; former director, New Jersey Society of Architects. Author, *Joint Ventures for Architects and Engineers* and *You and Your Architect;* chapter author, *Financing Real Estate Development;* former chairman, editorial board, *Architecture/New Jersey.* B. Arch., University of Pennsylvania, 1949.

Author, Chapter 2, "The Professional Organization."

PHILIP J. MEATHE, FAIA. President, Smith, Hinchman & Grylls Associates Inc., Detroit. Secretary, AIA College of Fellows; former director, AIA and Michigan Society of Architects; former president, Detroit Chapter AIA. Recipient, Edward C.

Kemper Award. B.A. Arch., University of Michigan, 1948.

Author, Chapter 3, "Project Delivery."

HAROLD L. ADAMS, AIA. President, Director, Chief Executive Officer, RTKL Associates Inc., Baltimore. Former chairman, AIA Task Force on the Future of the Institute; former director, Maryland Society AIA; former president, Baltimore Chapter AIA. B. Arch., Texas A&M University, 1962.

Author, Chapter 4, "Management Principles."

MacDONALD BECKET, FAIA. President, Welton Becket and Associates, Los Angeles. Former chairman, AIA Documents Board. B. Arch. and Cert. Bus. Econ., University of Southern California, 1952 and 1956.

Author, Chapter 5, "The Client."

PETER PIVEN, AIA. General Manager, Geddes Brecher Qualls Cunningham, Philadelphia. Chairman, AIA Financial Management Task Force; former chairman, AIA Task Force on Membership; former vice chairman, AIA Personnel Practices Committee. B. Arch., University of Pennsylvania, 1963; M. Arch., Columbia University, 1964.

Author, Chapter 6, "Financial Management."

DAVID M. BOWEN, AIA. Associate, The McGuire & Shook Corp., Indianapolis. Trustee, AIA Retirement Program; former chairman, AIA Personnel Practices Committee and Pension Task Force; former member, Joint Committee on Employment Practices; treasurer, Indiana Society of Architects; former president, Indianapolis Chapter AIA. B.S. Arch., University of Cincinnati, 1960.

Author, Chapter 7, "Personnel Management." Additional contributor: William R. Fleming, Director of Personnel, Smith, Hinchman & Grylls Associates Inc.

BERNARD B. ROTHSCHILD, FAIA, FCSI. Senior Vice President/Secretary, Finch, Alexander, Barnes, Rothschild & Paschal, Inc., Atlanta; Vice President/Treasurer, Associated Space Design, Inc. Former chairman, AIA Documents Board and AIA Nominating Committee; former member, AIA Task Force on Architect-Engineer Agreement; former director, AIA; former president, Georgia Association AIA and Georgia Chapter AIA. Former president, Construction Sciences Research Foundation. Recipient, Edward C. Kemper Award. Author, *Construction Bonds and Insurance Guide;* chairman, editorial board, *Architectural Graphic Standards.* B. Arch., University of Pennsylvania, 1937.

Author, Chapter 8, "Insurance Management."

RICHARD G. JACQUES, AIA. Principal, Richard G. Jacques Associates, Albany; President, Environment Systems International, Inc. Chairman, AIA Project Delivery Systems Task Force; former vice chairman, AIA Systems Committee; former president, Eastern New York Chapter AIA. B. Arch., Rensselaer Polytechnic Institute, 1959.

Author, Chapter 9, "Principles of Project Management."

CHARLES R. SIKES Jr., AIA. President and Chief Executive Officer, Neuhaus + Taylor, Houston. B. Industrial Arts, North Texas State University, 1949.

Author, Chapter 10, "Budgeting and Scheduling." Additional contributors: Victor A. Kormeier Jr., Treasurer and Senior Vice President, Neuhaus + Taylor; Jerry R. Lacy, Management Consultant.

HERBERT McLAUGHLIN, AIA. Principal, Kaplan/McLaughlin, San Francisco. Chairman, AIA Facility Programming Task Force. Former member, Ad Hoc Advisory Committee on Correctional Architecture, Law Enforcement Assistance Administration, U.S. Department of Justice. Author, *Programming, Planning and Designing the Community Mental Health Center*. B.A. and M. Arch., Yale University, 1956 and 1958.

Author, Chapter 11, "Programming."

JAMES Y. ROBINSON Jr., AIA. Principal, Ferebee, Walters and Associates, Charlotte, N.C. Former chairman, AIA Life Cycle Cost Analysis Task Force and Automated Practice Technology Committee; former chairman, North Carolina Chapter AIA Research Committee. B. Arch., Tulane University, 1963; M. Arch., Rice University, 1969.

Author, Chapter 12, "Construction Cost Control."

PEYTON E. KIRVEN, AIA. Partner, The Raymond Ziegler Partnership, Los Angeles. Former chairman, AIA Codes and Standards Committee and Fire Safety Task Force; former chairman, California Council AIA Codes Committee and Southern California Chapter AIA Building Codes Committee. B. Arch., University of Texas, 1948.

Author, Chapter 13, "Regulations Control."

HAROLD J. ROSEN, PE, FCSI. Construction Specifications Consultant, Merrick, N.Y. Former Chief of Specifications and Materials Research, Skidmore, Owings & Merrill, New York City. Author, *Principles of Specifications Writing* and *Construction Specifications Writing;* contributing editor/columnist, *Progressive Architec-*

ture. B. Ch. E., College of the City of New York, 1938.

Co-author, Chapter 14, "Information Resources." Additional contributors: Susan Cosgrove, AIA Librarian; Bess Balchen and Marion Mistrik, former AIA staff; Anne Hartmere, The Architects Collaborative; Katherine Hoester, Hellmuth, Obata & Kassabaum; Joy Taylor and Sid Smith, Caudill Rowlett Scott.

ROBERT F. MATTOX, AIA. Vice President, Colvin-Robinson-Associates, Ann Arbor, Mich. Former chairman, AIA Automated Practice Technology Committee; former member, AIA Task Force on Computerized Practice Aids and AIA Research Committee. B.A. and B.S. Arch., Rice University, 1960 and 1961; Dipl. Arch., Ecole des Beaux Arts at Fontainbleau, 1961.

Author, Chapter 15, "Computing."

JACK D. TRAIN, FAIA. President and Director, Metz Train Olson & Youngren, Inc., Chicago. Former vice chairman, AIA Automated Practice Technology Committee; former chairman, AIA Task Force on Study of Standards of Professional Practice and Task Force on Rewriting and Computerizing AIA Cost Accounting System; former director, AIA; former president, Illinois Council of Architects and Chicago Chapter AIA. Former director and chairman of the board, Production Systems for Architects & Engineers, Inc. Recipient, Edward C. Kemper Award. B.S. Arch. Eng., University of Illinois, 1944.

Author, Chapter 16, "Office Machines." Additional contributor: Gene L. Montgomery, AIA, CSI, Associate, Metz Train Olson & Youngren.

JAMES J. O'BRIEN, PE. Principal, James J. O'Brien & Associates, Cherry Hill, N.J. Chairman of the Board, Project Management Institute. Author, *Construction Inspection Handbook, CPM in Construction Management, Management Information Systems, Management with Computers* and *Scheduling Handbook;* co-editor, *Contractor's Management Handbook;* chapter author, *Creative Control of Building Costs.* B.C.E., Cornell University, 1952.

Author, Chapter 17, "Network Scheduling."

NED H. ABRAMS, AIA. Principal, Ned H. Abrams - Architect, Sunnyvale, Calif. Lecturer and instructor, seminars and continuing education laboratories on cutting production costs. B. Arch. and M. Arch., University of Pennsylvania, 1937 and 1938.

Author, Chapter 18, "Drawings."

PAUL HEINEMAN, FCSI. Principal, Heineman Associates, Baltimore; Manager, North American Construction Specifications. Former member, CSI Long-Range Planning Committee; charter member and former president, Baltimore Chapter CSI. Editor, *CSI Manual of Practice* documents on performance specifying and page formats.

Author, Chapter 19, "Specifications."

Chapter 1
The Business and Tools of Architecture

"Architecture as a profession is fascinating and fulfilling; as a business, it is demanding and difficult."
—MORRIS LAPIDUS, FAIA*

Business Management → PROFESSIONAL ORGANIZATION ← Design Delivery
Management Tools → ← Production Tools
Project Delivery → ← Project Management

As the architect's client becomes more sophisticated, the successful architect will develop a parallel degree of sophistication. The client's expertise in business matters must be matched by that of the architect. Attention to the business aspects of architectural practice may be demanding, but the process need not necessarily be difficult with adequate preparation and planning.

ORGANIZATION AND DELIVERY

Application of the business and tools of architecture centers in the professional organization. The way an architectural firm is structured and administered will frequently affect the outcome of such application. For example, a firm which has grown to the point of needing a professional business manager may suffer adversely if an architectural principal without formal business education continues to fill this role.

Operations of the architectural firm are affected by both external and internal influences. Ever-changing methods of project delivery can have a profound effect on the firm's organizational response and even on its survival. And the office's internal design delivery system should be planned and administered with the same degree of care given to responding to the client's requirements for a project.

BUSINESS MANAGEMENT

It has been said that lack of objective business planning is a major problem of

* From *Architecture: A Profession and a Business* by Morris Lapidus.© 1967 by Litton Educational Publishing, Inc. Reprinted by permission of Van Nostrand Reinhold Company.

many architects and that we as architects must earn the right to survive. Merely producing a good design is not sufficient reason to merit this right. The profession's stature is at stake if it does not have competence in the areas of all services offered. Proficiency is needed both as professional designers and as professional managers.

A basic understanding of management principles will go a long way toward reaching the goal of a good professional manager: astute and incisive management of the affairs of the firm and those of the client which are entrusted to the architect. A sound knowledge of such areas as financial, personnel and insurance management will provide the architect the groundwork needed to attain this goal.

PROJECT MANAGEMENT

Every project undertaken by an architect for a client ideally should be responsive to the objectives of both in respect to quality, cost and time. Effective control of design quality throughout the project is a primary responsibility of the architect: controls relating to function, esthetics, constraints, economy, durability, comfort and responsiveness of the design solution. Competent management of time and construction cost is of equal importance.

Many of the processes used for general management of the architectural firm are interrelated with those needed for management of the client's project. For example, planning and control of office cost and time inherent in project budgeting and scheduling are directly related to the firm's financial management system and inseparable from it.

Increasing complexity of the design and construction process demands increasing expertise in the management of projects in the architect's office, from initial programming as the beginning of the design process through all the phases to project closeout.

MANAGEMENT AND PRODUCTION TOOLS

Advanced techniques in general management of the architectural firm as well as in project management require advanced tools. In many cases, the tools used for one are equally applicable to the other.

Planning networks, most effective for scheduling project design, documentation and construction activities, can be used to good advantage as aids to general management tasks. Bird-dogging strategies and billing cycles are among the activities which can benefit from creative networking techniques.

Office machines and computers which increase administrative efficiency can often do double duty in enhancing the design and documentation process. Coupled with the human intuitive approach inherent in architecture, modern equipment innovatively employed with contemporary techniques can help to bring architectural practice to a new plateau.

The architect is both a primary user and a primary supplier of information. The better the quality of input, the better the potential for improved output. As professional information systems improve, so will the systems for communicating the architect's design decisions. The methodologies exist. All that remains is to apply them effectively.

PART ONE
ORGANIZATION
AND DELIVERY

Chapter 2
The Professional Organization

DAVID R. DIBNER, FAIA

For architects, whose professional lives are spent in planning for others, the first step toward their own survival is in planning for themselves. Each firm must plan and develop a successful management procedure in order to provide outstanding services to their clients while remaining a viable business entity.

The architect as a practitioner of a major art may be referred to as an artist, differing, however, from the usual definition of "artist" in that professional services are provided directly to a client in response to needs. Further, in dealing with matters such as budgets, estimates, costs and other items associated with the word "business," the architect in a sense must also be a businessperson. Sound business practice is not unprofessional. The architect's efforts must be organized to render services in the most effective manner, assuring the client of the best possible result and the practitioner of the best possible return, and for both, the fewest possible problems.

Because of the diversity of firm sizes, professional services, project types and state laws which govern the practice of architecture, only the highlights in the forms of office organization are covered. It is suggested that the practitioner, when contemplating a change in organizational structure, investigate the local regulations which apply and seek the advice of legal, financial and insurance counsel in assessing any such move.

The first step in the process is to determine the firm's goals. These include the type and size of projects, scope of services to be provided, area of specialization if any, and the extent of ownership and control to be shared with others.

PROFESSIONAL SERVICES

As a practitioner of the "responsive art," the architect must shape the scope of services to match the requirements of clients and their projects. As a result of clients becoming more sophisticated and projects more complex, involving advancements in technology as well as broader sociological aspects, the types of professional services to be provided become increasingly more varied and comprehensive. Therefore, the traditional definitions of architectural services may no longer fit the present-day demands by clients on the architect.

TRADITIONAL APPROACH. For many years, the services to be provided by the architect on a project were defined in the Standard Form of Agreement Between Owner and Architect, AIA Document B141, and its predecessors. This document carefully separated those services which the owner could expect to receive for the stated compensation (basic services) from those for which, if requested, would have to be paid for as an extra (additional services).

This method of division of services has long served the profession well, and its wide acceptance and use through the years formed the common basis of understanding between architect and owner. It also formed the basis for legal decisions and for the traditional methods of compensation.

NONTRADITIONAL APPROACH. With the increasing complexity of the design and construction process, many of the services which previously were unusual to a project, and were therefore listed as additional services, are now more usually required from the architect. This broadening of the scope of services has brought about attempts to redefine the method for contracting for services. In this new approach, a comprehensive list of *all services* which the architect may perform on the project is reviewed by the architect and the owner, and those required for a specific project are selected. In this way, the differentiation between basic and additional services is avoided. This method seems to have many advantages:

—Provides the parties to the contract with a "shopping list" outlining all the possible services to be performed.

—Educates the owner to a fuller realization of what an architect really does and what can be done on the particular project.

—Affords flexibility in that it can be modified and expanded as new services become necessary.

—Retains the traditional role of the architect as a professional adviser.

—Easily accommodates to a project in which only partial services or a typical service are required, e.g., research, feasibility studies.

—Offers an equitable basis for determining compensation for the architect's services.

This new approach to the definition of professional services and the establishment of equitable compensation which is consistent with these services has been defined in *Compensation Management Guidelines for Architectural Services*, AIA Catalog No. M188. These comprehensive guidelines are the initial step of an entire system which will include other elements such as documents, forms and programs to provide a completely integrated procedure for defining services and management of compensation.

While this movement to the broadening of professional services is widespread, there remains an opposite approach among some firms toward the development of specialties. Their concentration on one particular building type or one aspect of service affords them a depth of experience and knowledge. They thus become specialists in such fields as hospital design or in such services as construction management or site planning.

FORMS OF ORGANIZATION

The selection of the most suitable form of organization for the firm has important meaning not only to the principals of the firm but also to their clients, employees and even their heirs. As a result, this decision should be made only after a careful analysis of the principals' and firm's goals and in consultation with legal, financial and insurance counsel. While the choices to be made are relatively simple, the process for the determination of which form the firm should take requires much investigation, review and cogitation.

Most firms have three forms from which to choose: proprietorship, partnership and corporation. The decision over which one to select will involve a variety of factors, but first a review of these forms is in order.

PROPRIETORSHIP. This is the simplest form of organization. The firm is owned by one person who has complete undiluted control over its decisions and destiny, and personally has a legal and financial responsibility for all of the firm's actions. However, this form has a number of disadvantages. The sole owner must rely on personal expertise, except for the advice of employees. Everything depends on this single person whose capability may be stretched too thin because of many demands. Key staff members feel a limitation on their ability to move up in the firm and often leave because of lack of incentive. An individual owner often has limited sources for financing, and firm growth may suffer. Also, full control means full liability for all losses of the firm, claims against the firm and actions of the firm.

PARTNERSHIP. This is still the most commonly used form of organization for architects. As partners, several people share both the ownership of the firm and the liability for its acts. In fact, each partner is liable for the business actions and obligations of all of the partners. The partnership's profits or losses are credited or debited each year to each partner's account. Each partner's share of distributed or undistributed profit or loss from the partnership must be reported on the individual's income tax return. The partnership itself does not pay income tax. Although state licensing laws may differ on the name under which a partnership may practice, there is no state law which prevents the practice of architecture by a partnership, providing the partners are licensed to practice in the state.

CORPORATION. The corporate form of practice is fast increasing in popularity. The corporation is a separate legal, taxable entity. The principals who form the corporation become its employees and as such are eligible for employee benefit programs, which are usually the greatest advantage to be derived from incorporation. It was not until recently that many states passed legislation allowing the incorporation of professional practice. This form has created tax and benefit program advantages over other organizational types. There may or may not be some protection from certain liabilities depending on the applicable law. However, incorporation is not for every architectural firm, and all considerations must be weighed carefully before making the decision to incorporate.

DIRECT OR GROUP OWNERSHIP?

The first question in choosing the form of organization is to decide whether to practice alone or with others sharing ownership. In choosing to remain a sole proprietor or adopt a partnership or corporate form of ownership, a number of considerations should be pondered.

GOALS. One of the most important aspects to consider in this analysis is what the principal(s) wants to achieve. If the desire is to retain a small practice and be absorbed completely in all aspects, then sole proprietorship is the answer. If, however, the desire is to grow and expand into new fields, or branch out into new geographic locations, the responsibilities and the liabilities are often best shared with others, and either form of group ownership—partnership or corporation—would be better. This allows a broader coverage through the dividing of activities, increasing the firm's capital, and broadening of potential for employees to share the leadership. Principals are able to manage remote offices, provide varieties of expertise, and divide the responsibilities for procuring and developing the work.

PERSONALITY. This is often the prime factor to consider. Perhaps the individual can truly share leadership with others, or may possibly be a loner. On the other hand, there may be areas of practice in which the architect prefers not to engage. Fortunately, because of the diverse nature of the requirements within an architectural office, co-owners may often be found who complement the strengths of the others, thus forming a cohesive firm. For instance, the designer type may combine with a production type to provide complete services. Or the "inside" man may join with the "outside" salesman type to form a firm. However, no matter the type of combination of expertise, careful consideration of individual personalities should be given to the selection of co-principals.

FINANCIAL ASPECTS. The sharing of the ownership of the firm also means the sharing of the financial responsibilities. This allows for the acquisition of additional capital to operate the firm and to expand, and in bad times to provide the holding power necessary to overcome the unfortunate valleys of reduced income which all practices seem to have.

AGE. The older a professional gets, the more important a factor age becomes. Through group ownership, the opportunity arises to be able to convert into hard cash the goodwill and reputation which a personal practice has developed through the years. However, if the essence of the firm is vested in one individual and its entire identity revolves around that person, then the value of the firm to others becomes questionable.

FIRM SIZE. The size to which a firm has grown may have an effect on the decision regarding organizational form. At one time, only the largest firms incorporated. However, many small and medium-size firms recently have done so for tax or legal reasons. There are notable exceptions, however, such as Skidmore, Owings & Merrill, one of the country's largest firms with offices in more than a half-dozen cities both here and overseas, which continues to be a partnership by choice.

PRACTICE MIX. The type of services which the firm offers will be in large measure dependent on the capabilities of its principals. For instance, if architecture and engineering will be provided through in-house expertise, then it may be best to consider matching principals to the capabilities required. Similarly, if a firm engages in a specific area of architectural practice, such as health care facilities or shopping centers, it may be helpful to have experts in these fields as part of the ownership team. Of course, this distribution of expertise among the principals is not essential since these positions may be filled by employees, but it does help to establish credibility with a client when the co-owners possess these varied backgrounds.

GEOGRAPHIC LOCATION. The choice of a firm's location may be a factor in choosing the form of organization. If the desire is to have a multioffice operation in various locations, it may help to have at least one principal manage each office. This may help to insure greater produc-

tivity and efficiency in the branches and make it easier to develop new business.

PARTNERSHIP OR CORPORATION?

Once the decision about group ownership has been made, the question of whether or not to incorporate is likely to arise— probably one of the most frequently discussed subjects among professionals in recent years. Individual requirements should be carefully measured since the case for incorporation is not always clearly positive. The firm contemplating this step should proceed cautiously, aided by competent, unbiased legal and financial advisers.

In a number of states, architects may practice as a general business corporation. In practically every state, they may operate as a professional corporation. The main difference between the two types is the allowable makeup of the shareholders. In a professional corporation (PC)—in some states, professional association (PA)—only licensed professionals may hold stock. Most states limit an association or a corporation to members of the same profession. This restriction may not seem severe to those contemplating a change from partnership to a professional corporation until it is realized that persons such as a valued business manager, or other capable professionals such as a landscape architect or planner, who might be valuable assets to a firm would not be eligible to participate in the ownership of the architectural PC. Further, state laws have different definitions as to which disciplines constitute "the same profession," and many do not permit engineers, landscape architects, planners, etc., to join with architects.

Since a professional corporation rather than a general business corporation is possible in most states, the pros and cons of establishing the former are discussed here.

FINANCIAL ADVANTAGES TO PRINCIPALS. Probably the most important element to bear in mind in the election of the professional to incorporate rather than form a partnership is the ability through the corporation to provide, under current law, several forms of protection, while enjoying a tax deduction. Such provisions include health care and disability insurance. When death occurs, insurance also can protect the survivors and the estate. The cost of these benefits would be paid for by the corporation and deductible to it and would be free of income tax to the professional. This would not hold true in a partnership.

Contributions made by the corporation to an approved pension or profit-sharing plan are tax deductible by the corporation, and the earnings are free of personal income tax until the benefits are withdrawn after retirement. The benefits to participants are only taxable when and as received. As employees of the corporation, the principals stand to gain the most from the corporate form of organization. Contributions to a profit-sharing plan can be up to 15 percent of the employee's compensation or to 25 percent if combined with a pension plan. There can be proportionately greater benefits to the principals through "integrating" the corporation's retirement plan with Social Security payments or through the use of fixed benefit pension plans in which older employees have larger amounts set aside.

While on the surface, these financial benefits seem overriding in favor of corporate instead of partnership practice, several considerations must be taken into account by the principals. First, the principal who contributes to a corporate pension and/or profit-sharing plan must give up some spendable income. Is the individual willing to accept this reduced current income for long-term benefits? While a tax-free corporate retirement plan may look attractive, there may be ways such as investing in real estate to get a better appreciation and return on the same money. (However, the risk of such a decision should be carefully evaluated.) In addition, *all* the regular employees of the firm must be included in these plans, and since architectural firms usually have a high ratio of employees to principals, the cost on behalf of nonprincipals can become quite extensive.

A retirement plan is also available for sole proprietors and anyone who owns more than 10 percent of a business. Through the Keogh Plan, principals may set up an individual tax-saving retirement fund in which they may reserve up to 15 percent of their earnings with a top investment of $7,500 a year. In addition, any employee of a corporation (which would include the principals) or a partnership where no retirement plan exists may start an individual retirement plan. The yearly contribution to this plan is limited to 15 percent of the employee's salary with a maximum of $1,500. The money for both types of retirement plans is payable after age 59½ and must be paid starting at 70½.

Under all of these plans, one of the principal advantages is the postponement of income tax on the monies invested as well as the interest or dividend income for the period—often decades between the time of the contribution and the ultimate distribution after retirement.

PERPETUATING THE FIRM. One of the advantages of incorporation is that it is an effective way of perpetuating the firm. A process can be set up to have the younger principals buy out the stock of retiring principals so that each senior owner will be taxed on its appreciation in value as capital gains. Further, it is possible for the corporation to take out life insurance at its own expense to provide cash to purchase a deceased principal's stock.

PROFESSIONAL CONCERNS. Some architects have objected to the corporate form of practice because of their belief

that the image of a personal service profession such as architecture would be tarnished by practicing as a corporation. However, with the growing number of professional corporations, no such effect has become evident.

POTENTIAL DISADVANTAGES OF INCORPORATING. Several negative aspects of incorporating are:

—Compensation to officers of the corporation must be fixed at what the Internal Revenue Service considers "reasonable" levels in order not to be taxed as dividend income. No such problem exists with partnerships.

—The costs of incorporating are usually much higher than those of forming a partnership because of the necessity to respond to many more legal requirements as well as filing requirements with state authorities.

—Corporations cannot accumulate too much income without a penalty. On the other hand, since partnerships must treat *all* of the income as though it had actually been distributed to the partners at the end of each fiscal year, no tax-free accumulation in partnerships is possible.

—Corporations as legal, taxable entities pay taxes on income in addition to the personal income taxes which their employees and stockholders pay on salaries and dividends. Partnerships are not subject to this dual taxation.

—The corporate form is much more rigid than the partnership and involves many more technicalities such as requirements for board of directors' and stockholders' meetings, accounting reports, etc. Corporations generally receive closer scrutiny by the IRS.

OTHER ORGANIZATIONAL STRUCTURES

In addition to the three basic forms of organization, there are variations which may be utilized for practice.

JOINT VENTURES. These consist of temporary associations of two or more firms formed for the expressed purpose of providing services on a specific project. The venturing firms may be in any of the three organizational forms, but their combination is considered similar to a partnership. This is a useful device for a firm desirous of handling a project larger than it can itself produce, or working in an alien field of practice or expertise or in a remote location. The venture is formed using the Joint Venture Agreement, AIA Document C801, or a similar one, and once the project is over, the venture is dissolved. The same care should be taken in choosing partners in forming a joint venture as in developing a partnership or corporation.

ASSOCIATED PROFESSIONAL FIRMS. Sometimes several firms of varying disciplines associate to develop new business together, and, if successful, join in providing a continuation of services. Their association is often a rather loose arrangement which subsequently formalizes into a joint venture for a specific project. It is worthwhile, however, before the commission is received, to bind the interrelationship with a written agreement, thereby avoiding controversy when the work has to be done together.

MERGERS AND ACQUISITIONS. "The urge to merge is as old as Adam and Eve" is a saying which was popular several years ago when there was an unprecedented parade of firms forming mergers or acquiring other firms. This movement toward merger seems to have abated; recently, in fact, there seems to have been a movement to dissolve previous mergers. For the professional, there are basically two types of mergers possible: interprofessional and those between a professional and nonprofessional firm. The advantages of a merger include such benefits as broadening technical services, acquiring better management techniques, expanding markets and gaining financial security.

The nonprofessional ownership offers the greatest hazard to the professional firm in such aspects as loss of independence, undue emphasis on profit, less professional objectivity and possible future conflict of interest. When asked why he had repurchased his engineering firm from a major conglomerate, the professional principal summed it up: "Its people just didn't speak our language." This is typical of the problems of mixed mergers.

While the interprofessional merger would appear to have less of these problems, some still arise, especially with respect to who makes the management decisions. No matter what the merger or acquisition, it is wise to secure the best possible experienced professional advice available, to fully explore all aspects and to have all questions answered before the merger takes place. Mergers involving the receipt of securities require special care in view of the dependency on future income and capital value. It is always prudent to allow enough time for all parties to change their minds.

TEAM ENDEAVORS. In these days of ever-increasing technology and the broadening scope of architectural services into fields such as construction management, development building, design-build and turnkey operations, the architect is often involved in joint efforts with all sorts of other professionals and nonprofessionals. In providing a broad range of services, the architect must develop a firmly defined relationship based on delineation of the individual roles of the various participants in the project.

This relationship must be reduced to writing, with all parties agreeing to their individual and collective responsibilities, both technical and financial. In these instances, and in practically all others, the architect must make judgments and agreements on the advice of those competent to do so in legal and financial matters.

Awareness of the requirements of the state in which the project is being executed is essential to make sure that registration laws are not being violated. Furthermore, when the architect's seal is attached to the drawings produced on behalf of the entire team, the practitioner must realize that a responsibility is assumed beyond the compensation and interest in the project. Above all, professional liability insurance should be checked before entering into any contractual obligation to insure that coverage has not been forfeited because of the relationship itself or participation in project ownership.

BRANCH OFFICES. A not too unusual way for a firm to grow is to establish branch offices in different parts of the country and overseas. This is often the result of acquiring another professional firm in a remote area and operating it as a branch office of the expanded parent firm. At other times, branches are established remotely from the main office when a new large project opens up a geographic area.

Of extreme importance in establishing these branch offices is the need for proper management controls. Only if someone is placed in charge with a carefully defined scope of responsibility and the ability to act in carefully delimited areas does the branch office have a chance to operate efficiently. Often, in order to evaluate the value of branch offices, each is made a separate profit center. Other factors besides business aspects are also very important. Is the design quality of the new office consistent with that of the parent firm? Is it necessary to duplicate the various disciplines and administrative office functions in each branch as opposed to providing central services?

PUBLIC OWNERSHIP. A relatively few architectural firms have been restructured and have offered shares for sale to the public. A publicly owned corporation must be a general business corporation. While it may practice in the state in which incorporated, it may have difficulty (without changing form) in practicing in states not allowing general architectural corporation practice.

Among the advantages of going public are:

—The capital base expands and increases the firm's financial resources to expand, develop and acquire other firms.

—A method is provided to capitalize on a firm's reputation and goodwill.

—Supplementary compensation is available through stock option plans so that ownership can be spread widely, thereby providing better employee incentive.

—Continuous control can be maintained when the principals retain a majority ownership in the corporate stock.

—Public scrutiny tends to promote greater efficiency.

And there are several disadvantages to going public:

—High cost is involved in the reorganization of the firm and the maintenance of its records.

—Difficulty exists in establishing a broad market for the stock.

—Constant pressure mounts to show good earnings, which may affect the firm's professional practice.

COMBINATION OF FORMS. Many firms have found that combining several forms of organization best serves their purpose. A simple example is the partnership with an incorporated drafting room. The professional services partnership is maintained for personal client relationships, while the production arm is a corporation. Another example is the establishment of separate corporations to provide construction phase services or interior design services or construction management. These entities may be subsidiaries of the parent firm or they may be held by one

EXHIBIT 2-1. COMPARISON OF FORMS OF ORGANIZATION

	Proprietorship	Partnership	Professional Corporation	Business Corporation
Usual Firm Size	Generally small	Small to large	Medium to large	Medium to large
States Which Permit This Form of Practice	All	All	Virtually all*	Some
Personal Involvement of Principal	Maximum	Varies	Varies	Varies
Extent of Personal Liability (Business)	Maximum	Shared	Usually minimum	Minimum
Extent of Personal Liability (Professional)	Maximum	Maximum but subject to contribution	Slightly reduced	Slightly reduced
Potential Personal Tax Advantage for Principals	Minimum	Minimum	Maximum	Maximum
Potential Benefits for Employees	Usually minimum	Varies	Maximum	Maximum

* State laws vary, some providing for professional associations.

holding company. Because of the legal and financial complications involved as well as the varying state laws, careful study must go into any decisions regarding multiple organizations. And tax treatment of holding companies must be carefully investigated, particularly the especially high rates assessed against firms treated as personal holding companies. The trend is, however, with the field of architecture broadening, for forms of organization to become more complex.

INTERNAL OFFICE STRUCTURE

Just as the diversity in architecture stems from the many and varied challenges in response to the variety of owners' needs, so the organization developed for response to these needs has as many varia-

tions. The major trends which have appeared in recent years are discussed.

IN-HOUSE DISCIPLINES OR CONSULTANTS? The first decision to be made by the architectural firm in practice is what disciplines it wants to maintain in-house and which will be covered by consultants. The number of disciplines which are necessary for the full and complete practice of architecture is extensive and seems to be growing larger every day. Which disciplines should be represented as employees of the firm, as consultants, as joint venturers?

Because many of the consultants have areas of expertise used only rarely (when certain projects arise), no architectural firm will contain all. Therefore, the first basic decision is whether to employ on staff the most usual of the consultants:

the structural and mechanical-electrical engineers. Each firm must assess its own situation. Some of the ingredients in this decision making follow.

Firm Size. For small firms starting out, unless the principals are skilled in the engineering sciences, it is usually best for them to hire engineers as consultants. This cuts down considerably on the payroll, overhead expenses and liability. Such a move also permits the small firm the adaptability to take on all sorts of projects without worrying whether it can keep all disciplines busy all the time. With the use of consultants, the firm has "instant expertise" when needed and no obligations when not.

For medium and large firms, the decision is usually not that simple, and factors other than firm size should be taken into account.

Practice Mix. If a firm specializes, it is often helpful to have all the necessary disciplines available in the office. This should help to balance the workload since the ratio of personnel skills would be established for the requirements of the practice. However, if the practice is diversified, trying to keep everyone busy becomes a chore. Using consultants also allows the architect flexibility to choose the firm best suited to the specific expertise required by the project. For example, different engineering consultants may be retained for a hospital than for an office building.

Geographic Location. If common practice in the geographic location is to have a combined architectural-engineering in-house capability, it is hard to compete with other firms without having one's own engineers. In addition, if most firms in the area are combinations of architects and engineers, then it may be difficult to find competent consulting engineers due to the lack of available opportunities.

Other Criteria. Additional thoughts to ponder in making this decision might include these questions:

—How best will the architect serve the client?

—Does the architect want to share the compensation (and hopefully profit) with some consulting firm?

—Can the architect coordinate the work as closely and as well with a consultant as with an in-house staff? Will clients have the same opinion?

—Does the architect want to assume all the professional liability for both architecture and engineering or prefer to see it shared?

—Does a "professional stagnation" take place when consultants on the staff respond only to one architect's work, rather than having to remain competitively sharp in order to get work from many different offices?

—Can the architect offer the services of the in-house engineering staff to other architectural firms and thereby gain additional income?

—Can the architect finance the combined operation?

All of these factors and many more are worthwhile reviewing before deciding on the direction of the firm; and as it grows and changes, a periodic review of the situation may be in order. To assist in this review, Exhibit 2-2 lists many of the types of consultants which the architectural firm may call on from time to time.

TYPES OF INTERNAL OFFICE ORGAN-IZATION.
Having decided the types of service which a firm will provide, it is important to determine how the firm will be organized internally to turn out the work. As in everything else, this can take a multitude of different forms.

First it is important to talk about a key factor in any architectural office: management. As practitioners of one of the major arts, some architects often feel immune from the business aspects of the office.

Unless the firm is well managed, not only will profits diminish but services will also suffer. Under these conditions, the architect will not be effective in meeting client needs.

In recognition of this important factor, many firms hire professional managers as an integral part of their staffs. Such managers attend to the business and organizational aspects of the practice, while the architects concentrate on professional activities. As an alternative, functions of the firm's personnel may be reallocated to accomplish equivalent results. Many management consultant firms have been attracted to the field of architecture and engineering and have become specialists in the reorganization of professional design firms and reallocation of duties.

In all firms, there are two primary divisions of responsibility: administrative and technical. The administrative area includes accounting, financing, marketing, purchasing, contract management, personnel management and consultants' coordination. These functions are supervised in a variety of ways. Some firms appoint principals with the responsibility of overseeing some or all of these aspects. Other firms do it by committee, established to meet periodically for reviewing and setting policy for the particular areas under consideration. No matter what the method, the object is to make sure that these areas are being covered by a principal who will have responsibility for the firm's efficient operation of the office.

EXHIBIT 2-2. PARTIAL LIST OF CONSULTANTS

A list of consultants who may be employed by architectural firms in the interest of the project might contain those from the following areas:*

Acoustics	Interior design
Audiovisual equipment	Landscape architecture
Behavioral sciences	Life cycle analysis
Building types	Lighting
Civil engineering	Mechanical engineering
Codes and regulations	Mechanization systems
Color	Models
Communications	Photography
Computers	Planning
Construction costs	Process engineering
Conveying systems	Real estate
Development building	Renderings
Economics	Research
Electrical engineering	Scheduling
Energy conservation	Soils engineering
Environment	Space planning
Facilities programming	Special equipment
Financing	Structural engineering
Fine arts and crafts	Surveys
Fire protection	Traffic engineering
Food service	Value analysis
Graphics	

* This list does not include the normal legal, accounting, insurance, bond and tax counsel that most firms retain for periodic advice concerning their business and professional operations, nor related consultants in the areas of management, personnel, marketing, reproduction, specifications, etc.

In the technical area, which encompasses the responsibility for producing the work, there are many forms of organization. This aspect of the practice determines whether the firm will continue to survive and to grow. Despite the quality of the internal administrative procedures, if the resultant professional services are not of high quality, the firm will be going nowhere.

There are several different forms of internal technical organization. Some of these forms affect the administrative areas, but the difference is essentially in the varied relationships of the personnel involved in a project process: design, development of construction documents and administration of construction contracts. The two basic types of internal office organization are departmental and nondepartmental. There are also variations of these forms.

Departmental Organization. This type of organization separates the various functions which must be performed in the development of a project. Thus emerge a Design Department, a Construction Documents Department and a Construction Administration Department. A typical departmental organization is illustrated in Exhibit 2-3. Each is headed by someone-in-charge, usually a principal of the firm. Often each department is assigned a budget for the particular project and is required to stay within its designated portion of the overall budget.

One advantage of this system is that personnel can be selected on the basis of their particular skills and asked to concentrate their activities in the areas in which they are most competent. The department heads can maintain a close watch over their respective operations and establish performance standards. Each department can be set up as a profit center and, when not performing up to par, can be analyzed and changed as needed to guarantee the best results.

Other than the perennial problem of uneven work flow which affects all organizational forms, the disadvantages to the departmental system have mainly to do with the personalities of people. They do not like to be segregated in terms of specific processes. Many were trained in architectural schools to look at a project in its full context. They want to identify with an entirety, not just the working drawings or other segments. Also, the project at times may falter under such a system as it flows from department to department. There are certain aspects of the project which remain in the designer's mind, awaiting further development for expression. This professional, who likewise desires to follow the concept to its maturity, may be kept from supplying additional input as the project proceeds into the next phase.

And because of the sometimes intangible nature of architecture in progress, there may be a tendency for one department to forward problems to the next without solutions.

The departmental system is most often used in larger firms which can afford to hire employees with specialties. As with any combination of specialists, balancing personnel and workload so as to keep everyone busy and productive sometimes becomes a problem. In such a case, a nondepartmental structure may provide a better answer.

Nondepartmental Organization. To respond to the human needs for identity with a project, a different form of organization has resulted in some architects' offices. At the start, a team is created to de-

EXHIBIT 2-3. DEPARTMENTAL ORGANIZATION

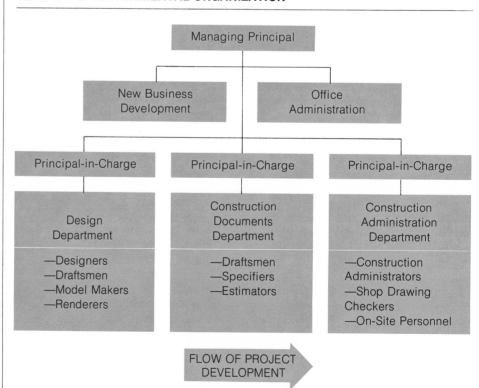

EXHIBIT 2-4. NONDEPARTMENTAL (TEAM) ORGANIZATION

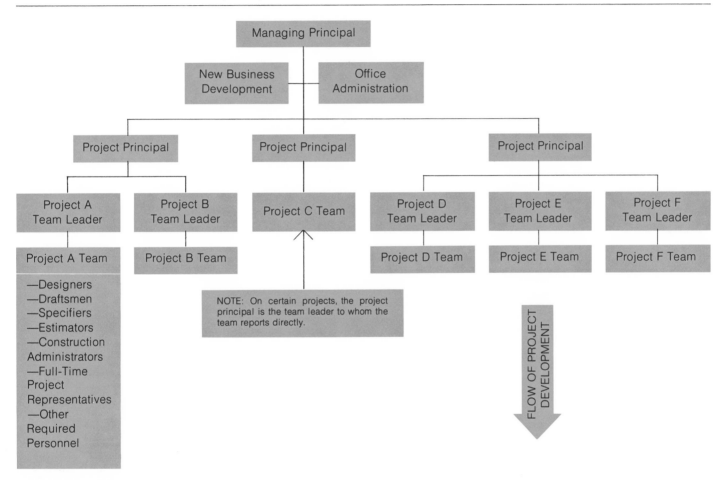

velop the project. A typical nondepartmental organization is illustrated in Exhibit 2-4. The team leader chooses people with varied skills to turn out the work. The main team members are the leader and the designer (sometimes the same person) who stay with the project from inception to conclusion. The team will expand with different members as the project progresses, with the number of team members varying in accordance with the requirements of each phase of the project. In this way, some of the disadvantages of the system are eliminated in terms of continuity and identity with the end results.

However, the nondepartmental system brings up other problems. These include such factors as control and maintenance of a uniform level of service. If each individual team leader is responsible for the entire project, how can the latter be expressive of the firm as a whole? Who will be responsible for the assignment of personnel to insure that some teams do not take up all the best people? Since various personnel are at various times assigned to different team leaders, what prevents them from being required to furnish different responses for different people on different projects? To whom should these

independent team leaders report and be responsible?

In an attempt to deal with the potential shortcomings of the two basic types of organization, there are variations in the structure which may be used.

Modified Team Organization. A combination of departmental and nondepartmental systems is often used in larger offices, preferring to use a form of the team system because it answers human desires for continuity and identity. However, to maintain a certain uniformity of services and to assure that some teams

EXHIBIT 2-5. MODIFIED TEAM ORGANIZATION

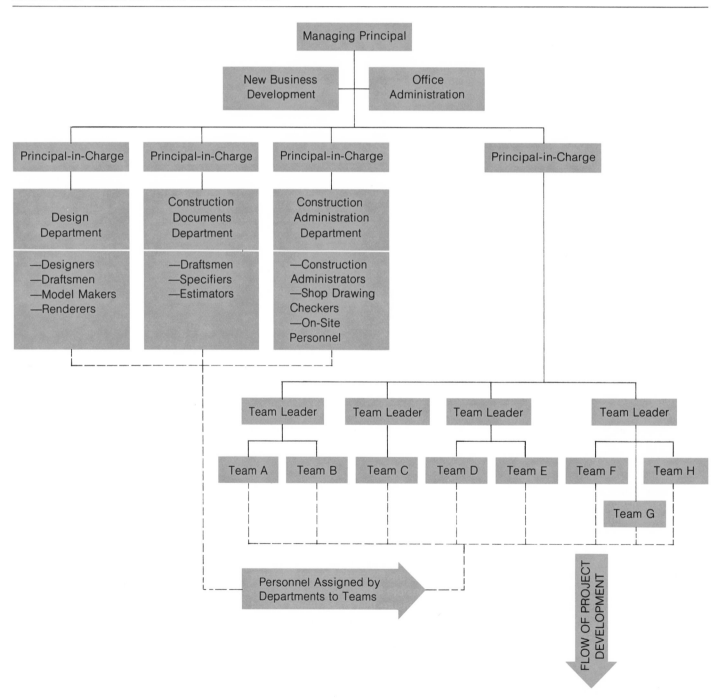

EXHIBIT 2-6. MODULAR ORGANIZATION

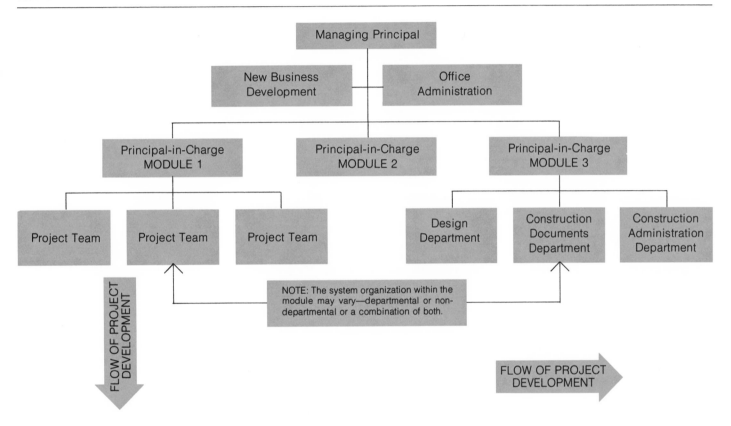

are not loaded with skilled people at the expense of others, they maintain a modified form of structure.

In this combined system, the leader is assigned personnel from each department as the need arises. When assigned to the team, employees take directions from the team leader. However, the various functions are monitored for conformity and completeness by the department head. A problem arises when there is a conflict between the team leader and the department head. This is solved in different ways, depending on the firm. In some offices, the responsibility for final decision is assigned to one or the other; in others, the adjudicating position is given to a principal, or the function is turned over to a committee for review and decision. In this combined form of organization, the project teams, in effect, are centrally administered and serviced. A typical modified team organization is illustrated in Exhibit 2-5.

Modified Departmental Organization. On the basis that the construction documents phase of practice is the one which most benefits from a departmental approach, some offices with remote branches organize their practice to capitalize on this advantage. They permit their branch offices to carry projects through the schematic and design development phases. When this work has been approved, the main office will then turn out the working drawings and specifications, using a corps of specialists in its construction documents department. The same office may also provide a reservoir of additional specialists for the branches such as experts in facilities programming, environmental impact, economics, etc. In this instance, the main office will bill the branches for consulting services and will provide accounting and many other administrative services as well.

Modular Organization. Another form which has become a method of operation within the very large firm is to divide the firm into modules, each run by one or several principals and each serving as a separate profit center. These modules may be based on the different areas of practice such as a health care facilities group, an educational group, etc. These modules usually contain the specific design expertise needed but are serviced by a central administrative group. They may include their own construction documents staff or may draw from a central pool of personnel. A typical modular organization is illustrated in Exhibit 2-6.

Other firms divide their offices into modules based not on a practice specialty but on a different principle. This arrangement draws its origins from the old atelier system in which various teachers ran their own design studios, attracting students to learn from the master. The extent of services provided by each group and those from central sources varies with the office. Again, technical quality control becomes an important requirement.

Whatever the method of organization, it is essential that there be a clear definition of the organizational structure and clearly defined lines of responsibility. There is nothing more unnerving for an employee than to be left floundering without an understanding of what is required and to whom to report.

The types of organization and internal structuring of an architect's office are many. Some can be more flexible than others, shifting with the changing requirements of the practice and the principals. None should be regarded as permanently fixed, but rather should periodically be reexamined in terms of satisfying the goals of the firm and responsiveness to new conditions.

For every professional services firm, these essential goals should always be kept in mind:
—Produce the best architectural results
—Achieve the best response to the client's needs
—Make the most money
—Avoid legal complications
Only through efficient organization can the architect produce a successful project for the client and run a successful practice.

BIBLIOGRAPHY

"Anatomy of a Merger: The Year of the Merger—and the Year After." *Consulting Engineer,* October 1971.
 Traces a merger from its outset, listing the effects on the personnel and firms involved.
Architect's Handbook of Professional Practice. Washington, D.C.: AIA, parts updated periodically.
 Current compendium of practice information; chapter on architect's office especially pertinent.
Architectural Practice. Clinton H. Cowgill and Ben John Small. New York: Reinhold, 1959.
 "Standard" text describing all aspects of architectural practice.
"Architecture in the 1970's—Gearing Performance to Needs." Walter F. Wagner Jr. *Architectural Record,* October 1970.
 General review of what can be expected in the architectural profession in the 1970's.
"Choose Your Partner." David R. Dibner. *AIA Journal,* March 1969.
 Concise review of the joint venture process, including benefits which can accrue to the large and the small firm.
Compensation Management Guidelines for Architectural Services. Washington, D.C.: AIA, 1975.
 Describes the new approach to establishing compensation through the review of services to be performed.
"A Hard Look at Incorporation." Leif C. Beck. *AIA Journal,* April 1971.
 Discussion of the aspects which should be investigated before incorporating.
"How Professionals Feel About Nonprofessional Mergers." R. M. Collie and William J. Fell. *Consulting Engineer,* January 1969.
 Description of the pros and cons of professional-nonprofessional mergers and generally develops a case for merger.
"Incorporating Professional Practice." Bernard Tomson and Norman Coplan. *Progressive Architecture,* October 1970.
 Concise review of the potential benefits and drawbacks of incorporation.
Incorporating the Professional Practice. George E. Ray. Englewood Cliffs, N.J.: Prentice-Hall, 1972.
 Written for all professionals who contemplate a change to a professional corporation or association.
"The Joint Venture: Prelude to Marriage and Growth." *Building Design & Construction,* June 1974.
 Story of one firm's use of the joint venture as a tool for growth.
Joint Ventures for Architects and Engineers. David R. Dibner. New York: McGraw-Hill, 1972.
 Detailed analysis of all aspects of the joint venture form of practice.
"Luckman Tells All About Ogden." Robert E. Koehler. *AIA Journal,* June 1970.
 Architect responds to 13 questions about his merger.
"Management Hints for Consultants." John D. Cole. *Consulting Engineer,* February 1970.
 Suggestions to the professional firm on various aspects of management.
"The Mechanics of Merger." Howard G. Shambaugh. *Consulting Engineer,* April 1969.
 Principal of an engineering firm relates from his experience the aspects to be considered while merging.
"Mergers Spur Professional Growth." *Consulting Engineer,* June 1972.
 Another firm describes the personal experience and benefits of merger as a method to expand practice capabilities.
"Need to Expand Your Practice? Profits?" John M. Dickerman. *Consulting Engineer,* October 1969.

How to structure a program to analyze a firm's expansion program.

"Organization for Professional Practice." Bradford Perkins. *Architectural Record*, June 1972.

Brief description of the various forms of organization for a professional firm.

"Practical Means to Higher Profits." Richard A. Enion. *AIA Journal*, November 1969.

Discussion of fees and internal organization of an architect's office and advantages of incorporation.

"Pros and Cons of Corporate Professional Practice." *Architectural Record*, March 1971.

Concise presentation of both sides.

"The Pros and Cons of Going Public." Louis Berger. *Consulting Engineer*, September 1969.

Discussion of what going public can mean to the personnel and growth potential of a firm.

"Some Thoughts on Starting Your Own Office." Earl R. Flansburgh. *Architectural Record*, April 1969.

Personal description of the decision-making process and problems encountered in starting one's own practice.

"Suggested Organization for Environmental Engineering Firms." George P. Fulton. *Consulting Engineer*, September 1973.

Discussion of office organizational structure in terms of interrelated functional teams.

"To Go or Not to Go." *Forbes*, October 15, 1973.

Review of the reasons why public stockholders of consulting and adver-

tising firms have not done well.

"To Merge or Not to Merge—A Growing Question for Design Firms." *Building Design & Construction*, August 1971.

Benefits and hazards of mergers and acquisitions reviewed in concise terms and history of 16 merger guidelines.

"What's Wrong with Corporate Practice in Pennsylvania." *Charette Journal of Architectural Practice*, September-October 1973.

Comparison of business and professional corporations for architects.

"Why and How to Plan Professional Firm Management." Bradford Perkins. *Architectural Record*, March 1972.

Short description of the management and control aspects of office organization, financial planning and new business development.

Chapter 3
Project Delivery

PHILIP J. MEATHE, FAIA

The architectural profession has been under severe pressure to find better overall answers to client demands for simultaneous handling of the intricate balance of time, quality and cost of projects. The ultimate goal is a facility that is delivered in the shortest possible time, at the lowest possible cost, with the highest possible quality and/or performance. But each of these standards is subjective, almost always having an effect on the other two.

The different weighting of time, quality and cost by the owner/user will influence the method by which the project is designed and built. For the purpose of this discussion, there are three primary methods by which all building projects are brought from the client's original decision, through the design and construction processes, to the owner/user's occupancy of that facility. Although other project delivery methods could be identified, many are simply variants of one of the three primary methods.

METHOD 1: TRADITIONAL LINEAR

The first method of project delivery is referred to as "traditional linear," through which the architect determines all of the client's physical and functional needs, creates a design, secures approval, draws up all necessary documents, then puts the project out for either competitive bids or a negotiated price. Upon the awarding of the contract or contracts, construction begins. Typically, the client's program is completely understood before design begins, design is completed before the project is priced, and prices are determined before construction begins.

METHOD 2: FAST-TRACK

The second method of project delivery calls for the acceleration and overlapping of the design and construction phases of the project, and is generally referred to as

"fast-track" or "phased design and construction." The intent is to shorten the time between decision and delivery of a project, which minimizes the period of cost escalation, provides earlier occupancy of the facility, and reduces the interest and carrying charges on construction financing. This method is exactly the same as the linear during the determination of the program and schematic design, but with the approval of schematics, the project is broken into the optimum number of bid packages rather than a single general contract or several simultaneous prime contracts. Each bid package is the definition of the work that will be put into place under that contract. These bid packages are awarded or negotiated in a predetermined order according to the construction logic so that earlier packages can go right into construction while later design packages are still being refined.

METHOD 3: DESIGN-BUILD

The third method of project delivery is generally referred to as "design-build," which has a number of variants, but essentially consists of the client being given a firm combined price for both the design and the construction of a project. Since the price is given at an early stage, there is limited definition of project program and criteria, and there will be single-point responsibility for its delivery. This single point can be either the architect or, more usually, a general contractor.

Although the client's individual prior-

ities toward time, quality, and cost will suggest a preference for one or another of these three *methods* of project delivery, they all share three separate and distinct *phases* in the delivery process. The primary distinction in each *method* of delivery is the timing and the relation of each *phase* to the other two.

PHASE 1: DESIGN/DOCUMENTATION

During the design/documentation phase, the program of the owner is articulated, defined and analyzed, and the input of all design disciplines is gathered. Economic feasibility is determined, the site studied (sometimes even selected), the owner's stated needs for space and/or function confirmed, schematic designs prepared for approval, and the basic design of all mechanical, electrical and structural systems determined and developed. At various points during this phase, cost estimates and time schedules are prepared or refined.

Either cost or schedule can have an appreciable effect on design decisions if the preliminary estimates show either being exceeded. The scope of the project may have to be reduced, or there may be substitutions of various materials or equipment in order to bring the cost or the schedule back into line.

Data- and criteria-gathering continues throughout the development of the design and the preparation of construction documents. With each bit of added facts and

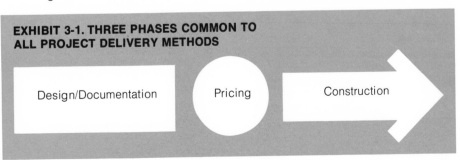

EXHIBIT 3-1. THREE PHASES COMMON TO ALL PROJECT DELIVERY METHODS

Design/Documentation　　Pricing　　Construction

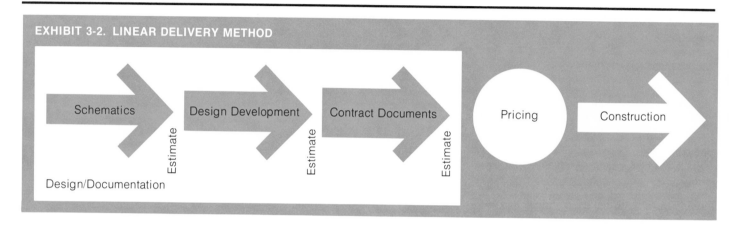

EXHIBIT 3-2. LINEAR DELIVERY METHOD

Schematics → Design Development → Contract Documents → Pricing → Construction

Estimate   Estimate   Estimate

Design/Documentation

their confirmation, cost estimates and time schedules become more reliable (as long as they are prepared by an experienced, professional staff of estimators).

PHASE 2: PRICING

The second phase of all three delivery methods is the pricing of the data and criteria already generated, and this occurs only with the acceptance of a firm bid by a qualified contractor (or the signing of a negotiated contract). Up to this point, estimates are just that, and while they may prove to be reliable and accurate, the marketplace is the final determinant of the actual cost of construction. Surely, the saddest words to architect and client are: "The bids came in over the budget."

PHASE 3: CONSTRUCTION

Although modern tools, methods and equipment have increased the efficiency of construction, the actual time required for the physical implementation of the project is not subject to major reduction and savings. If the architects and engineers have correlated their design for smooth interrelation in the field, and if the contractor uses modern management of both people and processes, lost time and expensive errors can be reduced to a minimum. The greatest contribution the

professional can make to construction is a set of error-free documents with no ambiguities or potential misunderstandings. Alfred Levitt, the architect-turned-builder, once said, "We must design our houses so the workman *cannot* install anything wrong, even if he tries."

So the building team of owner/designer/builder is confronted with three basic choices of project delivery *method*, but regardless of which is selected, the project must go through the above three broad *phases* of design/documentation, pricing and construction.

EFFECTS ON THE PROFESSIONAL ORGANIZATION

The various methods of project delivery will affect the architectural office in various ways.

LINEAR DELIVERY METHOD. If the project will follow the traditional linear method, the professional will be involved in the determination of the program to a greater or lesser degree. Some owners spend much time and money in writing a complete description of spaces and functions (hospitals and industrial plants are good examples). Others will ask the architect to start from page 1, helping to identify needs and establish the program.

The linear method is by far the most familiar to professional firms, and this straight-line process of designing the project, pricing it, then building it requires the least dislocation of operations. The level of professional personnel is distributed predictably throughout the length of the process, and the only lulls that must be anticipated in a smoothly flowing project during the design/documentation process are the relatively short periods of client or agency review at stated points.

If it is strictly an architectural firm, those engineering consultants who are called in for civil, structural, mechanical or electrical systems are engaged only as needed. The architect must provide expert management and correlation of the various design disciplines, but the problems of personnel utilization and financing of operations are largely shifted to the consultants.

When the pricing (estimates or actual bids or negotiated prices) indicates that the original budget is being exceeded, the client has the options of increasing the budget, or of redesign and/or reduction in project scope. At this point, a minimal financial commitment has been made but likely no construction commitment.

If a governmental agency is the client, the budget very likely will be a line item, not subject to expansion except in subsequent fiscal years, and it is incumbent on the design team not to exceed the appropriation. If the agency's program cannot be met by the available funds, it must be told this clearly and firmly, as early in the design phase as possible.

The simplest pricing in the linear method is by way of a lump sum general contract, under which a contractor agrees to build a facility according to complete drawings and specifications for a fixed price. Before submitting a bid or agreeing on a negotiated price, the contractor will have done more or less complete pricing of the various subcontracts, systems and materials. Factors based on specialized knowledge of the construction marketplace then are added. The contractor hopes that the bid price will be more than the total cost to construct, with the difference being profit. The risk lies in the construction costs exceeding the price, when normally there is no recourse to re-negotiation.

As is obvious, when the costs of the project exceed the agreed-upon fixed price, the general contractor is vulnerable to a substantial loss. As the size and complexity of projects increase, and as the factor of price escalation becomes largely unpredictable, many general contractors are less willing to bid a lump sum on a major project. They prefer bidding or negotiating on some type of a "cost-plus" basis. In these arrangements, the contractor will certify all costs to the owner for payment and will receive a fee as remuneration.

This doesn't mean the owner is buying blind. Under a cost-plus arrangement, the general contractor will have secured enough bids or estimates from the various subcontractors to give the owner an approximate cost. The owner, now becoming the possible victim of any cost or schedule overruns, may ask for the protection of an upset price, slightly higher than the estimate. If costs exceed this price, the financial responsibility shifts from owner to contractor.

But the knife cuts both ways; the owner would be the beneficiary of any saving of time or money. As a compensating incentive for the contractor to keep costs down, it is common practice for the owner to agree to share all monies saved under the agreed-upon upset price. The division of these savings is a matter of negotiation, but 50-50 is a common arrangement.

FAST-TRACK DELIVERY METHOD. The fast-track or accelerated and overlapped method is a direct response to the double-digit escalation of building costs over the past decade or so. It accepts the fact that little can be done about labor, materials or financing costs, and that the only feasible attack can be on shortening the time between decision to build and delivery.

The acceleration and overlapping means that at the completion and approval of schematic design, the project is broken into a number of bid packages, and the pricing of these packages is compressed backward into the design/documentation phase. Demands for personnel with specific skills become more concentrated, since more highly skilled designers (architectural and engineering) rather than draftsmen or less skilled personnel are going to be needed earlier than in the linear method. The scheduling of design personnel becomes of equal importance to the design itself because under this accelerated method, construction imperatives dictate design timing. For example, long-lead-time items and systems must be designed early enough

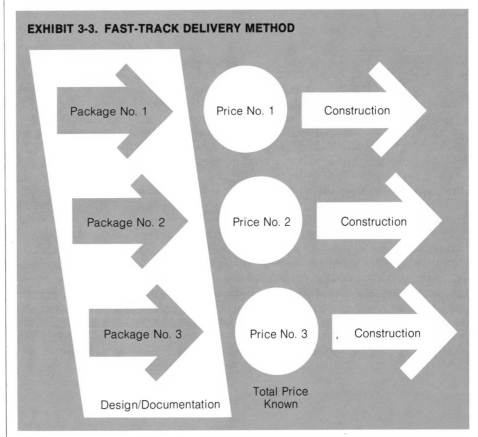

EXHIBIT 3-3. FAST-TRACK DELIVERY METHOD

Package No. 1 — Price No. 1 — Construction

Package No. 2 — Price No. 2 — Construction

Package No. 3 — Price No. 3 — Construction

Design/Documentation

Total Price Known

so that delivery and installation will occur when the construction logic dictates.

In the fast-track method, all of the design and documentation of the earlier bid packages must be complete since they are going to be priced before the entire design is completed. This means that the professional must anticipate the effects of early design decisions on later packages. To make such informed choices requires top-level people at an earlier and more concentrated point in the design process.

The pressure for acceleration of the design and construction phases has brought a number of new tools to enable the professional to meet this demand. Systems methods (often based on computer technology) in a number of areas must be widely used in fast-track projects. Cost control, accounting, design and construction scheduling, information retrieval and simulation tests are among the most prominent.

The impact on the professional firm is a dual one: First, it must now employ—or have access to—a number of new data processing and computer skills; second, its architectural and engineering designers must begin thinking in these new languages. They must understand the management process that controls and manipulates the design and construction of a facility related to the design and construction of various building systems.

The design of some building systems can be integrated with the purchase and installation of predesigned and manufactured items or complete systems. Prime contracts between owner and contractor or supplier can even be let on an installed basis, and with a performance specification rather than a prescriptive one. Again, the professional must have the kind of talent which enables one to think and to specify with performance in mind.

The use of multiple contracts in the fast-track method demands that a construction manager (CM) coordinate and oversee the performance of the contractors and the validity of cost and schedule. In effect, the CM performs the function normally carried out by the general contractor. The CM can be an architect, a general contractor, or even a management-oriented firm. Project cost control and management of the interface between the various prime contracts are the responsibility of the CM. As construction proceeds, there must be a feedback into the design process to maintain clear definition of the required contract packages.

Another skill that becomes more important is the professional firm's knowledge of the construction marketplace since design or specification decisions may be dictated by the realities of labor and materials supply in the project area.

Since it normally will take slightly more design man-hours to complete all the packages of a phased construction project than the linear method requires, the compression of schedule means that more highly skilled people are needed on board but for a shorter time. A higher volume of work would ordinarily be needed in order to justify this larger number of higher-caliber people in all of the disciplines. When the specialists are all outside consultants rather than internal staff, the responsibility is shifted across all the consultants concerned, but it does not eliminate it.

DESIGN-BUILD DELIVERY METHOD. It is in the design-build method of project delivery that the hardest crunch comes on the professional firm since the design decisions must be made on less information than the other methods. Because the program and criteria are limited, and because the design decisions must be backed by a firm bid, it is imperative that the design decisions are right the first time. All the most skilled specialists, in all of the design disciplines, are needed almost simultaneously in a concentrated effort. But once the project is priced and the owner has accepted it, lower-salaried personnel will constitute the majority of employees implementing changes that occur during the actual construction of the project. The professional as a member of the design-build team will play a continuing consulting role with the builder-partner. The latter brings to the team that knowledge of the marketplace that is so essential to a successful bid.

As the professional firm moves out of its traditional role of acting as the owner's agent, with the single responsibility of protecting that owner's interest, a number of conflicts of interest can arise. In many design-build projects, the incomplete program and criteria allow a great number of variables in the selection of materials, equipment and building methods. The design-build contractor reaps the benefits of any economies achieved during construction, and the designer could be forced to choose between the best possible alternatives from the owner's point of view and the profitability of the project to the employer: the contractor. This potential conflict of interest remains even when the choices are in the best interests of the owner and the project.

There are also some unclear legal implications as the professional firm moves out of its traditional role. Historically, any physical deficiency in a project would have to be corrected, which can be very expensive, and the responsibility for such corrections depends on whether there has been design or construction negligence. Normally, the architect's insurance provides protection against the former, and the contractor's bond against the latter. When these lines get blurred, questions of liability coverage arise.

The architect acting as the single point of responsibility in a design-build situation is responsible not only for the design but also for the construction and cannot be covered by professional liability insurance. If the contractor is the prime and subcontracts the design function to the professional firm, the arrangement more

EXHIBIT 3-4. DESIGN-BUILD DELIVERY METHOD

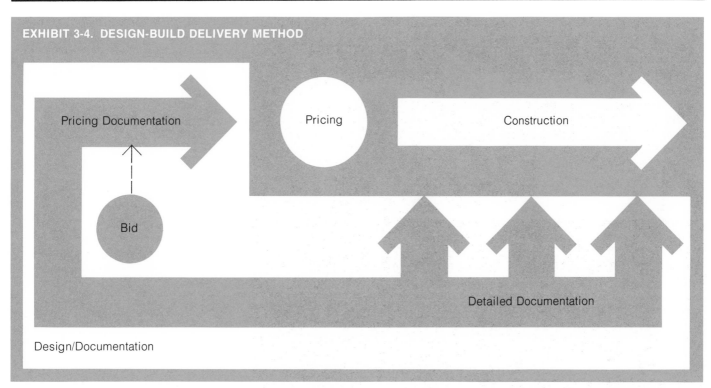

Pricing Documentation

Bid

Pricing

Construction

Detailed Documentation

Design/Documentation

closely resembles the traditional one. This role of the architect is normally insurable (the contractor being the client), although legal and insurance consultation should always be sought before a commitment is made.

Although the role of the architect in the design-build method is normally insurable (as long as the traditional architect-client role is retained with the contractor), it is necessary for the professional firm to see that the duties and responsibilities of the contractor team leader are not shifted to the design professional. Among the more dangerous clauses are those which would have the architect assume responsibility for project completion dates and costs, for project site safety, for code and standard compliance in construction, or for any indemnification of the owner through the contract with the general contractor. The surest protection for the architect is the use of the Standard Form of

Agreement Between Owner and Architect, AIA Document B141, and any change in this document requested by the team leader should be carefully reviewed with both legal and insurance counsel.

The growth of the design-build method of project delivery seems assured because of client demand for firmer guarantees of both price and schedule, and more and more design professionals will be exploring such ventures. But they should only be undertaken after the closest scrutiny by legal, insurance and financial advisers so that the potential risks, as well as the advantages, are known.

NO SINGLE RIGHT ANSWER

As has been explained, there are three primary methods of project delivery, and each has a different impact on the organization and management of the profes-

sional firm. The two less conventional methods—fast-track and design-build—are more demanding of large numbers of highly experienced (and highly paid) professionals earlier in the design/documentation phase of the project.

But selection of the method of delivery should be based on the client's needs and priorities, not the architect's preference. As a general rule, the client's varying concern with time, quality or cost of the project may point the way to determining the most satisfactory method. If the client's concern is for a great building, an important architectural statement, and the highest quality of materials and design details, the traditional linear method will *probably* be most satisfactory.

If, however, the client wants this same high general level of quality, but is willing to sacrifice the perfect resolution of all details in favor of reduced time and cost, the savings in overall project delivery time in

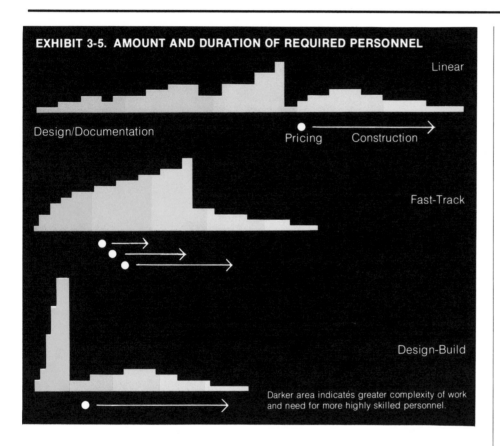

EXHIBIT 3-5. AMOUNT AND DURATION OF REQUIRED PERSONNEL

Linear

Design/Documentation

Pricing   Construction

Fast-Track

Design-Build

Darker area indicates greater complexity of work
and need for more highly skilled personnel.

the fast-track method will *probably* result in the optimum cost savings and a speeding up of beneficial occupancy.

But if time is everything to the client, if the building type is a relatively simple one and if a modest level of quality is acceptable, the immediate pricing and limited program criteria of the design-build method may fit the client's needs better than either of the other two.

Some public and private clients, as well as architects, are experimenting with delivery systems whose concepts and complexities go far beyond the basics examined in this chapter. New services such as construction management and project administration are emerging to respond to the more complex needs of these delivery systems. And offerings of complete design/construction/operation packages are appearing in many forms. All affect the architectural profession and its survival, requiring attention in such areas as ethics, professional competence, liability exposure and the like.

BIBLIOGRAPHY

AIA Guide to Improved Project Delivery Approaches (tentative title). Washington, D.C.: AIA, forthcoming.

Identifies best-known delivery systems and discusses conditions relating to them.

"The Architect and Construction Management." Peter C. Darin Jr. *Michigan Society of Architects Monthly Bulletin,* September 1974.

Step-by-step explanation of the duties and responsibilities of the construction manager.

"The Architect of the Future." MacDonald Becket. *Building Design & Construction,* April 1970.

Reinforcement of the "team" theory philosophically and in practice.

"Architecture in the 1970's—Gearing Performance to Needs." Walter F. Wagner Jr. *Architectural Record,* October 1970.

Summation of the changes facing the architect.

"Budget Control of the Phased Construction Project." William B. Foxhall. *Architectural Record,* October 1971.

Based on material from *Professional Construction Management and Project Administration,* AIA and *Architectural Record,* 1972.

"Design/Build." John McNichol. *Charette Journal of Architectural Practice,* January-February 1974.

Explanation by an exponent of the design-build method in the area of health facilities.

Design-Build-Bid: Task Force Report. Washington, D.C.: AIA, 1975.

Report of the special committee appointed to explore the ethical and economic effects of procuring professional services via the bidding of all service teams.

"Design-Construct." *The Contractor,* October 1974.

Pros and cons of design-construct.

"The Difference That Method Makes." Ewing H. Miller. *AIA Journal,* October 1973.

Defense of the traditional methods of providing professional services and a critical look at some of design-build's claimed advantages.

"Fast-Track Closeout." Richard L. Pearce, David W. Pearce and Donald C. Donaldson. *Architecture/Midwest,* August 1970.

How to wrap up the fast-track project to the satisfaction of all parties involved.

"Fast-Track to Construction." *Consulting Engineer*, November 1971.

Several case studies of the earliest effort in the method.

"It's a Wide Open Field: Construction Management." Philip J. Meathe, *AIA Journal*, March 1973.

How the architectural firm must structure itself in order to provide construction management services.

"Jefferson County Design/Build Program" *BSIC/EFL Newsletter*, April 1973.

Case study of how one county used the savings brought by design-build to enable them to have taxpayers pass a bond referendum they had previously turned down.

"Management Unifies Design and Delivery Process." *Architectural Record*, June 1973.

How a construction management program meshed the design and construction of a major U.S. airport.

"A State Construction Fund: Management for Quality." *Architectural Record*, January 1971.

Experience of the New York State University Construction Fund, the largest single user of construction management methods.

"On Track with Fast-Track." Francis G. Whitcomb and Stephen A. Kliment. *AIA Journal*, February 1973.

A dozen considerations that must be kept in mind if fast-track is to be used successfully.

PART TWO
BUSINESS
MANAGEMENT

Chapter 4 Management Principles

HAROLD L. ADAMS, AIA

Good management of an architectural firm is essential to survival. Principles of good business management are equally applicable to every size firm and type of organization. The major difference in applying management principles is in spreading the responsibility for implementation as the firm grows in size. The architect, then, needs commitment and understanding of organizational methods and supporting tools that respond to the demands of practice.

In the preface of his book, *Management: Tasks, Responsibilities, Practices,* Peter F. Drucker writes, "Management is tasks. Management is a discipline. But management is also people. Every achievement of management is the achievement of a manager. Every failure is the failure of a manager. *People* manage rather than 'forces' or 'facts.' The vision, dedication and integrity of managers determines whether there is management or mismanagement."

And later on, Drucker underscores and expands that point: "We further know that management is independent of ownership, rank or power. It is objective function and ought to be grounded in the responsibility for performance. It is professional—management is a function, a discipline, a task to be done; and managers are the professionals who practice this discipline, carry out the functions and discharge these tasks. It is no longer relevant whether the manager is also an owner; if he is, it is incidental to his main function, which is to be a manager."

The architect's traditional role of leadership in the design process seems to be challenged on all sides, and increasingly so. Added to this challenge is the public's attitude that practitioners have trouble making up their minds about decisions which appear to be the conclusion of mystical processes. Thus the architect does have reason to take stock.

To a significant extent, this condition exists because of the emphasis, during the architect's education and training, on the design of facilities without adequate regard for the complexities of the total building process required to control and produce a quality result. If the profession is losing stature, it is because of the lack of competence in some areas of services being offered.

IDENTIFYING OBJECTIVES

With the understanding of "professional" management as the primary tool, the architect is in a position to build an organization that works for everyone involved at all levels. The manager's most important responsibility is to establish realistic objectives for the firm. Plans must be carefully laid to achieve the objectives. But the lack of objective business planning is the architect's major problem, as one corporate executive in an allied field sees it.

The planning effort becomes merely an interesting exercise unless policies and procedures are established and coordinated. Execution follows inevitably whether planning has been done properly or not. But execution without provision for evaluation may be likened to a ship embarking on a lengthy voyage without proper navigation instruments. Unless there is a feedback mechanism that determines whether one is on course and progressing satisfactorily toward stated objectives, the pilot may very well be found out of fuel, adrift and headed for unknown ports. By the same token, the manager, with the proper set of indicators and performance measurements, is in a position to react to changing events and conditions. This provides an opportunity to replan accordingly and modify the organization as required and execute the necessary revised planning. Management's prime function should be to plan, organize, schedule, control and evaluate all work of the firm in order to assume the attainment of objectives which are then translated into specific goals.

Take an example. An architectural firm might have as an objective the creation of an organization at the highest level of competence to produce environmental change for the betterment of the quality of life: at the widest possible scale, within the largest possible territory and with the greatest possible speed. To achieve this objective, there are required resources: personnel, organization and hardware (limited).

The nature of the objective determines the character of personnel resources requiring:

—Disciplines to design (imagine and evaluate) "whole" alternatives to each proposed unit of environmental change—all design disciplines in addition to economics, sociology, behavioral science, ecology, etc.

—Disciplines to put in place a piece of the built environment, thought of chronologically as roughly market analysis through project completion.

The scale and the nature of the objective seeks a certain organization of these resources permitting:

—Growth at a digestible pace in order to preserve quality.

—The most rapid response to opportunities for achieving environmental change at a scale consistent with each such opportunity.

—Professional growth and the creative fulfillment of each individual within the organization.

The scale and nature of the objective also ascertains the extent of the hardware, or pieces of equipment, which under any circumstances in an architectural practice is limited in scope.

ACHIEVING OBJECTIVES

Business management is becoming a vital necessity to firms of all sizes. Operations management and design management are now necessary to establish standards of performance, effectiveness of personnel and profitability of operations. The emphasis must be placed here on methods that will meet the immediate needs of organization and management theories and practices to deliver known professional and technical knowledge in deference to an easy magic system.

Therefore, rather than looking for a "system," one should think in terms of management concepts, tools and techniques that embrace:

—Intuitive versus rational management
—Work planning
—Organizational development
—Conscious management
—Continuous management
—Management versus administration
—Management by objectives
—Management by exception
—Management for results

A total management approach must be supported by a management information system which incorporates an accounting system. A well-designed system will collect, store and process all relevant data such as:

—Management decision making
—Financial reporting and control
—Marketing
—Personnel

The basic elements of most management information systems include:

—A direct relation to on-going activities.
—An integrated operation whether by people or machines.
—A group of procedures to individually support each department and collectively support the major decision-making units of the organization.
—Timely reporting sequences.
—An organizational process for evaluating and making decisions based on the provided information.

The following are examples of questions each individual should ask in relation to one's own management operations:

—Is it better for the firm's manager to have basic training in architecture or in business, or both?

—How much business organization, planning, management and record keeping is necessary?

—What are the choices of business accounting systems, the advantages and disadvantages of each, and applicability in terms of office size, growth potential, tax liabilities, etc.?

—In starting a new practice, how much time and money should be allocated for business organization and management?

—What kind of time and cost accounting information will the architect need to manage the practice as compared with the information needs of the architect's accountants and tax consultants, and why are they different?

—What chart of accounts can be found that is tailored particularly to accounting for architectural practices?

—What indirect expense (overhead) items on the chart of accounts are a legitimate part of the cost of doing business but would not usually be allowed as overhead items by government auditors when services are provided to government agencies for compensation on the basis of costs?

—What are typical indirect costs as a percentage of direct (chargeable) time of the office staff, and how do they vary by type of office organization and equipment, services offered, size of staff and type of client?

—At what point in the growth of a practice is it necessary to initiate the following: a time accounting system and to what degree of sophistication; a comprehensive accrual cost accounting system to allow management of the practice by providing timely status reports on individual project profitability, office profit and loss, net worth, efficiency and status of indirect costs; a computerized versus manual system?

—What is the best method for the office to record time of principals, technical staff and nontechnical staff?

—How does the typical gross annual

compensation per staff member throughout the country vary by location, size, type of office and services rendered, and how does this compare with the firm's experience?

—Under what conditions should the firm borrow money to operate the practice and what are the ramifications of the various ways of financing?

—What are the peculiarities of the practice affecting return on investment, cash flow, etc.?

—What are the potential initial costs, operating costs and savings for introducing devices such as automated specifications, microfilmed or computerized information retrieval systems, computerized time and cost accounting systems, central dictation, automatic typewriters, sophisticated reproduction equipment, computer drafting and in-house printing?

—What guidelines are there on the reasonable ratios of various indirect expenses to billable or gross amounts?

—What ratio of accounts receivable to gross billings might be considered reasonable?

—What profit goals will keep the architect competitive, and what have the historic differences been between profit goals and actual profit?

—What are the financial outgrowths of branch offices, mergers and joint ventures?

—What marketing costs are reasonable as a percentage of gross income?

—What cost range is reasonable for brochures and other sales aids?

—At what stage of growth, taking cost implications into account, should the architect seriously consider incentive and retirement plans, employee evaluation procedures, personnel handbook development and professional testing?

INTERNAL RESOURCES

An architectural practice unlike many business ventures requires limited resources as measured by a banker's standard. Nevertheless, the lack of adequate internal resources is the usual reason for business failure in architectural firms. Internal resources include personnel, financing, commissions and counsel.

PERSONNEL. Without adequate, properly trained, experienced personnel, an office has little reason for being. People are often overlooked as a resource of quantifiable value. Perhaps finding another partner of a different experience or area of knowledge can often be worth more to a firm than dollars in the bank. Human talent, therefore, is the key resource to a successful firm, and management must be extremely sensitive to this aspect of its business.

FINANCING. Capital is needed for salaries and expenses to finance receivables and to purchase a few fixed assets. Through investment by its founding members, project profits which are retained, and borrowings from either commercial banks, friends or family, a firm should have a minimum of from 25 to 33 percent of its anticipated annual billings in capital in order to operate comfortably. Tendencies toward profit squeezes may require substantially larger capitalization.

COMMISSIONS. The projects for which the firm is commissioned will formulate the office's experience resources. Each should be viewed as a step forward in the practice through another commission and/or a recommendation; the accomplishment of an added experience to be better qualified for the next project; a higher level of quality (a design award perhaps) or a technological achievement of merit; profitability which means an increase in financial resources.

In planning for one's commissions and/or one's market, it is important that the market research be realistic, taking into consideration any and all opportunities and restraints such as geographical and

EXHIBIT 4-1. COMPARISON OF APPROACHES TO BUSINESS DEVELOPMENT

PROJECT PRIOR WORK — A Satisfied Client	PUBLICITY — Speeches / Articles / Other
	PERSONAL — Business / Nonbusiness / "Cold" Visit
PROJECTS — Visability / Other	REFERRAL — Personal / Client

PROMOTIONAL EFFORTS AIM TO ACHIEVE KNOWLEDGE OF FIRM BY CLIENTS

COMMISSIONS

MARKET RESEARCH EFFORTS AIM TO ACHIEVE KNOWLEDGE OF CLIENTS BY FIRM

PRIOR WORK	PUBLICITY
	PERSONAL
RESEARCH	REFERRAL

economic factors, as well as the prognosis for the future of the project type. Diversity of type, size and location may be selected as the firm's goal; however, this approach probably would require more key personnel than a more conventional one. And the possibility of not being generally recognized as an "expert" in any given field could become a liability. Exhibit 4-1 illustrates the two different sets of information resulting from market research and promotional approaches to identifying potential new commissions.

COUNSEL. Other resources not often recognized by practitioners are the various kinds of counsel available which can add a great depth of experience and new knowledge to the firm at a cost that is usually minimal when compared to the benefit.

Legal counsel, perhaps the most obvious, is frequently underutilized by the architect except in time of trouble when counsel is most expensive and necessary for survival. A capable business attorney can serve as an extra set of eyes, ears and hands. This is a resource as valuable as the most talented designer and even more necessary in these days of steadily growing legal, fiscal and compliance responsibility being placed on the architect's shoulders.

Tax-financial counsel will most often be found in an accountant, and every firm should have one as an on-call adviser in major management decisions, not just a person to come in at year-end to close the books and prepare tax returns. Such an individual should have management training as well as an accounting background.

Investment counsel is of importance when a firm starts thinking about establishing an employee pension and/or profit-sharing program. A word of warning: Do not rely on advice from the most aggressive salesperson; seek help from a banker, lawyer or accountant who is qualified to advise on investments. Another possible area of investment is real estate development. This is an area fraught with danger for the inexperienced (and for the experts). It is a situation in which one should seek the advice of counsel before moving too fast since the wise placement of excess cash in real estate demands great skill and intuitive ability.

Insurance counsel serves an area where many practitioners need professional help, as is emphasized in Chapter 8. Oftentimes, too much faith is placed in the advice of a talented salesperson whose livelihood depends on sales commissions when an independent insurance counselor should be engaged.

Management consultants can reduce the agony of a necessary transition in size and organizational structure and also help plan for growth. A person and/or firm with a working knowledge of the architectural profession should be used when possible.

MANAGING THE RESOURCES

The basic resources as defined are an asset only if handled responsively within the firm's organization. The problems of successful management may be compounded by the need for more sophisticated management techniques as the firm increases in size. Conversely, overly sophisticated techniques could be detrimental to a firm not able to handle them. Architects quickly discover that what is good management and organization for 15 to 25 persons will not work for, say, 50, and will realize that the organization required for that number is usually top heavy, requiring further growth for support. This last point is borne out by the AIA's recent survey of the profession which shows that the earnings per owner dip during these organizational transition periods.

A good organization should provide:
—An atmosphere conducive to creative efforts
—An organizational umbrella that will relieve the professional of administrative detail while providing necessary data
—A sound financial base to meet the firm's objectives
The chronological resolution of an organizational structure comes from:
—Definition of firm objectives
—Realization and agreement of need for organization
—Position descriptions of required personnel
—Sufficient time allocated to plan the new organizational structure without pressures of daily operation

QUALITY CONTROL. The word "quality" in an architectural office is often thought of in terms of design excellence as represented in awards won or in technical competence (buildings that don't leak, for example). Quality, and its control or monitoring, should be thought of in more extensive terms. One architect defines quality as "the implementation of an innovative but functional design, using advanced, competent technology while providing superior professional services and maintaining adequate monetary reward." A checklist of basic areas affecting the quality of an office's end result follows.

Project Administration. There are at least seven steps:
—Contract/proposal (guidelines, personnel selection, production schedule selection, post-mortem)
—Compensation/budgeting monitoring and recording
—Production monitoring and recording (see Exhibit 4-2)
—Personnel responsibility definitions and relationships (leadership, project and office)

EXHIBIT 4-2. PROJECT MONITORING AND RECORDING

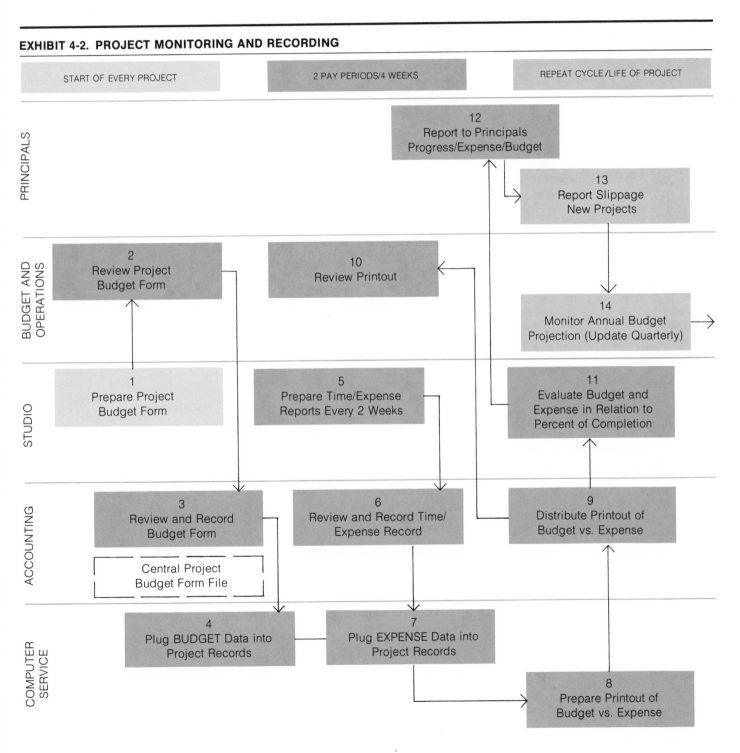

START OF EVERY PROJECT   2 PAY PERIODS/4 WEEKS   REPEAT CYCLE/LIFE OF PROJECT

PRINCIPALS

12
Report to Principals
Progress/Expense/Budget

13
Report Slippage
New Projects

BUDGET AND OPERATIONS

2
Review Project
Budget Form

10
Review Printout

14
Monitor Annual Budget
Projection (Update Quarterly)

STUDIO

1
Prepare Project
Budget Form

5
Prepare Time/Expense
Reports Every 2 Weeks

11
Evaluate Budget and
Expense in Relation to
Percent of Completion

ACCOUNTING

3
Review and Record
Budget Form

6
Review and Record Time/
Expense Record

9
Distribute Printout of
Budget vs. Expense

Central Project
Budget Form File

COMPUTER SERVICE

4
Plug BUDGET Data into
Project Records

7
Plug EXPENSE Data into
Project Records

8
Prepare Printout of
Budget vs. Expense

EXHIBIT 4-3. DEVELOPMENT STEPS IN THE DESIGN PROCESS

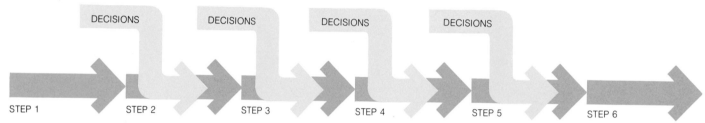

STEP 1

PROJECT
ORGANIZATION
The design team is
selected and the
mechanics of coordina-
tion and decision
making are established
by consultation with
the client.

STEP 2

RECONNAISSANCE
The design team
assembles existing
reports, studies and data
which relate to the
project, surveys physical
characteristics of the
project site and identifies
special study needs.

STEP 3

OBJECTIVES AND
STRATEGIES
The design team
develops basic alterna-
tive objectives, considers
priorities, feasibility,
options, givens and
constraints.

STEP 4

DESIGN CONCEPTS
Based on the objectives
and strategies selected
in the previous step,
the design team develops
alternative concepts of
development and inventory
of implications.

STEP 5

DESIGN DEVELOPMENT
The design team
develops the selected
design concept in detail.

STEP 6

IMPLEMENTATION
Final documents are
prepared and
implementation begins.

—Professional practice education
—Marketing monitoring
—Personnel monitoring (morale and evaluation)

Design. In this area, there are three distinct aspects:
—Design (review system, guidelines, cost control, legal regulations evaluation education, production systems)
—Design education
—Post-mortem process

Implementation. Again, there are three factors similar to the above:
—Implementation process (review system, guidelines, cost control, legal regulations evaluation education, production systems)
—Implementation education
—Post-mortem process

Offices are developing processes and systems whereby in-house quality control can reduce the chance of errors or omissions during the development of contract documents. It has been pointed out by Charles B. Soulé, FAIA, past chairman of the AIA Insurance Committee, that 65 percent of the claims filed against architect-engineers have been due to errors in preparation of drawings and specifications. An example of a design process that carries a project through logical development steps which require team member review and client concurrence as each phase is completed is shown in Exhibit 4-3.

HANDLING PERSONNEL. Since human assets are the major resource to be managed, it is important for management to recognize the need for professional growth within the firm, sensitivity to change in areas such as ethical standards and licensing, and a plan for succession. Further aspects of personnel management are discussed in Chapter 7.

IMPROVING CAPITALIZATION. There has been a great deal of talk and thought in the architectural profession about mergers into publicly owned companies, or for a few even going public on their own as a means of acquiring growth capital. Although these approaches may be viable, the need for greater capitalization is even more important in these days of slow turnaround in receivables and high interest cost on borrowed money. From where and how can a firm increase its needed capital other than retained earnings which are also hard to come by with profit margins under their own pressures?

One method to broaden the ownership base of the firm is to sell stock (assuming a corporation) to a group larger than the founding principals. Another method worth considering is to establish an IRS-qualified employee stock bonus plan and trust which purchases the stock in the corporation with borrowed money that would be repaid out of the firm's earnings at the maximum rate of 15 percent of payroll per year. The result is that the loan is paid off with before-tax dollars, and the firm ends up being owned by the employees, creating a powerful incentive to improve production.

SEEKING NEW MARKETS. Today's architect must become more aggressive, creative and flexible in today's changing world, endeavoring not only to expand the market but to get a larger piece of it by offering a broader base of services. It is only by keeping and increasing a comfortable flow of new work that architectural firms may prosper and grow.

For many years, there has been a prevailing attitude among architects that it is unprofessional, and almost unethical, to take the business management aspect of a practice very seriously and to talk and write about it. And all too often the results have been unhappy clients and a profession that suffers a poor image.

The practitioner who is to avoid becoming a business casualty or a professional basket case learns something about the business of architecture and strives to learn some more. Awareness of management principles prepares the architect to deal with realities and opportunities when the goal of running one's own practice or being a principal in a firm is reached, even when management skills themselves must be found elsewhere.

BIBLIOGRAPHY

"Architectural Firms Needn't Be Poorly Managed." *Building Design & Construction.* November 1974.
> Description of a management by objectives (MBO) program.

"Business Managers: A New Discipline Enters the Architectural Office." David A. Vachon. *Charette Journal of Architectural Practice,* July-August 1972.
> Brief profiles of nonarchitects who serve in this role, with job descriptions of administrator and manager types.

"Management and Control for the Consulting Firm." A. R. White and Charles H. Kruse. *Professional Engineer,* January 1971.
> Delineation of responsibilities and authorities in two sets of job descriptions for all key personnel: client oriented and company oriented.

Management: Basic Elements of Managing Organizations. Ross A. Webber. Homewood, Ill.: Richard D. Irwin, Inc., 1975.
> A complete introduction to and survey of management.

"A Management Compendium." Robert W. Richards, *Consulting Engineer,* October 1971.
> Commentary intended to clarify the understanding of management.

Management: Tasks, Responsibilities, Practices. Peter F. Drucker. New York: Harper & Row, 1974.
> Must reading for anyone who takes this business function seriously.

"Planning for Growth: Managing Change." Clint Page. *Progressive Architecture,* March 1972.
> A look at growth—a natural tendency and goal for architectural firms.

"Room at the Top: The Rise of the Professional Manager." Clint Page. *Progressive Architecture,* December 1972.
> Analysis of the management role as a full-time responsibility.

"Why and How to Plan Professional Firm Management." Bradford Perkins. *Architectural Record,* March 1972.
> Overview of the planning process.

Chapter 5
The Client

MacDONALD BECKET, FAIA

Business development and client relations are two interrelated subjects which thrive on communication, mutual respect and clearly defined interpersonal relationships. From the pursuit of new clients to the successful completion of their projects, these matters are of the utmost importance to the architect.

GETTING THE CLIENT

All too often architects approach the generating of new business haphazardly instead of in a well-organized manner. They maintain that they are professionals, not business- or salespersons, and that projects miraculously will appear after expending the minimum amount of effort. This is seldom true in today's competitive world, and it is doubtful if it ever was to any great extent.

When architects, who are unfamiliar with ordinary business techniques, pursue new clients, they often do so without logical preplanning, distinct direction or definite goals. For instance, architects, accustomed to designing speculative-type buildings, may continue to seek such projects long after this particular market has diminished or vanished in a certain region. Possessing little, if any, marketing knowledge, they may look for projects that are either nonexistent or unfeasible from a competitive or cost point of view. Or, without reviewing the capabilities of their offices, they may decide to pursue a very complex project when their staff's expertise and experience do not reflect such capabilities.

Successful architects must know their firm and themselves, and they must balance their creative design abilities with keen business sense. In addition to competent design, the key to a successful, thriving architectural firm depends on knowledge of the building market, salesmanship, promotion and plain hard work. This holds true whether the office be large or small.

PEOPLE RESOURCES. What emerges are three primary resources which help architects develop new business: the principal, the internal staff and the business development team. The firm that recognizes and makes use of these resources, rather than simply surviving, will find itself designing an ever-increasing number of viable projects with an ever-expanding repertoire of creative opportunities.

The Principal. Possibly *the* major requirement of a good client relationship is the continual, personal involvement of the principals of the architect's and the client's firms. At the very least, the architectural principal assigned to the project should be present at the signing of the contract and at ceremonials: the groundbreaking, the dedication and perhaps the topping out. In between these milestones, the principal should make personal contact other than by telephone.

One of the hallmarks of good client relationships is for one principal of the client and one of the architectural firm to get together regularly to discuss current construction or design problems and to establish a personal rapport which may lead to a long-term relationship. The client becomes assured of the architect's sincere interest in the project, which is often difficult to demonstrate when the practitioner's time is overscheduled.

After a project reaches completion and for an indefinite period of time afterward, it is important that the architect maintain personal contact even though the client does not foresee additional building. A former client is a reference, and references are the lifeblood of architects.

Internal Staff. Perhaps the most overlooked "business development persons" in any architectural firm are the ones without the title, the employees who work on individual projects. Often, during the course of a project, responsible em-

ployees develop close personal relationships with the client's representatives. This is a natural occurrence, and architects should encourage their employees to maintain such contacts after the project has been completed. Contacts may take the form of a lunch, a dinner, periodic telephone calls or a stop at the new building for a visit. The client's representatives may know the building market better than the firm's principals and can be an important source of information.

Employees may be less valuable in a small architectural firm as business development persons because often the client expects to deal directly with the individual whose "name is on the door."

Business Development Team. In most small architectural firms, the principals (usually registered architects) comprise the business development team. In larger firms, the trend is toward hiring people with business and marketing backgrounds who possess more than a casual knowledge of the architectural profession.

Whether principals or professionals with architectural backgrounds, members of the business development team ideally should have credibility, poise and the sensitivity to talk the language of each prospective client. For public work, they should understand the inner workings of local, state and national politics as well as the administrative bureaucracies. They should have the capacity to thoroughly perceive the current market situation and the economy both regionally and nationally, and comprehend financial and fiscal policies.

As part of its credibility, the business development team should not promise a client what the firm cannot deliver. It must constantly monitor the personnel available for a project since capabilities of a firm may rapidly change, especially in a small or medium-sized firm when an especially qualified staff member leaves. This monitoring also involves a familiarity with projects currently in design and production, making mandatory an accurate schedule projected at least a year in advance. All firms should acquaint themselves with each service they feel capable of handling at a given time and in the foreseeable future.

In addition to capabilities, personnel and services, members of the business development team should know the firm's policies, standards, traditions and factors during contract negotiations with a client. Concurrent with knowledge of their own firm, they should generally understand the capabilities of other architectural offices (both as competitors and as potential joint venturers) and the major qualified consulting firms in the area. Finally, business development persons should enjoy the challenge of meeting and winning over a constantly changing stream of prospects and clients.

A well-organized business development team directs its energies full time in the following areas: territory; market research; new and repeat clients; public and community relations; and business development aids.

TERRITORY. Every architectural firm should identify physical boundaries and areas of interest for its business development effort. A logical framework to organize time and effort should be developed.

A large office with a number of business development persons may divide the country into geographical regions. These individuals become experts on their particular region, concentrating their efforts on making and keeping client contacts in each geographical area. Yet they remain aware of the larger national picture because of its effect on the region.

Many large architectural firms employ a full-time person who only pursues government work because of its intricate nature, involving all levels and agencies. Other firms, whether large or small, may emphasize one or two building types, and their business development persons become experts in, say, hospitals, office buildings or schools. However, commitment to a single building type invites danger, especially if the market shifts in the region or otherwise dries up.

MARKET RESEARCH. Through market research, architectural firms may identify the types of available work they prefer and the potential clients for such work. Many smaller practitioners without the benefit of structured research usually have to "work the territory." But in larger firms, this research helps to crystalize goals by defining the outer limits of expertise. In part, this is determined by the architects' ambitions and the talent available to them. Market research also should include an estimate of how many projects are needed to reach a projected annual gross.

Before developing a particular area of interest, such as educational facilities design, business development persons should ascertain that a market exists. They must determine the availability of work within the market; competition; the scope of services required and whether their firm can provide them; and the potential compensation for professional services.

Market research involves a thorough knowledge of national and regional economic indicators and constant monitoring of published opinions. It means assembling and systematizing this information, then making a decision based on the facts and the architect's experience. If activity within the market meets the business development team's criteria, contact may be made with potential clients.

An important part of market research is culling published material on proposed projects. The real estate section of local newspapers may carry an occasional report, while the general news sections may mention grants received and bond issues approved. Construction-oriented newspapers and magazines usually report projects in progress, but there may also be sporadic reports on proposed projects for which an architect has not been selected.

Notices of proposed federal construction projects requiring architect-engineer services are listed in *Commerce Business Daily,* available on subscription from regional Department of Commerce field offices or the Superintendent of Documents, Government Printing Office, Washington, D.C.

Although architectural marketing newsletters such as *The Coxe Letter,* published in Philadelphia, do not usually provide direct leads to specific projects, they do provide valuable tips for bird-dogging new markets and analyses of many different current potentials for new construction programs. Publications such as *The Client Prospect Directory* produced by Guidelines Publications in California list company executives who screen design firms for potential work. Annual reports of corporations and published budgets of political subdivisions may produce additional leads.

NEW AND REPEAT CLIENTS. Seeking clients entails bird-dogging or discovering prospects; learning the wants and needs of clients; writing letters of interest to clients; filling out government forms, answering questionnaires and submitting brochures; representing the firm at client interviews; and negotiating contracts for execution by a principal.

Bird-dogging can assume many faces. If an architectural firm has been in business for a number of years, a business development person should first analyze its current and past clients. Repeated contact with past clients is essential because an architectural firm's capabilities may change, and the former client may not have an awareness of this new expertise. The client also may assume that no contact means no interest.

In addition, even though past clients do not contemplate a project in the near future, they may serve on the board of a hospital, school or another community or private agency which does plan a building. Architects' membership in civic and community organizations frequently proves useful since many other members are local business leaders possessing invaluable insight into the future building market.

Business development persons should identify the decision makers on the client's staff and assess their feelings about architectural firms. Who will finally decide on the choice of the architect? How satisfied are the clients with their present architectural and engineering services? What is their feeling about out-of-state firms, joint ventures, branch offices, combined architectural-engineering firms, new firms, separate design offices, and importing and exporting talent?

Before meeting past clients again, business development persons should check whether the accomplished project was satisfactory, seeking answers to questions that might arise. Did maintenance problems develop after the project was finished? When the roof leaked, and the contractor was "unavailable," how did the architect respond? Was there a personnel problem which was never solved?

In addition, business development persons should look into the expansion and growth of past clients' business and industries of which they are a part. They should inquire at length about future work which could require the firm's additional services and inform clients of what services the office now provides. After all meetings, business development persons should record the time and place and a short description of what happened; and then keep these observations in a central file and constantly update them as priorities demand.

Statistics gathered by the author's firm

show that some 80 percent of all new contacts made through bird-dogging result in the architectural firm being considered when the prospects have work. In turn, some 10 to 20 percent of these clients have work; some 10 to 20 percent of these clients should have work pending; and some 30 percent of those who have work pending should offer the architectural firm a contract. A business development person needs to analyze statistics such as these to determine how much time to spend pursuing a particular project.

The best way to maintain the respect of repeat clients is to solve their problems, complete their project on time, stay within the predetermined budget, and accomplish it in the most efficient way possible.

PUBLIC AND COMMUNITY RELATIONS.
While public relations efforts seldom bring work directly into an architectural office, these functions often help reinforce the reputation of the firm in the mind of the potential client. Basically, public relations is another service provided by the architect, and one that requires organization, coordination and a keen sense of priority in that it is desirable to tailor part of the program to the marketing effort.

Among the public relation tools—surely one of the least expensive—is the news release which helps to generate articles in newspapers and magazines, giving recognition to both the architectural firm and the client. A news release is not a 200-word essay on design. Rather, its intention is to mark project milestones from design to completion.

Aside from news releases, a firm may provide the media with information on personnel appointments; professional, civic, academic or project awards; professional papers; and speeches by principals and employees.

In general, public relations endeavors to create a climate of credibility, trust and integrity with the press and with existing and potential clients.

Community relations is involvement of the firm's principals and employees in local affairs, including an interest in local government and its politics and policies long before a project is on the horizon. It might extend to inviting visitors—especially students and other young people—to tour the firm and to lending office facilities for community events. Some larger architectural firms award scholarships, often in memory of a deceased principal, to encourage promising students to enter the fields of architecture or urban design.

BUSINESS DEVELOPMENT AIDS. To support the business development effort, an architectural firm may use a number of tools, depending on the size of the office and on the variety of clients and projects.

Audiovisual Equipment. A typical office may possess simple or sophisticated audiovisual equipment such as 35mm slide or 16mm motion picture projectors or videotape for use in presentations to prospective clients.

The least expensive, most flexible method is the color slide show. The slides may present photographs of current or past projects which relate directly to what the client wants and of architects and engineers in a working environment to give the impression of office procedures. The business development person can either talk directly to the client about the slides or a prerecorded tape can offer a general description.

The motion picture or videotape presentation, usually with sound, is more impressive than slides but can quickly become obsolete. Partly because these methods lack flexibility, the costs are considerably higher. In addition, to impress the client, the firm may resort to rear-screen projection, two-or-three screen projection, or a combination of slides and motion picture or videotape projection.

Although the slide show can be flexibly assembled to identify with the program needs of the potential client, if not carefully considered and lightly presented, it can literally put viewers to sleep. Slides which glorify the architect's talents, those of latter-day masterpieces and dynamic ones which "turn on the architect," may be unappreciated by outside viewers.

Brochures. Often the general office brochure is the first impression a client has of an architectural firm. Because of this, it should reflect a high degree of professionalism and uphold the office's standards and traditions. Brochures come in all sizes, shapes and colors. Some firms prefer the horizontal legal size, others the vertical letter size or a square format; some select soft covers, others hard; some use loose-leaf, others bound; some adopt bold, bright colors, others select more dignified, darker tones. In all cases, the firm's logo is prominently displayed, usually on the cover. Preferences are as diverse as the firm's principals and the image they wish to convey.

Most brochures show renderings and photographs of selected projects of architectural significance, usually illustrated in black and white; interiors, however, are best presented using the four-color process. Photos should include people, where possible, and give a clear idea of how a building works and/or how it fulfills the user's needs. Other features may be photos of the principals and employees in working situations, biographical information, and standard introductory pages that include a description of services and a list of projects, and a short statement of philosophy. Written material should be clearly written, concise and kept to a minimum.

Some brochures subtly educate a client in what an architect does: A few pages are devoted to a small, easily understood segment of a project, first in bubble diagrams, then in schematics, working drawings and, finally, in a photograph of the completed building—from concept to

reality. Brochures serve only as a starting point, with details filled in verbally at a later date.

Aside from the general office brochure, which usually follows a set format, the architectural firm will often assemble timely customized brochures geared to a client's particular area of interest. A flexible loose-leaf general office brochure often will meet this need by the simple rearrangement of the individual pages, e.g, emphasizing hospitals rather than office buildings, and adding new pages and other information. Some type of prototype layout will facilitate the assembling of special brochures. Slip cases may be used to hold individual booklets or folders which show examples of a particular building type; the folders contain sets of loose pages which are flexible enough to be updated at minimum cost and delay.

Brochures are important in that they can capsulate a firm's experience and capability. Other than for establishing an initial set of credentials for consideration, expensive-looking brochures prepared for specific projects can become a disadvantage. A high-budget brochure does not equate with a low-budget project.

A brochure introduced and circulated at a meeting can be detrimental to the presentation process. Literally, as each of the building committee members are politely turning the pages of the promotional piece, they are neither hearing the accompanying verbal remarks by the

EXHIBIT 5-1. ORGANIZATION OF A GENERAL BROCHURE

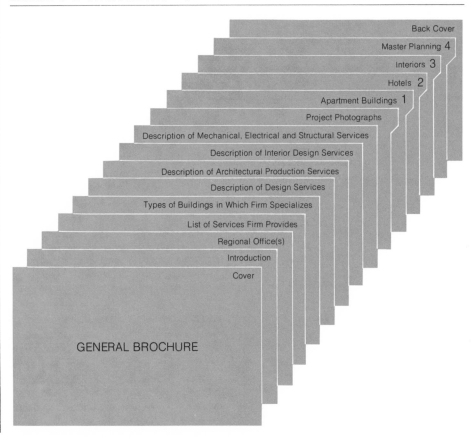

architect nor are they in fact having the opportunity to evaluate the content. It may be desirable to distribute such material after the presentation.

Supportive Material. The business development office also should develop separate backup and illustrative material to send to prospective clients and to keep current and past ones abreast of the firm's activities. Such material may include in-house publications covering current projects in design and under construction; special pamphlets on the firm's lesser known special capabilities, e.g., graphics and furnishings; reprints (with a facsimile of the cover) or tearsheets of newspaper and magazine articles written about the firm or by its personnel; in-depth technical reports; and speeches delivered by principals or employees. This material is also useful for external newsletters.

A well-organized architectural firm maintains thorough, up-to-date project files which should contain information on every project for the past 15 or 20 years. Aside from general descriptive materials—press releases, fact sheets, design concept pieces, feature articles and background material on the client's firm —these files should include complete sets of black-and-white photos, both exterior and interior; sketches and renderings; and 35mm color slides. Occasionally, 4x5 color transparencies, used to produce color prints, are part of the files.

GOALS AND BUDGETS. To weave together the various elements that generate new business, it takes a well-thought-out, long-term plan with identifiable goals. The business development team should anticipate at least a six- to nine-month lead time—occasionally as long as two years —in developing new business and should not feel discouraged if results are not immediately forthcoming.

The budget should allow for ample personnel and expenses to coordinate and follow through on a business development plan. (During slow periods, the business development staff should grow.) Figures gathered by the author indicate that firms with yearly grosses of $100,000 to $500,000 spend 5 to 10 percent for business development. Above that, expenditures average out to about 5 percent. Another set of data points out that the majority of architectural-engineering firms with public relations programs allocate 1 to 3 percent of their annual budget for this purpose and more than one-third of them from 4 to 6 percent.

By surveying the past performance of repeat and referral clients, it is possible to project gross compensation as much as a year in advance. For established firms, some 60 to 80 percent of all work can come from repeat clients. With a well-organized business development effort, the percentage can substantially increase.

KEEPING THE CLIENT

The key to effective client relations can be found in *communication*—frequent contact which enables client and architect to identify problems and other areas of mutual interest. This signifies a partnership based on active participation of the client in the design and construction process and entails sharing information, experience and expertise.

In the ideal situation, architect and

EXHIBIT 5-2. ORGANIZATION OF A SPECIAL BROCHURE

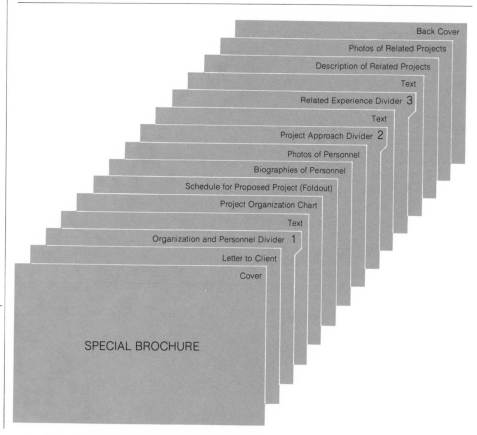

Back Cover
Photos of Related Projects
Description of Related Projects
Text
Related Experience Divider 3
Text
Project Approach Divider 2
Photos of Personnel
Biographies of Personnel
Schedule for Proposed Project (Foldout)
Project Organization Chart
Text
Organization and Personnel Divider 1
Letter to Client
Cover

SPECIAL BROCHURE

client "educate" each other, keep each other abreast of developments, and make decisions together in an atmosphere of understanding and common knowledge. Nothing will come as a surprise to a client who continually works in concert with the architect's team and is kept informed of the project's progress. For instance, if the budget and the program initially prove incompatible, the client readily will see the reasons because of participation in the process that resulted in that decision. It is up to the architect to discuss with the client all problems as they occur and all phases of the work as the project progresses. This allows for the most rapid decisions to take place in an atmosphere of congeniality and lessens the possibility of misunderstanding.

NEGOTIATING THE CONTRACT. Client relations will proceed in a smoother manner if both parties clearly understand the ramifications of a well-defined contract.

Scope. Before determining compensation and the type of contract, the architect should practice certain mandatory ground rules:

—*Know the client:* Ask some questions. Is the client a developer with building experience or a private individual or corporation with little or no experience? Is it a government agency—local, state or federal—which has unusual requirements? The major question is: How knowledgeable is the client about architecture, engineering and financing?

—*Know the scope of the project:* Quiz the client on all known details. Are one, two or three buildings planned—for construction immediately or ultimately? Why did the client arrive at the size of, say, 126,000 square feet? Who did the preprogramming? Who owns the site? Who owns the client's company? Is financing set and a bond issue required (if government work)? What is the zoning? Who is

to be the one point of contact for the client, and does the person have authority and experience? What is the method of project delivery? The architect who does not fully understand the scope of the project should keep asking the client pertinent questions. All clients tend to underplay the scope at this point, but the more they talk the larger the project becomes.

—*Know the scope of services:* The architect should not assume anything when discussing this area. Determine if the project will include master planning, site evaluation, promotional services, existing structural evaluation, programming, interiors, furnishings and graphics in addition to the normal schematics, design development, contract documents and services during construction. Also, identify the disciplines involved: architectural, mechanical, electrical, structural and civil engineering. Find out who is to select or coordinate the special consultants: traffic, parking, landscape and acoustics. *Compensation Management Guidelines for Architectural Services,* AIA Catalog No. M188, emphasizes these points.

When the architect knows the client, the scope of the project and the scope of services, it is then time to discuss compensation and the type of contract.

Compensation. The principal point made in the AIA's manual on cost-based compensation, *Compensation Management Guidelines,* is that the architect's remuneration should be directly related to the cost of providing agreed-upon services rather than to some arbitrary yardstick. It is essential that a reasonable margin of profit is valued for in determining the worth of these services. A project should not be negotiated at a reduced fee with the naive thought that it might bring future business.

In an article in the November 1973 *AIA Journal* titled "Agree Cautiously!" by Thomas Nathan, AIA, 11 points relating to compensation are cited in relationship to

use of non-AIA agreements:
—State the amount of compensation in positive terms.
—If the basis is stipulated sum (also known as lump sum or fixed fee), define the scope of the project and make allowances for adjustment if the scope changes substantially.
—If the basis is percentage of construction cost, define cost to cover all conditions.
—If the basis is professional fee plus expenses, follow procedures for stipulated sum and define expenses.
—If the basis is multiple of direct personnel expense, define terms and make sure other direct expenses are either reimbursable or paid by the owner.
—Don't confuse direct and indirect expenses.
—Clearly set out the method of payment and relate it properly to scope of services.
—Make sure the method of payment covers certain contingencies if the project is abandoned.
—Do not agree to an indefinite or contingent payment based on the owner's or contractor's action (taking title to land, securing zoning, etc.).
—Make sure the other party to the contract is solvent.
—Establish provisions for additional work, including unreasonable and unforeseeable time overrun of construction administration.

In determining method of compensation, the multiple of direct personnel expenses seems to work best when the scope of a project is vague. The stipulated sum method has its advantages when the scope of services is in detail, but is not necessarily the best contract. Cost per square foot is popular with some clients—especially for large uncomplicated projects such as factories or warehouses—but it may not account for inflation, and problems sometimes arise in determining net versus gross square feet.

Terms of the Agreement. A contract (agreement) between owner and architect should have clarity of language that facilitates understanding of all aspects of a proposed project. The AIA publishes standard forms of agreement that cover these contracts as well as an entire series of interrelated documents (architect-consultant, owner-contractor, etc.).

The AIA has, in recent years, made a concerted and continued effort to update and coordinate all of its documents, with the consistent help of attorneys and others knowledgeable in the field. Thus it is strongly recommended that architects take advantage of these documents, certainly as a base from which to start.

While the AIA recommends the standard form contract, many large architectural firms have developed their own variations based on their individual needs, and some clients have a preference for their own agreement forms. In all cases, it is wise to have legal counsel, experienced in architectural and construction terminology, assist in preparing the contracts. Many firms follow the philosophy: "Lawyers do contracts, architects do buildings."

In owner-architect agreements, there are five basic cautionary areas:
—Definition of the project's scope and the services to be performed
—Duties of all parties
—Amount and method of compensation
—Adherence to the budget as a condition of the contract
—Time

Under the duties of parties in the previously cited article by Thomas Nathan, 15 distinct warnings are given:
—Do not guarantee construction costs.
—If meeting the budget is a condition of the contract, make sure it is realistic for the time and place, has some degree of latitude, is flexible to variations in the scope of the project, and, if exceeded, the architect has the right to make revisions with the owner's cooperation.

—Do not guarantee accuracy of cost estimates. Even without a "guarantee," the client believes that the information from the architect is reliable, and the latter is often hard pressed in explaining more than minimal differences in cost.
—Do not assume responsibility for topographic or survey information or soils reports.
—Do not agree to provide services not defined in the agreements.
—Do not agree to "supervise" the construction.
—Do not assume any responsibilities which are the contractor's or anyone else's.
—Do not guarantee the performance of any contractor, subcontractor or their employees.
—Do not guarantee quality of workmanship.
—Do not guarantee or certify to the use of funds paid to the contractor.
—Do not agree to become liable to the owner for damages arising out of "stopping work."
—Do not agree to conditions in the agreement which conflict with the general conditions without specific stipulation.
—Do not agree to the owner's general conditions without first checking for differences with the AIA's general conditions.
—Make sure the duties and responsibilities of the owner are understood.
—Do not agree to surrender ownership of documents or the reuse of documents without appropriate safeguards and compensation.
During negotiations, the architect should be candid and should try to avoid feeling intimidated. Other general hints:
—Get dates in the contract to account for inflation.
—Do not pretend to have the final word, i.e., have an "out," such as "I have to check with partners" or "certain points with the attorney," or "redoing the figures will take more time."

—Always have a number of concessions ready to give and know the value of each.
—Do not concede too rapidly, yet do not argue too much.
—If the mood is not right, break off the negotiations and ask for more time.
—Argue with facts, not with emotions.
In short, make a *good* deal—not just *a* deal. More loss situations are determined at the negotiating table than at the drafting board.

These are only some of the areas in which architects should protect themselves when not using a standard AIA agreement form. When in doubt, it is best to consult an attorney who is familiar with construction contracts.

WORKING WITH THE CLIENT. Following selection of the architect and negotiation of the agreement, most projects proceed along a well-known phased path of services from the initial programming to beyond occupancy: predesign, site analysis, schematic design, design development, construction documents, bidding or negotiations, construction contract administration and post-construction. Both the architect and client will benefit from a thorough knowledge of these phases and their timing and sequence. The *Project Checklist*, AIA Document D200, and the already cited *Compensation Management Guidelines* are useful tools in implementing the major project milestones and the communication required to achieve them.

Predesign Services. The initial phase establishes the project program, financial and time constraints, and other requirements prior to the beginning of design.

At the beginning of the predesign services phase, the architectural firm assigns a person—partner or project director (titles vary)—to administer the project. This individual details the program with the assistance of the client, reviews all legal ramifications, establishes a completion date for each phase of the project, and determines tentative space and volume requirements. It is the partner-in-charge or the project director who attends all meetings and has communication on a day-to-day basis with the client's representative. This is the direct and most important link between client and architect.

Once a contract has been agreed on, too many times an architect rushes to the design board without a thorough critical review of the program. If, due to this over-zealousness, the architect errs in the interpretation of the program, it can cause a substantial loss of time and, consequently, money.

To avoid this occurrence, it is desirable to encourage the client's participation in the project from this point until the completion of construction. During the programming phase, the client and architect collaborate on quantity, size, technical, human and physical requirements of each type of space; functional interrelationships among spaces; requirements for flexibility and expandability; needs relative to special equipment and systems; and site requirements. They also review space schematics and flow diagrams to determine the project's internal functions; human, vehicular and material flow patterns; and general space allocations. This often includes a detailed analysis of the client's operating functions and studies of adjacencies, circulation and traffic.

Following the establishment of the program, the architect begins to assist the client in preparing a mortgage package to take to a lending institution to obtain financing if this is part of the agreed-upon services. Two comprehensive reference sources for this activity are two AIA books: *Financing Real Estate Development,* edited by Harry A. Golemon, FAIA, and *Development Building: The Team Approach,* by C. W. Griffin.

A typical mortgage package contains a general description of the project; out-lines of construction and equipment or material; basic design concept documents (site plan, vertical sections through the buildings, principal floor plans, elevations, general descriptive views, illustrative sketches, models, renderings of the exterior, and actual photographs of the existing site and surrounding area); a statement of probable construction cost, including data from consultants; and background information on the development team (partners, developer, architect and contractor, if selected) and what function each would perform.

The general description includes architectural and structural information, neighborhood characteristics, legal information, outline specifications, survey reports and comparisons of land values in the general vicinity of the project. Often architects can direct clients to available sources of financing within the community.

After identifying the lender, loan applications and negotiations proceed simultaneously. However, before approval of the loan application, the project's economics are more thoroughly projected, based on the potential loan commitment. In a later phase—schematic design services—the architect completes schematic drawings, and construction costs are estimated in order to obtain greater accuracy. Project costs and the potential loan commitment are reconciled, and the client accepts the interim or permanent loan commitment.

Marketing studies are often submitted as part of the mortgage package. Basically, these economic, social and political feasibility studies are in-depth looks at the advisability of placing a project in a certain area at a certain time. They are conducted by either the architect or, more often, by an independent outside consulting firm. A small firm's capability in this area should be verified; the effort may not justify the liability. Marketing studies attempt to predict, as accurately as pos-sible, whether clients will receive the best dollar return by locating their projects in a particular area.

Taken into account in this study are land values, interest rates, availability of money, proximity and the market for the type of service offered by the client.

If the studies pencil out favorably, then the client would include it within the mortgage package; if not, the client should forget the whole project.

Assuming the economics of the project are favorable, the architect now looks to the overall planning approach. What is the best way to save the client money? Before signing the owner-architect agreement, it has been determined whether or not to use such devices as construction management, fast-track techniques and network scheduling.

The client may hire an outside consultant to manage a project, entirely independent of the architect or the contractor. The consultant becomes the owner's agent. This is commonly known as construction management, a highly organized effort to treat all aspects of a construction project as a coordinated process, from feasibility studies up to and including occupancy in some cases. Construction managers review all programs, designs and suggestions developed by the project's architects, engineers and contractors, enabling them to advise the client in choosing the most desirable building options (usually from a cost standpoint).

Assuming the owner has delegated this job to a highly competent agent, such an approach may produce the best possible choice of materials and systems, the greatest cost benefits and the shortest construction cycle, all with concern for the building's operation and maintenance after construction.

Cost savings are obtained by identifying all systems and materials in the original scope and budget, establishing the total cost and evaluating it against the yardstick of a minimal-cost building. Construction managers may encourage input from contractors, subcontractors and material vendors. They consider any practical suggestion that accomplishes the intent of the design, proper building function and reasonable maintenance, and saves the owner money by carefully analyzing both first costs and operating/ maintenance costs (life cycle cost analysis as discussed in Chapter 12).

Fast-track techniques may require sophisticated programming capabilities and long experience in the building industry to produce an effectively directed and administered phased design and construction schedule. Use of this concept permits the start of construction prior to the completion of working drawings. The fast-track method saves substantial time in the overall project which results, especially in an inflationary market, in saving considerable money. At the same time, fast-track scheduling requires great skill on the part of the architect.

Network scheduling is a simple, logical master plan for the development of a construction project which provides a general framework for accomplishment. It provides the mechanism for both client and architect to know the work completely before a project starts. The network schedule constructs a framework to assist in planning the numerous and complex activities of the design process, the overall project development and the schedules of events. It establishes a format for making more accurate estimates of costs.

Site Analysis Services. The architect may provide the client with agreed-upon services necessary to establish site-related constraints during the site analysis phase. During this phase, the architect works with the client on locating, evaluating and finally selecting a site, if not already acquired. Services may include detailed studies of topographic and sub-

surface conditions, utilities, zoning, land use requirements, parking and traffic flow regulations, and determination of deed restrictions and existing and proposed easements. The architect, or special consultant, may also study labor potential, availability of specific skills, labor relations and public relations—all with input by the client. (Note: the architect's professional liability insurance policy should be checked for coverage of additional services not normally included.)

Schematic Design Services. At the beginning of the schematic design service phase, many architects call an "organization" meeting to familiarize the client and all consultants and team members with one another as well as with the overall program. During this phase, the architect prepares drawings and other documents for approval by the client. The architect and client continue with practically day-to-day communication and contact. Since this has been the case throughout the first two phases of the project, where the architect has been retained for these phases, the client will thoroughly understand that wants and needs, outlined in the program, have been adequately met.

(Throughout this phase as well as all other phases, the architect periodically reviews the internal office budgets and production schedules, and checks against the actual progress of the project, maintains expense accounting records and submits monthly statements to the client, including reimbursable items.)

Design Development Services. Prior to starting the design development phase, the architect reviews the schematic design checklist and ensures that all required data has been obtained and assimilated. With the client's input, the architect delineates additional or special requirements, reviews the program and verifies compliance, rechecks the schematic documents against all codes and

regulations, selects additional special consultants (the architect ascertaining who pays for these services), and re-examines all miscellaneous data received from the client and consultants. It then becomes practicable to develop the documents in greater detail.

At this point in the traditional linear process, the architect confirms with the client whether to use a single or multiple contract system. Because the client has continually participated in all the previous phases, it should take little explanation to reach decisions.

During this phase, the client and architect should consider initiation of a comprehensive public relations program, using either an in-house staff or outside counsel. Actually, some preliminary public relations work may have occurred in the early phases—announcement of selection of architect, construction manager, etc.—but the client can say nothing substantial until after the approval of the schematic design. This program should receive the same care as the building design. The architect's public relations staff or agency should consistently maintain contact with the client.

The client and architect should define their "publics," i.e., the segment of the population each wishes to reach. A strong public relations effort will enable clients to reach the media with news releases and demonstrate to the general public their concern for the community. Public relations information, disseminated during the program, goes to the client's employees as well as to the local press. The *story* told in the release may explain the reasons why the client is moving from, say, the inner city to the suburbs or why a plant expansion will help to create new jobs for citizens. This is basically "hard" news and will appear on the front pages of smaller newspapers and on the business/ financial pages of larger ones.

In general, the client wants the new building known to the public for such reasons as these: Stockholders are interested in a management philosophy geared toward a functional, efficient, flexible and consolidated operation; employees are concerned with an attractive and healthy working environment; community leaders, viewing the immediate and long-term welfare of the community, see it as a handsome contribution to the environment and a sizable financial investment.

Image and prestige within a community also are of client concern. The architectural firm can assist by having its public relations staff or consultant contact national architectural magazines and other publications regarding the design of the building. The key to public relations, architecturally speaking, is not to attempt to "sell" or promote the design of a building. If the design is a good one, the architectural publications may publish it, although space is always a factor. A poor design published through pressure or promotional methods does more harm than help the reputations of the architect and the client.

The public relations program allows the architect to show interest in the client. Aside from distributing information on the design of the building to the press, such an effort also can offer services to the client, among them setting up ground-breaking, topping-out or dedication ceremonies. Public relations staffs can handle all details to ensure the function's smooth and efficient operation.

Construction Documents Services. Before entering the construction documents phase, the architect reviews all previous checklists and the program and checks the documents against all codes and regulations. If not already determined, the architect should discuss the client's requirements for phased occupancy and what items the client may wish to furnish. It is also appropriate at this time to assist the client's legal counsel in determining

a suitable type of construction contract.

During this phase, the architect prepares final drawings and a project manual that includes specifications. All completed documents are checked for coordination, compliance with the program and accuracy. The architect reviews the cross-coordination program with the engineers and consultants. Each consultant furnishes a further statement of probable construction cost. The architect prepares testing and quality control program budgets, and final calculations on net and gross area and on volume. The architect and client should jointly review these items as well as a list of potential contractors and their qualification statements.

Bidding or Negotiations Services. Each construction project requires a general contractor (or two or more prime contractors) and a number of subcontractors. The architect's role in the bidding or negotiations phase is to advise the client on the best course of action. Selecting contractors can be done in three ways:

—Open competitive bidding, which is used mainly for public projects. The architect advises the client on publication of an advertisement in local papers and solicits statements of qualifications from interested contractors/bidders. In most cases, the architect is the best judge of the bidder's qualifications. The low bid is not necessarily the best bid; the architect takes into account the bidder's experience, available personnel and expertise.

—Invited competitive bidding. Selected bidders are notified by the client or architect as to the general scope and time schedule of the project and asked to submit their proposals. The same rules apply as in the case of open competitive bidding.

—Direct selection. Commonly used in larger projects, the direct selection system of construction award requires negotiation with a selected contractor. The architect recommends the most qualified

contractor and obtains the client's concurrence.

The architect may hold a prebid conference to make sure that all documents are understood; assists in receiving, tabulating and analyzing bids; advises the client on acceptance or rejection of a particular bid; and notifies successful bidders of acceptance.

Construction Contract Administration. Prior to the start of construction, the architect obtains, reviews and forwards the contractor's performance bond and labor and material payment bond (if requested) to the client. If required by the contract documents, the architect also has the contractor file a certificate of insurance with the client and has the contractor secure and pay for all required permits. The client is also alerted to insurance to be carried as required by the contract and that recommended for additional protection. The architect also should review the contractor's list of subcontractors, schedules of values and estimated progress schedules, discuss them with the client and act on them in accordance with the contract documents. Copies of all required construction documents should be furnished to the contractor by the architect at this point.

During the construction period, the architect visits the site at intervals appropriate to the stage of construction, occasionally with the client. The architect reviews the contractor's proposals for changes, prepares change orders for the client's approval, and transmits the client's orders and instructions to the contractor. The architect has the power to reject work not in conformance with the contract documents and, by issuing certificates for payment, determines the amounts to be paid to the contractor.

Shop drawings and materials submissions are reviewed from time to time. When construction nears completion, the architect assists the client in obtaining a certificate of occupancy, receives the contractor's written notice that all work has been completed and makes a final inspection of the project. More often than not, the "punch list" of items to be completed or corrected takes many weeks to complete; many problem items emerge only after occupancy.

Post-Construction Services. If applicable, during post-construction services, the architect may serve as a trouble-shooter during initial occupancy and until proper operations are established. The architect also may consult with the client if some building element fails to function properly. Post-construction services may include the evaluation of the initial program versus actual use of a facility; the operation and effectiveness of the various building systems and material systems in use; the functional effectiveness of the facility plan; and the application and effectiveness of the design/construction process.

Just as a high level of professional competence is required in the design and documentation effort, so should such a level be applied to business development. The energy and expertise expended in this area will return dividends that include better community relations, increased number of clients, and an opportunity for architects to concentrate their talents on the practice itself.

During the course of the project, the client and architect are drawn closely together in a cooperative effort. All major decisions are made jointly, and the full participation of the client becomes a positive contribution to the end result.

BIBLIOGRAPHY

"Agree Cautiously." Thomas Nathan. *AIA Journal,* November 1973.

Excellent checklist on the pitfalls to avoid when negotiating a non-AIA contract.

Architect's Handbook of Professional Practice. Washington, D.C.: AIA, parts updated periodically.

Current compendium of practice information; chapters on client, public relations and marketing especially pertinent.

Compensation Management Guidelines for Architectural Services. Washington, D.C.: AIA, February 1975.

Concise manual on cost-based compensation, divided into easily understood sections; section on negotiating especially pertinent.

Comprehensive Architectural Services. William Dudley Hunt Jr., ed. New York: McGraw-Hill, 1965.

Written by architects in practice, stressing architectural services.

Consulting Engineer. Barrington, Ill.: Technical Publishing Co., November 1975.

Major part of the issue devoted to new business marketing.

Effective Public Relations. Scott M. Cutlip and Allen H. Center. New York: Prentice-Hall, 4th ed., 1971.

How to organize and manage a comprehensive public relations program.

Financing Real Estate Development. Harry A. Golemon, ed. Washington, D.C.: AIA (Aloray Publisher), 1974.

Informative section on preparation of mortgage packages.

"Flexible System Gets the Most from Firm Brochures." Don V. Roberts. *Consulting Engineer,* February 1969.

Summary of components which make up a general office brochure.

The Guidelines Architectural Letter. Orinda, Calif.: Guidelines Publications, October 1973.

Imaginative tips on what to guard against when negotiating contracts.

The Guidelines Architectural Letter. Orinda, Calif.: Guidelines Publications, December 1973.

Touches on client search methods and information-gathering techniques.

How to Market Professional Design Services. Gerre L. Jones. New York: McGraw-Hill, 1973.

How and where to find potential clients and how to sell them.

Marketing Architectural and Engineering Services. Weld Coxe. New York: Van Nostrand Reinhold, 1971.

A good how-to book.

"Project Checklist." Washington, D.C.: AIA, 1973.

Outline of tasks to be completed during phases of a project.

"Public Relations." Andrew Warren Weil. *Consulting Engineer,* a continuing series.

Concise tips on all aspects of the subject.

"What It Takes to Have a Marketing Program." Weld Coxe. *Charette Journal of Architectural Practice,* July-August 1973.

Views the framework necessary to establish a successful program.

"Why and How to Plan Professional Firm Management." Bradford Perkins. *Architectural Record,* March 1972.

Comments on a management approach to business development.

Chapter 6
Financial
Management

PETER PIVEN, AIA

The first and most important action in the development of any financial management system—in fact, in any decision to *have* such a system—is to establish a clear and simple statement of the firm's objectives and then the policies to be implemented in reaching them. Clearly, one of any architectural office's goals must deal with the financial aspects of the existing practice or practice-to-be, especially as regards profit. Profit is vital for capital growth, reward for risk and return on investment.

Peter F. Drucker, writing in *Management: Tasks, Responsibilities, Practices*, expresses this somewhat differently, indicating that any "Business needs a minimum of profit: the profit required to cover its own future risks, the profit required for it to stay in business and to maintain intact the wealth-producing capability of its resources." He further states, however: "Profitability is not only a need, it is also a limitation. The objectives of a business must not exceed the profitability with which it can expect to operate."

Following the development of a statement of overall goals, which must include those for profit, and the balancing and resolution of inherent conflicts that result, the firm should take the next step and develop a subprogram for the financial management aspects alone. How are the firm's financial aspects to be managed? By whom? On what schedule? With what results? The answers to such questions constitute the first step of what management of any kind is all about: planning.

THE PROFIT PLAN

Planning income, expenses and profit constitutes the profit plan, which formalizes the financial objectives of the firm. It identifies the profit goal and the required income and expense levels necessary to attain that goal. As an integral part of the overall technique for management planning and control for the year, it becomes the basis for the periodic (usually monthly) budget used to control all expenses—direct (project) and indirect (overhead)—and then becomes the measuring tool for evaluating the results.

Preparation of a profit plan can begin at either top or bottom: projected income or desired profit. Ultimately, it must be worked back and forth to generate a plan which recognizes a reasonable income projection and matches expenses and profit to it. In the alternative, it must establish a profit goal and tailor expenses to it or identify the need for additional income.

The essential concept in the profit plan is the interrelationship between total income and total expense and, more particularly, between net income from projects (also known as gross margin) and indirect expense. It is commonly accepted that profit is earned when gross income exceeds gross expense. In the architectural profession, income is largely a consequence of project compensation, and consequently profit is earned when the net income from projects—the amount left after direct expenses—exceeds the firm's indirect expenses. The profit plan should be a guide to determine requisite action to keep the firm on target by cutting direct project expenses to increase net income from projects; cutting indirect costs to reduce overhead; creating new income; or, if all else fails, revising the profit plan to reduce profit.

Once completed, the profit plan should be used as the firmwide guide to identify the need for new income generation and create parameters for establishing and monitoring project budgets as well as general and administrative expense. The profit plan as documented in a projected 12-month income and expense statement will identify all planned income, direct and indirect expense items, and the relationships between them in percentages. Key profitability indicators, which are discussed later, become explicit; overhead factors are identified. Projects can then be budgeted in direct proportion to the firmwide plan, and monthly income and expense budgets can be prepared for monitoring actual activity against the plan at monthly intervals. The office is in a position to plan the work and work to the plan.

ORGANIZATION AND PEOPLE

The firm must organize in a manner that facilitates and encourages effective management. Who will develop and monitor the firm's management policy and, for the larger firm, the financial management system? Who will decide on the kind of accounting and control systems that will be employed? Who will be responsible for day-to-day financial management decisions?

In small proprietorships or partnerships, the organization is explicit and obvious: Proprietors or partners are responsible for establishing the management policy of the firm and exercising direct control. They establish accounting procedures with the help of a consulting accountant, make decisions incorporating management policy and monitor the results.

As the firm grows, the principals will probably devote more time to administrative tasks. Despite project and other overhead activities, the ultimate management decisions are the consequence and responsibility of ownership and cannot be delegated entirely to others. However, the implementation and control functions begin to require significant amounts of time in a specialized area in which the principals may be little qualified or interested. At this point, the introduction of a second management level may be desirable. On projects, implementation and control functions are most ordinarily the responsibility of project managers. In the firm's administration, there may be a need for a

EXHIBIT 6-1. EXAMPLE OF CASH FLOW PROJECTION—1973

	June	July	Aug.	Sept.	Oct.	Nov.	Dec.
Cash Inflow							
Cash Balance	$5,000						
XYZ Project		$1,000	$3,000	$3,000	$3,000	$3,000	$ 5,000
A.C. Project		1,000	–0–	–0–	–0–	–0–	20,000
Total	$5,000	$2,000	$3,000	$3,000	$3,000	$3,000	$25,000
Cash Outflow							
Staff Cost	$3,000	$3,000	$3,000	$3,000	$3,000	$3,000	$ 3,000
Overhead	2,000	2,000	3,000	2,000	2,000	2,000	3,000
Total	$5,000	$5,000	$6,000	$5,000	$5,000	$5,000	$ 6,000
Net Cash Inflow							
(Outflow)	–0–	($3,000)	($3,000)	($2,000)	($2,000)	($2,000)	$19,000
Accumulated		($3,000)	($6,000)	($8,000)	($10,000)	($12,000)	$ 7,000

This analysis indicates that starting July 1, outside cash will be required until late in December. Furthermore, it appears that the practitioner will need at least $12,000 to cover expenses during this period.

Source: *Financial Management Concepts and Techniques for the Architect*, by Thomas J. Eyerman, Skidmore, Owings & Merrill, Chicago, 1973.

manager who implements financial management policy, maintains the financial management system, oversees other administrative staff, especially the bookkeeper, and reports to the principals.

The larger firm is likely to be departmentalized, and may be divisionalized, to create separate profit centers of its various internal disciplines. More and more, the larger firm tends to incorporate under the general laws of incorporation or the recent ones legislated to permit practice in the form of a professional corporation. Ownership may have been widely distributed to shareholders either within or outside the firm. Previously centralized ownership and responsibility may have become diffused requiring new and distinct management personnel. A president or other chief executive officer is appointed to manage the firm for the board elected by the shareholders. In turn, there may be a general manager or, in some cases, a business manager who may supervise an accounting, bookkeeping and clerical staff.

What kind of people are these? Today's principal of an architectural firm is likely to have been educated in a program which probably omitted any formal management training whatsoever. Duties as a manager probably suggest attempting to build on basic abilities as a planner in the broad sense by developing an awareness of good management principles.

The general manager, who is responsible to the principals, should probably be either an architect who has accumulated experience as a manager and/or has had special management education, or a business-trained nonarchitect who has developed sensitivity to the special conditions and needs of the professional firm. Overall obligations are apt to include financial and operational management encompassing process planning, project manpower planning, personnel administration and accountability for the firm's central administrative services. Accordingly, one's background should be founded in the spheres of both architecture and business.

The business manager, who is responsible to the general manager or chief executive officer, preferably should have a background in accounting or systems analysis to carry out assignments which are heavily in the areas of financial systems and controls.

The accountant provides invaluable assistance in establishing accounting systems and procedures and in providing regular auditing, especially for tax purposes. This individual offers information, advice and help in budgeting, controlling and making special decisions. It would be wise to consider pairing an aggressive accountant with conservative legal counsel or vice versa.

ACCOUNTING PRINCIPLES

In his book, *Accounting for Management Control*, Charles T. Horngren emphasizes that the manager must have an overall perspective of the entire organization, understanding the financial goals and their relationship to other goals. That individual must develop a plan to attain these objectives, execute the plan and appraise the conformance of actual performance to the plan. The division of the management process into *planning* and *control* provides the concept for effective decision making which is the nucleus of the management process.

The *data base* for effective decision making is accounting. And, as Horngren points out, it is through the financial accounting process that the accountant accumulates, analyzes, quantifies, classifies, summarizes and reports events and their effect on the firm.

Cash basis accounting recognizes income or expense when cash is received or paid. This method may be adequate for accounting in very small firms, taxation reportage or cash flow projections (the forecast of the office's cash position resulting from anticipated receipts and expenses, as illustrated in Exhibit 6-1). In general, however, the cash basis is an inadequate and misleading method of accounting for the professional services firm. It fails to recognize the important principle of work-in-process (unbilled services) so vital because billings usually follow services. Even operating under cost-based compensation (the means of analyzing compensation generally based on the costs involved in performing services), which method prompts frequent, regular billings, not every firm will be able to bill out every active project at the end of every accounting period.

Accrual basis accounting recognizes the impact of events on assets and equities when services are rendered or utilized. *Assets* are economic resources expected to benefit future activities: things of value *owned*. *Equities* are claims against, or interests in, the assets: things of value *owed*. For an architectural firm, income is accrued when it is earned, and expense accrued when it is identified as having been expended, regardless of actual receipts or disbursements.

There are occasions when a large account payable, such as a major bill from a consultant, may seriously alter a firm's financial position when the bill is paid. This is one problem with cash basis accounting. When preparing periodic financial statements, firms on a cash basis may want to consider recognizing major accounts payable to better reflect their financial positions.

Work-in-process or unbilled services is that portion of the firm's direct project labor cost which has been expended in the interest of income-producing work but not yet billed to the client. The difference in current and previous work-in-process levels is the amount of uninvoiced income. The firm's invoiced and uninvoiced income constitute its total income from projects, exclusive of nonproject income, e.g., investments, honorariums, rents, etc.

Accounting principles in general include all the conventions, rules and procedures that comprise accounting practice; they become "generally accepted" by agreement and are codified by the Financial Accounting Standards Board, the governing body of the accounting profession. Some of the more common ones include the principles of realization, a stable currency, going concern, consistency in reporting, objectivity, conservatism and materiality. Detailed explanations may be found in any good text on accounting.

REPORTS

The manager uses various reports to monitor the activities of the firm. Three of the most important are the balance sheet, the income and expense statement, and the office earnings report.

BALANCE SHEET. The statement of a firm's financial status at a (any) specific time, the balance sheet has two counterbalancing sections: assets, and liabilities and equities (sometimes called capital or net worth). Assets include all goods and property owned as well as claims against others yet to be collected. Liabilities are claims against the assets, or debts due; equities are the amounts the owners (stockholders or partners) would divide if the business were liquidated at the value shown on the balance sheet.

The fundamental balance sheet equation is:

$$\text{Assets (A)} = \text{Liabilities (L)} + \text{Stockholders' Equity (SE)}$$

From this equation is derived the essential balance of the report in which total debits (entries on the left) always equal total credits (entries on the right).

The balance sheet is an excellent report for determining the real value of a firm at any given time. When compared with other balance sheets at regular intervals, it is an effective way to measure and chart the firm's growth or decline. It is effective in measuring the financial result of operations of the firm but ineffective in measuring and controlling the operations. For that, an income and expense statement (I&E), sometimes called the profit/loss statement (P&L), is needed.

INCOME AND EXPENSE STATEMENT. The record of a firm's operations at a (any) specific time, the I&E is the key indicator of the financial success or failure of the firm as recorded in the bottom line: profit or loss.

A good I&E for an architectural firm would record on both a monthly and year-to-date basis the following:

—The various income accounts, e.g., invoiced, uninvoiced income, investment income.

—The various direct project expenses, including labor, consultants, travel, reproductions, etc.

—The difference between the above two items, sometimes called gross margin or net income from projects.

—The various indirect expenses or

overhead accounts, including indirect (nonproject) labor, benefits, general and administrative expense.

—Profit or loss.

A better I&E would record the percentages of total income for all accounts below the income line, and a still better one would show, on a separate report, budgeted versus actual expenditures for the accounting period reported and year-to-date. The AIA standardized accounting system, both manual and computer-based, provides these features.

The I&E records the financial effect of the operations for the entire firm. Architects are project oriented and tend to relate better to individual project accounts than to officewide ones. The office earnings report (OER) developed as an integral part of the AIA computer-based financial management system (CFMS) presents project descriptors and critical financial indicators for all projects active in the office.

OFFICE EARNINGS REPORT. Among the items listed on the OER for each project on a project-to-date basis:
- —Project number
- —Project name
- —Fee (referring to total compensation)
- —Income type
- —Earned income
- —Billings
- —Receipts
- —Work-in-process
- —Accounts receivable
- —Expenses
- —Profit/Loss

For each project on a year-to-date basis, the OER indicates earned income, expenses and profit/loss. By looking at one report, the firm's management—manager and/or principals—can monitor the total financial operations on a project-by-project basis and, by noting the changes in successive accounting periods, can develop a thorough understanding of the effects of individual projects and all of them on the office as an entity.

INDICATORS

The manager requires information first to plan and then to control. Accounting formalizes plans as budgets; accounting formalizes control as performance reports which compare results with plans and which spotlight exceptions: deviations or variances. The manager comes to rely on certain numerical results as key indicators of the firm's operations. With total income shown as 100 percent on the I&E, the ratio of direct job labor (DJL) and then of total labor (DJL plus indirect labor) to total income is critical. Depending on the size of the firm and degree of in-house consulting disciplines, DJL/total income might range from 20 to 40 percent, and total labor/total income proportionally higher. The manager will very soon learn at what level the firm must operate for profitability. Firms which require greater numerical sophistication can derive other productivity indicators from DJL/expense figures, including:
- —Earning capacity as a multiple of direct personnel expense
- —Employee productivity as billings per employee
- —Employee effectiveness as profit per employee
- —Project efficiency as income from projects (gross margin) as a percentage of billings
- —Project labor productivity as billings per labor dollar expense
- —Project labor effectiveness as profit per labor dollar expense

The project hours/total hours ratio provides another good indicator worth monitoring. As one of the possible output reports generated by time sheet input, these ratios aid in the evaluation of individual personnel but, more significantly, serve as a succinct but reliable indicator of the firm's overall productivity.

For most firms, a ratio of project hours/total hours, i.e., technical versus total labor, falling below 62 percent will generally record unprofitable operations, while a ratio that exceeds 63 percent will indicate a profitable one. Also, the productivity spread between project-related personnel and all personnel, including administrative and clerical, will be on the order of 20 percent, i.e., if the ratio for all employees is 65 percent, that for project-related employees should approximate 85 percent. These indices will vary as to firm and as to the firm's policy in recording time.

Specific indicators aside, the most important aspect of financial monitoring involves the variances between planned (budgeted) and actual operations. Many of the architect's standard reporting forms, but especially the I&E, lend themselves to this kind of reporting. The specific areas which require financial management control will come through analysis of the variances: the differences between budgeted and actual items, both income and expenses, for each of the accounts on the I&E. The AIA CFMS has an I&E analysis that does precisely that.

CASH MANAGEMENT

Whether on a cash or accrual basis of accounting, the management of the firm's cash is essential.

BILLINGS, ACCOUNTS RECEIVABLE AND BACKLOG/CASH FLOW. The cash flow cycle starts with *billings:* turning the value of unbilled services into cash for the firm's operations. The importance of a regular, i.e., timely, billing and collection procedure, cannot be overemphasized. The billing responsibility should rest with a specific individual—generally the principal, general manager or bookkeeper—and, if performed by clerical personnel, should be reviewed by the principal or general manager. The significance of

EXHIBIT 6-2. TYPICAL FINANCIAL PLAN

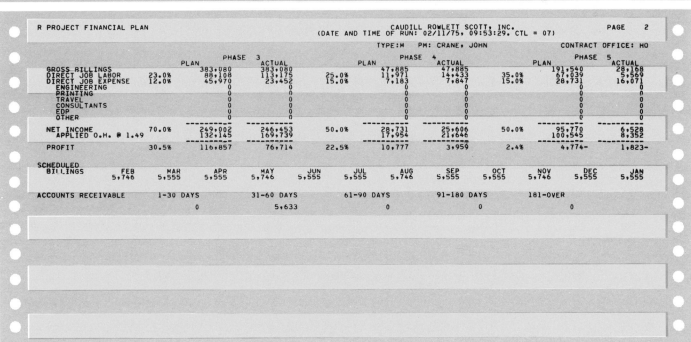

Source: Caudill Rowlett Scott, Inc.

regular billings has been recognized by some firms to the extent that project income is declared only as a function of billings, thereby imposing on the project schedule a billing schedule which serves to hasten project development in the interest of increased income and improved cash flow.

A report of *accounts receivable* should be generated by the billing process for management review. That report should show uncollected funds by project for the current period and spread by age for prior months to use as a basis for follow-up calls and short-term financial planning. The collection process cannot be routinized to the same degree as the billing process; collections must be pursued by the people responsible for projects, usually principals-in-charge.

Backlog is the difference between total committed compensation and total billings. Easily calculated, it is a good indicator of the firm's total future cash resources and, even more important, it provides the best indicator to the marketing staff of the gap between actual and projected (budgeted) income. Billing projections relate backlog spread by age for future months, generally for one full year. These projections chart the firm's future income and identify potential inadequacies in the firm's cash resources for the stipulated period. Along with the aged accounts receivable report, it offers a good basis for the identification of resources to document applications for credit or loans, to meet deficits or, in the alternative, to establish the need for a short-term investment plan for excess funds. The larger firm will wish to prepare a cash flow statement (Exhibit 6-1) to provide cash planning information to the principals, such as:
  —Cash income (billing projections)
  —Cash requirements
  —Cash balance
  —Recommendations for dealing with surplus or deficit

Forecasting is the identification of future income beyond the study of backlog and is possible to some extent in a review of the firm's marketing history: the predictability pattern of potential income from the firm's success rate in developing new business. The managed firm will have a clear idea of its success rate in promoting new business and be able to plan on compensation that may be generated by marketing activity in progress or being planned: contracts, interviews, proposals, etc. Although more a marketing function than one of pure financial management, the two are closely related. Decreasing income will identify the need for heightened new business development activity; an increase in the latter will identify potential new income for the firm.

LINES OF CREDIT AND INVESTMENTS. The successful firm seeks vehicles for the protection and expansion of surplus capital. Firms that are just beginning or those with poor cash positions require interim funding.

Professionals beginning a practice will require adequate cash resources for initial capital investment, trade accounts and suppliers, payroll and benefits at the very least. In periods when money is readily available and cheap, i.e., interest rates are low, the architect's personal bank should be a good funding source. In periods of tight currency, major lending institutions will not regard the new practitioner as highly and will more closely examine credit safety. Good personal credit ratings, tenure in business, contracts with large, secure owners and cash flow position will all be important in evaluating loans. Newer, more aggressive banks may be a useful source, and one should not completely discount the value of the personal extended credit checking account.

The architectural firm with a strong cash position will look for vehicles to make its money work. Although some state banking laws prevent corporations from owning passbook savings accounts, that rule generally does not apply to proprietorships and partnerships. Commercial paper, treasury bills, certificates of deposit, bankers acceptances—in fact, all money-market funding sources—are available to all types of firms, and, for the longer run, stocks and bonds may be considered.

In general, architectural practice will reflect the total economy. The practitioner might well consider the advice of competent investment counsel both to help forecast possible economic decline and to recommend investment vehicles in times of surplus.

EXPANDING OWNERSHIP. Regardless of the original form of practice, the growing architectural firm ultimately will face a decision regarding the opening of ownership to others in the firm. Chapter 2 suggests that the corporate form of practice will permit change with least disruption. What are the financial considerations affecting the expansion? Once the basic decision to expand has been made, the firm must be evaluated to establish the worth of the holdings of the present principals who own the business. Although the balance sheet will establish the net worth as the difference between assets and liabilities, this so-called book value does not reflect any increment for goodwill. Thomas J. Eyerman, AIA, in an article on "Methods of Establishing a Firm's Value," published in the August 1974 *AIA Journal,* offers the capitalization rate method as one reasonable way to deal with the problem of including subjective values in assessing worth. The formula

Capitalized Earnings

$$= \frac{\text{Average Earnings}}{\text{Capitalization Rate}}$$

where 20 percent, i.e., five times earnings, is given as a conservative capitalization rate for the architectural profession.

EXHIBIT 6-3. PROJECT STATUS REPORT—EXAMPLE NO. 1

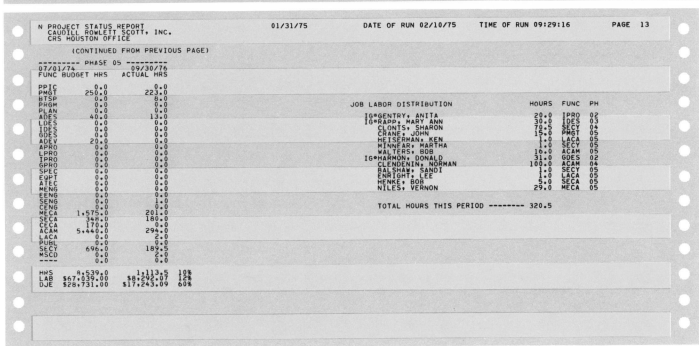

Source: Caudill Rowlett Scott, Inc.

EXHIBIT 6-4. PROJECT STATUS REPORT—EXAMPLE NO. 2

```
SASAKI ASSOCIATES, INC.              PROJECT STATUS REPORT     06/28/75  PROJ NO. 5105           PAGE 315

PROJECT NUMBER   5105      PROJECT NAME    JACKSON DESIGN CONSULTATION

MANAGER   0287    James Alexander         STATUS 4 CONTRACT      BILLING CLASS  43        CONTRACT DATE 06 04 75
DIRECTOR  0287    James Alexander         STATE CODE    53 - WISCONSIN                    CONTRACT AMT   12,000

WORK SUMMARY FOR PERIOD: 06/28/75 - WEEK NO. 26

CLOCK  E M P L O Y E E       ACCT. REG HRS O.T.HRS          AIR FARE     LODGING    MEALS  GRND TRVL      OTHER

299 2  Frank Jones              11    30.00
 28 7  James Alexander          17     4.00
 28 7  James Alexander         500                          192.73       223.56     27.10    25.00
299 2  Frank Jones             500                          160.73                  10.74    19.70

                                     34.00                  353.46       223.56     37.84    44.70

CUMULATIVE COST SUMMARY
CONTRACT COSTS

ACCT                     BUDGET    BILLING    %    BUDGET    %   OVER/UNDER                CLIENT   LAST
NO. DESCRIPTION          AT B/R    EXPENDED  EXP   BALANCE COMPL AVAIL BUDG    S&D COST     BILLED  BILLING

11 SCHEMATICS                     2,425.50         2,425-        2,425.50-    1,690.50
17 GENERAL               10,000   1,567.50   15    8,433        1,567.50-     1,032.50
   DIR LABOR             10,000   3,993.00   39    6,007        3,993.00-     2,783.00

96 PROJECT C & N            480     412.50   85       67          412.50-       287.50
   N/B LABOR               480     412.50   85       68          412.50-       287.50

   TOTAL LABOR          10,480    4,405.50   42    6,075        4,405.50-     3,070.50


520 AIR FARES                       353.46          353-          353.46-       353.46
521 LODGING                         223.56          223-          223.56-       223.56
522 GROUND TRAVEL                    44.70           44-           44.70-        44.70
523 MEALS                            37.84           37-           37.84-        37.84
525 TELEPHONE       *                39.17           39-           39.17-        39.17
528 PHOTOGRAPHY OUT *                 2.70            2-            2.70-         2.70
    UNDISTRIB. EXP.                 701.43          701-          701.43-       701.43

   TOTAL UNDISTRIB.                 701.43          701-          701.43-       701.43

624 TRAVEL OTHER         2,000                     2,000            .00
    REIMBRS. EXP.        2,000                     2,000            .00

   TOTAL REIMBURS.       2,000                     2,000            .00

   TOTAL CONS & EXP      2,000      701.43   35    1,299          701.43-       701.43

   TOTAL LABOR&EXP      12,480    5,106.93   40    7,374        5,106.93-     3,771.93

   NET ADJSTMNT                      11.26           11-            .00          11.26
```

Source: Sasaki Associates, Inc.

Eyerman proposes further that the ability to establish worth by negotiation not be discounted. In a closely held company, that negotiation will be between the selling principal(s) and those to whom shares or partnerships are being offered. For those firms offering shares to the public through investment bankers, the negotiation aspect appears first in the price per share established by the banker and the offering firm, and second in the actual price paid by the individual investor.

Once a formula has been derived to value the firm and to create a basis for later resale, the firm will require a funding mechanism so the actual purchase and transfer from present to prospective owner can be effected. One such method involves the funding of the buy-out with pretax dollars through increased salaries to the selling principals. Other means are possible, and expert legal and accounting advice should be sought.

COMPUTER APPLICATIONS. At one time, the small architectural firm may not have needed nor been able to afford detailed project and office accounting reports. In a climate of increased competition, the well-managed firm, regardless of size, will find an advantage in access to detailed financial data about itself. For the middle-sized and larger firms, a computer-based financial management system is a necessity. The mass of data and level of detail required for effective management and control makes computerization a virtual necessity. Many firms have developed proprietary programs which incorporate features unique to their own practices (see Exhibit 6-2 for a typical financial plan and Exhibits 6-3, 6-4 and 6-5 for examples of project status reports).

Of particular importance to the profession, however, is the AIA computer-based Financial Management System originally developed by Dr. G. Neil Harper from the AIA book, *Financial Management for Architectural Firms*, by Arthur Andersen &

EXHIBIT 6-5. PROJECT STATUS REPORT—EXAMPLE NO. 3

```
THE ARCHITECTS COLLABORATIVE, INC.         CAMBRIDGE, MASSACHUSETTS  3/31/72

                          PROJECT STATUS BY PHASE
                          -----------------------

NAME - ELEMENTARY SCHOOL                             NUMBER         - 70020-0
TO   - D. SHEFFIELD, R. CRANE                        PERIOD ENDING -  3/24/72

-----------------
CONTRACT SERVICES
-----------------

                       --------------PER CENT-------------   OFF   --HOURS---
                       0  20   40   60   80  100  120  140 SCALE  USED  LEFT

52-  SCHEMATIC DESIGN  *%%%%*%%%%*%%%%*%%%%*%%%%*    *    *          663   989
                       *$$$$*$$$$*    *    *    *    *    *
                       *TTTT*TTTT*TTTT*TTTT*TTTT*    *    *

53-  DESIGN DEVELOP.   *%%%%*%%%%*%%%%*%%%%*%%%%*    *    *          302   752
                       *$$$$*$    *    *    *    *    *    *
                       *TTTT*TTTT*TTTT*TTTT*TTTT*    *    *

55-  CONSTRUCTION DOC  *%%%%*%%%%*%%%%*%%%%*%%%%*    *    *         3599   -53
                       *$$$$*$$$$*$$$$*$$$$*$$$$*    *    *
                       *TTTT*TTTT*TTTT*TTTT*TTTT*    *    *

58-  CONSTRUCTION      *%%%%*%%% *    *    *    *    *    *         1779   659
                       *$$$$*$$$$*$$$$*$$   *    *    *    *
                       *TTTT*TTTT*TTTT*TTT  *    *    *    *

-------------------
ADDITIONAL SERVICES
-------------------

                       --------------PER CENT-------------   OFF   --HOURS---
                       0  20   40   60   80  100  120  140 SCALE  USED  LEFT

701  CHANGE ORD. PREP  *%%%%*%%%%*%%  *    *    *    *    *          175    99
                       *$$$$*$$$$*$$$$*    *    *    *    *
                       *TTTT*TTTT*TTTT*TTT  *    *    *    *

730  BIDDING           *%%%%*%%%%*%%%%*%%%%*%%%%*    *    *          655  -655
                       NO BUDGET ESTABLISHED
                       *TTTT*TTTT*TTTT*TTTT*TTTT*    *    *

799  CLERK OF WORKS    *%%%%*%%% *    *    *    *    *    *         1824  1154
                       *$$$$*$$$$*$$$$*    *    *    *    *
                       *TTTT*TTTT*TTTT*T    *    *    *    *

-----------------
NON-LABOR EXPENSES
-----------------

                       NON-REIMBURSABLE        REIMBURSABLE
                            $      %                $      %

INCREMENTAL BUDGET       4927  100.0             4025  100.0
SPENT TO DATE               0    0.0                0    0.0
                      -------  -----          -------  -----
BALANCE                  4927  100.0             4025  100.0

                        WHERE:   %  =  ESTIMATED PERCENT COMPLETE
                                 $  =  PERCENT BUDGET SPENT
                                 T  =  PERCENT BUDGETED CALENDAR TIME ELAPSED
```

Source: The Architects Collaborative, Inc.

Co. It provides a complete range of integrated project and office financial reports, among which are:
—Project detail report
—Project progress report
—Cash journal
—Direct expense summary
—Journal log
—Invoice log
—Balance sheet
—Income and expense statement
—Office earnings report
—Aged accounts receivable report
—Expense analysis
—General ledger
—Time analysis report
This and other similar systems afford the architect a way not only to *account* but to *manage*.

The various specific reports and methods discussed are all tools for use in the two key management tasks: planning and control. Financial management requires establishing financial objectives, especially profit; planning the firm's practice to generate that profit; and controlling activities to ensure it. Successful financial management can create the solid base to support the totally successful practice.

BIBLIOGRAPHY

Accounting for Management Control. Charles T. Horngren. Englewood Cliffs, N.J.: Prentice-Hall, 3rd ed., 1974.

Although not oriented specifically to architects, a useful, informative detailed treatise on accounting practices.
Compensation Management Guidelines for Architectural Services. Washington, D.C.: AIA, February 1975.

Concise manual on cost-based compensation.
"Computer-Based Financial Management." G. Neil Harper. *AIA Journal,* December 1972.

Discussion on implementation of AIA's financial management system.
The Economics of Architectural Practice. Case and Company, Inc. Washington, D.C.: AIA, 1968.

Early guide to financial management for architects.
Financial Management: Concepts and Techniques for the Architect. Thomas J. Eyerman. Chicago: Skidmore, Owings & Merrill, 1973.

SOM's manager's view and a very good one.
Financial Management for Architectural Firms: Computer Users Manual. G. Neil Harper. Washington, D.C.: AIA, 1971.
Financial Management for Architectural Firms: A Manual of Accounting Procedures. Washington, D.C.: AIA and Arthur Andersen & Co., 1970.

Above two manuals present AIA's best look at profit planning and a complete financial management system.
"Financial Management of the Professional Firm." Bradford Perkins. *Architectural Record,* May 1972.

General information on management principles.
Management: Tasks, Responsibilities, Practices. Peter F. Drucker. New York: Harper & Row, 1974.

Best book on management history and principles available by the authority in the field.
Management Controls for Professional Firms. Reginald L. Jones and H. George Trentin. New York: American Management Association, 1968.

By two partners of the accounting firm Arthur Andersen & Co., not written specifically for architects but strong on control aspects.
Profit Planning in Architectural Practice. Case and Company, Inc. Washington, D.C.: AIA, 1968.

Useful reference on the contribution method of profit planning.
Standardized Accounting for Architects. Washington, D.C.: AIA, 1976.

A manual of accounting procedures, with forms and instructions for use.
"A User's View of Computer-Based Financial Management." Peter Piven, *AIA Journal,* July 1973.

Introduction to the AIA's computer-based financial management system.
"Why and How to Plan Professional Firm Management." Bradford Perkins. *Architectural Record,* March 1972.

Good general information on management principles.

Chapter 7
Personnel
Management

DAVID M. BOWEN, AIA

The architectural profession's principal asset is people and their expertise. Relations with people is the core of effective management. The ability to properly manage human resources is directly reflected in the firm's morale, effectiveness, productivity and efficiency.

The best reputation that an office can have in regard to employer-employee relations is being recognized as a good place to work. Equitable salary and benefit arrangements are important to that achievement but, attractive as they may be, do not replace individual recognition, challenge and freedom to develop.

MANAGEMENT PHILOSOPHY

In his book, *Up the Organization*, Robert Townsend points out that the rewards offered to employees today are higher wages, medical benefits, vacations, pensions, etc.—none of which can be enjoyed *on the job*. It follows, then, that a good solid personnel program acts as a rudder and steers the interests of both employer and employees in a common direction. A comparison of employer and employee interests is illustrated in Exhibit 7-1.

No personnel program can be isolated to a single one of these interests, nor is any staff or individual employee concerned with only one need at a time. Each person is an entity and wants to be treated as such, even though part of a group.

Management therefore, must get to know the firm's employees, their weaknesses and strengths, and what they expect from their jobs. Such knowledge helps to create a climate in which they will motivate themselves to assist the employer reach stated objectives. A common understanding or philosophy of purpose must be developed which gains the endorsement of a majority of the employees, thereby becoming the guiding principle of the firm.

PARTICIPATIVE MANAGEMENT. Work is a very human activity and involves close and intimate relationships between people. In recent years, there has been a trend toward more participative management in the operation of a business. When developing this philosophy, the greatest and most difficult change for management is that of moving away from controlling employees toward trusting them.

Participative management attempts to do the following:

—Establish a commonality of interest, mutual trust and interdependence between employees at various staff levels.

—Improve the value of the human resources by removing conditions which inhibit self-development and growth.

—Aid employees, through in-house training, to use their creative potential to assist in the solution of management problems.

—Allow employees to improve their work situation and share experiences through team efforts.

Care must be taken when attempting such a program since some employees are not prepared to accept the responsibilities and tend to sink rather than swim.

LEADERSHIP. An important consideration in management philosophy is the attitude of those who lead. It is easy to fall into the trap of developing policies that are not really geared to the benefit of the followers but to the enrichment of the leaders. The qualities of a good leader include respect for people, loyalty, judg-

ment, fairness and humility. Compensating rewards are found in seeing improvements in performance by those being led.

There are some distinct differences between a boss and a leader which are listed in the box below. When the best leader's work is done, the employees say, "We did it ourselves," for management objectives become their own.

INTERPERSONAL RELATIONS

As defined in the field of psychology, the interpersonal theory states that personality development and behavior disorders are related to and determined by relationships between persons. Whether one subscribes to that theory is not the issue here, but the concept does focus on the importance of interpersonal relations. In personnel management, these might involve at least four factors: communication, evaluation, motivation and advancement.

COMMUNICATION. A strong communications program is imperative to maintain a common ground between employer and employee. At the bottom of many communication gaps lies the problem of an employer viewing an employee's grievance as misbehavior rather than as an intended positive feeling toward a final goal.

A study of 379 union organizing campaigns by the University Research Center in Chicago found that not one executive in 10 is aware of employee complaints,

BOSS	LEADER
Drives employees	Coaches them
Depends on authority	Depends on goodwill
Inspires fear	Inspires enthusiasm
Says "I"	Says "we"
Knows how it is done	Shows how it is done
Makes work a drudgery	Makes work an experience

EXHIBIT 7-1. COMPARISON OF EMPLOYER AND EMPLOYEE INTERESTS

EMPLOYER INTERESTS

Lowest unit personnel costs
Maximum productivity
Employee stability
Employee loyalty
Employee cooperation
High organization morale
Intelligent initiative
Profits
Growth

Personnel Program

Motivating Force

EMPLOYEE INTERESTS

Information on firm activities
Opportunity for advancement
Individual recognition
Opportunity for expression
Economic security
Interesting work
Good work environment
Fair and efficient leadership
Freedom to be creative
Control over own destiny

even after hearing them. Listening to employees should not be confused with interrogation. Instead, it should be approached on a systematic basis.

Techniques. In numerous cases, owners and/or principals are never involved until a complaint turns into a problem. Thus exposure to certain employees is more often in connection with trouble than it is with success. One system used to listen to employees is the old-fashioned suggestion box. To be successful, it must have top management support and prompt acknowledgement with an explanation when a suggestion is rejected, as this practice often indicates the first glimmer of a problem.

Some offices have employed a plan by which genuine participation can be experienced through the formation of committees composed of employees and management. Each committee keeps minutes of discussions and distributes them to the other employees. Recommendations are sent to management which must be prepared to react, sometimes to proposals of a seemingly negative nature.

A good many firms attempt to provide a mechanism for dealing with dissatisfaction by an open-door policy, meaning that employees are told orally or through written statements that any of them can,

at any time, call on the officers or principals to present and discuss their grievances or suggestions for improvement. This system seems to work fairly well, but its weaknesses should be acknowledged. Employees may feel, rightly or wrongly, that the door is closed to any matter of real substance; or they may be reluctant to "stick their necks out" as individuals— a fear that could spawn unionization if they are convinced that there is less jeopardy in approaching management as a group.

Other, more common, means of prompting employer-employee interchange are regular staff meetings, supervisory reports, team projects and periodic social get-togethers. Unfortunately, the busier and larger a firm becomes, the more difficult is the communication process.

An employee newsletter or magazine is regarded as an important communication vehicle in many firms, with monthly and quarterly dates of issuance appearing to be the most popular. Such a publication is a combination of human interest items

and news of professional activities.

Reprints of articles written by members of the firm for distribution to clients and prospects can serve effectively, too, as an internal tool, yet management often overlooks this relatively simple and inexpensive procedure. The same can be said for promotional pieces. It should be remembered that employees themselves can play a significant role in any public relations effort.

Common Understanding. A basic difficulty in communication is that the meaning which is received by one may not be what the other intended to send. This point is illustrated in the box below.

The greater the gap between the employer's background and experience and that of the receiver, the greater the effort must be to establish some common ground of understanding. Sometimes it is better to communicate outside the work environment, particularly with an obviously frustrated employee, perhaps at lunch, or enroute to a construction site. In every circumstance, the receiver should have an opportunity to ask questions. Feedback is an important tool to find out if a point is being made.

Insights into the value of effective employee communication was offered by Stephen C. Rafe, public relations manager of Amerada Hess Corporation, when he analyzed 1,000 interviews with employees who had resigned. Writing in a 1972 issue of the *Public Relations Journal*, he explained that the interviewer encouraged the subjects to respond beyond routine reasons of money and job advancement. The results showed that 36 percent admitted they were leaving

SPEAKER		LISTENER	
Intent (motive) ⟶	Expression (what is said) ⟶	Impression (what is heard) ⟶	Interpretation (meaning assigned)

because of the lack of information regarding changes in work policies and procedures; 36 percent said they had received insufficient direction; 22 percent listed dissatisfaction brought about by conflicting instructions.

Program Considerations. The following factors are among those to be considered when developing a communications program:

—A clearly defined approach, regardless of firm size, must be taken.

—Top management has to lead and demand middle-management cooperation in larger offices.

—The goal is to reach *all* the employees since some individuals are not always tuned in.

—A normal resistance to change arouses questions of negative impact which should be dealt with beforehand.

—An employee versus management syndrome seems to exist in the majority of people.

It cannot be emphasized enough that communication within a firm does not happen by accident but results from a conscientious effort on the part of everyone concerned. It is rarely as good as it can be, and few employers give this program the significant place it deserves on the overall priority list.

EVALUATION. An evaluation system, and it should be just that, is crucial if motivation and advancement are to be put in their proper context. It offers these benefits to the employer and employee:

—Serves as an employee rating procedure for employers.

—Brings attention to employee weaknesses and strengths.

—Indicates character traits in employees.

—Provides employees with objective feedback as to value of their performance.

—Affords a basis for a salary scale based on merit.

—Requires department heads or employers to become more acquainted with employee goals.

—Offers employees an opportunity to see how they are doing and where they are going.

—Permits quick response to good performance.

It is evident from the foregoing that evaluation has little value if the results are not discussed with the employee. Firms which have such systems normally evaluate new employees at the end of three months and then on the average of twice a year thereafter. Some have two evaluators for each employee, giving the task to the immediate supervisors who are best able to assume the responsibility; others evaluate by committee to eliminate bias.

There are several evaluation systems which can be utilized. Using a general rating scale for all employees has severe limitations. It assumes each category is of equal importance for a particular position. Some firms employ a numbering system and assume totals are additive, while others use "unsatisfactory" to "outstanding" for each category. Subjective-type essay questions give a more complete picture and require thought processes to be documented.

As a minimum, the rater should be required to comment on the reasons for selecting an above-average, average or below-average performance for the rated employee. Exhibit 7-2 is an example of an evaluation form providing that kind of input while retaining a simple format which should be well understood by the users.

A follow-up interview should be conducted to enable the evaluation to serve as a means of feedback by charting the progress and standing of the individual, and by giving the manager an opportunity to counsel the rated employee on improving performance. A commitment must be made at the top to have a strong evaluation system. It works best when the intent is to help subordinates improve

themselves. Evaluation to merely establish wage rates is not true evaluation but classification.

It is through an evaluation system that the strengths and weaknesses of employees are discovered. It is then the responsibility of the employee, with the cooperation and encouragement of the employer, to work on eliminating those weaknesses and develop personally and professionally.

MOTIVATION. Another prominent link between the employer and the employee is motivation. Unfortunately, as already mentioned, most rewards or benefits for service must be enjoyed *off* the job. All too often, little effort is spent on making the job itself more rewarding. Some hold the philosophy that high wages, fair treatment, good benefits, etc., will automatically motivate employees. These things do bolster the firm's reputation in the community, attract better workers and reduce turnover. But, they provide little direct motivation for personnel to contribute more than minimum effort.

Some major motivators might include achievement, recognition for that achievement, interest in the task, responsibility for an enlarged task, and growth and advancement to higher-level tasks. Properly implemented, a team-type system can provide an ego-building environment in which all or most of these motivational factors might be present. Ideally, the harmonious and supportive group assists the employee to build self-confidence.

Recognition. Most firms differ to the extent in which they allow their employees to be recognized for their achievements as individuals. Some choose to recognize publicly the individual contribution, while others work very hard to maintain the "we-the-team" approach. Recognition is important both internally and externally. Everyone has an ego—some are just more in evidence than others.

EXHIBIT 7-2. EMPLOYEE EVALUATION REPORT

Employee Name			Discipline/Group		Division		Classification
Evaluator				**Date**		**Date Discussed With Employee**	
Evaluation Narrative	**Exceptional**	**Good**	**Average**	**Poor**	**Narrative**		
Quality Of Work Describe accuracy, thoroughness and neatness of Employee's work	Consistent highest quality work; errors and omissions are rare	Work is consistently good; errors and omissions are infrequent	Work is usually acceptable; meets normal standards	Work is often below accepted normal standards			
Knowledge Of Work Describe Employee's understanding of the responsibilities undertaken	Thoroughly outstanding knowledge of his and related work	Very knowledgeable in his work	Average or required knowledge	Needs significant improvement			
Volume Of Work Describe quantity of work which meets professional standards	Consistently top output	Unusually high output	Satisfactory output	Regularly below acceptable output			
Initiative Describe the originality and enthusiasm with which Employee approaches assignments	Almost never needs supervision or encouragement	Requires relatively little supervision	Requires average amount of supervision	Generally only follows supervision			
Judgement Describe soundness and maturity of Employee's decisions and actions	Almost never faulty	Decisions are well considered	Judgement and soundness of decisions is normally reliable	Decisions are often faulty			
Cooperation / Dependability Describe Employee's willingness to accept and work with others and the ability to accomplish assigned tasks	Accepts and fulfills all assignments at superior level	Willingly handles all responsibilities	Normally willing and dependable	Sometimes unreliable and uncooperative			
Client / Colleague Relationships Describe Employee's ability to build and maintain positive contacts with clients and co-workers	Builds and maintains outstanding relationships	Usually has good rapport	Satisfactory relationships	Has some problems with others			
Potential Describe Employee's possible future growth at SH&G	At the top; exceptional potential	Above average potential	Average potential	Not to be counted upon			

Source: Smith, Hinchman & Grylls Associates Inc.

Beyond compensation adjustments, directly related to employee performance and the assignment of greater responsibility, more ego-oriented methods of recognition might include:

—Listing of employees with tenure on office stationery
—Assignment, where feasible, of personal stationery, business cards, etc.
—Individual nameplates at work areas
—Placement of employee names on the drawings

Economic Aims. Some individuals are motivated primarily by economic drives. They desire security, both financial and occupational, and are willing to work hard in order to achieve it. They may have been active in changing jobs to get experience and may demonstrate interest in getting training for better positions.

Noneconomic Aims. Others are motivated principally by noneconomic goals. They seek the recognition already cited and will respond well to praise and appreciation for work well done, and frequently tend to make suggestions. In this category are those who desire to improve their positions, to increase their prestige, and to exercise more responsibility.

Some have a pronounced need for companionship and friendship, both on and off the job. If individuals feel a strong need to work with other people, they will dislike being placed on jobs where they are isolated or work alone. Under such circumstances, their productivity and morale frequently will suffer.

In employee selection, it is of great importance to appraise carefully the individual's motivation needs. It is these which help produce action, providing incentives to perform to the best of one's ability and beyond.

ADVANCEMENT. When one talks about an employee moving ahead personally and professionally, monetary rewards generally come to mind. And these often are geared to a promotion within a job classification or to a higher position. Another important aspect of advancing in a firm is the development of an individual's capabilities without particular regard to compensation, which is covered in the next section. The superior performing individual receives the ultimate in inner satisfaction—really the greatest personal reward—when achievement is recognized by fellow employees and management, and is accorded advancement through the assignment of more complicated tasks that in turn will allow more decision-making situations.

Professional Development. In this area, continuing education can play a significant role. Many offices establish a liaison with nearby universities, colleges and schools of technology to keep current with courses offered which might help their personnel. Employees are encouraged to enroll in night courses and occasionally even day courses which relate directly to job descriptions. Some firms pay 50 to 100 percent of tuition fees on successful completion; others provide in-house courses or obtain outlines of seminars developed by professional organizations and conduct in-house sessions on a voluntary basis. Both are good methods of relating textbook teaching to practical experience.

An office may establish a library or reading service to aid employees in their pursuit of information, technical and/or general. As a secondary benefit, such a service represents an outlet for constructive use of leisure time.

Numerous firms have instituted the exclusive "brown-bag club." Members are encouraged to bring their lunch and engage in discussion on current projects, view films on products or design, or just talk about the profession of architecture. What makes this effort particularly worth-

while is when a principal becomes involved in the program.

Participatory Activities. Offices may foster membership in professional societies by assisting with dues and, as a public relations tool, by suggesting participation of key personnel in the myriad of service clubs that are available. Others promote esprit de corps, possibly by giving financial support, through such activities as in-house musical groups; drama, art and camera clubs; and team competition in bowling, softball and tennis.

OFFICE OPERATIONS

Once a management philosophy has been established and interpersonal relations have been acknowledged and implemented, an overall personnel program must be translated into something tangible by means of a definite plan.

ORGANIZATIONAL STRUCTURE. No matter how carefully a firm's structure has been organized, complete with defined areas of responsibility, authority and accountability for each position, it is the employees who give that structure vitality. Every executive should ask, "Is my office organized for hierarchical structure, or is it designed to accomplish the necessary tasks?"

The structure of an organization is essentially the relationship between the various tasks necessary to accomplish the objective of a firm and those individuals who perform the tasks. Any organizational chart should be designed to provide a system for coordinating the total efforts toward a common goal. It must also be designed to foster cooperation and establish formal channels of communication.

The classical structure reflects "rule from the top." It does not work well where operations change constantly, where relevant technology may be accessible to

well-informed, intelligent subordinates as well as to supervisors, and where adaptability to local considerations can be important to successful operations. This latter set of conditions, most often found in an architectural office, mandates a less structured, more flexible organization as being the more practical.

The flexible organization encourages group influence and enables the charge of decision making, once the exclusive property of top management, to be shared by those individuals who can make meaningful contributions.

The organizational concept shown in Exhibit 7-3 defines the groups, or teams, involved in the overall operations of a firm and their interrelationships. The illustration should be recognized as a concept that might be utilized; it must be molded to fit each particular office.

PERSONNEL POLICY MANUAL. A professionally developed personnel policy manual, prepared for both employee and employer alike, recognizes the responsibility one has to the other. The employer must fairly and adequately compensate employees to achieve goals beneficial to the public and the profession. The professional employee must understand the economic and political constraints on the employer.

The purpose of a manual is to clarify procedures and policies and eliminate as many misunderstandings as possible. Every employer has to make decisions on employee policy: by fielding questions on a day-to-day basis or developing a guidebook of personnel policy and distributing it to employees. One of the most important entries is a clear definition of the purpose and objectives of the office.

Guidelines for a Personnel Practices Manual, AIA Catalog No. M138, has been published to suggest the subjects which might be covered, and it is just that—a guideline, no more. Richard A. Drever Jr., AIA, in a review of the manual, calls it "a basic building block for both good business practice and improved employer-employee relations."

A personnel policy manual should be reviewed at least semiannually, and a legal adviser should be retained to check the manual for compliance with local and federal laws relating to employment practices. It can also be used as a tool when recruiting by showing the potential employee exactly what may be expected and what will be the basis for evaluation.

The format for a manual should include good graphics and a loose-leaf format to facilitate change. Detailed explanations of insurance and similar programs should be handled in separate pamphlets.

COMPENSATION. Employee compensation, sometimes referred to as direct personnel expense, is made up of salaries and benefits. The current edition of the standard form of Agreement Between Owner and Architect, AIA Document B141, states: "Direct Personnel Expense is defined as the salaries of professional, technical and clerical employees engaged on the Project by the Architect, and the cost of their mandatory and customary benefits such as statutory employee benefits, insurance, sick leave, holidays, vacations, pensions and similar benefits."

When mandatory and customary benefits are combined, they could range as widely as 18 to 40 percent of base income in architectural offices. Firms with sophisticated computer programs figure each employee separately, but most of them use an average percent for all personnel. When negotiating a government contract, these figures must often be justified; definitions of compensation-related terms in this context can be found in the Federal Procurement Regulations.

Salaries, Bonuses and Profit Sharing. Monetary rewards, of course, can be accomplished by several different means, including a raise in pay, conversion from an hourly wage to a salary, and participation in bonus or profit–sharing plans. (In addition, remuneration may include the opportunity to buy stock, to exercise an option or to receive partial payment in company stock; the provision of an automobile or membership in a private club; or, as has been suggested earlier, the chance for additional education with the tab being picked up by the office.)

A few words about profit sharing plans are in order. They are of three basic types: cash payment (taxable income), deferred payment (retirement income) and stock ownership. The motives for such plans are a sense of partnership, group incentive and employee security.

A successful profit–sharing plan contains the following characteristics:
—Analysis of profits is fairly done.
—Amount of compensation is related to employee performance.
—An explanation is given each employee regarding the portion received or why a proportional share was not received.
—Exceptions are not made when a formula is employed.
Among the dangers of profit sharing:

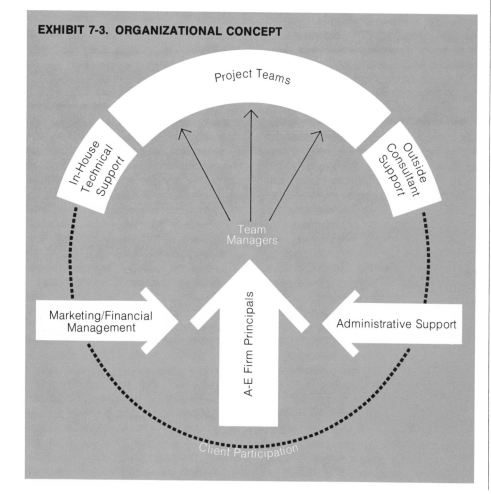

EXHIBIT 7-3. ORGANIZATIONAL CONCEPT

Project Teams

In-House Technical Support

Outside Consultant Support

Team Managers

Marketing/Financial Management

A-E Firm Principals

Administrative Support

Client Participation

—Programs are so structured that employees get to a point of expecting a share of the profits periodically, even if not deserved.

—Employees may resent receiving no payments when there are no profits.

—Employees may feel that they have made extra efforts while profits decline for extraneous reasons.

Statutory Benefits. Often referred to as mandatory benefits, these include "payroll taxes" paid by the employer, such as FICA, Workmen's (also known as Worker's) Compensation and Unemployment Compensation.

Since 1948, all states have provided for Workmen's Compensation furnishing protection related to on-the-job accidents and occupational hazards. An employer is permitted to obtain security for payment through three general methods: private insurance, a public insurance system (mandatory in some states) and self-insurance. Since compensation laws vary from state to state, the employer should know the requirements of any jurisdiction in which an office is located.

Through the authority of the Social Security Act, all states have enacted Unemployment Compensation legislation. All employers are required to pay a percentage of a defined amount of wages paid to each employee during the calendar year.

Paid Time Off. This is an area which must clearly be spelled out in a firm's personnel policy manual, whether in reference to leave time, vacations or holidays. The AIA manual underscores the importance of such policies when it comments: "The absence of a formal sick leave policy can work a hardship on staff members who suffer bona fide illnesses. However, formal policies for sick leave and personal emergencies should not be confused with time off for vacations or leaves of absence. If the purposes of each type

of time off are emphasized, abuses and morale problems will be minimized."

Leave time is used for sickness or personal time off. The amount of leave time granted (many firms restrict to illness) varies from one half-day to one day per month. Some employers allow leave time to accumulate up to a maximum number of days. Leave time, like vacations, may be considered as a reward for service where employees are compensated for time earned, whether used or not. Under this approach, the cost can be included as a direct personnel expense as defined in AIA Document B141.

Some employers give each employee a "bank" of leave-time hours for the year. If the employee exceeds the time in the bank, additional absence is reflected in a deduction of pay. If, on the other hand, all of the hours are not used, the employee is paid at the current hourly rate for those remaining. A number of offices supplement this system with a group disability income plan to cover those instances of extended absence due to sickness or accident.

The average paid vacation period is 14 days, according to statistics taken from the 1974 Survey of the Membership, AIA Catalog No. M177, developed by Case and Company. Exhibit 7-4 indicates personnel benefits reported by respondents as being provided by their firms. Some firms credit an employee with a fixed number of hours per month worked so that no conflict arises regarding the amount of vacation time earned when a termination occurs. Few offices allow employees to receive pay in lieu of vacation.

The number of holidays granted varies from 5 to 11, with the AIA survey showing the average to be 7.3.

Insurance Programs. Among the various types of coverage provided by employers are the following (see Chapter 8 for additional details):

—Hospital insurance: a program which

may cover employees only or may include dependents. Many small firms seek to join a group for lower rates and higher benefits through AIA components or other associations. Of the AIA members responding to the survey, 47.8 percent are covered for hospitalization.

—Major medical insurance: the least expensive and some say the most important of all coverages. Over half—54.5 percent—of the respondents are provided with this insurance.

—Dental insurance: a new program and becoming more common, but is at the moment expensive.

—Life insurance: generally based on the salary of the individual employee when the employee has the privilege of naming the beneficiary. Of the respondents, 51 percent are covered by a life insurance plan.

(Related to the first three but not insurance in the usual sense, preventive care is a multiphasic health testing program whose purpose is early detection of possible health care problems.)

Retirement Plans. The AIA survey indicates that 27.9 percent of the respondents are enrolled in a retirement program, with different levels of contribution by their employers. There are a number of plans, the most common being:

—Fixed benefit plan: Benefits are set according to a predetermined formula based on actuarial studies. Annual contributions to fund the benefits are made in accordance with what an employee will receive at age of retirement geared to a salary-related formula.

—Money purchase plan: Contributions are set as a fixed percentage of covered payroll. Benefits are the amounts that have accumulated in employee accounts at retirement.

—Deferred profit sharing plan: This is similar to the money purchase plan, but contributions are expressed as a percentage of profits.

EXHIBIT 7-4. PERSONNEL BENEFITS (Percentage of survey respondents reporting benefits provided by firm)

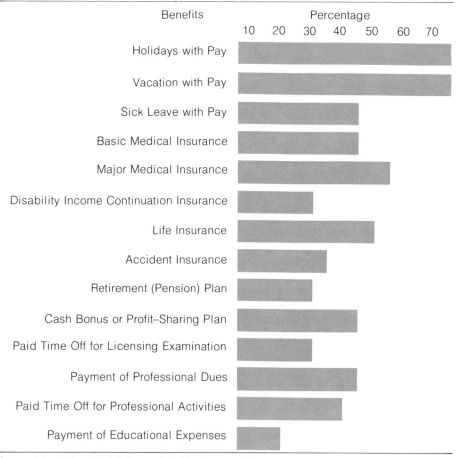

Source: Adapted from the AIA *Survey of the Membership*, 1974.

—Deferred thrift plan: This is similar to the profit sharing plan, but contributions are a fixed percentage of required employee contributions.

Whatever the type, the sole purpose of a retirement plan is to provide retirement income for employees. To be workable, one of the significant features of such a program in the highly mobile architectural profession is portability. If a benefit like this is indeed a form of compensation, then it seems only fair that an employee should not sacrifice eligibility or accumulated benefits when changing employers.

Legislative Considerations. One of two recent pieces of legislation which might have an impact on a firm's package of benefits is the Health Maintenance Organization (HMO) Act of 1973, applicable to every firm which employs an average of 25 or more employees in a calendar quarter and which is required to pay the minimum wage specified in the Fair Labor Standards Act. Such an employer must include in any health benefit plan offered by the firm the option of membership in one type of a qualified HMO during the following calendar year to the extent that it serves the area in which the employees reside. Payment to an HMO on behalf of the employee does not have to exceed the employer's normal contribution to the in-house hospitalization program.

The second, and a complex measure indeed, is the Employees Retirement Income Security Act of 1974 (ERISA) covering basically *all* employee benefit plans. Since it places a fiduciary responsibility on sponsors of such programs, employers should consult legal counsel for a proper understanding.

CLASSIFICATION. Often used to establish wage rates and to assist in employee evaluation, a classification system should indicate personnel relationships, responsibilities and specific duties that constitute a given job or position. It should answer these questions: What gets done? How is it done? Why is it done?

A separate job title or position description should be created only when the scope of responsibility is sufficiently different to warrant that specific title. To assign a title such as project architect, job captain or department head is not enough. Information on functions performed and pertinent aptitudes required should be included.

"A Classification System for Architectural Personnel," by Roger W. Boe, AIA, published in the June 1974 *AIA Journal*, can be used to evaluate an individual's position in the firm (Exhibit 7-5). It serves as a tool to indicate promotional opportunities, permit the employee to understand the responsibilities and establish a wage scale which grows with experience and education.

WORK WEEK. While the majority of firms remain on the traditional five-day week, some have been experimenting with other schedules.

The most popular thus far has been the four-day week which, in some instances, appears to decrease absenteeism and

EXHIBIT 7-5. EMPLOYEE CLASSIFICATION SYSTEM

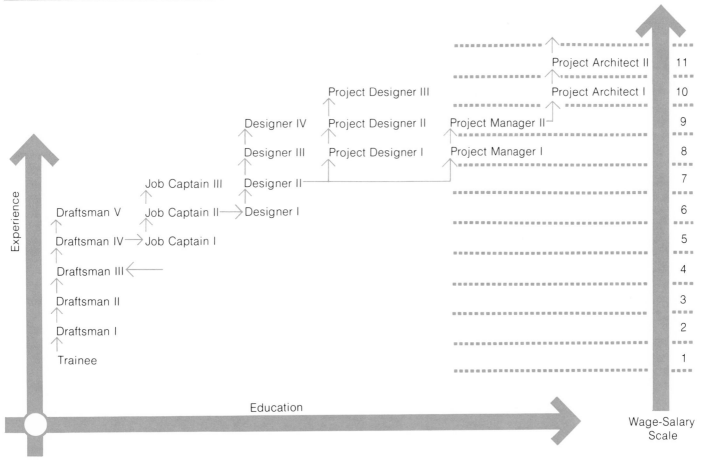

Source: *AIA Journal,* November 1974.

increase recruitment possibilities. Offices may compromise by establishing a 4½-day week in order to maintain a 40-hour week but limiting the workday to a maximum of nine hours. This seems to be especially popular during the summer months.

Another concept that is gaining momentum, particularly since experimentation in various U.S. government agencies has been underway, is known as "flexitime," a European idea which permits employees to tailor their work hours to personal needs. It differs from the four-day week, or some form of staggered work hours, although it might combine features of both. In a few cases, office hours are extended and employees are permitted to arrive as early or depart as late as they wish. However, they are encouraged to be on the job between, say, 10 a.m. and 3 p.m., and firms rarely allow personnel to work the required number of hours in four days in order to have a full day off. For many employers, flexitime may be a real morale booster in relieving the stress of rigid schedules, rush-hour traffic, etc.

Those firms which have been most suc-cessful with uncommon work schedules have taken extensive precautions to orient both the employers and the clients with the new system. And none of these programs should be considered without understanding the Department of Labor's rules on overtime pay.

The Fair Labor Standards Act says that among those exempted from the overtime provisions of the act are executive, administrative and professional employees. All employers should be familiar with those sections of the act which define exempt and nonexempt employees.

The work week is the term applied to a period of 168 hours during seven consecutive 24-hour periods. It may begin any day of the week or at any hour as established by the employer.

"Hours worked" includes all of the time an employee is required to be on duty, or on the employer's premises or other prescribed places of work, and any other additional time the employee is required or permitted to work for an employer. Non-exempt employees must be paid at least 1½ times the regular rate of pay for all hours worked over 40 in a work week; they cannot be given time off as credit for overtime in subsequent weeks as some employers misconceive.

The fact that an employee is on salary is not automatic exemption from the overtime provisions of the act. It is much safer and easier, and a good personnel practice, for employers to pay all employees at a rate of 1½ times for work over 40 hours.

As an extension of the work week, moonlighting deserves a passing mention. Most architectural firms do not encourage this practice, and for a very good reason. Many an employer who has suggested that an employee do some moonlighting to help a friend or pick up additional money, has suddenly been found on the other end of a lawsuit. Policies about moonlighting should be put in writing.

INTEROFFICE POOLING. Since the practice of architecture is subject to many outside influences that can alter the workload, many firms adopt a system for the temporary placement of personnel during periods of slow and/or expanded workload. This pooling of personnel between offices provides a more stable employment base and continuity of benefits for the employee. It also allows the employer to retain competent personnel without the economic loss of a nonproductive payroll and, conversely, to temporarily augment staff without the necessity of a long-term economic commitment. For such a system to operate effectively, a spirit of cooperation between the participating firms and a written agreement are desirable.

Although this practice might be considered normal in populated areas, it can be a very traumatic experience for the "loaned-out" employee, whose reaction may be a feeling of being unneeded or unwanted. At such a time, employer-employee communication takes on added importance.

EQUAL EMPLOYMENT. Firms which employ 15 or more employees in each of 20 or more calendar weeks of the year are subject to Title VII of the Civil Rights Act of 1964. The act prohibits any discrimination with respect to employment on account of an individual's race, color, religion, sex or national origin. By law, the Equal Employment Opportunity Commission has the authority to investigate and conciliate complaints or bring civil actions against employers on behalf of aggrieved persons.

The best and most economical method of self-protection and defense to a charge of discriminatory practices is a full knowledge of that which is allowed and that which is not under the act as amended. Since the refinements of the law change quite frequently, just a few important areas where adequate precautions should be taken will be considered.

Generally speaking, an employment application seeking to elicit information not directly needed for some purpose connected with the process of hiring can be discriminatory.

A written test is probably one of the most frequently challenged as a discriminatory practice in employment litigation. Even if the test can be validated against job performance, it still cannot be imposed on any individual if other employees or job applicants have not been subjected to it.

Any employer with group benefit plans for employees such as profit sharing, hospitalization, etc., should be careful in structuring them so as to avoid a charge of discrimination.

And every employer should be prepared to demonstrate persuasively that substantial efforts have been made to attract minorities and women in the recruiting program.

Title VII of the Civil Rights Act of 1964 guarantees equal employment opportunities for employees in private employment. Executive Order 11246, revised, on the other hand, carries forward a program of equal employment opportunity in employment under federally assisted construction contracts.

EMPLOYMENT CYCLE

All three stages of the employment cycle —recruitment, retention and termination— are vitally important in the overall personnel program, but somehow hiring and, most definitely, firing tend to get short shrift from a good many employers.

RECRUITMENT. Employment should be based on professional competence and ability to perform assigned responsibilities adequately, with employee qualifications and employment opportunities represented in a factual and forthright manner. Recruiting should be done by plan, not by chance.

The employer, or personnel manager in larger firms, should be prepared to explain the nature of the position, salary prospects, available benefits, office policies and objectives, personal and professional opportunities, and career potential. The employer in turn should be prepared to be rated by the prospect on the firm's reputation, communication, salary and benefit levels, and the initial discussion.

It is helpful to have the potential employee talk with those persons most closely associated with the job to provide a better understanding of what the work is really like. This is a protection against misunderstanding or, in some cases, misrepresentation by an eager recruiter.

Successful recruiting programs through architectural schools often involve a third-party relationship with a dean or professor. This has the advantage of closer academic/professional ties and provides the recruiter with a deeper knowledge about the education and background of a candidate. On the other side of the coin, the dean or professor should understand the philosophy of the firm to have a better idea of the type of person being sought.

Those who seek employment unsolicited should receive the same professional respect as the recruited individual. Cooperation should be sincere and honest, and the wise employer does not suggest that something might "open up" when applicants do not meet the desired qualifications.

As an operating base for recruiting, the employer should ask: "From what sources and by what methods has our office secured the most valuable employees?"

Handling of the recruitment interview is most important. (Interviews are held for a number of reasons other than for employment. Among them are to handle grievances, take disciplinary action, evaluate, assist with personal problems, transfer or promote, or to terminate.) For any purpose, the basics for a good interview are:

—Clearly establish objectives to be gained or purposes to be served.

—Give the interviewee advance warning which is reassuring, not alarming.

—Hold the interview in quiet, secluded and comfortable surroundings without interruption.

—Use straightforward words and phrases so that the interviewee gets the proper meaning.

—End the interview with a definite conclusion.

The interviewer should:

—Have respect for the individuality and confidentiality of the interview.

—Prepare for the interview by reviewing pertinent information about the interviewee.

—Make the interviewee feel at ease and encourage free discussion.

—Listen patiently and offer thoughtful advice for solving problems presented.

—Promise no more than can actually be delivered.

—Evaluate the interview.

If the interviewer keeps in mind the aims of achieving understanding and mutual respect, most interviews can be a satisfying experience in human relations.

RETENTION. All of the facets of the personnel program which have been discussed thus far, of course, have a direct bearing on this phase of the employment cycle. Suffice it here to say a few words about what happens once employment has been accepted since the introductory procedure is vital to the new employee's attitude.

The newcomer should be introduced to the principals and fellow workers, be shown the facility, and have explained the operation and the firm's goals. The office's communication channels and the employee's responsibilities and opportunities for development should be covered. It is essential that the new employee completely understands all personnel benefits: a misunderstanding and resultant financial loss to an employee which can result in a legal claim if the employer is found to be negligent in this particular area.

Some personnel managers suggest employment contracts. In any event, management must keep the climate challenging and invigorating and the rewards commensurate with employee performance. The most effective way to achieve these aims is through the evaluation system discussed in an earlier section.

TERMINATION. The third stage in the employment cycle should not be an unpleasant and neglectful act, either on the part of the employer or the employee. If poor judgment has been made about an individual's ability, then continued employment is unfair not only to the employee involved but to others as well.

When termination occurs—whether by dismissal, resignation or retirement—it should be handled positively, helping the individual to preserve self-respect. Management should be honest and should perform the following:

—Allow the employee reasonable time to find new employment. If termination is the result of reduced workload or other reasons not in the control of the employee, take that into consideration.

—Extend the insurance protection beyond the termination date where legally permitted. This could be the period of time that the coverage is needed the most.

—Offer severance pay commensurate with the contributions of the employee, with a minimum of two weeks' pay if for reasons other than cause.

—Reimburse the employee for benefits earned but not received.

—Make certain the employee understands clearly the reason for termination and establish responsibility since problems could arise if actions were found to be discriminatory.

—Maintain a record of the action taken and the events leading to the action.

—Assist the employee in finding a new job where that person's strong points can be maximized.

Retirement as a form of termination is too often given little attention in architectural offices. Here again, a procedure should be formulated that goes beyond any retirement plan suggested as part of employee benefits.

Many firms make it a practice to conduct termination or exit interviews since the employee has gained valuable data, ideas and insights which are wasted if not shared with management. In some cases, the departing employee may be reluctant to talk due to hostile or otherwise negative feelings; in others, the individual may be more willing at this particular time to freely express thoughts and opinions, especially if confidentiality is assured.

In a profession which is somewhat fluid, the termination process becomes even more critical. It is quite possible that many employees, particularly those laid off, will be rehired. Therefore, the points outlined are designed to offer a termination procedure which is professional and positive in its various aspects.

RATING THE OFFICE

To help rate its personnel practices, management should determine whether the office:

—Has a policy based on a careful analysis of the objectives and ideals of the firm—a policy known and understood by all who must work with it or are affected by it.

—Gives employees a chance to talk and listens to them.

—Has a periodic job evaluation and advancement program, and offers counseling and encouragement to employees to move up.

—Assigns responsibility that reflects dignity and prestige.

—Keeps abreast of what other employers are paying.

—Selects supervisory personnel on the basis of their management ability as well as their technical skills.

—Reviews benefits to offer the best package possible.

—Sets forth policies in writing, distributes them and sticks to them before situations arise.

—Encourages professional activity.

—Steps back and looks at the firm through the eyes of the employees.

Offices that do all of the above con-

scientiously not only will have a high rating for good personnel practices from a management point of view but also will get a top score from employees themselves.

When the late Robert F. Hastings, FAIA, addressed the Joint Committee on Employment Practices in 1968, he sounded a warning that can serve to keep interrelationships in focus. He talked about the multitude of problems that arise in any office and the "ingenious" personnel programs developed to normally cope with them. But mankind's desires are never fulfilled, and that goes for employees and employers alike. And so to believe that a problem is solved once and for all, that it and the solutions can be put in a convenient cubbyhole and completely forgotten, is one of the greatest errors of management that can be made.

BIBLIOGRAPHY

"Alternatives to Unionization." Proceedings of annual meeting. Washington, D.C.: Joint Committee on Employment Practices, c/o National Society of Professional Engineers, 1968.

Examination of employer-employee relationships.

Architect's Handbook of Professional Practice. Washington, D.C.: AIA, parts updated periodically.

Current compendium of practice information; chapter on architect's office especially pertinent.

"Building Solid Employee Relations." William R. Fleming. *AIA Journal,* September 1973.

Discussion of the three R's of personnel practice: recruiting, retention and release.

"The Cafeteria Approach to Executive Compensation." C. T. Hellmuth & Associates Inc. *Executive Newsletter,* April 1974.

Summary of principal benefits in

use today for key personnel and a brief description of their tax consequences.

"Communicating Within Your Own Office." Andrew Warren Weil. *Consulting Engineer,* August 1972.

Insight into the values of effective communications between top management and employees.

"Communications—Key to Effective Management." Andrew Warren Weil. *Consulting Engineer,* October 1970.

Tips on reaching employees at all levels.

"Employee-Employer: A Relationship in Transition." Proceedings of annual meeting. Washington, D.C.: Joint Committee on Employment Practices, c/o National Society of Professional Engineers, 1969.

Examination of development of a proper climate to promote a professional partnership.

"Employment Discrimination and the Small Businessman: An Unavoidable Pitfall?" Benjamin F. Small III. *Digest 74—Indianapolis Chamber of Commerce,* September 1974.

Points out that hiring people is no longer a simple procedure.

"Examine Your Communications Process." Andrew Warren Weil. *Consulting Engineer,* October 1973.

Some ideas on developing in-house communication media.

"Fair Labor Standards Act." *Federal Register,* Vol. 38, No. 87, Part II. U.S. Dept. of Labor, May 7, 1973.

Guidelines for a Personnel Practices Manual. Arthur T. Kornblut. Washington, D.C.: AIA, 1972.

Skeleton for building an office's own manual.

"Guidelines on Employee Selection Procedures." *Federal Register,* Vol. 35, No. 149. Equal Employment Opportunity Commission, August 1, 1974.

"Guidelines to Professional Employment for Engineers and Scientists." *Professional Engineer,* February 1973.

Developed jointly by 16 professional engineering societies to establish mutually satisfying relationships between employees and employers.

"Health Maintenance Organization Act of 1973." C. T. Hellmuth & Associates Inc. *Executive Newsletter*, February 1974.

Brief look at the options available to the employee and the employer under the terms of the Act.

"The Human Factor in the Engineering Office." Richard A. Enion. *Professional Engineer*, July 1972.

Discussion of personnel problems encountered in professional offices and recommended solutions.

Human Side of Enterprise. Douglas McGregor. New York: McGraw-Hill, 1960.

A look at the people aspect.

"Individualized Engineer/Employer Relationships." Louis A. Bacon. *Professional Engineer*, February 1973.

Examines techniques of employee evaluation.

"Is Architecture Unfair to Architects?" Clint Page. *Progressive Architecture*, June 1972.

Discusses professional employees who are finding a voice for their complaints in a growing labor movement.

"The Issue—Personnel Practices." David M. Bowen, Peter A. Ekstein and William R. Fleming, *AIA Journal*, August 1972.

The approach toward unionization and the options.

"Making the Four-day Work Week Work." Robert S. Lundberg. *AIA Journal*, September 1972.

Problems that a firm encountered in establishing a four-day work week and their solutions to success.

"Participative Management: New Approaches to Human Work Resources." Sidney P. Rubenstein. *Professional Engineer*, December 1972.

The role played by the Japanese work force and techniques used to solve work-related problems.

Personnel Administration, A Point of View and a Method. Paul Pigors and Charles A. Myers. New York: McGraw-Hill, 1973.

A comprehensive and consistent point of view at the policy level and a brief analysis of techniques and procedures.

Personnel, The Human Problems of Management. George Strauss and Leonard Sayles. Englewood Cliffs, N.J.: Prentice-Hall, 1972.

Places personnel problems in the context of management problems and deals with issues of motivation, leadership, communications and control.

Personnel Management. Michael J. Jucius, Homewood, Ill.: Richard D. Irwin, Inc., 1971.

Seventh edition of a college textbook.

"Personnel Practices in Professional Firms." Bradford Perkins. *Architectural Record*, August 1972.

Discussion of policy problems when analyzing a benefit structure and effective counters to low morale.

"Picking Your Own Work Time." *Nation's Business*, September 1973.

How flexible hours make happier employees and happier companies.

"Retirement—A Necessary Fringe Benefit." Anthony G. Maletta. *Consulting Engineer*, June 1969.

A look at different kinds of pension plans.

Survey of the Profession: Individual Members. Case and Company, Inc. Washington, D.C.: AIA, 1974.

Personnel data especially pertinent. Also includes questionnaire.

Up the Organization. Robert Townsend. New York: Knopf, 1970.

A bit contradictory to everything else one will read but refreshingly written by a successful businessman.

Chapter 8
Insurance Management

BERNARD B. ROTHSCHILD
FAIA, FCSI

Although the services rendered are professional in nature, the architect's office operation is in fact an ongoing business enterprise. The practitioner is thus subject to the usual risk of peril with which any other business venture—commercial or industrial—has to contend. In addition to these normal exposures, the architect is also faced with the unique area of liability that is assigned to those who practice professions.

None of these perils is a respecter of size. The one-person firm, literally, is exposed to the same hazards as the practice with hundreds of employees. Slippery floors or misplaced decimal points are prepared to haunt any office. Fire, smoke and water can play equal havoc with the drawings for a summer cottage or a large industrial complex. Juries return verdicts in amounts far beyond the most nightmarish expectations for loss or injuries that all too often appear not to be the responsibility of the architect-defendant. The practitioner must be prepared to evaluate these many exposures whether usual or unique and must develop the capability of making risk management decisions on how potential losses are to be offset.

EVALUATING THE PROGRAM

In all matters of risk management evaluation, there are several alternative methods of approach:

—Avoid risk by eliminating from the firm's practice those things which create a hazard.

—Ignore risk by accepting the fact that a loss might occur—in effect, be self-insuring.

—Reduce risk by taking loss-prevention steps to lessen the chance that a loss would occur.

—Transfer risk by making another party accept responsibility for the chance of loss via a hold-harmless agreement.

—Insure the risk.

Any one of these may be a valid method for handling a given type of peril, but all should be given due consideration in the evaluation of the overall program of risk management.

For most architects, however, insurance programs are generally used as the principal risk management tool since a majority of design firms do not have sufficient capital assets to set up self-insurance programs, and, more often than not, it would be impossible to revise an ongoing practice so that the exposure to claims of liability would be minimized or eliminated. There is no hard and fast rule as to what coverages must be carried and what the limits of liability should be. Insurance programs relating to the architect's practice are as varied as the individual firms. These will be governed by the size of the office, size and scope of the practice, capital assets and number of employees, as well as the economic status of the practitioner and the office. With all of this taken into account, there are still certain basic coverages which would apply to every firm, i.e., public liability, professional liability, fire.

It is important to recognize that this discussion is not intended to be a textbook on insurance and does not attempt to detail all of the potential coverages. It is rather a guide and checklist for the architect and the insurance counselor to use jointly in developing an adequate insurance portfolio. When coverages have been determined, specimens of all the policies should be reviewed item by item so that the specific terms as well as exclusions and available extensions are understood: Take absolutely nothing for granted.

COUNSELING

The architect must make certain basic management decisions concerning the handling of perils, looking to legal counsel, the accountant and occasionally even the banker for assistance in determining the exact extent of overall exposure. Once this is determined, the practitioner should obtain qualified insurance counseling.

Insurance is a tremendously complex subject, and architects often tend to view the advice of people in the insurance business as primarily sales oriented. This is more the exception than the rule, and the practitioner must have confidence that the recommendations of a competent person are in one's best interests. Just as an accountant and an attorney are retained because they are skilled professionals in their respective fields, so also the qualified professional insurance counsel should be engaged to assist in establishing the needs of that program.

It must be remembered that an individual who specializes in one field of insurance does not necessarily have the qualifications to provide overall counseling service in all areas of coverage. In selecting an insurance counselor, one important factor would be whether or not the individual or firm being considered possesses any of the professional designations which are used within the insurance industry. This would include, for example, those who are designated Chartered Property and Casualty Underwriter (CPCU), which marks persons who, in addition to having met certain experience requirements, have also passed a comprehensive set of five examinations in insurance-related subjects. Individuals with this designation generally will be able to provide counseling service in areas involving property and casualty insurance. A similar designation is provided within the life insurance industry and is known as Chartered Life Underwriter (CLU).

An important responsibility of the insurance counselor is to have a thorough knowledge of the business of insurance, especially if that party is the broker or agent actually placing the coverage. (There are firms which give advice, evaluate risks and analyze available cover-

EXHIBIT 8-1. COMPONENTS OF AN ARCHITECT'S INSURANCE PROGRAM

PROPERTY DAMAGE COVERAGES

Fire Insurance
—Extended coverage
—Vandalism and malicious mischief
—Improvements and betterments coverage
—Sprinkler leakage coverage
—Business interruption
—Extra expense
—Demolition endorsement
—Electronic data processing equipment
Valuable Papers
Boiler and Machinery Policy
Fine Arts
All Risk Policy

THIRD PARTY LEGAL LIABILITY COVERAGES

Comprehensive General Liability Policy
—Operations-premises
—Fire legal liability
—Contractual
—Premises medical payments
—Personal injury endorsement
—Host liquor liability
—Nuclear energy liability exclusion
Professional Liability Insurance
—Contractual liability
—Joint ventures
—Retroactive coverage
—Retired or inactive architects coverage
—Nuclear energy liability exclusion
Directors and Officers Liability Policy
Umbrella Excess Liability Policy
Workmen's (Workers') Compensation
—Employer's liability
—Longshoremen's and Harbor Workers' Act coverage
—Additional medical benefits endorsement
—Executive officers endorsement
Automobile Physical Damage
Comprehensive Automobile Liability
—Protection against uninsured motorists
—No-fault automobile insurance
—Fleet automatic coverage (automobile)
Aircraft Insurance
Watercraft Insurance

CRIME COVERAGES

Mercantile Robbery Policy
Mercantile Safe Burglary Policy
Paymaster Robbery Policy
Broad Form Money and Securities
—Broad Form Personal Theft
Comprehensive Dishonesty, Disappearance and Destruction Policy
Fidelity Bond
—Individual and scheduled bond
—Commercial blanket bond
—Depositors forgery bond
—Credit card rider
Package Policies

EMPLOYEE BENEFITS

Key Man Life Insurance
—Waiver of premium
Group Life Insurance
Key Man Disability Income Protection
Group Disability Income Protection Plan
Accidental Death and Dismemberment Insurance Protection
Basic Medical Plan
—Basic hospital insurance
—Surgical insurance
—Major medical plan
In-Hospital Income Plan
Retirement Programs
Employee Benefit Plans Liability

NOTE: The above list relates to insurance which the architect purchases directly. Additional protection may be afforded to the architect through owner-furnished insurance and contractor-furnished insurance.

ages but do not actually sell insurance.) The insurance industry is regulated by the individual states, each of which has its own insurance code as well as a regulatory body which deals with policy terms, rates and licenses, and stipulates the resources and assets of insurance companies which qualify to do business within the state. The insurance counselor should have the necessary background information about the various insurance companies which will be given consideration in the implementation of the architect's insurance program.

In addition, the insurance counselor should have broad experience in the processing of claims so as to advise the architect about the claims-handling needs of the various insurance companies and, in the event of a claim, vigorously assist in the negotiation of a settlement. Just because a company is licensed in a state and can meet the regulatory requirements does not necessarily indicate that it will provide the type of service which the architect may need for a given type of insurance. The mere existence of a policy and continued premium payments does not guarantee prompt settlement of a claimed loss. It may be necessary to investigate circumstances, the extent claimed and whether the loss is covered. As stated before, an insurance counselor in whom the architect places complete confidence and trust can help immeasurably in looking out for the latter's interests during the investigative and settlement phases of a claim.

DEVELOPING THE PROGRAM

The insurance which the architect purchases directly can be broken down into four categories: property damage coverages including consequential loss, third party legal liability coverages, crime coverages and employee benefits. These are detailed in the ensuing sections and listed in Exhibit 8-1.

While no one can foresee all of the problems that might arise, the practitioner in the role of business manager must take the time and effort to be sure that a careful analysis of all areas of exposure have been accomplished. The necessary insurance must then be provided to assure that, except under the most unusual and totally unforeseen circumstances, the architect will "survive" the comparatively minor claims most often asserted.

In making this analysis, the practitioner and the insurance counsel, along with the accountant and the attorney, should attempt to pinpoint the various potential risk sources as well as the potential extent of liability. This procedure should be an ongoing one so that all of the architect's advisers can be kept alert to any changes which might require new or different coverage.

This is best illustrated by casualty policies which are generally written on a limited, relatively short-term basis, i.e., one year, three years, etc.; this permits changing conditions to be covered on a reasonably frequent basis. However, when at any time during the specified term of a policy a situation develops which changes the conditions that existed at the policy's inception, the new facts can be discussed with the insurance counselor to determine if there is need for an amendment. This can be especially true of fire insurance which is most often written on a three-year basis. If the policy's terms require coinsurance, it might be important, in view of escalating costs, to evaluate the replacement costs on an annual basis and, if warranted, increase the value shown in the policy. Several insurance companies (but not all) offer an automatic escalation endorsement, i.e., 1 percent every three months, to reduce the possibility of being underinsured in the event of loss.

RISK ANALYSIS. The process for developing insurance coverage is called risk

analysis. The Asset-Exposure Analysis checklist (Exhibit 8-2) is intended to be a guide in the development of the architect's insurance needs. The checklist may, at first reading, appear to have in it much extraneous material. However, risk analysis must probe deep into potential areas of exposure. Items seemingly unrelated to the practice of architecture as, for example, an office-sponsored baseball team or a reflecting pool adjacent to the suburban office, can produce risks which must be evaluated.

In addition to insurance as such, the architect must consider other methods of handling the risk of perils, including self-insurance by way of deductibles or transferring the risk, if possible, by contractual agreement. As insurance coverages are determined to be necessary, the broker or agent will present an insurance package designed to provide the needed protection. The architect should require that several alternatives be proposed so that the premium dollars paid out for coverage may be evaluated in relationship to the self-insured loss potential in order to arrive at maximum acceptable protection with lowest overall costs.

An example will make the point. In establishing the amount of Professional Liability Insurance to be carried, quotations of premium costs would be obtained for various top limits of coverage with varying amounts of self-insurance (deductibles) in order to determine which is the best coverage for the maximum economically acceptable premium dollar. A smaller firm with restricted capital funds and relatively modest exposure to loss might prefer to pay a few extra dollars in premium cost for adequate coverage with a comparatively small deductible sum, payment of which would do minimum damage to its cash position. On the other hand, a larger firm with a strong fiscal background and with relatively greater exposure potential might prefer to take the premium savings brought about by a substantial deductible sum and pay toward higher limits. It might also be able to put the full amount of the self-insurance for one claim in an interest-bearing account and use the earnings to help offset the premium cost.

In the course of this analysis, all firms, small and large, should evaluate the possibility of having clients, by terms of the agreements for professional services, reimburse the architect's cost for Professional Liability Insurance coverage for specific projects, thereby effecting a reduction in the practitioner's insurance costs.

POLICY PITFALLS. The architect should not assume that because policies exist the coverages are assured. Changed circumstances, often occurring innocently, can nullify the terms of the coverage; e.g., driving an automobile across the border into Mexico which is outside the territorial limits of the usual automobile liability policy. It is almost more important to be fully aware of what the policy does *not* cover than to know what is covered. Perhaps this can be best illustrated by describing a few not unusual situations for many architectural firms:

—The large firm with offices in several states need be concerned with each jurisdiction's requirements for Workmen's Compensation, particularly if one of the offices is in a state which has a monopolistic fund and will not accept the otherwise practical all-states Workmen's Compensation policy endorsement.

—When firms work abroad, especially if a temporary office is set up in the alien country, all policies should be checked for "Policy Territory." Most policies, including Professional Liability Insurance, limit coverage to the United States, its possessions and territories, and Canada.

—The incorporated firm may not be able to practice as a corporation in another state and must create a partnership to do so. The corporation's Professional

EXHIBIT 8-2. ASSET-EXPOSURE ANALYSIS

This checklist is intended as a guide to risk analysis and should be used in conjunction with other detailed checklists or questionnaires which require actual listing of assets and exposures. It is not intended to be accepted as totally complete but should be used as a stimulus to a logical and systematic interpretation of *all* exposures to loss. Since this is a generalized list, there may be items shown which are—or seem to be—inappropriate for an architectural practice. However, in the course of running an office, architects often invest in nonpractice-related property, e.g., undeveloped land, office or mercantile buildings, mineral rights, patents, etc. It is important that these items be disclosed and evaluated for their effect on the insurance coverages required.

In this list, assets are divided into physical—real, personal and miscellaneous property—and intangible in an attempt to bring out *all* assets for review, whether or not they may properly be considered insurable.

Exposures are broken down into three areas: direct, indirect (or consequential) and third party liabilities. Again, the purpose is to cover all fortuitous exposures to loss of assets or earning power, even to including some exposures which are somewhat speculative in nature.

LIST 1—ASSETS

A. Physical Assets
   1. Real Property
     a) Buildings

1) Under construction	6) Garages and hangers
2) Owned or leased	7) Dwellings-farms
3) Manufacturing	8) Tanks, towers and stacks
4) Offices	9) Wharfs and docks
5) Warehouses	10) Pipes and wires (above ground)

     b) Underground property

1) Cables and wires	4) Mines and shafts
2) Tanks	5) Wells, ground water
3) Shelters, caves, tunnels	6) Piping and pipelines

     c) Land

1) Improved	2) Unimproved

   2. Personal Property (on and off premises and in transit)
     a) Equipment and machinery
       1) Machines and tools
       2) Dies, jigs, molds, castings
       3) Boilers and pressure vessels
         (a) Fired vessels—steam and hot water boilers
         (b) Unfired vessels—steam and hot water boilers
       4) Mechanical electrical equipment (transformers, generators, motors, fans, pumps, compressors)
       5) Engines—diesel, gasoline, steam
       6) Meters and gauges
       7) Turbines—steam, gas, water
       8) Conveyors and lifts, trams, elevators

Liability policy would have to acknowledge, as an additional named insured, such other partnership.

—The firm which takes all or a portion of its compensation in the form of stock or capital interest in a project may find that, depending on the percentage of ownership, it is not covered by the Professional Liability policy for damages related to negligence attributed to performance under the owner–architect agreement. The same would be true if a partnership existed between a contractor and an architect mutually involved in a project since the architect's *professional* acts are not covered if the firm is in any way related to the construction process.

—Agreements for joint work with other firms should make clear that the master-servant (principal-consultant) relationship is intended. If the agreements are found to create a joint venture for Professional Liability Insurance purposes, no coverage would be provided unless modified by specific endorsement.

It is no coincidence that most of the foregoing examples relate to the Professional Liability policy. It is startling to note the number of insured practitioners—and, perhaps equally as important, their key personnel responsible for preparation of the construction documents—who do not realize that the statement of what is covered by that policy takes one-half column of print and what is excluded takes one and one-half columns! It may be correct to assume that losses attributable to errors and omissions committed in the course of one's practice are properly insured against, but a quick reading will show that such things as patent infringement, insurance advice, timely completion of drawings and specifications, and express warranties are *not* covered.

As tedious as it may seem, reading the restricting clauses in *all* insurance policies is absolutely essential if one is to avoid that bone-chilling answer to a claimed loss: "So sorry but coverage is

EXHIBIT 8-2. ASSET-EXPOSURE ANALYSIS (CONTINUED)

    b) Furniture and fixtures
    c) Electronic data processing equipment
    d) Improvements and betterments
    e) Stock—supplies, raw materials, goods in process, finished goods
    f) Fine arts—antiques, paintings, jewelry, libraries
    g) Safety equipment—instruments, apparel, alarms, installations
    h) Valuable papers

1) Tracings, prints, specifications	6) Tapes, cards, discs, programs
2) Formulas	7) Own securities—negotiable and non-negotiable
3) Accounts receivable	8) Other corporate securities
4) Patents and copyrights	9) Cash (indicate currency)
5) Titles and deeds	

  3. Miscellaneous Property
    a) Vehicles (including contents)

1) Commercial	3) Contractors' equipment (licensed)
2) Private passenger	4) Warehouse equipment

    b) Aircraft

1) Missiles and satellites	3) Aircraft—jet, piston, fixed wing, rotary wing
2) Lighter-than-air	

    c) Animals
    d) Antennas
    e) Crops, gardens, lawns
    f) Fences
    g) Firearms
    h) Nuclear and radioactive property—isotopes, tracers, reactors, cyclatrons, accelerators, betatrons
    i) Promotional displays—signs, models, plates, handbills, exhibits
    j) Recreational facilities—parks, gyms, lakes, cafeterias
    k) Watercraft (including contents)—boats, yachts, barges, ships, submersibles, buoys, drilling rigs

B. Intangible Assets
  (Assets not necessarily shown on balance sheet or earnings statement)
    1. External Assets
      a) Markets
      b) Resource availability

1) Suppliers	4) Public utilities
2) Transportation	5) Public protection
3) Employees (full-time and temporary)	

      c) Communications—telephone, teletype, television, radio, newspaper
      d) Location—climate, political, economic and social stability, currency convertibility
      e) Counsel and specialists—legal, engineering, accounting, insurance, real estate, general management, marketing, advertising, public relations, banking

excluded under the terms of your policy." If the circumstances of a firm's practice include situations or risks which are normally excluded, the insurance counselor should be asked to determine if removing the exclusion from a policy by endorsement and additional premium payment is economically justified.

One cannot insure against all possible risks or magnitude of loss: The cost would be prohibitive. There are ways, however, such as "umbrella" policies, to provide more than mere minimum protection, both in terms of dollars and exposure, and use of such policies should be carefully evaluated before any basic insurance is purchased or existing policies are modified.

BASIC COVERAGES. There is no hard and fast rule or outline for the architect's insurance program. However, the following are the basic needed coverages which should always be considered in the initial program development:

—Fire, Extended Coverage, Vandalism and Malicious Mischief on buildings and contents, and improvements and betterments on leased property
—Valuable Papers coverage on existing drawings, papers, books, etc.
—Comprehensive General Liability coverage for both premises and operations exposures
—Broad Form Professional Liability coverage
—Workmen's Compensation and Employer's Liability coverage
—Comprehensive Physical Damage and Collision coverage on autos
—Automobile Liability coverage, including Nonowned Automobile coverage and Medical Payments coverage
—Crime coverages
—Employee benefits programs including life and medical programs

The general method of providing these basic coverages is to place them in combination or comprehensive policies which cover several perils under one broad in-

EXHIBIT 8-2. ASSET-EXPOSURE ANALYSIS (CONTINUED)

2. Internal Assets
    a) Research and development
    b) Goodwill and reputation
    c) Financial
        1) Credit cards
        2) Credit lines (received)
        3) Insurance
        4) Customer credit
        5) Employee benefit program
        6) Royalties and rents
        7) Leasehold interest
        8) Ownership of stock
        9) Company foundations (nonprofit)
        10) Tax loss carry-forward
    d) Personnel (employees and executives)
        1) Education and training
        2) Experience
        3) Key employees
    e) Rights
        1) Mineral and oil rights (aboveground, underground and offshore)
        2) Air rights
        3) Patents and copyrights
        4) Royalty agreements
        5) Distribution agreements
        6) Manufacturing rights

LIST 2—EXPOSURES TO LOSS

A. Direct Exposures
    1. Generally uncontrollable and unpredictable
        a) Electrical disturbance—lightning, burnout, sun spots, power surge, demagnetization of tapes
        b) Falling objects—aircraft, meteors, missiles, trees
        c) Land movement—earthquake, volcano, landslide, avalanche
        d) Sound and shock waves—sonic boom, vibration, water hammer
        e) Subsidence—collapse, settlement, erosion
        f) War, insurrection, rebellion, armed revolt, sabotage
        g) Water damage—flood, rising waters, flash flood, mudslide tidal waves (tsunami), geyser, ground water, sprinkler leakage, sewer backup
        h) Weight of ice, snow
        i) Windstorm—typhoon, hurricane, cyclone, tornado, hailstorm, rain, dust
        j) Nonowned automobiles of employees, agents and others
    2. Generally controllable or predictable
        a) Breakage of glass—other fragile items
        b) Breakdown—malfunction of part, lubricant, etc.
        c) Collision on and off premises—watercraft, aircraft, vehicles
        d) Contamination--liquid, solid, gaseous, radioactive, pollution
        e) Corrosion—wear, tear, abuse, poor maintenance
        f) Employee negligence, including nonowned automobiles
        g) Explosion and implosion

surance contract. For the architects, this could include the following types of package policies among others:

—Comprehensive General Liability policy
—Comprehensive General-Automobile Liability and Physical Damage policy
—Comprehensive Dishonesty, Disappearance and Destruction (3D) policy
—Blanket Crime policy
—Office package Special Multi-Peril policy

A listing of various insurance options which are usually available for the architect's direct purchase if recommended follows. This is not necessarily the full spectrum of coverages. If one is willing to pay the cost, almost anything and any circumstances can be insured. Those mentioned here are more typical of an architect's practice.

PROPERTY DAMAGE COVERAGES

Property damage insurance embraces those coverages which insure against the peril of direct damage to real or personal property. In addition, contingent loss policies are also included under the definition of property insurance. These policies cover the architect in the event a loss is suffered from a direct peril, such as fire, wind or hail, and as a result the firm must either suspend the business operation or set up temporarily in another location. Such unexpected costs or losses arise not directly from the peril itself but rather in an indirect, contingent manner and are referred to as consequential losses.

FIRE INSURANCE. These policies cover damage or loss to the architect's office or office building due to fire or lightning. They can be expanded to include contents such as furniture and furnishings up to specified amounts. No coverage written is all-inclusive so it is important to review any proposed policy form with insurance

EXHIBIT 8-2. ASSET-EXPOSURE ANALYSIS (CONTINUED)

    h) Failure of environmental control—temperature, humidity, pressure
    i) Fauna—animals, rodents, insects, pests
    j) Fire
    k) Installation and construction hazards—dropping
    l) Intentional destruction—jettison, backfiring, etc.
    m) Perils of sea—pirates, rovers, barratry, etc.
    n) Physical change—shrinkage, evaporation, color, mildew, expansion, contraction
    o) Rupture, puncture of tank, vessel
    p) Smoke damage, smudge
    q) Spillage, leakage, paint spray
    r) Structural defects, crane or elevator fall
    s) Transportation—overturn, collision
    t) Unintentional error—employee, computer, counsel
    u) Vegetation
    v) Vandalism, malicious mischief, defacing of property
    w) Riots, civil disorders, strikes, boycotts, curfews
3. Primarily financial in nature
    a) Employee dishonesty—forgery, embezzlement, larceny
    b) Expropriation—nationalization, seizure, exercise of eminent domain, confiscation
    c) Fraud, forgery, theft, burglary, robbery
    d) Invalidity of deed, title, patent, copyright
    e) Inventory shortage—mysterious disappearance, loss or mislaid property
    f) Obsolescence
B. Indirect or Consequential Exposures
    a) All direct exposures as they affect
        1) Suppliers   4) Transportation (personnel and
        2) Customers   property)
        3) Utilities   5) Employees
    b) Extra expense—rentals, communication, product, etc.
    c) Concentration of assets
    d) Change in style, taste, desire
    e) Bankruptcy—employee, executive, supplier, customer, counselor
    f) Disruption of education system (racial, political, economic)
    g) Economic fluctuation—inflation, recession, depression
    h) Epidemic, disease, plague
    i) Increased replacement cost, depreciation
    j) Invasion of copyright, patent
    k) Loss of integral part of set, pair, group
    l) Loss of rights resulting from records destruction
    m) Managerial error in
        1) Pricing, marketing   6) Political predictions
        2) Distribution   7) Investments
        3) Production   8) Dividend declaration
        4) Expansion   9) Tax filing
        5) Economic predictions

counsel to determine if any of the exclusions or limiting policy terms should be brought under the policy by specific endorsement. An important exclusion deals with cash and securities; if this is a potential risk, other coverage must be obtained (see Broad Form Money and Securities Insurance).

When a building is insured, there are two methods of payment available for loss covered by fire insurance policies: actual cash value or replacement cost. The actual cash value is the cost of replacement less depreciation. Replacement value is the full cost of replacement. The insurance counselor must assist the architect in thoroughly evaluating the economic portent of each of these methods before the decision on basis of coverage is made.

Under usual policy terms, in the event of a claim, the insurance company will pay 100 percent of the property loss up to the policy limits only if the amount of insurance carried is equal to a specified percentage of its value (known as the co-insurance clause). The insured would have to buy coverage in an amount not less than the stipulated percentage—most often 80 percent—of the actual cash value (or replacement cost) of the property insured in order to obtain maximum settlement in the event of an insured loss. More than the required amount may be purchased, but if less is carried, the insurance will not pay the full value of the loss. Thus a $200,000 property (either actual cash value or replacement cost depending on the terms of the policy) with an 80-percent coinsurance clause would require insurance in the amount of $160,000 to be paid with no participation by the insured. On the other hand, if only 60 percent ($120,000) were carried on this $200,000 property, intentionally or through failure to reassess property values, the insurance would pay 60/80th or 75 percent of the loss, and the insured would pay the other 25 percent, with the

EXHIBIT 8-2. ASSET-EXPOSURE ANALYSIS (CONTINUED)

    n) Recall of product
    o) Spoilage
C. Third Party Liabilities (compensatory and punitive damages)
  1. Aviation Liability
    a) Owned and leased aircraft
    b) Nonowned—officers and employees licensed
    c) Grounding and sistership liability
  2. Athletic
    a) Sponsorship of teams, recreational facilities, etc.
  3. Advertiser's and Publisher's Liability
    a) As agents
    b) Libel, slander, defamation of character
    c) Media used—radio, TV, newspaper, samples, exhibits
  4. Automobile Liability
    a) Operation of vehicles—owned and nonowned
    b) Loading and unloading
    c) Dangerous contents—flammables, explosives
  5. Contractual Liability
    a) Purchase agreements
    b) Sales agreements
    c) Lease agreements—real or personal property
    d) Performance or service
    e) Loans, mortgages, notes
    f) Hold-harmless clauses
    g) Surety agreements
  6. Easements
    a) In gross
    b) Appurtenant
    c) Positive or negative under common law
    d) Rights to access to light, water, drainage, support
  7. Employer's Liability
    a) Workmen's Compensation or similar laws
    b) Federal Employees Liability Act
    c) Common law
    d) Longshoremen's and Harbor Workers' Act
    e) Jones Act
    f) Defense Bases Act
    g) Outer Continental Shelf Act
    h) Unemployment Compensation
    i) Discrimination in employment
  8. Fringe Benefits Plans Liability
    a) Pensions, trusts, profit-sharing plans, investments
    b) Insured—life, accident, health, etc.
    c) Credit unions
  9. Malpractice Liability—Errors and Omissions
    a) Architectural
    b) Medical—doctors, nurses, specialists

insurance company's payments not to exceed $120,000. (For example, assuming a $100,000 loss, the insurance company would only pay 60/80ths of the loss or $75,000, and the insured would have to pay the other $25,000.)

Extended Coverage. As an extension of the fire policy, this covers additional hazards such as windstorm and hail, smoke, explosion (as limited by terms of the endorsement), riot, riot attending a strike and civil commotion, aircraft and vehicles (when the insured property is damaged by physical contact with these conveyances). Losses by flood or earthquake are not included. Coverages for these exclusions can be purchased, but, obviously, where they are needed, the cost will be high. Firms faced with floodwater problems would be well advised to investigate federal government assistance in insuring against flood loss.

Vandalism and Malicious Mischief. As an extension of the fire policy, this covers loss or damage to the insured property caused willfully by vandals. It does not cover glass breakage, theft or inventory shortage even though such losses may appear to be malicious acts on the part of the perpetrator, and it does not cover any of the recognized losses if the premises had been left vacant as defined in the policy for over 30 days.

Improvements and Betterments Coverage. This extension modifies the basic fire policy when the insured is not the building owner and is intended to provide coverage for losses resulting from the named perils to "improvements and betterments" owned by an insured who is a tenant in the premises.

Sprinkler Leakage Coverage. As an extension of the fire policy, this covers property loss brought about by accidental leakage or discharge of water from a

EXHIBIT 8-2. ASSET-EXPOSURE ANALYSIS (CONTINUED)

      c) Lawyers
      d) Engineers
      e) Trustees of pension plans
      f) Patent infringement
10. Ordinary Negligence
      a) Of employees
      b) Of agents
      c) Of invited or uninvited guests
      d) Of contractor or subcontractor
      e) Failure to provide safety equipment, warnings, etc.
      f) Inadequate enforcement of regulations
      g) Improper preparation of food
11. Nonownership Liability
      a) Leased real or personal property
      b) Bailee's liability
      c) Employee's use of vehicle, aircraft, watercraft
12. Owner's Liability
      a) Attractive nuisance
      b) Invited guests
      c) Trespassers (false arrest)
      d) Rights of others—riparian, mineral, light, air, view, lateral support, easements, party walls, licenses, drainage, eminent domain
13. Products Liability
      a) Implied warranty
      b) Express warranty
         1) By agents—sales, advertising or general
         2) By employees
         3) Of merchantability
         4) Of suitability or fitness for use
         5) Of title
14. Protective Liability
      a) Industrial contractors hired
      b) Construction or demolition
15. Railroad Liability
      a) Sidetrack agreements
      b) Right-of-way
      c) Grade crossings
16. Director's and Officer's Liability (stockholder derivative suits)
17. Watercraft Liability
      a) Ownership, leased, operation
      b) Types—boats, yachts, ships, submersibles

Source: Adapted with permission of the publisher from *Fact-Finding Techniques in Risk Analysis* by Bernard Daenzer © 1970 by the American Management Association, Inc.

sprinkler system due to a breaking of any of its parts or due to freezing.

Business Interruption. Also known as Use and Occupancy or U&O, this policy is a form of coverage protecting against loss resulting from the interruption of a business or practice caused by damage to real property insured under the fire policy. An architectural firm would require the Gross Earnings Form for mercantile and nonmanufacturing risks—Form No. 3 —and the insurance counselor would have to evaluate the potential of loss to determine the basis, i.e., Agreed-Amount Clause or Earnings Insurance which pre-determines maximum payment to be made in event of a loss, and amount of coinsurance to be required as well as the specific perils to be named. The exclusions in the policy as well as the one-year-of-coverage time limit should be studied to determine if the specific needs of a firm are covered.

Extra Expense. The miscellaneous extra costs involved in maintaining the office operation in the event of disruption due to a loss caused by an insured peril are covered by this insurance. Such items as extra salaries on account of overtime, added personnel, extra rent, additional telephone service, cost of moving to temporary quarters, etc., are involved.

Demolition Endorsement. An extension of the fire policy, this provides coverage for loss caused by demolition of an un-damaged part of a building because of the enforcement of a law concerning construction or repair.

Electronic Data Processing Equipment. Most Business Interruption and Office Equipment Fire policies have a limitation on coverage for EDP software or equipment. Firms which maintain EDP equipment on the premises should carry specific insurance to cover total destruction or loss of use of such equipment.

In evaluating replacement cost for stored media, e.g., programmed tapes, the cost of potential reprogramming and operation at another location should be considered. (Although not an insurance item, it should be emphasized that the best "insurance" for computer programs is a duplicate set of tapes stored in a fireproof vault off the premises. It is also important that an arrangement be made at other locations for emergency use of equipment which would be compatible with in-house equipment and media.) When a service bureau is used in lieu of leased or owned equipment on the premises, the amount of insurance carried by such a bureau should not be relied on for protection, and the tapes or other software containing the office's programs should be covered by the architect's own policy.

VALUABLE PAPERS. The value of documents lost or destroyed because of any of the perils insured against are covered under this policy. The nature of an architect's operation is such that frequently many of the most valuable documents are those in the preparation stage, and protection is required. It is important to investigate the various forms of coverage which are available: Scheduled, Blanket or Reporting Form (indicating periodic changes in value). This insurance should be written to cover the detailed costs of preparation, including research, labor and material, for replacement of destroyed documents. Stored material relating to completed work as well as any of the client's documents which the architect might have in temporary custody may be insured.

BOILER AND MACHINERY POLICY. This insurance covers loss of the insured's property on account of an insured accident, cost of temporary repairs, damage to property of others and legal defense in the event of a related suit. The architec-

tural firm which owns its own building would possibly need this coverage because of heating, air conditioning and electrical apparatus which would be specifically covered by the policy.

FINE ARTS. An Inland Marine Form, this provides coverage up to a predetermined value for items of a special value such as antique furniture, paintings, art objects and oriental rugs for which there is insufficient coverage under the usual fire policies.

ALL RISK POLICY. The insured is protected from loss arising from any cause other than those perils or causes specifically excluded by name.

THIRD PARTY LEGAL LIABILITY COVERAGES

Third party legal liability insurance concerns itself with two basic areas of loss which the insured would suffer because of property damage or either bodily injury or physical harm to other persons. The first area deals with those liability claims which arise out of the insured's day-to-day operations and the fact that the architect is operating a business. This would include not only exposure at the place of business but also the exposure (other than professional liability) which exists on the project site. In addition to this general liability exposure, the architect, by virtue of architectural licensing statutes, has a responsibility to perform in a professional manner, with reasonable competence and without negligence. This duty creates the second liability situation which is covered by a separate broad form insurance contract dealing specifically with professional liability exposures.

COMPREHENSIVE GENERAL LIABILITY POLICY. This insurance provides sums for which the insured becomes legally liable to pay as damages on account of bodily injury or property damage, subject to specified exclusions and limitations. (The usual coverages related to the architect's office follow as separate titles.)

Operations-Premises. Coverage is provided for bodily injury or property damage to persons or property other than the insured's own employees or property in the insured's care, custody and control caused by an occurrence on or away from premises owned, leased or occupied by the insured. It is extremely important to understand that this insurance does *not* insure the property of the insured or the insured's employees.

Fire Legal Liability. Loss to premises which the architect may lease but which is property of others is covered under this policy. By its terms, Fire Insurance may cover only contents and the architect's personal property. Under Comprehensive General Liability, property damage coverage would exclude property in the architect's care, custody and control, i.e., the premises that are leased. Fire Legal Liability is an extension of property damage to protect the architect from subrogation in the event the landlord's fire insurance coverage pays the loss and the carrier seeks to recover that loss from the lessee, assuming the damage was caused by the lessee's negligence. (In lieu of this insurance, the lessee can be protected by a hold-harmless agreement executed prior to a loss or contained in the lease or by being named in the lessor's policy as coinsured.)

Contractual. As it relates to General Liability Insurance, this covers loss resulting from an agreement to hold another party harmless from perils associated with bodily injury and property damage. Contractual Liability is broken down into three classes:

—Broad form hold-harmless wherein one party assumes liability and holds harmless a second party for all claims against either regardless of which party's negligence is responsible for the occurrence.

—Intermediate form hold-harmless wherein one party assumes liability and holds harmless a second party for all claims against either even when the second party's negligence is contributory, but not when it is the primary cause of the occurrence.

—Limited form hold-harmless wherein one party holds a second party harmless from claims arising solely out of the first party's negligence.

General Liability coverage is available for all three of the above classes, but only Limited Form Contractual coverage is normally available under the Professional Liability policy. If the owner or others should insist on a hold-harmless agreement which would be insurable as an extension of the Comprehensive General Liability policy, the architect is well advised to seek legal advice before signing such an agreement to be certain the particular hold-harmless is a legal one and that no greater liability will be imposed by the agreement than would be imposed by law.

Premises Medical Payments. Coverage is provided for bodily injury caused by a condition on the premises or within the operations of the insured.

Personal Injury Endorsement. This policy covers three specific categories of injury with the short titles: False Arrest; Libel and Slander; Wrongful Entry. The endorsement excludes employees of the insured, and it is strongly recommended that when this exposure is insured, the architect have the exclusion waived. (An employee discharged for public drunkenness who actually was suffering from insulin shock can sue the employer for slander and undoubtedly win a comfort-

able settlement in a court contest.) Often the terms personal injury and bodily injury are used interchangeably, although in the usual General Liability policy they have specific, and quite different, definitions. The exact extent of coverage insured as Personal Injury in a policy should be examined to be certain the proper perils are specified.

Host Liquor Liability. Law in about a dozen jurisdictions imposes liability for the negligent acts of a guest or others to whom the insured has offered and given intoxicating beverages. If a firm customarily hosts many social gatherings or even office parties, it would be well to determine the extent of liability existing and whether or not this coverage is warranted.

Nuclear Energy Liability Exclusion. All General Liability policies contain this exclusion. If an architect or engineer becomes involved in any way with a nuclear facility, it may be necessary to insure such exposure with the special group of underwriters who write this coverage. Evaluation of potential risk on account of such exposure should be performed by the insurance counselor (see also this exclusion under Professional Liability Insurance).

PROFESSIONAL LIABILITY INSURANCE. This policy covers legal liability for damages caused by errors, omissions or negligent acts arising out of the performance of the architect's professional services. In the event of alleged negligence which is not proved, it will pay claims expenses subject to the deductible clause. It is imperative that the architect read this policy and be thoroughly familiar with its provisions, especially the exclusions. It should be specially noted that, by terms of the AIA-commended policy and unique among insurance contracts, the insurance carrier cannot settle a claim without the consent of the insured and must defend the insured in court actions. The reason for this is that settlement of a claim can be construed as admission of fault and thus damage the insured's professional reputation. When the right to either reject or demand arbitration of a claim exists in the agreement for professional services, the insurer has the right to make the decision whether or not to arbitrate.

Contractual Liability. With reference to Professional Liability Insurance, the basic policy excludes coverage for hold-harmless clauses. Limited form Contractual Liability coverage can be obtained by endorsement to the basic policy.

Joint Ventures. For purposes of Professional Liability Insurance, joint ventures must be separately endorsed in the policy, except for those joint ventures formed prior to a date specified in the policy which may be automatically covered by terms of the policy.

Retroactive Coverage. For qualified firms, the Professional Liability policy can be endorsed to cover completed projects going back to the firm's first years at the current policy limits and subject to the current restrictions therein. This must be specifically included in the policy by endorsement.

Retired or Inactive Architects Coverage. When a member of a firm retires or an individual practitioner who has carried Professional Liability Insurance ceases practice, arrangement to continue the coverage should be made. This may be done at nominal cost and should even be recommended to executors for estates of deceased architects. Where statutes of limitations do not restrict the length of time for filing suit in the event of alleged negligence, an architect, even though long retired, can be sued for prior participation in performing professional ser-

vices. This is equally true for a deceased practitioner, and the executors should be made aware of this potential exposure.

Nuclear Energy Liability Exclusion. With respect to the Professional Liability policy, this exclusion contains the standard wording applicable to other casualty insurance. If a firm becomes involved in design of nuclear facilities, the need for this special coverage should be evaluated by the insurance counselor (see also this exclusion under Comprehensive General Liability Insurance).

DIRECTORS AND OFFICERS LIABILITY POLICY. This insurance is an errors and omissions form covering claims arising against the insured because of activities as an officer or director of a corporation.

UMBRELLA EXCESS LIABILITY POLICY. In consideration of the escalation of amounts awarded by courts in satisfaction of various suits, the architect and the insurance counselor should examine carefully the limits of those policies which are subject to catastrophic disasters that cannot be reasonably evaluated or predicted to see if there should be some protection beyond the usual limits. Such additional protection is afforded by an Umbrella Excess Liability policy.

The policy forms for this insurance vary considerably, and only by specific inquiry can the exact extent of the potential coverage and exclusions be determined. When this is written as Excess Over the Primary Insurance, it covers only those hazards specifically insured by the primary insurance (called underlying policies) and starts when the maximum limits of those policies are reached. This is often referred to as Following Form Excess Liability. If this form of Umbrella is used, the limits of the underlying policies will be stated on the face of the covering policy. These limits *must* be maintained during the policy life of the Umbrella coverage

and must not be changed without proper notification to the excess carrier. It is also possible to broaden the Umbrella coverage to protect against those hazards excluded from the base policies or not covered at all. When these additional risks are insured, a specified and generally substantial amount of self-insurance is required, e.g., $10,000, $25,000, etc., before the Umbrella policy can be called upon.

WORKMEN'S (WORKERS') COMPENSATION. Compensatory payments by employers to employees for job-related physical harm are required by statute in all the states and in many foreign countries, thereby eliminating the necessity of the employee suing the employer to recover for damages. Workmen's Compensation, currently being referred to in the industry as Workers' Compensation although only a few insurance jurisdictions have officially changed their statutes, is the coverage necessary to insure the employer's legal liability. Large companies occasionally choose to self-insure this risk.

This coverage compensates an employee or the heirs for medical expenses, loss of wages and death benefits arising out of or directly related to employment and is Coverage A of the policy. The amounts are stipulated by each statute and will vary from state to state. Payment of a claim under the Workmen's Compensation Act precludes the employee from suing the employer, although an employee may waive protection of the Workmen's Compensation statute if this is done at the outset of a term of employment and prior to any claim. Statutory requirements usually exclude small firms with less than a specific minimum number of employees, but these firms may voluntarily obtain this insurance coverage.

When a firm contemplates expansion of its operations into unnamed states during the policy year, an All-States Endorsement should be considered which automatically accommodates those jurisdictions where private companies are permitted to insure this coverage; obviously a firm with offices in several states should maintain such an endorsement. Eighteen jurisdictions have state compensation funds; six of these do not permit Workmen's Compensation coverage to be carried by private insurance companies. The architect's insurance adviser will have the necessary information if a practice branches into an unfamiliar state. When performing services outside the continental United States, the requirement for Workmen's Compensation in foreign countries should be investigated since they may, if this coverage is mandatory, also demand that it be carried in a local company or in their own monopolistic fund.

Employer's Liability. Coverage B provides for injury or loss to an employee for which the insured may be legally liable and which is not covered under the basic Workmen's Compensation policy. This is usually subject to a limit of $100,000 which may be increased when advisable.

Longshoremen's and Harbor Workers' Act Coverage. This insurance is for firms with work which will involve employees boarding watercraft or working on piers or around or near water. It is an endorsement to the Workmen's Compensation policy and must be specifically purchased since coverage is not automatic.

Additional Medical Benefits Endorsement. This coverage allows an increase in payments for medical expenses above statutory maximum costs where Workmen's Compensation Acts have such monetary limits.

Executive Officers Endorsement. This coverage provides for partners or company officers in states with laws which

allow the firm to elect to include such principals under the benefits of Workmen's Compensation insurance.

AUTOMOBILE PHYSICAL DAMAGE. Owned, nonowned and hired vehicles are protected against any loss or damage to them. This policy can be written with Comprehensive (loss on account of all risks, including fire, lightning or transportation; theft; towing and labor; fleet automatic) and Collision (usually with a deductible amount) terms. If vehicles are leased for a long-term period, it is generally a requirement of lease contracts that the leasing company be included as an additional insured interest. When hired or nonowned vehicles are used, this insurance becomes excess coverage over any basic insurance carried by these other owners. For example, an employee's own automobile insurance generally covers accident claims to the limits of the policy, and the employer's nonowned vehicles policy operates as excess coverage above the employee's coverage to protect the firm when the automobile is being used on the firm's business. (This coverage is discussed in this section rather than in the preceding one on property damage coverage because this and the coverages below are normally included in the same insurance policy.)

COMPREHENSIVE AUTOMOBILE LIABILITY. This insurance covers bodily injury and property damage on account of an occurrence involving owned or long-term leased vehicles and can be extended to cover hired (short-term rental) and nonowned vehicles. As indicated above for Automobile Physical Damage Insurance, when hired or nonowned automobiles are insured under a separate policy, this insurance becomes excess over the other available forms.

Protection Against Uninsured Motorists. The insured is covered for loss which

may be caused by a third party who is uninsured for loss or by an unidentified, unapprehended vehicle used in a hit-and-run.

No-Fault Automobile Insurance. This is not a policy title but a reminder that multistate firms or firms with out-of-state resident personnel who drive automobiles on company business should be alert to the need for expanded coverage required by states which have adopted so-called "no-fault" laws.

Fleet Automatic Coverage (automobile). Under this policy, 30 days' automatic coverage is provided for new cars.

AIRCRAFT INSURANCE. Covering loss or damage to the aircraft, property damage on the ground and public and passenger liability, this policy is written in two separate parts. Under the first, the hull may be insured against named perils or for all risks on the ground except when moving on the ground under its own power; or for all risks on the ground, including when moving on the ground under its own power; or all risks, ground and airborne. Under the second part, public liability coverage insures harm to persons not in the aircraft and damage to property other than the aircraft itself; passenger bodily injury liability is also written separately. Since this insurance is quite special, it is usually written for the specific insured and may contain requirements of pilot warranties as well as geographic limitations.

WATERCRAFT INSURANCE. These policy terms are similar to Aircraft Insurance.

CRIME COVERAGES

Criminal dishonesty insurance contains those coverages which the architect needs for protection against criminal loss not only involving one's own employees but also outside criminal losses such as burglary or robbery. The necessity for much of this will be governed primarily by the size of the firm. Larger firms with more persons responsible for fiscal activities will need more comprehensive protection.

MERCANTILE ROBBERY POLICY. This insurance covers loss on or off the architect's premises when property is taken by stealth or force. Policy terms define coverage for inside and outside robbery.

MERCANTILE SAFE BURGLARY POLICY. Protection is provided for loss of property from within a vault or safe by safe burglary or an attempt thereat.

PAYMASTER ROBBERY POLICY. Loss within the premises of money or checks intended for payroll is covered. If both the paymaster and employees who have just been paid are robbed, the employees' losses are protected as well as that of the insured employer.

BROAD FORM MONEY AND SECURITIES. This form combines Mercantile Safe, Paymaster, Inside Robbery, Outside Robbery and other specified coverages. Protection for money and securities is on an all-risk basis, with loss due to certain risks related to dishonesty excluded. This is important coverage in the event of loss by fire since money and securities are excluded from the standard fire policy but are covered under the terms of this policy.

BROAD FORM PERSONAL THEFT. Coverage is provided for loss by theft or mysterious disappearance of items of a personal nature either at identified premises or away therefrom. Personal property of the architect or employees is not covered under terms of various mercantile crime policies and would have to be taken care of individually by means of a policy such as this one owned by each individual.

COMPREHENSIVE DISHONESTY, DISAPPEARANCE AND DESTRUCTION POLICY. This includes in a single policy, but on an optional basis, many of the coverages described herein related to dishonest acts such as fidelity, burglary, robbery, theft, forgery, disappearance and destruction. The cost is based on the coverages elected so this so-called 3D policy is no less expensive than separate policies for each. However, by placing all of these in one insurance company, it does avoid the problem (and usual subsequent delay in settlement) of several companies trying to determine which policy covers a loss when it might be interpreted as coming under more than one coverage, e.g., disappearance versus employee dishonesty.

FIDELITY BOND. Loss due to dishonesty of an individual is covered; while it would depend on the size of the firm and the nature of the practice, in general all persons who receive or disburse office funds should be bonded. Each bond is written in the name of an individual employed for a specific job.

Individual and Scheduled Bond. This is a fidelity bond written to cover an individual in any position that person may hold, or may be written to cover any individual who holds a specific position.

Commercial Blanket Bond. Since all officers and employees are covered without listing specific names or positions, the use of this bond may be the most practical approach for the average architect's office.

Depositors Forgery Bond. This bond covers forgery involving checks paid out by the firm and protects the bank on payment of such forged items.

Credit Card Rider. As an addition to the Depositors Forgery Bond, this rider covers losses due to unauthorized use of the firm's credit cards.

PACKAGE POLICIES. It is often possible to include in a single policy, usually identified as a package policy, many of the previously described coverages as well as coverage for separate properties. These can include property damage, liability and crime coverages. Workmen's Compensation, however, cannot be written under package policies. The special Multi-Peril policy is the best known of these package programs and covers building collapse in addition to the other perils already noted.

EMPLOYEE BENEFITS

Employee benefits must be carefully reviewed by the architect as an owner of a business and as an employer of other persons. These include hospitalization, health-related benefits and salary continuation, as well as pensions and life insurance coverage, and are appropriate for all offices, small or large. The AIA has for many years endeavored to arrange for group programs which would reduce the insuring costs and allow firms to provide attractive benefits, hopefully helping to reduce employee turnover. Information on these programs can be obtained by contacting the Professional Practice Department, AIA Headquarters.

KEY MAN LIFE INSURANCE. This is life insurance carried by a firm on partners, principals and other key employees to provide, on the death of such a key person, funds for the firm to use for expenses in connection with the replacement of the individual or satisfaction of obligations to the deceased's estate. This is usually straight life insurance (rather than the more limited "term" insurance) and has the advantage of accruing a cash value that can be borrowed against should the need arise.

Waiver of Premium. When key man insurance is purchased as straight life insurance, a rider is available which waives premium payments on proof of permanent disability. Some life insurance companies furnish this automatically.

GROUP LIFE INSURANCE. Life insurance is available to specific groups of people, like AIA members, with a premium which is generally lower than for insurance purchased on an individual basis. There are usually limitations on maximum amounts, e.g., $30,000 for principals and lesser amounts for employees. This is generally written on a term insurance basis.

KEY MAN DISABILITY INCOME PROTECTION. This insurance relieves the firm of having to continue the salary of a key person who has suffered extended or permanent disability. (This can be an important factor in retaining top employees on the staff.) Under certain circumstances, even if a firm has Group Disability Income Protection covering all of its employees, it may be desirable to provide greater coverage under an individual policy on selected persons in order to be sure of the adequacy of the proceeds in the event it is necessary to call on this insurance. As an option, when straight life insurance is purchased for key personnel (instead of term insurance), a rider on that policy is obtainable which would provide a monthly payment, on proof of total disability, as a supplement to Key Man Life Insurance. This is usually a monthly amount per thousand of the face amount of the policy and may have age restrictions on length of time the payments will continue.

GROUP DISABILITY INCOME PROTECTION PLAN. Continuation of income during periods of disability is provided by this plan. It is written on a group basis for firms in order to offer a range of options

at less cost than if it were done on an individual basis; the provisions frequently are broadened for larger firms. There is generally a designated waiting period during which the firm will continue to pay the salary and after which the insurance takes over. The federal tax laws exempt up to a specified amount of this form of income from computation of gross income, i.e., as of 1975, the first $5,200 is exempt from taxation. The AIA has a commended plan in this category.

ACCIDENTAL DEATH AND DISMEMBERMENT INSURANCE PROTECTION. This coverage is for accidents which are so serious as to cause death or loss of sight or limb, and can contain provisions for monthly income payments. The AIA commends such a policy which provides income payments after the first 12 months of disability.

BASIC MEDICAL PLAN. Although plans vary widely, they generally cover part, and occasionally all, of doctors' fees other than surgical for most types of illnesses, but with certain common exclusions such as pregnancy, childbirth and normal dentistry. Payments usually cover hospital, office or home visits. The amount paid is normally a per visit sum with a limitation on visits.

Basic Hospital Insurance. This policy covers room and board and many of the hospital's extra charges; it may include provisions for nurses. This coverage is usually written on a reimbursement basis rather than providing for direct payment to the hospital. The allowable amount per day is stipulated, and the coverage is usually for a semiprivate room. This coverage and the Basic Medical Plan are available as group plans.

Surgical Insurance. Schedules of costs for various operations are contained under a separate policy since the Basic

Medical Plan does not usually include surgeons' fees. However, surgical coverage is an option available with some Basic Hospital Insurance.

Major Medical Plan. This coverage is offered to offset the high medical costs resulting from serious injury or prolonged illness, costs which could become catastrophic in nature. It can be written as a total coverage or as an "umbrella" over Basic Medical and Hospital Insurance and is usually subject to high deductibles, with the insured participating in a portion of the balance. Because of the high deductibles, this insurance can be written for larger limits while keeping premiums within a reasonable range. Group plans, such as the one commended by the AIA, frequently provide substantially better benefits than others available on an individual family basis.

A reminder about group plan benefits: When two or more group plans having similar benefits are participated in by the same family, the plans will only participate proportionately. However, family policies, purchased on an individual basis, will not affect payments under group plans and are themselves usually not affected by payments on the group account. In connection with all of the medical, hospital, surgical and major medical plans, the most common exclusions are pregnancy, childbirth and usual dental expenses, and there is limited coverage for mental illness. These may be brought into programs as options but, as might be expected, in comparison with usual coverages, at a substantial increase in premiums.

IN-HOSPITAL INCOME PLAN. This coverage provides a stipulated daily amount for each day, commencing with the first, that the insured is hospitalized for any reason. These payments are not affected by those from other policies. AIA members have such a commended plan.

RETIREMENT PROGRAMS. The methods of making income or capital available to older, retired persons vary so considerably that the discussion here is limited to being only a reminder of this form of employee benefit. The AIA has a commended Retirement Investment Program as well as a Tax-Qualified Retirement Program (Keogh Act). Programs can be insured or uninsured, qualified or unqualified, or can be a deferred profit-sharing plan. The advice of competent insurance counsel as well as knowledgeable attorneys and bankers should be sought to determine the best and most appropriate plan for any individual practice.

EMPLOYEE BENEFIT PLANS LIABILITY. Although this insurance would be an endorsement to the Comprehensive General Liability policy, discussion here appears appropriate after listing the various forms of employee benefits. Coverage provides for claims which may arise due to alleged negligence in administering these various benefits, e.g., loss attributable to claimed medical expense of an employee who is not insured under major medical coverage because of the firm's failure to enroll the employee at once on becoming eligible. Included are such things as counseling employees about benefits, handling of records in connection with any program, enrollment procedures, etc.

RELATED INSURANCE

Oversimplified, the insurance purchased by the architect is primarily intended to protect both the firm and its employees from risks attributable to the operation at the physical location of the office. When a project enters the construction phase, the architect is exposed to a different class of risk arising out of the work performed by other parties; the third party legal liability insurance carried by the architect will only cover in a general way some aspects of liability exposure during construction. In order to have some protection under the terms of a contract to which the architect is not a party, reliance must be made on special reference for inclusion in the insurance coverages carried by the owner and contractor. Usually the insurance furnished by them for a specific project will more directly protect the architect from alleged job-related involvement. These coverages are Property Insurance (Builders Risk), Owners Protective Liability and Contractual Liability.

In the General Conditions of the Contract for Construction, AIA Document A201, Article 11 deals with insurance in broad terms. The architect incorporates in the supplementary conditions the decisions of the owner and the owner's insurance counselor with regard to specific kinds of insurance as well as dollar limits for each coverage. In Property Insurance, the architect can be protected, as the owner's representative, by the waiver of subrogation contained in paragraph 11.3. The owner's Protective Liability coverage can be written to include the architect in the event of nondesign-related claims. The contractor's responsibility in Article 4 for some project-related lawsuits, such as for bodily injuries to workers, is insured by Contractual Liability required in paragraph 11.1.

The foregoing coverages are not specifically part of the architect's insurance portfolio, and should not be considered a substitute for the architect's own insurance. On any project where the owner requires the use of general conditions other than the current AIA document, the architect should make certain that the waiver of subrogation and the contractual liability provisions appear in the documents which are used. These could have an important bearing on the architect's own insurance coverage, and inadvertent omission of either could possibly be reflected in future increased premium costs. More complete information on the overall subject of construction-phase insurance can be found in *Construction Bonds and Insurance Guide,* AIA Catalog No. M163.

OWNER-FURNISHED INSURANCE. During the period of construction, the owner usually insures the property being constructed against loss by fire and other related perils. Assuming that AIA Document A201 is used as the general conditions, paragraph 11.3 pertains to this insurance requirement, and it includes a requirement that the owner, contractor and all subcontractors waive their rights, each against the other, in the event of an insured loss. Such a waiver eliminates the insurance company's right to assume the place of the injured party (subrogation) in order to sue a third party to recover monies paid out in the event the insured loss was due to the negligence of that third party and on the condition that both the damaged and negligent parties have signed such a waiver prior to an occurrence.

By modification in the supplementary conditions, the architectural firm and its employees should also be included in this waiver as the owner's representative (see Guide for Supplementary Conditions, AIA Document A511). The architect, by virtue of being specifically included, can avoid such a suit should the architect's negligence be alleged as a contributing factor in the loss. This might be said to be "insurance coverage by inference" rather than any direct policy protection.

The AIA general conditions further recommend that the owner carry a policy which will offer protection from claims which may arise out of the operations of others under the construction contract. Since these are usually third party suits in which the contractor agrees to defend the owner (see Contractual Liability below), the Owner's Protective Liability policy acts to provide the necessary legal work to have the direct suit dismissed in favor of the contractor's agreement to hold the owner harmless. The architect, by being named as an insured in this policy, also receives similar legal representation. In the event that such a suit is not dismissed, the owner and architect will be defended under the terms of this policy. The dollar limits for such coverage are usually similar to those required of the contractor in the General Liability policy and are set by the owner and the insurance counsel.

CONTRACTOR-FURNISHED INSURANCE. Again, assuming use of AIA standard construction-phase documents, paragraph 4.18 of the general conditions imposes liability on the contractor for certain claims, damages, losses and expenses (including attorneys' fees) arising out of or resulting from the performance of the work. This is insured by furnishing Contractual Liability coverage as an extension of the contractor's Comprehensive General Liability policy. The requirements of paragraph 4.18 should be carefully checked against the coverage provided under the contractor's policy, as well as against any relevant statutory limitations on contractual liability.

Broad form hold-harmless agreements which may be required by owners are void by statute in several states, and the contractual liability provision would be neither enforceable nor insurable. Where such a statute exists, neither the owner nor the architect can be protected by agreement from suits arising out of the contractor's performance, and both have to look to the adequacy of their own insurance programs to be certain of coverage for any situation which may arise.

In addition, it should be noted that none of the insurance protection provided under coverages furnished by the owner or contractor cover claims alleged to be on account of the architect's professional negligence. When this allegation occurs, it would be defended in accordance with the terms of any Professional Liability policy the architect carries.

Although insurance may appear to merely create a nonproductive outflow of cash so far as the architect's fiscal position is concerned, its value is never realized until a crisis arises. Insurance is not an investment; it is not a scheme to make money; it cannot be counted on for windfall profits. Rather, it is a method of cooperatively spreading the risk among many parties, which has the effect of protecting any one of them from being wiped out should a catastrophic accidental loss be sustained.

The most effective "insurance" program any architect can institute is the elimination from drawings and specifications of design risks brought about through carelessness in the drafting room. This is closely followed by providing employees with a truly safe place in which to work. When these two goals are achieved, the architect's insurance programs described in this text really become what they are intended to be: a hedged bet against unforeseen disaster.

BIBLIOGRAPHY

Architect's Handbook of Professional Practice. Washington, D.C.: AIA, parts updated periodically.

Current compendium of practice information; chapter on insurance especially pertinent.

Construction Bonds and Insurance Guide. Bernard B. Rothschild. Washington, D.C.: AIA, 1973.

Discusses bonds and insurance related to construction projects with suggestions for modifications (supplementary conditions) to the General Conditions of the Contract for Construction; has glossary of terms.

Guidelines for Improving Practice. Washington, D.C.: Victor O. Schinnerer & Co., Inc.

Monthly pamphlets which discuss architects' exposure to liability and counsel on methods to reduce it.

The Hold-Harmless Agreement. Georgia Chapter CPCU. Cincinnati: National Underwriter Co., 2nd ed., 1973.

In-depth study of hold-harmless agreements both construction-related and other; also contractual liability insurance in detail.

Insurance for Contractors. Walter T. Derk. Chicago: Fred S. James Co., 4th ed., 1974.

Discusses broad aspects of contractor's insurance, not just construction phase, including items pertinent to architectural practice.

Insurance and Risk Management for Small Business. Mark R. Greene. Washington, D.C.: U.S. Government Printing Office, Small Business Management Series No. 30, 1970.

Guide to business insurance requirements, comprehensive in scope but in less detail than Athearn's *Risk and Insurance*.

Risk and Insurance. James L. Athearn. New York: Appleton-Century-Crofts, 2nd ed., 1969.

Typical of college textbooks on risk analysis, dealing with all aspects of insurance buying and characteristics of all types of coverages.

PART THREE
PROJECT
MANAGEMENT

Chapter 9
Principles
of Project
Management

RICHARD G. JACQUES, AIA

Since the early 1960's, the design professions have been profoundly affected by external societal forces that have begun to alter, in a basic way, the overall process of delivering the built environment. It is now possible to look backward and forward in an effort to identify at least several forms these forces are taking:

—The increasing pressure of users, owner and government on the design professions to deal simultaneously with the complex (and sometimes conflicting) goals of time/quality/cost: the need for reducing total delivery time, improving the overall building quality (performance) and delivering within realistic short- and long-term cost constraints.

—The complexity of environmental problems brought on by enlightened consumer demands; by increasing scarcity of natural and man-made resources; by shifting user preferences and lifestyles; and by the general instability of the economy and of the building industry.

—The realization that planning/design/construction must be carried out within the context of regional and national goals with a clearer understanding of the probable long-term impact of today's decisions.

—The rise of a diversified and dynamic society that presents a challenge to develop physical environments that are more sensitive to human needs.

SYSTEMS APPROACH TO PROJECT MANAGEMENT

External forces began to clearly manifest themselves in the late 1950's and early 1960's when it was recognized that conventional solutions to building programs would fall short of meeting the demands being created by the forces. In the United States, two simultaneous innovative public building programs were initiated to deal head-on with the emerging demands: the California School Construction Systems Development (SCSD) program and the New York State University Construction Fund (SUCF) program. Although the physical results (buildings) generated by these programs are by no means identical, both programs developed mechanisms (processes and methodologies) for dealing effectively with complex issues of time/quality/cost. In retrospect, it can be said that SCSD and SUCF adopted a systematic or rational approach to problem solving, program management and project development. Inherent in these efforts were varying permutations and combinations of these specific techniques and technologies:

—Increased concern for and commitment to user needs as a basis for design.

—The development of reliable methods for identifying and choosing among alternatives to planning/design/construction.

—The use of sophisticated performance criteria and performance specifications as a means of defining program goals and objectives.

—The utilization of comprehensive long-range program planning and physical planning procedures.

—The development of high–performance, flexible building systems utilizing the full technological capacity of industry at the time.

—The utilization of nonconventional program phasing procedures such as prepurchased building systems and fast-track scheduling.

—The application of comprehensive construction management skills to assist in meeting compressed budgets and schedules.

—The use of feedback and evaluation techniques as a basis of improving future building program performance.

Taken collectively, these techniques and an almost infinite number of variations have evolved during the last 10 years into what can be called, for want of a better name, "systems techniques." And when these techniques have been used in the solution of complex time/quality/cost problems in the building programs, it is reasonable to say that the programs have been dealt with in a systematic or systems way.

An essential characteristic of SCSD and SUCF is that both programs evolved as management-intensive efforts aimed at solving problems in a systematic way that would allow the more effective mobilization and concentration of material, human and financial resources in the building industry. And, as with the most successful business enterprises, large-scale ongoing research programs were an inherent part of SCSD and SUCF activities.

During the past 10 years, the steady evolution of a more systematic approach to complex problem solving in the profession has generated an almost infinite array of specific improved practice techniques, many of the basic techniques having evolved from the SCSD and SUCF programs. These have been developed, tested and refined by firms and organizations of all sizes, in the public as well as in the private sector of the building industry.

In terms of today's problems and potentials, the efforts of the General Services Administration's Public Buildings Service (PBS) are particularly noteworthy. The PBS program has taken a national leadership position in applying systematic approaches to its overall building effort for projects of all sizes, both new and rehabilitated facilities. And, like SCSD and SUCF, PBS is clearly demonstrating that a high level of quality is not inconsistent with a management-intensive program.

When one steps back and tries to sum up the real meaning of these techniques in a way that is meaningful to the average practicing architect—whether in an architectural firm, in government or in industry—the one basic element that begins to knit all the techniques together is that of the greatly increased utilization of improved project management techniques. To a large degree, the profession has borrowed these techniques from external professional management experience that has had a profound impact on all of society in this century. The whole management phenomenon has, in fact, become one of the most clearly distinct characteristics of this age. At all levels, it is now recognized that management is an essential, creative tool which is utilized to assist in the attainment of complex program and project goals.

ESSENTIAL ELEMENTS OF PROJECT MANAGEMENT

Project management in the practice of architecture must be viewed within the framework of both process and product. That is, architects must evolve a value system that does not lead to obsession with process (methods and techniques) at the expense of the quality of their product (architecture). Therein lies a great opportunity and responsibility for integrating a concern for management within day-to-day practice.

Effective project management demands a concern for certain tasks and activities regardless of the size and complexity of the project. In the case of each project, only the depth of analysis will vary. In broad terms, these tasks consist of the following elements:

—Project program planning
—Evaluation of conceptual alternatives and tradeoffs
—Project implementation and execution
—Project evaluation and feedback
—Project cost control

These tasks (sometimes referred to as project development milestones) imply a rational decision-making process which organizes decisions in an orderly sequence, dealing with the larger issues first, then progressing to more detailed ones. The discipline demanded of this approach has been difficult for many architects to accept. Yet this process is so essential to effective project management that it must be stressed. An example of this idea in practice can be demonstrated by understanding the futility of advancing a project into the construction documents phase when the basic structural system has not been selected or when the program budget has not been established and agreed to between owner and architect. Both examples indicate the failure to deal with and resolve basic issues at the early level of project development. A systematic approach to project development means that all of the significant design parameters are considered in each phase of project progression.

Looking at the traditional design process represented in Exhibit 9-1, one sees that decision making becomes more complex as the architect moves forward from phase to phase. Relatively few concerns are faced in the initial phases; more are added at each new phase. Because both architectural education and the practice of architecture have tended to focus on overall design and form considerations, it is understandable that in many instances the architect has tended to not consider all of the critical aspects of the project at each phase of development. With the increased pressures of time and cost, the architect is increasingly forced to take a more rational approach to decision making and to go significantly beyond traditional design and form considerations to ensure that no major aspect of the project will be overlooked during the project development sequence.

EXHIBIT 9-1. TRADITIONAL DECISION PROCESS (Different major considerations are introduced at different phases and at different levels of detail)

Subject*	Program Phase	Schematic Approach	Schematic Design	Design Development	Construction Documents
Lighting					
Traffic					
Acoustics					
Esthetics					

* These are but a few of the many concerns which must be faced in design and are chosen only for illustration.
Source: Adapted with permission from *A Guide for Facilities Planning, Interim Report,* © 1970 by State University Construction Fund, as are Exhibits 9-2, 9-3, 9-4 and 9-5 and portions of text on pages 98–103.

To achieve the goals of time, quality and cost, the architect must view the design process somewhat differently. Each major parameter is considered during each phase of the project; only the level of detail related to each concern increases from phase to phase. This is indicated in Exhibit 9-2. This approach applies to all concerns in planning, design and construction, and has as its objectives to:

—Insure that no major decision is overlooked.

—Allow architect and consultants to get projects under complete control early.

—Permit decisions made in one phase to serve as boundaries or parameters for those to be made in the next phase.

—Assure that commitment to a specific solution is made at all points along the way and not reserved until the very end.

—Avoid the constant redesign which occurs when new information is introduced late in the design process.

For the critical design phases (schematic approach, schematic design and design development), Exhibit 9-3 shows how this systematic decision process translates into the primary considerations the architect must deal with in an orderly and thorough way. Note that the use of the term schematic approach does not suggest a completely separate and new phase of project development in addition to those normally used by the AIA. The idea of the schematic approach milestone was to a large degree a result of the vast experience in SUCF where it was realized that the tasks of schematic design really break down into two subtasks: the first being one of developing a very generalized approach or concept for the project and the second being that of developing what is normally understood as schematic design information. It was found that, by introducing the schematic approach step, both the owner's and architect's attention could be focused on the basic concept and that, by getting collective agreement at this point, the ability to proceed

smoothly with further project development would normally be assured.

Exhibit 9-3 is, in a sense, a checklist useful for project management reference. Exhibit 9-4 indicates how the decision-making approach discussed above is applied to one parameter of project development: acoustics.

Although Chapters 10 through 13 are concerned with specific and comprehensive *tools* of project management, the following overview of the five primary project management *tasks* outlined above provides a context for discussion of these tools. While this overview does not represent an exhaustive framework or checklist for every aspect of project management, it does suggest a framework for the project manager to carry out decisions and responsibilities most effectively. In

terms of more specific coordinating and management information, the Project Checklist, AIA Document D200, has been found to be extremely helpful as a tool for assisting in the orderly processing of most projects done in architectural firms. The overall organization of the materials that follow are consistent with the major sections contained in the Project Checklist, and the two guidelines, when used together, should result in significantly improved approaches to project management. The architect is encouraged to utilize the Project Checklist whenever possible, although it may have to be modified to suit unique projects or very large-scale projects.

PROJECT PROGRAM PLANNING. In the initial task of project management, the

EXHIBIT 9-2. SYSTEMATIC DECISION PROCESS (Each major consideration—such as acoustics—is considered in every phase and at an equivalent level of detail)

Subject*	Program Phase	Schematic Approach	Schematic Design	Design Development	Construction Documents
Lighting					
Traffic					
Acoustics					
Esthetics					

* These are but a few of the many concerns which must be faced in design and are chosen only for illustration.

Source: Adapted from *A Guide for Facilities Planning, Interim Report,* State University Construction Fund, 1970.

EXHIBIT 9-3. SYSTEMATIC DEVELOPMENT FOR CRITICAL DESIGN STAGES

	Schematic Approach	Schematic Design	Design Development
Landscape and Site Development	Basic site concept in plan Massing and spatial development Circulation patterns Grading and planting concepts Relation to existing utilities Soils investigations initiated	Detailed siting concept Grading and planting plans Selection of general site materials Soils investigations conducted	Detailed site plan Detailed planting plan Typical sections and details Outline specifications for site materials
Spatial Organization	General design concept General architectural statement Rough layouts and plans Three-dimensional organization Access patterns	Elaboration of design concept Floor plans, showing spaces, circulation, openings, etc. Schematic sections Room layouts as required Overall dimensions Provisions for handicapped	Detailed floor plans Detailed sections Dimensional control
Exterior Form and Elevations	Massing Views from surrounding points General approach to elevations	Articulation of form Character of elevations (solid-void, textures, shades and shadows) Selection of exterior wall	Detailed elevations Selection of elevation materials Outline specifications for exterior wall system
Interior Design	General approach to interior design (light-dark, textures)	Selection of wall systems and of general finish materials	Special interior elevations Reflected ceiling plans Door and finish schedules Furniture selection Detailed color and graphics
Building Construction Systems	Program or site influences on selection of systems	General selection of wall, floor and roof systems	Outline specifications for wall, floor and roof systems Materials selection Finish schedule
Basement and Foundation	Effects of program and site on basement and foundation Allocation of activities to basement area	General basement plan Refinement of special foundation requirements	Basement floor plans Foundation plan

overall goals, objectives and constraints of the project are identified, documented and agreed to by all key participants in the development process. It is the framework for making all important decisions in the life of the project.

Those areas to be dealt with at this level should include at least the following issues:

—Definition of the broad scope and scale of project, taking into account the relationship of the project to other projects or to existing or proposed larger-scale plans.

—Development of a realistic and reliable program budget, taking into account both initial (capital) and long-term (operating) costs associated with the project.

—Establishment of a probable overall schedule for project development, including major phase or activity milestones.

—Development of a comprehensive statement of user needs and requirements, including assessment of flexibility requirements to respond to changing user needs throughout the projected life expectancy of the facilities.

—Identification of all codes, regulations, standards and policies that will have direct impact on the planning, design, construction and operation of the project.

EXHIBIT 9-3. SYSTEMATIC DEVELOPMENT FOR CRITICAL DESIGN STAGES (CONTINUED)

	Schematic Approach	Schematic Design	Design Development
Structural System	Selection of basic structural system Relation of structure to spatial organization, elevation, etc.	Reflection of structural module in design	Floor and roof framing plans Important structural details
Mechanical Systems	Identification of required mechanical systems General systems selection General distribution concept Impact on design concept, elevations	Spaces for mechanical systems indicated on plan, including recognition of required volume	Details of systems Distribution and riser diagrams Equipment lists
Lighting	Use of natural light Approach to artificial light Effects on design concept	Character of lighting in specific spaces Elevation and fenestration	Room lighting layouts
Acoustics	Effects of noise generated in and out of the building on siting, elevations, basic organization Implications for room shapes	General acoustical character of spaces	Room finishes Special physical provisions
Equipment	Special influences on design concept	Room layouts	Final room layouts Outline specifications Final equipment lists

Source: Adapted from *A Guide for Facilities Planning, Interim Report,* State University Construction Fund, 1970.

—Identification of anticipated internal and external and human and financial resources likely to be needed by owner and architect to ensure successful carrying out of activities from inception to completion of the project.

—Clear delimitation of roles, responsibilities and authority of all probable participants in the project development process. Lack of concern of architects and owners to this important and critical area is a point of great weakness in project management, yet the early resolution of this area will go a long way toward minimizing conflict, tension and misunderstanding within the development of each project.

Additionally, the programming phase must be viewed as a mutual orientation period: in the first instance, for the owner and architect; in the second, for all key participants in the project development team. For the architect, this is a period to become fully immersed in the scope of the proposed project. And this is a time for getting everything on the table between owner and architect.

As a tool of reference, Exhibit 9-5 identifies the critical concerns the architect should have early in project development.

Comprehensive project program planning is relatively new to project management in architecture. However, two publications by SUCF, *A Guide for Campus Planning* and *A Guide for Facilities Planning,* represent significant efforts to document program planning experiences in terms meaningful to architects in practice.

EVALUATION OF CONCEPTUAL ALTERNATIVES AND TRADEOFFS. This early step in the design process is aimed at seeking the most appropriate and vi-

able concepts that have the potential of responding to the time/quality/cost constraints stipulated in the project program documents. It is at this level that it is possible to explore basic cost benefit tradeoffs, particularly as they relate to concepts of life cycle cost analysis and value analysis discussed in Chapter 12.

Increasing economic pressures and diminishing natural resources have brought about increased awareness of the importance of assessing conceptual alternatives for project design and development, for it is only as a result of this exercise that the architect may be confident of satisfying program requirements in a responsible way, and the owner may be confident of getting the highest payoff on investment.

Within the definition of traditional AIA phases or milestones, the evaluation of conceptual alternatives and tradeoffs is

EXHIBIT 9-4. DECISION MAKING—ACOUSTICS

Program Phase	Schematic Phases	Design Development Phase	Construction Documents

Site, facility programs are analyzed in terms of sound generation characteristics and isolation requirements. Unalterable conditions affecting solution are identified and analyzed.

Noise producing and noise sensitive activities, propagation influences, off-site developments are analyzed for effects on siting, massing, organization and other schematic design issues.

Materials, surfaces and location of equipment are determined, in part, by acoustical requirements and criteria.

Solutions developed in the preceding phases are communicated via drawings and specifications.

Source: Adapted from *A Guide for Facilities Planning, Interim Report,* State University Construction Fund, 1970.

addressed during the schematic design phase. In terms of systematic project management, SUCF and large building clients have found it useful to break this phase into two components: schematic approach and schematic design.

Schematic Approach. While the program phase stresses analysis and interpretation of information about the project, the objective of the schematic approach phase is *translation*—translation of digested information into an outline approach to solving the problem. This is a conceptual level of thinking and takes into account:

—The design concept: basic spatial organization, exterior form, massing, views and approach to interior design.

—The site concept: approach to massing of man-made and natural forms, circulation, access and location of site elements.

—The systems concept: the general approach to construction, structural, mechanical and electrical systems.

The following checklists may be used as a management tool to ensure that the most important considerations are dealt with under each of the preceding conceptual areas, and it is suggested that these considerations be coordinated with portions of the AIA Project Checklist.

The design concept is the architect's general approach to solving the statement of the problem. The emphasis is on

the organization and the qualities of the physical solution—and not on its details. Some issues include:

—Functional relationships
—Role of the facility in the community and region
—Inherent organizational concepts
—Vertical organization of physical solution
—Access and circulation
—Form and massing
—Relation of exterior to interior
—General character of elevations
—Approach to interior design
—Pattern of light and shade
—Use of materials and textures

The design concept is a project's unifying element. It provides the context within which more detailed decisions can be made as design proceeds.

The site concept, which is closely allied with the building design concept, is the general approach the architect wants to take to siting the building and other site-related considerations identified in the program. Siting issues during the schematic approach phase usually include:

—The design concept and its implications for siting.

—Building articulation and massing, particularly relating to solids (buildings, plant massing, site features, etc.) and voids (spaces) which exist before the project is placed there and which will be created once the project is built.

—Site circulation patterns for pedestrians, bicycles, motor vehicles and any other transportation forms involved.

—Building access patterns, including views of the building as it is approached from surrounding areas.

—Views from the building.

—Site acoustics or the control of noise which might influence building layout and design.

—Plant material massing, grading and natural forms as they relate to the building and to the surroundings.

—Utility systems or routes and connections to major connecting lines.

The site concept is, of course, not conceived in a vacuum. Of utmost importance is contiguous development, as viewed by the architect during visits to the site. Existing and proposed circulation paths and utility routes are also important parameters in developing the site concept.

The impact of subsurface conditions on the site concepts must be carefully considered while developing a schematic approach to siting the building. The location of the building on the site must be justified on both economic and functional bases.

The systems concept is the architect's general approach in relating the implications of physical systems to the design concept. As a solution begins to emerge, so do many of the architect's and engineers' conceptions about the building and environmental systems.

The general types of systems to be used, transfer of load concepts, distribution patterns and many other conceptual aspects of these systems must be determined early in design, in the schematic approach phase. It is not necessary, however, to develop details until later phases. The importance of considering the major building systems as part of the initial design concept was mentioned earlier and further explained in Exhibit 9-2. Increasingly, it is the experience of design professionals and owners that the essential nature of these basic building and environmental systems has significant impact, not only on design but also on the issues of time, cost and overall building performance. It is, therefore, essential that the architect come to grips with at least a basic understanding of the implications of these systems as they affect the overall project.

The usual approach to communication at this stage is a carefully developed mixture of words, diagrams, schematic drawings, massing models, line perspectives and other tools which fit the level of detail involved.

Schematic Design. The objective of the schematic design phase can best be described as *expansion*. The acceptance of the schematic approach indicates that architect and client agree on the conceptual solution to the problem.

As concepts are expanded, the architect and consultants must be careful to:

—Maintain the integrity of the project. Building, site, systems and budget must be developed together, assuring that the project remains a coherent whole.

—Insure that all program requirements are reflected in the developing proposal.

—Make many new decisions without changing old ones. The object is to infill among existing important decisions without changing them.

—Rigorously test the concept developed to assure that the project coincides with the time/quality/cost objectives of the owner.

By the time the schematic design phase is concluded, the building systems should be selected and their outline descriptions developed. As part of the proposed solution, the architect should indicate what materials, assemblies or techniques have been chosen for such systems as:

—General structural system
—Foundation system
—Floor system
—Roof system
—Exterior wall system
—Interior walls and partitions
—Stairs
—Circulation equipment
—General equipment
—Plumbing
—Heating, ventilating and air conditioning systems
—Electrical systems
—Special services systems
—Site construction
—Lighting
—Acoustics
—Interior finishes
—Graphics

The schematic design proposal is one of the most important proposals in the entire planning and design effort. Once it

EXHIBIT 9-5. PROGRAM PHASE CONSIDERATIONS

CONTEXT
Concepts Behind the Project in General
—Functional, circulation, social patterns
—Building character and massing
—Spatial character and massing
—Relation of natural, man-made items

Role of the Project in the Plan
—Role in functional, circulation and social patterns
—Relation to structures already built
—Relation to spaces already formed
—New spaces to be formed
—Relation to future growth

USER NEEDS
Role and Purpose of the Project as a Series of Parts
—Activities to be accommodated
—Spaces required
—Site features required
—Space types or site features requiring additional research

Role and Purpose of the Project as a Whole
—Interrelationships
—Search for organizing factors
—Implications for environmental systems
—Site use and circulation patterns
—Relation of building to site

ECONOMIC FACTORS
Analysis of Owner Input, Including Evaluation of
—Special demands of large-scale plans
—Soil and foundation problems
—Special site development work
—Special program requirements
—Special demands on environmental systems

Preliminary Analysis of Possible Market Influences on Costs

Identification of Special Cost or Market Studies Required

CONTROLS
Identification of Applicable Regulations, Codes and Procedures

SCHEDULE
Analysis of Design and Construction Timetables, Evaluating the Effects of
—Special site or program requirements
—Need for special studies
—Construction market conditions

Development of Staffing Plan, Including All Consultants

Source: Adapted from *A Guide for Facilities Planning, Interim Report,* State University Construction Fund, 1970.

has been accepted by all parties involved, the architect enters a period of refinement. This implies that all major decisions about the project have already been made. Because the schematic design is a catalog of those decisions, it is imperative that it be communicated fully and well.

The schematic design must include whatever information the architect feels is necessary to communicate the selected approach such as:
— Project description
— Program revisions
— Site description
— Site plans, sections, details
— Building description
— Massing study
— Plans, elevations, sections
— Room layouts
— Systems description
— Interiors description
— Equipment description
— Summary of code problem areas
— Area analysis
— Statement of probable construction cost
— Schedule
— Marketability

The product of this rigorous activity of choosing among alternatives brings the project to a level of development where owner and architect have such confidence that the normal project execution and implementation process can be initiated. Relative to the AIA Project Checklist, this would put the project at the end of the schematic design phase. It is also at this point that a firm commitment would be made to the most appropriate project delivery procedure to be used.

This has become a most important consideration of building projects today because it has become increasingly apparent that the traditional methods of project delivery are not sufficient to satisfy the time/quality/cost goals of many clients. The architect must come to grips with the reality of the project in the building market and quickly assess which planning, design and construction procedures are most suited to the particular project. In the past five years, increasing importance has been given to nontraditional building delivery procedures such as phased design and construction, systems building and design-build procedures.

PROJECT IMPLEMENTATION AND EXECUTION. This element encompasses the phases normally called design development, construction documents, bidding or negotiations, and construction contract administration. Each activity, in sequence, represents a further refinement and development of these broad ideas and concepts decided on by the end of the design period. It is unlikely, if the project has been brought along in a rational and systematic way, that any major changes would occur during these activities.

It is essential, as part of this process, to continuously test decisions against program goals and objectives so as to ensure basic adherence to time/quality/ cost constraints.

In a strict management sense, the implementation and execution phases are viewed as pragmatic production efforts and as an important part of the project development process where rigorous quality control procedures must be used.

Design Development. There is a major shift in attention from the schematic phases to the design development phase. Emphasis moves from overall context (building layout, systems outlines, site concepts) to more detailed concerns. The framework developed in earlier stages is now ready for infilling or development into a complete solution.

Hundreds, perhaps thousands, of decisions are made during design development, but they are always made within the context of the conceptual decisions made and affirmed earlier. If at any point the architect finds that this context is not clear, there should be conscious return to the appropriate earlier phase to clarify the conceptual intent in relation to the other decisions made at that time.

The work during design development is best characterized by the condition in which the architectural solution must be when the phase is completed. It must be developed to the point where all major decisions are made and working drawings and specifications can begin. This suggests that:
— A full site design has been developed. Building location and access, circulation, planting, grading and utilities have been fully thought through and interrelated.
— A full architectural solution has been developed, with all spaces firmly located and dimensioned and with all section and elevation features thought through.
— Building systems (structural, mechanical, electrical and equipment) have been fully and carefully thought through and integrated.
— Building interiors have been integrated with the overall architectural planning. Room layouts, materials, textures, furnishings, equipment, color coordination and provisions for the handicapped have all received careful attention.
— A full set of outline specifications has been developed.
— Cost implications of all design decisions have been considered and recorded.
— A confirmation has been received of tentative decisions regarding bid packages and bid form.

If the design development phase is successful, the architect will find that the construction documents phase to follow can be largely limited to finalization and production. It should not be necessary to cycle back into design to make decisions which should have been made there in the first place.

Construction Documents. The principal activities during this phase include:

—Completion of the contract documents

—Preparation for bidding or negotiation of the construction contract

—Preparation for construction

Each of these activities is critical. The first should be relatively easy since all major decisions have been made by this time. The second is more complex because the owner and the architect share responsibility for developing the building package. The third activity is necessary to lay the appropriate groundwork for constructing the project.

The finalization of the construction drawings and specifications should pose no significant problems. One of the express purposes of the previous phases is to assure that all major and most minor decisions about the project are made before final construction documents are prepared. If the owner and the architect have been successful in this regard, the construction documents phase should be largely dedicated to *production*—and not decision making.

An important aspect of this finalization process is the cost estimate; all questions and issues relating to the cost of the project should be ironed out with the owner at this time.

The bidding and construction schedule must also be finalized. This is not only to establish the bidding dates but also to assess the cost implications of market conditions on this schedule. Because the occupancy of the project is often a point of great concern to the owner, suggestions for schedule changes should be thoroughly discussed before they are implemented.

Bidding or Negotiations. The architect's first responsibility during bidding is effective advertisement and monitoring of the bidding process.

The architect is also charged to con-tinue the work begun during the construction documents phase to stimulate qualified contractors to submit bids on the work and to keep the owner posted of efforts and results in this vital task. The attraction of qualified contractors to the work is critical to meeting time/quality/cost goals. Where markets are tight or over stressed, fewer contractors may bid. Studies have shown that the number of bidders can have a significant impact on the cost of the work.

It is possible under nontraditional building delivery procedures that the architect's role may be modified or even significantly different. For example, if the owner has effected an agreement directly with a construction manager, it would normally be the manager's responsibility to undertake all of the market research and contractor interest stimulation. It is conceivable that if the architect is providing more comprehensive services that include construction management, then the architect's role will be expanded beyond those activities listed above.

Construction Contract Administration. Careful administration of the construction contract or contracts will greatly contribute to the effective and timely completion of any project. Good management begins with the owner and the architect, for it is their approach that will set the tone for the construction period.

The first essential is that the owner, architect and contractor be philosophically and organizationally prepared to undertake the management and construction of the work. Issues at stake include:

—Architect organization of field operation

—Orientation of all parties involved

—Contractor readiness to begin work

—Contractor preplanning of the project

—Owner participation in overall decision making

—Owner-architect sharing of management responsibility

Central to effective construction contract administration is communication among everyone involved. Each party must know what is going on, the particular role of each party, and what potential trouble spots may be developing. This suggests that:

—The instruments of communication must be formalized to some extent. Job meetings, correspondence, logs, records, planning and scheduling tools, approval submissions, drawings, tests, general notices, requisitions and other pieces of communication become important.

—Communication must be channeled, i.e., specific pieces of project information must travel along specific routes.

The foregoing guidelines for project implementation and execution provide an overall framework for project management decision making. They stress the primary concerns the architect must have if any project is to meet the time/quality/cost goals developed and agreed to between owner and architect in the program phase. In conjunction with the general framework for project management, it is suggested that the architect utilize on a continuous basis the materials contained in the AIA Project Checklist and the family of related documents developed for assistance during this phase.

PROJECT EVALUATION AND FEEDBACK. This significant activity in the systematic approach to delivering the built environment has the effect of closing the project management loop and providing an objective basis for making judgments as to the validity of previous planning, design and construction decisions.

It has become increasingly apparent to both architects and building users alike that it is not sufficient to develop an efficient management system for building delivery. It is equally important to extend this management effort to encompass the evaluation of the appropriateness of fit between architecture and user, and to evaluate buildings in use in terms of overall performance achieved. To do otherwise is to assume that the practice of architecture is a static rather than an ongoing, dynamic, human enterprise.

Although architects have developed reasonably reliable methods of measuring technical building performance (wear, cost, etc.), the topics covered in Chapter 11 on programming indicate the urgent need for getting a better grip on human/behavioral aspects of evaluation.

PROJECT COST CONTROL. This element is an essential activity which pervades the overall function of project management. Current experience of the profession has disproven earlier notions that cost control and quality design are in conflict; in fact, one is very much part of the other. A valid initial budget which is constantly evaluated, updated and accepted by the architect as a design objective can result in architecture of the very highest quality—on time and without costly redesign and rebidding.

There are three major elements in an effective cost control system: budget development, evaluations during design, and award flexibility. Within each element, the project manager's attention must focus on key areas.

Budget Development. A successful approach to design cost control begins with a carefully developed budget. Work on the budget should begin before the architect embarks on design, and is accomplished in parallel with the development of the project program. It is essential that the architect, consultants and owner understand what items are included and excluded in the project budgets.

All budgets should provide for some adjustment for project timing and location. Probable escalation of labor and materials costs, as well as regional variations in labor, materials and purchasing power, are taken into account.

While many owners are constantly striving to improve their own capability to predict market factors, a major responsibility for this task falls to the architect. The architect should have a knowledge of anticipated regional market conditions, make design decisions accordingly and report probable cost influences to the owner.

Evaluation During Design. The architect's and owner's commitment to project budget as a design objective demands that both continually evaluate developing solutions against the budget.

This evaluation can be thought of as a testing process. The budget and its parts are considered as target objectives, and the probable cost of each of the major building systems in the project should be evaluated and related to these objectives at each design phase. This approach is designed to pinpoint potential trouble spots early in the design so the solution (or, in some cases, the budget) can be adjusted.

Where the owner-architect agreement provides for engaging a cost consultant, such consultant becomes a key participant in this evaluation process with a role far more than that of a quantity surveyor. The cost consultant must be able to cope with the problems of cost in the very early stages of design as well as in later stages where details are available. The cost consultant proves valuable in assessing market influences on such cost-related decisions as timing, bid packaging and selection of major construction systems, assemblies and materials. Estimated cost is considered in greater detail at each succeeding phase of design and documentation.

Award Flexibility. Even when design cost control is carefully followed, it is still possible that the acceptable low bid may exceed estimates. In order to assure that the owner-architect goal of time and quality will not be abridged through redesign and rebidding, it is necessary to build award flexibility into projects.

This is accomplished through two means: alternates and contingencies, including those for market abnormalities. Experience has also proven that a percentage of appropriate alternates in the bid proves invaluable in moving the project forward and meeting essential project goals.

In response to the concept of dealing with each major design issue at each phase of the project, alternates should not be left to the end, but considered at each point along the way. They should be investigated in early phases, proposed and developed in the intermediate phases, and finally selected and presented in the construction documents.

Control During Construction. To a large degree, the control of project costs during the construction phase is the responsibility of the contractor or the construction manager. Assuming that the architect has utilized a comprehensive and rational approach to design and project development, the construction documents should so clearly delineate the scope of the project that no major factors should arise during construction that would necessitate major additions to the project budget.

The primary area of probable construction cost change would be due to unforeseeable site conditions or program or scope changes initiated by the owner on the project. If the owner has been deeply involved on a continuing basis in the development of the design, it is highly unlikely that any major changes will precipitate during the construction phase.

In any event, it is essential to maintain a close monitoring of project costs during the construction period and to carefully document any project changes having economic implications. Scope or cost changes should be agreed to by all parties involved in the project and should be documented. The *Architect's Handbook of Professional Practice,* AIA Catalog No. M104, discusses these issues in detail, and several standard forms have been developed to implement recommended procedures. Some offices have developed their own versions of these forms to aid the communication and documentation process; however, the basic principles should be followed to avoid fragmentation of communication and control.

As projects become more complex, architects may become increasingly responsible for the overall monitoring of the project costs, including direct construction costs and a variety of indirect project costs. And, with the increased utilization of phased design and construction involving an increasing number of prime contracts, the architect will naturally be in a position of having to effect more careful and accurate overall control of costs, not only during design but also during the construction period. As a tool in helping to organize this project cost information, the architect should consider utilization of a project cost report similar to that shown in Exhibit 9-6, which indicates a meaningful way in which to organize cost-based information. In addition to providing a basis for immediate project cost control, this data is also useful for providing a basis for future project budgeting for both construction and professional services compensation.

Taken together, the foregoing five elements and activities can be viewed as basic to a systematic management effort for any project. Within the context of these activities, the following section is aimed at focusing on the roles and responsibilities of managers and management.

RESPONSIBILITIES OF MANAGEMENT

As the practice of architecture becomes increasingly complex and subject to

EXHIBIT 9-6. SAMPLE PROJECT COST REPORT

RICHARD C. JACQUES ASSOCIATES

CURRENT STATUS   APRIL 1, 1975   (All amounts in $1000's)

CONTRACTS AWARDED		ESTIMATE	ORIGINAL CONT. AMT.	CURRENT CONT. AMT. (%)	CURRENT TOTAL BILLED
PHASE L-1					
L-1.1	Excavation	81	145	144	144
L-1.2	Concrete	233	244	236	236
L-1.3	Str. Steel	575	423	422	422
PHASE L-2					
L-2.1	Concrete	429	435	444	444
L-2.2	Masonry	693	545	556	556
L-2.3	Lt. Mtl. Fr.	48	47	50	50
L-2.4	Steel Stair	87	54	53	53
L-2.5	Roofing	118	98	98	98
L-2.6	Ext. Drs. / Win.	349	269	274	274
L(GA)-5.3	Glass/Glazing	15	14	14	14
L(GA)-5.4	Toilet Ptns.	10	10	10	10
L(GA)-5.5	Conc./Earthwk.	69	50	51	51
LOFT Subtotal		4807	4286	4390 (25.3%)	4375
CUMULATIVE SUBTOTAL				4390 (25.3%)	4375

ITEM	INITIAL ESTIMATE	CURRENT ESTIMATE (%)	CURRENT TOTAL BILLED
OTHER OBLIGATIONS			
Legal Services	30		
General Administration	20		
Insurance	66	80	80
Reproduction and Reimbursible Expenses		80	75
Professional Services			
Planning and Design	1300	1282	1259
Construction Management	575	570	553
Furnishings	70	38	35
Subtotal	2061	2050 (11.8%)	2002
CUMULATIVE SUBTOTAL		15860 (91.4%)	15527
ON SITE EXPENSES			
General Accounts	743	823	
Miscellaneous Work		25	
Standby Electrician		35	
HVAC Maintenance		15	
Security		30	
Subtotal	743	928 (5.3%)	883
CUMULATIVE SUBTOTAL (CURRENT CONTRACTUAL OBLIGATIONS)		16788 (96.7%)	16410
WORK REMAINING			
Future Contract Adjustments		110	
Furnishings (Miscellaneous)		217	
Credits			
Insurance Claim Davis		(4)	
Subtotal		323 (1.9%)	
CUMULATIVE SUBTOTAL		17111 (98.6%)	
CURRENT CONTRACT RESERVE		240 (1.4%)	
ESTIMATED TOTAL PROJECT COST		17351 (100%)	

NOTE: Estimates are based on information available as of report date.

rapid change, the focal point of discharging the architect's primary professional responsibility must happen at the level of project management. This level is increasingly becoming the center of action and decision making in architectural firms relative to the carrying out of projects.

The evolution of the importance of project management has come about as a means of coping with effective multidirectional communications: upward, downward, sideways, internal and external. The project manager assumes a position at the center of these lines of communication and is in a unique position to control, direct and energize to the outer limits of these lines, and is thus able to have a great impact on overall project performance.

Traditionally, managers in all sectors of the economy have been primarily concerned with communications and relationships with those above and below them in organizations. Although this was satisfactory in the management of simple tasks, the complexity and constant changing environment in today's practice demands that the manager come to grips with the need for multidirectional communications noted above. Conceptually, the manager is at the center of a sphere as opposed to the traditional position of being somewhere on a line. This is shown in Exhibit 9-7.

In actual fact, the composition of the owner, design and construction teams is more complex than that shown in the diagram. For example, the design team would include all the traditional and special design disciplines and consultants, and would certainly include a whole range of activity such as programming, design, production and contract administration. In the case of the owner team, the composition would include the primary owner or owner group as well as a multitude of potential users of the facility whose needs must be taken into account in the design and execution of the proj-

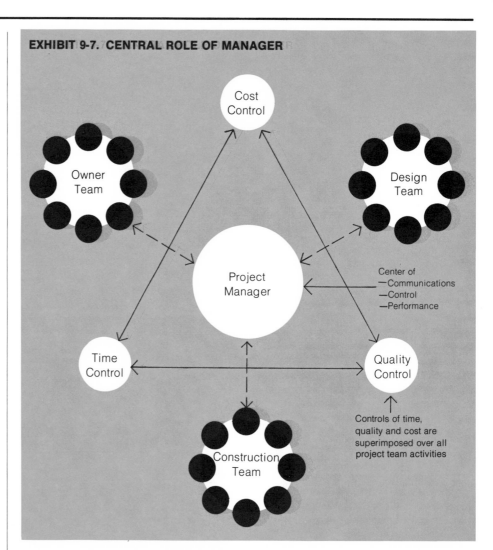

EXHIBIT 9-7. CENTRAL ROLE OF MANAGER

Cost Control

Owner Team

Design Team

Project Manager

Center of
—Communications
—Control
—Performance

Time Control

Quality Control

Controls of time, quality and cost are superimposed over all project team activities

Construction Team

ect. In the case of the construction team, the group would include both primary contractors and subcontractors, manufacturers and installers.

Depending on the complexity and nature of the project, the role of project manager might be assumed by any one of the three teams. In actual practice, this responsibility normally is that of the architect. Therefore, it is essential that the architect become increasingly competent and efficient in this area and understand all the implications of this responsibility

as it relates to day-to-day practice.

In theory, this idea is very sensible within the framework of today's architectural practice. In reality, it is essential that the project manager be given the tools and authority to work to full potential in carrying out the primary responsibilities of the assignment. It is essential, in this regard, that the manager participate in the early development of project goals, for it is only with a total commitment to these goals that the manager will reach a high level of performance in meeting the time/quality/cost requirements of each project.

An equally essential requirement of high manager performance is that of personal and professional accountability. Lacking such accountability, the manager is not motivated to become a driving force behind the project. It has become evident that with accountability goes concern, commitment and care, all essential to managers and management. This point cannot be overemphasized, for it is not merely procedures that ensure high project performance but human commitment to the task. This is not to diminish the importance of the various management tools covered in this and other chapters but rather to recognize that a tool is useless if not in the hands of a firm, sensitive craftsman.

Like design, project management demands great creative effort, and the profession has only recently begun to recognize this need. The traditional role of supervisor or job captain falls short of the mark of putting the project manager in proper context and importance in the practice of architecture.

The project manager must have a comprehensive grasp of the broad technical aspects of project development as well as the human motivational aspects so essential to getting the job done within program constraints. The ability to mobilize resources effectively is essential to attaining project goals. At the same time, the manager's contribution to the overall performance of the organization must be recognized above and beyond the demands of the immediate project. In this sense, the project manager undoubtedly, as a "working manager," can contribute certain personal expertise to the firm as a critical member of the management team.

The task of developing many projects today is beyond the capacity of a single person or a single firm. Increasingly, complex and unique projects require skills, expertise and experience as-sembled specifically to meet the demands of the project. Because of this, the notion of team effort has been stressed, as well as broad management guidelines for the project team and project tasks.

Early involvement of everyone on the team cannot be overemphasized. Very early project decisions will influence siting, building systems, cost and other areas of competence on the team. The early application of that competence can preempt many of the conflicts which traditionally arise in the later stages of design. The architect usually must engage consultants necessary to provide a project team of the quality required. As projects become more complex, the successful architect-consultant relationship is forged from the outset of the project—one of the most important keys to success.

Much can be said about coordination with other disciplines (consultants), but the key to an effective and productive working relationship has largely to do with the early participation of the consultant and the continuous communication between architect and consultant. This relationship is essential to implementing the systematic decision-making concepts expressed in previous exhibits.

The emerging role of the project manager clearly leads to increasing responsibility for the project as a profit center of the organization. The manager is in the best position to control the outcome of the project relative to client satisfaction and is in a position to influence dramatically the profitability of the project.

Project management, to be effective, must be a continuous process with a parallel assignment of single-point staff responsibility. It is a task of operating in the present with a view to the past and future, always striving to anticipate what is coming. Each project manager must develop an early warning system, a thinking process that causes flags to be thrown up well in advance of impending prob-lems related to project development. The difficulty in coming to grips with what may come was eloquently stated by the late Anthony G. Adinolfi, general manager of SUCF: "To look ahead seems to be the most trying task for a man who's trying to figure out what to do today."

BIBLIOGRAPHY

Architect's Handbook of Professional Practice. Washington, D.C.: AIA, parts updated periodically.

Current compendium of practice information; chapter on construction contract administration especially pertinent.

"Architecture in the 1970's—Gearing Performance to Needs." Walter F. Wagner Jr. *Architectural Record*, October 1970.

Definitive work assessing the demands shaping the present and future practice of architecture.

A Guide for Campus Planning. Albany: State University Construction Fund, 1967.

Based on the actual experience in planning 37 university campuses.

A Guide for Facilities Planning, Interim Report. Albany: State University Construction Fund, 1970.

Outlines the Fund's approach and represents the experience of work with architectural firms on a wide variety of building types and sizes.

Management: Tasks, Responsibilities, Practices. Peter F. Drucker. New York: Harper & Row, 1974.

Landmark study of management as an organized body of knowledge.

"Project Checklist." Washington, D.C.: AIA, 1973.

Guide for project managers on tasks during each project phase for which the architect is responsible.

"Project Management." Klaus C. Ruhland. *Consulting Engineer*, April 1970.

Discussion on coordinating the various disciplines.

Chapter 10
Budgeting and Scheduling

The desire to reduce voluminous data to a very simple analysis may lead management to ask: "What is my break-even point, and at what level do I reach it?" These two key questions are at the heart of of the most sought-after management information.

Like any other business or profession, the architect must develop a general framework within which the office and projects are managed. Personnel, physical resources and fiscal resources must be budgeted, scheduled and carefully monitored to achieve desired results on a consistent basis. Both office and project management require input to and information from other principals, administrative and technical personnel, the general accounting system (receipts, disbursements, general ledger, payroll, etc.), the project accounting system and the budgetary systems. Too often, the displacement of these various activities, data and personnel make insurmountable the management tasks of being current at the right level and spending time on important items.

An integrated systems approach is needed to meet resource management requirements and to develop the general framework for a comprehensive management system. Such a system should achieve orderly budgeting, scheduling and measurement of performance.

FORECASTING MANPOWER AND COST

The managing principal must provide a plan with which the results of the office can be measured over a period of time. Ideally, the plan summary should be reduced to a single page and, more importantly, to a few indicators which measure performance relative to budget. The key indicators are staffing levels, average labor rates, man-hour utilization, accounts receivable collection ratios, expenses

EXHIBIT 10-1. OVERALL BUDGET

Level	Category	A No. of Staff	B Annual Salary (Avg + 4%)	C Average Overtime (%)	D Total Salary *(No O.T. Pay)	E Available Hours	F Projected Utilization (%)	G Direct Cost (D × F)	H Direct Hours (E × F)	J Hourly Cost (G ÷ H)	K Annual Direct Payroll (A × G)	L Annual Payroll (A × D)
1	Officers	3	$60,000	10	*$60,000	2112	50	$30,000	1056	$28.40	90,000	180,000
2	Senior Vice Presidents	5	40,000	10	* 40,000	2112	80	32,000	1690	18.93	160,000	200,000
3	Vice Presidents	7	35,000	10	* 35,000	2112	80	28,000	1690	16.57	196,000	245,000
4	Project Managers	15	28,000	10	* 28,000	2134	90	25,200	1920	13.13	378,000	420,000
5	Project Architects	20	20,000	10	* 20,000	2156	90	18,000	1940	9.28	360,000	400,000
6	Senior Draftsmen	25	16,000	10	** 18,400	2156	95	17,480	2048	8.54	437,000	460,000
7	Intermediate Draftsmen	30	12,000	10	** 13,800	2156	95	13,110	2048	6.40	393,300	414,000
8	Junior Draftsmen	35	10,000	10	** 11,500	2156	95	10,925	2048	5.33	382,375	402,500
											$2,396,675 Direct Technical Payroll	$2,721,500 Total Technical Payroll

** O.T. pay calculated at 1½ times normal rate

Average Budget Multiple	2.50	2.71	3.00
Assumed Professional Fees	$6,000,000	$6,500,000	$7,190,000
Direct Expenses			
Salaries	2,396,675	2,396,675	2,396,675
Job Costs	400,000	400,000	400,000
General and Administrative Expenses			
Salaries (Indirect technical)			
Salaries (G & A)			
Payroll taxes and fringe	3,203,325	3,203,325	3,203,325
Occupancy etc.			
.			
.			
Bonus and profit sharing			
	6,000,000	6,000,000	6,000,000
Earnings Before Taxes	$ 0	$ 500,000	$ 1,190,000

Indirect Technical Payroll = $2,721,500 − 2,396,675 = $324,825

$$\text{Average Budget Multiple} = \frac{\text{Professional Fees}}{\text{Direct Labor}}$$

$$\text{Break–Even Multiple} = \frac{\$\,6,000,000}{2,396,675} = 2.50$$

and average project budget multiple. In the smaller office, the key indicators are often based solely on intuitive feelings. However, where top management is removed from the direct day-to-day activities, reliance must be placed on an information system.

OVERALL BUDGET. An overall office budget should be prepared on an annual basis parallel to the office's accounting and tax period. This is the primary tool from which all other information is derived and against which such information is measured. A sample one-page summary of this budget is illustrated in Exhibit 10-1. The upper portion indicates the projection of revenue for budgeting purposes; the lower left portion shows expense budgets, with earnings projections at various income levels indicated at the bottom based on different projected budget multiples, i.e., 2.50, 2.71 or 3.00. In determining the input for the annual budget, careful consideration must be given to a number of factors.

Staffing. Personnel staffing assumes average numbers of employees for the projected period at each level and is generally stable at the upper or management levels with maximum variance at the minimum experience levels due to mobility and workload factors. These assumed averages must take into account planned growth, new project requirements and planned promotions.

Utilization. An architect, like other service professionals, inventories only man-hours for future service. Unused or misspent man-hours cannot be regained; therefore, careful budgeting and use of time are most important. Budgeted utilization percentages are based on historical averages for the architect's office, but should reflect the expectations of management for each level or member of the staff.

Accurate historical data should tend to indicate that utilization within various levels will remain fairly constant and decrease as one assumes more marketing and administrative responsibility. Once accurately established, the utilization factors as key indicators are remarkably reliable.

Labor Rates. Average labor rates are composites of the existing payroll average, anticipated new staff members during the projected period and planned salary adjustments during the projected period.

Average Budget Multiple. This multiple is the best barometer for measuring performance of the office as a whole and for measuring individual project performance. It allows accurate comparison of dissimilar projects in relation to the overall goal. The average multiple is derived from historical performance for each architect's office. It is projected based on the economic outlook, competition and other factors which enter pricing decisions. The calculation is simply

$$\frac{\text{Architect Fees}}{\text{(Less Consultant Fees)}} \Big/ \text{Direct Labor Cost}$$

Using this concept, each office can derive a break-even office multiple for the period, i.e., an average multiple which just covers all costs for the period. With a projected profit for the period, the architect can calculate the average project multiple performance necessary to meet the overall projected profit.

Expenses. These can be classified as direct (job related) or indirect (general and administrative—G&A). Direct expenses are further broken down as reimbursable by the client or nonreimbursable. The nonreimbursable project expenses must be budgeted in addition to G&A expenses. These budgets must provide additional pricing guidelines in fee negotiations during the period.

BUDGET MULTIPLE. This provides a basis for measuring "apples to apples" relationships. Too often, systems measure only hours, and the cost of hours may vary by a factor of 8 to 10 times. The quantity as well as the quality must be accounted for to achieve a sophisticated level of management. Also, some project types are substantially more profitable than others and should be budgeted to reflect the expected higher profit multiple. The budget multiple is a simple device for budgeting purposes, monitoring projects and measuring performance. Exhibit 10-2 shows a sample budget of available fee dollars for distribution to various func-

EXHIBIT 10-2. PROJECT BUDGET USING BUDGET MULTIPLE OF 3.0

Compensation per Owner–Architect Agreement	$400,000
Less Consultant Fees	120,000
Net Architectural Fees	$280,000
Less Nonreimbursable Expenses	7,500
Net Fee Available for Labor Calculation	$272,500

$$\frac{\$272,500}{3.0} = {}^*\$90,833$$ (Labor cost available at 3.0 multiple for budget distribution to various functions and levels.)

* Direct labor costs are multiplied times the budget multiple (3.0 in this example) for reporting purposes to measure project performance to date in terms of fee, i.e., when $272,500 have been spent in direct labor ($90,833 cost × 3.0), the project should be complete.

EXHIBIT 10-3. COMPARATIVE REPORTING

Projected Multiples
(Based on Cost to Complete)

ABC ARCHITECTS PROJECT STATUS SUMMARY 10/31/74

LOS ANGELES OFFICE

PROJECT NO.	PROJECT	PD	PROJECTED MULTIPLE	BUDG MULT	% COMPL	ABC NET FEE $						UNBILLED HOURS
						BUDGET	PRIOD	TO-DATE	EARNED	VARIANCE	BILLED	
78132-00	RIVERSIDE HOSPITAL	CRSVAKJRLJMR	3.16—	3.65	96.0	106225	710	118142	101976	16166	104550	696
78132-01*	RIVERSIDE MED PARK	CRSVAKJRLJMR		3.00	DPE							
78132-02*	REV BY STATE & OWNER	CRSVAKJRLJMR		2.95	DPE			6128	6128		5942	
78132-03*	MP JAMES JUSTICE	CRSVAKJRLJMR		2.95	DPE			4707	4707			
78132-04*	CONFIRM STRUCTURAL	CRSVAKJRLJMR		2.95	DPE			12442	12442		5000	
78132-05*	RADIOLOGY DEPT REVS	CRSVAKJRLJMR		2.95	DPE			2302	2302		2300	
78159-00	101 HILLTOP TOWER	BEBCEBBMZ	4.62—	4.83	79.0	452600	13053	372815	357554	15261	475636	273
78159-02*	ATHLETIC CLUB ON GRG	BEBCEBBMZ		2.50	DPE			231	231		254	
78159-03*	HELISTOP	BEBCEBBMZ		2.50	DPE			600	600		614	
78159-04	ESCALATOR	BEBCEBBMZ		2.50	DPE		100	1506	1506		1630	5
78159-05	BANK TENANT	BEBCEBBMZ		2.50	DPE			678	678		783	
78159-06*	LWR LVL CAFETERIA LSE	BEBCEBBMZ		2.50	DPE			240	240		296	
78159-07	CONSTRUCTION SIGNANGE	BEBCEBBMZ		3.00	DPE			903	903			48
78159-08	BANK TENANT PROPOSAL	BEBCEBBMZ		2.50	DPE			625	625		638	
78159-09	WINDOW WASH ANCHORS	BEBCEBBMZ		2.50	DPE		60	237	237		173	3
78159-10	TENAT CONTR ADMIN	BEBCEBBMZ		2.50	DPE			420	420		250	
78160-04*	CONFIRM STRUCTURAL	GRTHCH		3.00	DPE							
78167-00*	JONES & JONES	LLF	2.51—	2.51	100.0	18300		18308	18300	8	15224	
78170-24*	RADIOLOGY LAB	BEBGRTHS		3.00	DPE			1970	1970			
78171-00*	OAKCREEK PARK	HCH		3.00	DPE			6055	6055		5523	
78173-00	UTOPIA CNTR	HCHGRTMLC	5.40—	5.38	92.0	226816	9969	210548	208670	1877	216521	200
78173-02*	MODELS	HCHGRTMLC		2.95	DPE			4425	4425		4799	
78173-03*	SITE PLAN REVISIONS	HCHGRTMLC		2.95	DPE			1875	1875		2801	
78173-04*	LEASE BACKGROUNDS	HCHGRTMLC		2.95	DPE			988	988		988	
78173-05*	DESIGN SITE SIGN	HCHGRTMLC		2.95	DPE			93	93		93	
78173-06*	TRASH CHUTE-L DOCK	HCHGRTMLC		2.95	DPE			2969	2969		2975	
78173-07	BASEMENT FLOODING	HCHGRTMLC		3.00	DPE			240	240		205	

Blanks Indicate Projects Based on
Direct Payroll Expenditures

tions and levels. Rather than cost measurements, the budget multiple allows the matching of performance in terms of fee.

Net Architect Fee. For budgeting purposes, the net architect fee is calculated as gross fee less fees to consultants. Consultant fees are excluded from the calculations of either average or project budget multiple.

Direct Labor. Average labor costs for each level can be used for appropriating man-hour costs for each level budgeted. Depending on personnel availability, the project manager can select personnel knowing in advance the approximate effect of each hour charged to the project. For detailed reporting purposes, the average for each level can be used (without disclosing individual salaries), inflated by the budget multiple to equate with fee. Likewise, projected man-hours at each level through project completion provide the basis for periodic calculations of projected multiple to compare with budget multiple. Exhibit 10-3 is an example of comparative reporting.

DETAILED PROJECT BUDGET. Project budgets can be determined in various ways. Some architects take time to prepare a detailed budget preparatory to negotiating an owner-architect agreement. Other architects use experience in negotiating compensation based on a percent of construction or standard rates for labor levels with a maximum fee not to be exceeded. With either method, a detailed budget can be formulated similar to Exhibit 10-4 to provide the basis for the work plan.

Consultant Fees. Since major portions of the work may be planned for consultants, the fee set aside for their payments should be allocated as soon as possible with corresponding consultant agreements prepared and signed as confirma-

tions. Scope of consultant work becomes an early checklist requisite for both budgeting and work plan requirements, as discussed in the project flow diagram section.

Nonreimbursable Expenses. Expenses which are not reimbursed by the client reduce project and office profitability. Travel, printing and other expenses not to be reimbursed, as spelled out in the owner-architect agreement, must be budgeted and carefully monitored to achieve expected results.

Available Man-hours. Exhibit 10-4 illustrates the calculation of fee dollars available for labor. These fee dollars when divided by the budget multiple provide the labor basis at cost for planning man-

hours, which at a general labor average can be used for a first estimate of their availability. However, as assignments are made, number of documents estimated, etc., the detailed estimate at average level costs can be compared to budget available and compared during the project for status.

Man-hour allocation is generally first made by phase of work and then to each function (employees performing work) involved in the phase. For instance, the schematics phase may represent 15 percent of the fee and will be performed entirely by the design function. The design development phase, however, may represent 20 percent of the fee, but requires 60 percent participation by the design function and 40 percent by the production function. With these general allo-

EXHIBIT 10-4. DETAILED PROJECT BUDGET

Net fee available for labor calculation from Exhibit 10-2 = $272,500

PHASE	PERCENTAGE	FEE
Schematics	15	$ 40,875
Design Development	20	54,500
Construction Documents	40	109,000
Bid and Negotiation	5	13,625
Construction Services	20	54,500
	100%	$272,500

Using the hourly cost data from column J, Exhibit 10-1, multiplied by an assumed budget multiple of 3.0, the following rates become valid for budget hours at each level.

LEVEL	HOURLY COST FROM COLUMN J EXHIBIT 10-1	COST INFLATED TO FEE @ 3.0 BUDGET MULTIPLE
1	$28.40	$85.20
2	18.93	56.79
3	16.57	49.71
4	13.13	39.39
5	9.28	27.84
6	8.54	25.62
7	6.40	19.20
8	5.33	15.99

Use these rates for establishing or checking hours available for each level for phase allocations above.

EXHIBIT 10-5. FUNCTIONAL PROJECT FLOW DIAGRAM

Sequenced Action Items
(Timing of events is
sequence as shown)

Corresponding Checklists

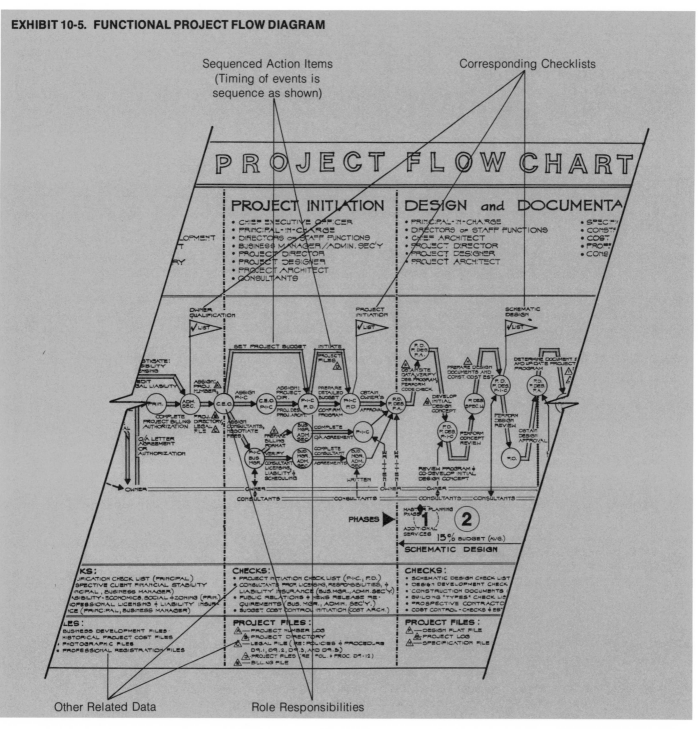

Other Related Data

Role Responsibilities

cations, the project manager can budget to the personnel levels involved and more specifically to planned participants.

STRUCTURING A PROJECT FLOW DIAGRAM

The flow of a project through an architect's office consists of several actions from client contact through project completion. The actions required may vary in complexity between projects. However, the phases, activities and action items follow an organized pattern within an office as illustrated in the functional project flow diagram shown in Exhibit 10-5. This diagram provides a frame of reference for sequenced action items, role responsibilities, timing of events, corresponding checklists and other related data. With this flow chart, each individual project can be planned, assigned, scheduled and monitored throughout its progress.

SEQUENCED ACTION ITEMS. Action items in Exhibit 10-5 are sequenced precedent to, concurrent with and subsequent to the normal occurrence of other items required to complete the project. The flow diagram, then, provides the precedence chart necessary to plan complex project activities which might otherwise require PERT, CPM or other network planning techniques discussed in Chapter 17. An office may prepare a separate

flow diagram depicting its approach to fast-track construction; additional diagrams may prove useful for joint venture projects or specialty services such as programming or interior design.

ROLE RESPONSIBILITIES. Probably the most important technique of the functional project flow diagram is the assignment of responsibilities to each action item as illustrated in Exhibit 10-6. These assignments provide the necessary link of who normally does what in a project unless specifically stated otherwise in the work plan or schedule of assignments. The assigned action items further provide a basis for describing specific role descriptions when placed in a secondary format for hiring, training and performance measurement purposes.

A member of the staff is not necessarily identified in a role; to the contrary, a member may provide multiple functions, particularly on smaller projects. For instance, a senior staff member might be the project manager and the project architect on Project A, the project manager on Project B, and perhaps the construction architect on Project C. Hence, even though the assignment of the individual varies, the requirements of each role in each project can be specifically stated so everyone will know which individual is to do what and when by knowing which role each is to play.

TIMING OF EVENTS. In some offices, the assignment of dates to action items on a flow diagram proves adequate for planning and control purposes. A summary of these actions may be depicted as a project phase schedule on the project status report (Exhibit 10-10). Other offices prepare detailed bar charts for each major phase with symbols and shading depicting action items and status.

CORRESPONDING CHECKLISTS. Since the action items referenced in the flow diagram are summary items, the checklists provide detailed reference of tasks to be performed. The flow chart illustrates the grouping of checklist items into related sets for routine checkoff during the projects. These related sets are flagged on the flow chart as action items to be performed prior to proceeding with the next project activities. Exhibit 10-7 shows a chosen format for checking, signing and dating or noting "N/A," not applicable. Certain checklist items may refer to more detailed specialty checklists such as codes, safety standards, consultant requirements, etc.

OTHER RELATED DATA. Other flow chart data which may be illustrated for reference is average phase allocation of budget, participants within each phase, owner and consultant coordination, major control documents and files prepared and

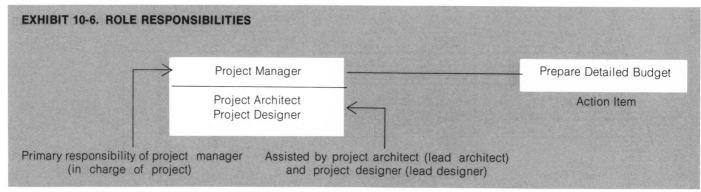

EXHIBIT 10-6. ROLE RESPONSIBILITIES

Project Manager

Project Architect
Project Designer

Prepare Detailed Budget

Action Item

Primary responsibility of project manager (in charge of project)

Assisted by project architect (lead architect) and project designer (lead designer)

EXHIBIT 10-7. TYPICAL PROJECT CHECKLIST

ABC Architects Architectural Handbook

Revision Date: 9/74

Approved By: *ER*

Section: CHECK LISTS

Section No: E21

Subject: TRADITIONAL/FASTRACK/INTERIORS SERVICES

Page 3 of 10 pages

SCHEMATIC DESIGN/MORTGAGE PACKAGE

- Verify completion of Project Initiation checklist. _____ N/A

- Verify completion of Programming and Space Planning check list (Interiors only) _____ N/A

- Verify execution of O/A Agreement. _____ N/A

- Verify signator's proper authorization by Owner. _____ N/A

- Verify Owner's written authorization to proceed with schematic design, mortgage package, or space planning-conceptual design. _____ N/A

- Assemble governing codes and regulations. _____ N/A

E3.4 E3.5 E3.6
- Verify checks of building code, zoning ordinances, deed restrictions, Fire Marshal, Dept. of Health, Traffic, Transportation, Water Department, labor department, OSHA, EPA, and where applicable, FAA, Corps of Engineers, State Highway, Handicapped, A.N.S.I. Elevators Escalators Dumbwaiters and Moving Walks A17.1-1971. _____ N/A

- Establish project timetable. Distribute to Owner, staff, consultants (and general contractor - Fastrack only). _____ N/A

- Document all meetings. _____ N/A

- Distribute synopsis of O/A Agreement to Staff and Consultants on need-to-know basis. _____ N/A

E3.7
- Verify Owner's furnishing of complete site topography, utilities and boundry survey, and a preliminary soils investigation report. Verify data per check list. Distribute to staff, consultants (and contractor-Fastrack only). _____ N/A

- Review site with staff, consultants (and contractors - Fastrack only). _____ N/A

- Review Owner's Project Requirements with staff, consultants (and contractor - Fastrack only) and co-develop initial design concept (and space allocation-interiors only). _____ N/A

- Verify design staff review of initial concept (and space allocation - interiors only) and obtain Owner's approval. _____ N/A

EXHIBIT 10-8. WORKING DRAWINGS STATUS CHART

ABC
Architects
Planning Consultants

Project Name : XYZ MANOR   Report No . 8

Project No.: 75053   Page 1 of 1

Sequence	Sheet Number	SHEET TITLE	Assigned to	Est. sht.M.H.	Act. compl Manhours	Percent Complete	Completion Number	Total hrs remaining
	A1-1	INDEX - PROJ. DATA	AS	16	4		5	12
	A2-1	SITE SURVEY	LC	8	2		10	6
	A2-2	SITE PLAN	"	56	44		7.5	12
	A2-3	SITE DETAILS	"	32	4		5	28
	A3-1	GR. FL. & TYP. FL. PLAN	BK	72	80		9.5	0
	A3-2	PTHSE & ROOF PLAN	"	72	41		8.5	31
	A4-1	APT. A,B & C PLAN	BK	72	74		9.5	0
	A4-2	APT. D, CORE PLAN	"	40	24		7.5	16
	A6-1	BLDG. ELEV & SECT.	JR	32	24		7.5	8
	A8-1	WALL SECTIONS	BK	32	30		9	2
	A8-2	EXT. WALL DET'LS.	JR	56	31		4	25
	A8-3	" " "	JR	40	24		5	16
	A8-4	ROOF DETAILS	JR	24	8		5	16
	A9-1	GLAZING DET'LS.	AS	32	41		9.5	0
	A9-2	ENTRANCE DET'LS.	AS	24	18		7.5	6
	A10-1	INTERIOR ELEVS.	JR	32	18		7.5	14
	A10-2	" "	"	40	9		4	31
	A10-3	" "	"	24	10		6	14
	A11-1	STAIR PLANS & SECTS	BK	24	27		9.5	0
	A11-2	STAIR DETAILS	"	16	22		9.5	0
	A12-1	ELEV. SECT & DET'LS	BK	40	25		7.5	15
				804	560	T O T A L	154	252

Percent Complete scale: 0, 25, 50, 75, 100
Completion numbers: 0 1 2 3 4 5 6 7 8 9 10
COMPLETION NUMBERS

% Complete = (Total of completion numbers) / (Total Number of sheets) × 10   **Remarks**

= 154 / 21 × 10 = 73.3%

Submitted by

PRODUCTION DRAWINGS REPORT

3/22/75

Date

EXHIBIT 10-9. MAN-HOUR SUMMARY REPORT

Levels

ABC ARCHITECTS MAN-HOUR UTILIZATION 10/31/74

LOS ANGELES

17504

	HOURS THIS PERIOD							HOURS FISCAL YEAR-TO-DATE								USE Y-T-D	
	EDUC & UNAS	VAC, HOL, SICK	ADM & PROM	SPCL PROJ	CHRG PROJ	BASE HRS	O.T. PAID -REF-	EDUC & UNAS	VAC, HOL, SICK	ADM & PROM	SPCL PROJ	CHRG PROJ	TOTL HRS	BASE HRS	O.T. PAID -REF-	% UTIL	% CHRG
OFFICERS																	
A	8	46			129	90		16	16	91		330	453	450		73	73
B						90		45	16	123	18	301	503	450		71	67
C	8	55			17	90			32	334		74	440	450		16	16
TOTAL ☆☆☆☆☆☆☆☆☆☆☆☆	16	101			146	270		61	64	548	18	705	1396	1350		54	52
SR. VICE PRESIDENTS																	
A	8	2			77	90		4	16	34	4	434	492	450		97	96
B	8	12			60	90			76	60		304	440	450		68	68
C	8	4			72	90		2	16	104		330	452	450		73	73
D	10	11		1	60	90		12	70	99	17	236	434	450		56	52
E	16			15	49	90			73	8	99	268	448	450		82	60
TOTAL ☆☆☆☆☆☆☆☆☆☆☆☆	50	29		16	318	450		18	251	305	120	1572	2266	2250		63	58
VICE PRESIDENTS																	
A	8				72	90			16			424	440	450		94	94
B	8	3			71	90			42	9		393	444	450		87	87
C	8	12			60	90		2	32	48	14	348	444	450		80	77
TOTAL ☆☆☆☆☆☆☆☆☆☆☆☆	24	15			203	270		2	90	57	14	1165	1328	1350		87	86
DESIGN																	
SR PROJECT DESIGNER																	
A	8		1		78	90			24	3	30	423	480	450		101	94
B	8				72	90		12	24			407	443	450		90	90
TOTAL	16		1		150	180		12	48	3	30	830	923	900		96	92
PROJECT DESIGNER																	
A	8				72	90			24			416	440	450		92	92
B	8				72	90			24	11	26	379	440	450		90	84
C	8				76	90			16		31	354	401	450	5	86	79
D	8		1		76	90			8	1		76	85	90		86	84
TOTAL	32		1		296	360			72	11	58	1225	1366	1440	5	89	85
SPECIFICATIONS																	
SENIOR SPEC WRITER																	
A	8	18			60	90		59	42	39		333	473	450		74	74
TOTAL	8	18			60	90		59	42	39		333	473	450		74	74
SPEC WRITER																	
A 2	10				78	90	10	97	18			369	484	450	44	82	82
TOTAL 2	10				78	90	10	97	18			369	484	450	44	82	82
TOTAL ☆☆☆☆☆☆☆☆☆☆☆☆ 2	18	18			138	180	10	156	60	39		702	957	900	44	78	78
TECHNICAL TOTAL 32	567	444		415	3476	5400	10	515	2167	2371	2629	21555	29237	29520	129	82	73

Levels

Functional Activities

Levels within Functional Activities

Total for all Levels

used. This data may prove useful for the training of new staff members and for showing prospective clients how the office performs project activities.

SCHEDULING

Scheduling is probably the most difficult of all systems to maintain consistently due to the requirements of holds (stalled projects), deadlines, meetings, travel, owner financing, sickness and other unknown factors. Personnel scheduling has proved to be most successful when performed on a flexible day-to-day basis by a senior member of the firm with knowledge of staff capabilities, project schedules and priorities as determined by the managing principal.

FUNCTIONAL ACTIVITIES. Functional activities are best scheduled using known workload, available hours of personnel and priorities. Information can be gathered for project requirements from project manager cost-to-complete estimates (Exhibit 10-10) and regular project status meetings. Estimates of man-hour requirements should be carefully prepared by the project manager. Exhibit 10-8 provides a formal approach to such a determination.

PERSONNEL. Assignments of personnel, depending on the size of the office and the number of projects, may be made on a daily basis, or at least modified daily. Unexpected holds may be placed on the project by a client phone call. Likewise, other project changes may require additional personnel than previously anticipated.

COMPUTER SCHEDULING. Time-shared computer programs used for scheduling and other routines are most likely to be found in large offices of approximately 100 professional employees or more, performing perhaps 20 or more projects at any given time. Factors used in qualifying computer scheduling include project complexity, degree of office departmentalization, computer turnaround time, and styles of office management and project management.

MAINTAINING CONTROLS AND REPORTS

The integrated systems approach referred to earlier requires that the controls and reports produced by the office's standard accounting and reporting systems access the indicator's data necessary to monitor both office and project performance relative to their respective budgets. The pyramiding of a sound data base allows the summarizing of key information for each budgeted area, while providing the detail which is necessary for project management as well as normal administration requirements.

MAN-HOUR UTILIZATION. Exhibit 10-9 illustrates the pyramiding effect of summary reporting. The managing principal is interested first in the use of all technical man-hours for the period which reads as a single percentage. Further, if more than one office is involved, it is desirable to determine the contribution of each to the overall percentage, with every office having a calculated percentage for technical man-hours' use.

Data is available to show contribution to the total or each office percentage by level or staff category. As shown in Exhibit 10-11, the various levels are budgeted at different utilization percentages due to administrative and business development requirements.

Data is also accessible by functional activity, e.g., design, interiors, etc., to provide a basis for measuring performance of scheduling ability. Last, the lowest level of data is a recap of an individual's time report input to show individual use of man-hours' inventory.

PROJECTS. The project status report illustrated in Exhibit 10-10 gives the project manager a recap of the project to date and the basis for an estimate of overall schedule, cost to complete and billing information. The areas shaded on the exhibit depict the project manager's input information, and the remainder of the report is computed and printed for project use.

Project Budget Multiple. The budget multiple is printed as shown and indicates the factor used to compute charges from average costs of each labor level. Average costs by levels are used to maintain confidentiality of individual salaries. This multiple could be revised during the project if the project scope changed or if the budget proved unrealistic, but its use is intended for measurement only in comparing charges to fee budget.

Projected Cost to Complete. Two areas of input by the project manager shown in Exhibit 10-10 allow for the estimated man-hours to complete by month and a distribution of those man-hours by level. The system extends these hours by average level costs to determine cost to complete. Data available to the project manager in return includes the total cost at completion and a projected multiple based on the input.

Projected Multiple. The projected multiple is an exact indication of performance to budget and in turn profitability. The overall budget computations have determined a break-even multiple, and this projection shows how much contribution the project will provide toward the overall budget. The impact of this project is simply the net architect's fee for the project divided by the annual projected net architect's fee.

Projected Workload. A further summary of total hours projected by period for all

EXHIBIT 10-10. PROJECT STATUS REPORT

```
                    ABC ARCHITECTS    PROJECT STATUS REPORT            10/31/74                          PAGE   86
                                                                                           OFFICE - LOS ANGELES
  78132-00    RIVERSIDE HOSPITAL FEE $140,000 NO REIMB EXCEPT PLANS & SPECS OVER 15 SETS, BILLINGS MONTHLY       I/C - CRS VAK JKL JMR
                            BASED ON / COMPLETE                                                                  ---
                      THIS PERIOD       TO DATE          BUDGET         HOURLY PROJECTIONS BY PROJECT MANAGER    ESTIMATED    BILL THIS
                      -----------     -----------      ----------                                                   %           %
  PHASE    EMPLOYEE   HOURS CHARGES   HOURS CHARGES   CHARGES HOURS    NOV  DEC  JAN  FEB  MAR  APR  OTHER       COMPLETE     COMPLETE

  01 MAST PLAN/MORT PKG                  2    550      6800   285                                                  100          100
     8632 SMITH, ANDREA
  02 SCHEMATICS                        537  17674     10000   420                                                  100          100
  03 DESIGN DEVELOPMENT                440  12233     10600   445                                                  100          100
  04 CONSTRUCTION DOC.    2    73     2731  69332     64500  2700       4    6   16   12                            99           99
     4526 RICHARDS, EDWAR  2    73
  05 BID AND NEGOTIATE
  06 CONSTRUCTION SERV   17   637      622  18350     13600   570      16   18   32   32                            87           87
     3352 CULVERSON, CHAR 14   549
     4526 RICHARDS, EDWAR  2    73
     8632 SMITH, ANDREA    1    15
  99                                                   725

            TOTALS       19   710     4392 118142   106225  4420       20   24   48   44
```

```
  FEE BILLINGS -ABC -@ 75%        7650        104550                            HOURS TO COMPLETE      136    PROJECTION
  FEE BILLINGS -GROSS-           10200        139400                                                          BY RATE LEVELS
  REIMBURSABLES -CONSULT-                                                                                     -----------------
  REIMBURSABLES -OTHER-            80          1174                                         LEVEL  HOURS               CHARGES
  REIMBURSABLES BILLINGS         200          1029                                          1-OFF
  NONREIMBURSABLES -CONSULT-                  8660                                           2-SVP
  NONREIMBURSABLES -OTHER-         28          6894                                          3-VP    66                  2589
                                                                                            4-PD    30                  1095
                                                                                            5-PA    40                  1168
                                                                                            6-SD
                                                                                            7-ID
                                                                                            8-JD
                                                                                            TOTALS  136                 4852
```

```
  SCHEDULE            NOV  DEC  JAN  FEB  MAR  APR  MAY  JUN  JUL  AUG  SEP  OCT   START FINISH

  01 MAST PLAN/MORT PKG                                                              /    /
  02 SCHEMATICS                                                                      /    /
  03 DESIGN DEVELOPMENT                                                              /    /
  04 CONSTRUCTION DOC. -------------*                                              3/73  12/74
  05 BID AND NEGOTIATE                                                               /    /
  06 CONSTRUCTION SERV. ----------------------------*                              7/73  2/75
```

```
  LEGAL FILE STATUS                                                            BUDGET MULTIPLE       3.65
                                                                               PROJECTED MULTIPLE    3.16
  PROJ BILLING AUTH    O/A AGREEMENT      BUDGET    CONSULTANT AGREEMENTS       UNBILLED HOURS        696
  REVISION DATE     PREPARED  EXECUTED   PREPARED   NAME           PREPARED      EXECUTED   AMOUNT

    1   02/18/74    02/01/73  02/01/73   02/18/74   JONES STRUCTURAL  02/19/74   02/21/74   10,500   1
                                                    FRANK'S MEP SHOP             01/10/73   24,000   2

  REMARKS:  CONSULTANT (#2) AUTHORIZATION BY LETTER FROM CONSULTANT 1-10-73.
```

EXHIBIT 10-11. PROJECTED WORKLOAD SUMMARY

Actual Personnel
Projected

ABC ARCHITECTS MANHOUR PROJECTION SUMMARY 10/31/74

LOS ANGELES
CURRENT PROJECTS PROJECTION SUMMARY

	NOV	DEC	JAN	FEB	MAR	APR	OTHER
ACTIVE PROJECTS -HRS-	5753	4785	4202	3282	2754	3184	17173
MANMONTHS -HRS/180-	31	26	23	18	15	17	95
MANMONTHS @ 80% UT.	39	33	29	22	19	22	119
SPECIAL PROJECTS -HRS-	389	365	303	196	172	170	
MANMONTHS -HRS/180-	2	2	1	1			
MANMONTHS @ 80% UT.	2	2	2	1	1	1	1
PROSPECTIVE PROJECTS -HRS-							
MANMONTHS -HRS/180-							
MANMONTHS @ 80 % UT.							
TOTAL HOURS	6142	5150	4505	3478	2926	3354	17173
TOTAL MANMONTHS -HRS/180-	34	28	25	19	16	18	95
TOTAL MANMONTHS @ 80% UT.	42	35	31	24	20	23	119

(Projects can be coded as prospective)

NEW WORK PROJECTION SUMMARY -BY PROJECT

	NOV	DEC	JAN	FEB	MAR	APR	OTHER
SEATTLE HOTEL				150	150	150	6000
BOARD STREET OFFICE BLDG	—	—	100	100	200	250	4500
	6142	5150	4605	3728	3276	3154	27673
100%	34	28	26	20	18	21	154
80%	42	35	32	26	23	26	192

Completed by Business
Development Function

projects is a direct indicator to management of the backlog of known work. This backlog of hours, when divided by both average hours available for each individual, and the average utilization budget percentage, depicts the man-months of work available for each period. Exhibit 10-11 shows this summary for one office. A combined summary for all offices would be shown on a separate printout. Extra space is provided on the report for potential projects not presently in the project system which are added by the business development function with some comments regarding probability of work and the approximate scope and timing of it.

PROJECTED REVENUE ACCRUALS. In addition to man-hour backlog computations, the input cost-to-complete data also provides the ability for the system to compute revenue projections over the next several periods for known projects. This data offers to management a current projection of office performance for the near future.

OTHER GENERAL REPORTS. A system with this general data base also provides:

—Project status summary, a one-line report which shows projected multiple compared with budgeted multiple, budgeted net fee, charges to date, computed percent complete and pertinent billing information.

—Current projects list, a one-line project summary which can be used directly for distribution as a current listing of active project numbers, name, office assigned and in-charge personnel.

—Project closeout analysis, a report

prepared at completion which establishes project profitability as related to the budget multiple, the actual multiple at completion, a multiple based on collections and a combined multiple including extra services performed.

The principles of applying an integrated approach to resource management as it relates to budgeting and scheduling are of value to all size firms. The process remains the same for either manual or automated techniques. The basic fee-to-cost relationship should remain constant for all firms with a reasonable flow of projects.

The overall budget provides key ratios for measuring the performance of manpower utilization, labor rates, receipts and expenses. The budget multiple allows the responsible architect to measure performance in terms of fee particularly as cost-to-complete projections are updated. The functional project flow diagram provides the continuity of project scheduling in terms of sequenced events, responsibilities, timing of activities, the use of detailed checklists and other related project data. Finally, the formatting and timeliness of performance reports are the true measure of the effectiveness of the integrated approach as a tool in the management of the architect's office.

BIBLIOGRAPHY

"Breaking Even on Professional Services." William R. Park. *Consulting Engineer,* July 1973.

A look at break–even analysis as a tool in defining and understanding a firm's economic situation.

"Computer-Based Financial Management." G. Neil Harper. *AIA Journal,* December 1972.

Emphasizes the range of management controls made possible by the AIA financial management system.

"A Consulting Engineering Office Should Be Managed, Not Engineered." James R. Reid. *Professional Engineer,* July 1972.

Discussion of a firm's goals and objectives and controls needed to measure performance.

Management: Tasks, Responsibilities, Practices. Peter F. Drucker. New York: Harper & Row, 1974.

A basic reference on the subject.

"Management and Control for the Consulting Firm." A. R. White and Charles H. Kruse. *Professional Engineer,* January 1971.

Comparison of management controls of client-oriented versus company-oriented firms.

Management Controls for Professional Firms. Reginald L. Jones and H. George Trentin. New York: American Management Association, 1968.

Good points on financial aspects of control.

Managing Professional Services Enterprises. Robert E. Sibson. New York: Beekman Publishers, 1971.

Discusses whole range of consultant services, including financial aspects.

"A User's View of Computer-Based Financial Management." Peter Piven. *AIA Journal,* July 1973.

How the AIA system is used and how it has affected one firm's practice.

Chapter 11
Programming

HERBERT McLAUGHLIN, AIA

In reality, programming is design, particularly contemporary programming which has become increasingly comprehensive and complex. Architects must therefore be deeply involved in programming—and to do so they must develop new skills and attitudes.

ROLE OF PROGRAMMING

A contemporary program usually goes well beyond the traditional lists of the size and character of spaces and interrelationships. It describes, among other things, the functional and design intent of a building, often suggests forms and materials which are appropriate, the organization and interrelationship of component parts, costs, finishes, construction systems and timing. Such a document, then, defines many basic design options. Decisions as to whether a building is high rise or low, or a combination of both, or whether a project consists of one building or more are made when programming defines net-to-gross ratios and project budgets. The program frequently decides, for instance, how dormitory bedrooms relate to a lounge—whether it states so directly or sets up a series of functional imperatives which force the solution.

The existence of such a document in many ways seems to intrude on the architect's traditional freedom. It firms up design decisions very early, bringing the client and user deeply into the design process since the document should be couched in terms both can understand.

Further, the evolution of the document increasingly involves social scientists, cost estimators, building managers and professional programmers, whose views certainly complicate and may frustrate the architect's traditional processes and solutions.

For those clients increasingly determined to control or influence the design and construction process more aggressively, programming is the most oppor-

tune time to provide input to the design process—before the project submerges in the mysterious rituals of the architect's office. Thus the program becomes the focal point of design input from a great variety of sources.

The architect who realizes that programming is design, and participates fully, need not feel threatened. Architects should be eager to share design with others: clients, users, consultants. Programming can serve to facilitate these necessary communications; to articulate, organize and make public many of the private, seemingly instinctive processes of design; and to bring to client and user a sense of opportunity, to expand the often sharply limited confines of their experience and expectations.

The latter is critical. Designs are formed and limited by expectations, prejudices and predilections which have emerged through experiences of all concerned: client, user, architect, consultant. The selection of a particular architect and consultant is usually accomplished on the basis of the client's strong sense of congruity of attitudes and experience. Shared attitudes can then stifle each other, limiting exploration.

Programming can be a methodology for breaking through preconceptions. The process is uniquely suited to abstract and clearly defined problems, to provide architect and client with a fresh sense of purpose and with data to implement new design approaches.

Programming is also a critical tool in which the scope of a project can be dramatically reshaped from its original conception. For instance, it is the architect's responsibility to build very differently, to build less or not to build at all. Projects which threaten the environment are obvious examples.

Many projects may not have to be built or can be reduced in size through the reuse of older buildings or reorganization of facilities. Three smaller schools, two of

which exist, may be a better solution than one big, new one. Jails which tend to be overbuilt can be reduced in size with beneficial effects in cutting budgets and speeding the process of justice.

The role of programming focuses on those recently developing and emphasized aspects which move the process toward innovation, principally through the incorporation of client, consultant and user need input.

PROGRAM COMPONENTS

The standard AIA contract documents describe programming as an additional service, but give the service little precise definition. *Compensation Management Guidelines for Architectural Services,* AIA Catalog No. M188, lists "facility programming" under predesign services, pointing out that it "may be staged to provide only basic requirements initially, with more detailed requirements established as needed."

BASIC ELEMENTS. The 1969 AIA publication, *Emerging Techniques 2: Architectural Programming,* defines those elements which are the client's responsibility and those which are the architect's.

Within the client's realm are:
—Client philosophy and objectives
—Functional relationships
—Facility space requirements
—Client background and research
And those which are the architect's responsibility:
—Specific facility requirements
—Site development requirements
—Characteristics of the occupants
—Characteristics of the site
—Objectives of the master plan
—Relative location and interrelationship of spaces
—Functional requirements for the facility
—Flexible needs for future growth and changes

PROGRAMMING 121

—Priority of need among requirements
—Special restrictions and limitations
—Budget

The inference is that the client work precedes that of the architect, although the architect may have a role in evolving the client's program.

MERGING OF RESPONSIBILITIES. The above separation of components and responsibilities is impractical and ill-advised. The architect is needed to give definition to those areas which are defined as the client's responsibility but, more importantly, to explore possibilities of form and organization which can alter the client's perception of what is possible. Client lack of experience can lead to overplanning and excess scope so that the project must be cut back and much of the work painfully redone. Definition of budget at the outset is a critical case in point. Construction cost increasingly defines the feasibility of a project from the outset. The amount of square footage and the quality of construction should be determined congruently, not after the client has done studies of philosophy, relationships and space.

The client needs information concerning how design options affect operations and costs. Planning cannot be done in a conceptual and experimental vacuum. In a hospital project, the decision to utilize all private bedrooms will reduce the number of beds and at the same time increase construction and operational costs. In a school, the decision to go to open planning will often increase land coverage. This requires design decisions.

In essence, the client's traditional functional program, the architect's design program and the master plan are beginning to merge into one effort.

ADDITIONAL ELEMENTS. As a result of merging of efforts, the basic elements referenced in *Emerging Techniques 2* are often augmented by the following:

—A code and governmental restriction statement which can have substantial impact on cost and timing.

—Outline specifications which describe building systems in detail so that costs can be accurately derived and client expectations of building character and performance can be realistic. Such specifications may require a great deal of time to develop, particularly if sophisticated equipment such as transportation systems are included in the building.

—Schedules of construction and occupancy which are vital in determining construction and financing costs.

—Detailed "soft" cost budgets and schedules of expenditure. Such costs as architectural and legal fees, owner expenses during construction and interim financing loan fees can amount to 25 to 30 percent of construction costs. It is necessary to establish their scope and timing.

AMPLIFIED ELEMENTS. Another result of merging of efforts is amplification and development of the basic programming elements.

Space Descriptions. The "traditional list" of rooms which describes square footages, occupancy type, dimensions and perhaps finishes and equipment is often supplemented by a very detailed document which may systematically describe rooms in such terms as requirements for furniture, environmental controls and number of air changes. The document may also include plan and elevation drawings showing such items as doors and equipment locations. This data can then be used to establish detailed construction/equipment budgets. Such programming is usually limited to repetitive but complex building types—hospitals, for example—and may be facilitated by the use of computers. The amount of data generated may seem to be overwhelming or unnecessary. Once standardization at this level is accepted, and computer

capabilities utilized where possible, such data can be extremely helpful.

Market Research and User Need Data. This amplified element is receiving increasing emphasis. Widespread dissatisfaction with building performance has stimulated academic and client interest to increase the use of this technique particularly in so-called "compulsory" buildings such as hospitals, public housing and schools in which the users have little choice as to what building they will occupy or how it is to be designed. Research into user preference has, of course, existed for some time in free-market buildings, e.g., speculative housing or shopping centers, which have been most sensitive to user needs because the user can exercise the option to buy or not.

(Relative to later statements about client education and the necessity for more client input, developer clients for free-market buildings have been most forceful and sophisticated in working with architects to generate specific programs and designs. From necessity, these clients have had to learn a great deal about architecture and how to work effectively with architects. It is indicative of needed reforms in working relationships that architects generally view developer clients as among their most difficult. This is due not only to the low prevailing compensation for professional services but also to the client's knowledge that allows and even seems to encourage "control" of the architect—to demand justifications for all aspects of solutions. This is perhaps not such a bad thing.)

Clients, such as public agencies, who have been in the past generally unconcerned about user need data are now showing great interest. Social scientists, specialists and consultants of all sorts are moving into the field. The information they develop is often minimally useful as well as time consuming to deal with. It would then seem wise for the architect to help create useful and concise information rather than expensive and incomprehensible reports which now so often confuse design issues.

Design Guidelines. This material adds to an analysis of the client's philosophy and objectives, plus market research and user need data, and makes specific statements about the following:

—Desired imagery, emotional messages, etc., of the building forms which suggest whether the design be exciting, calm or institutionally austere.

—Traditional architectural methodologies for achieving emotional effects such as an exploration of the impacts of various materials and forms. Architects certainly know that some design features are perceived as cool, even brutal (raw concrete, for example); symmetry is generally seen as more authoritarian than is irregularity. This information can be derived from general experience and/or user need studies and shared intelligently by client and architect.

—Analysis of existing solutions to similar design problems. This exploration can range from detailed evaluation studies of specific buildings to a general survey of existing prototypes, their strengths and weaknesses.

—Generally desirable design characteristics of buildings based on the above. Precise references to desirable scales, materials and sequences of visual experiences are possible. Such specificity might at first seem limiting, but, in fact, it is merely an articulation of the processes that architect and client go through informally in the evolution of a design. Development of explicit guidelines should not impede creativity.

PROCESS

Two hundred years ago clients could have had a considerable role in design because problems were simpler and normal solutions well known. Today, the complexity of projects makes such insight possible only through considerable effort, and programming is the logical time for it to occur. A number of tools can be employed by the client, user, architect and other professionals to develop the required data and interchange.

MANAGEMENT. Inevitably one firm and one individual will dominate whether by omission or commission. Knowledge and position obviously are the keys to success. If one excludes work for developers in which the client is almost always dominant, the architect tends to emerge as the logical choice for this role, being the ultimate user of programming data. The latter is accustomed to the management of consultants, working to a schedule and, more particularly, to demanding precise and usable data, something that many socio-economic consultants find difficult. To achieve leadership, the architect must become knowledgeable about the disciplines involved.

The techniques of management in programming are not complex; they are similar to those of an architectural project. However, greater familiarity with the techniques and language of consultants is required because the relationship is closer to 50-50 than the usual architect-engineer collaboration. Most frequently a melange of specialties is involved. For instance, in a hospital project, the team should include representatives from the administrative, nursing and medical staff, the financial world, the public and medical program planning. In a school, it might include students, teachers, administrators, sociologists and environmental psychologists. In any field, a professional programmer may be included.

The independent professional programmer ranges in background from the academic to accounting/management consulting work. Such a person may have little experience with design options, opportunities or costs, or the full range of data which a practicing architect requires.

The architect should be careful to insure that these weaknesses, if they exist, are taken into account. In any event, the architect *must* work with the independent programmer from the start so that the preconceptions and limitations of either of them do not limit exploration. The processes indicated below should always be followed to assist in broadening the exploration.

SELF-ANALYSIS. At the project's beginning, all concerned should define, in writing, the limitations which their prejudices, experience and self-interest might place on them.

EDUCATION. The great majority of clients and users are unaware of the potentials and scope of contemporary architecture and techniques of its practice. The architect is generally conscientious in attempts to learn the nature of client/user activities, but effective interaction is limited by a lack of knowledge of the architect's craft by others. This one-way communication system must be altered.

Projects can begin with a short, organized course on principles and history of contemporary architecture, with special emphasis on building types contemplated. This can involve such teaching tools as visits to other buildings and presentations by consultants. At the same time that client and architect are sharing an education in the general nature of architecture and of past architectural treatment of the particular problem at hand, they will be sharing in learning the various aspects of building function. The users are well served by expanding this unusually limited operational experience. They are educated not only in the wide possibilities of architectural plan, function and form but also in organizational procedures.

Three examples from practice are hopefully instructive on how users can be educated and how this can facilitate participation in programming and thus design.

In the programming of a jail and prior to providing design input, groups of exconvicts toured with the architects through modern jails and parallel institutions such as mental health centers. Their inputs also evolved from questionnaires and group sessions. The impact of the tour on these users was considerable. It made clear to them that there was a wide range of environmental choices in what they had perceived as a very limited field.

Architects, in another instance, had a series of group sessions and individual interviews with people who had or were about to undergo surgery in a large outpatient clinic. These users were shown slides of various comparable environments. The rationale and function of the clinic were explained. The users were then able to be very explicit about the desirable character of their experiences: when they needed companionship and warmth, when a sterile atmosphere was most reassuring. They were also able to be explicit and descriptive about particular features and images which conveyed these feelings.

In the design of a mental health center, a short course in the forms of contemporary architecture was developed so that the client could have a vocabulary in terms of forms and design options. Clear criteria of design performance were set, and general design notions evolved in terms of scale and materials. Next, specific design guidelines in terms of scale, qualities of asymmetry, diversity of form and degree of access to the neighborhood were established.

Later phases involved the client in active development and review of alternative schemes, portrayed by a sequence of rough and then detailed models of the buildings. Comments were based on re-view of these models, their function and form. Criteria developed earlier served as a checklist throughout design. These criteria ranged from the general (The buildings should have a "campus" quality.) to the somewhat specific (The roof profile should be irregular.) to the very specific (All major public corridors should have an outside view at the end or at one side.).

Exhibit 11-1 illustrates interdepartmental relationships for a health care facility developed during the programming process.

DATA GATHERING. "Hard data," facts about operations and communications, requirements of materials for low maintenance, etc., are relatively easy to come by. It is somewhat more difficult to gather user need data which clarifies preferences for basic planning alternatives, e.g., the choice of open offices versus enclosed in a commercial building, or mid rise versus high rise in a residential development. It is most difficult to get at the differences that various design "treatments" of similar basic solutions can make. There are several techniques generally thought to be useful in this area.

Structured Interviews and Questionnaires. Formats and standards for questionnaires are well known to specialists available for consultation by architects. All questionnaires should include provision for some open-ended and associational responses. Semantic differential questions can be particularly revealing, although many social scientists feel that they lack reliability.

Nonstructured Interviews. These are vulnerable to a great play of expectations and past experience, but can be more revealing of actual feeling, particularly among less vocal users who tend to be disinterested in questionnaires, remain silent or agree with stronger individuals at group sessions.

Group Sessions. Almost inevitably differences are suppressed and agreement sought. Group sessions must be controlled to avoid domination by a strong leader who is often the most articulate. Unfortunately, the leader may also be anxious to protect power in the status quo. To minimize such problems, it is desirable to organize several groups, some of which represent similar experiences and perceptions and some dissimilar.

Observation/Behavior Mapping. The observation and recording of activity and reaction patterns in various environments can be very valuable in discovering design preferences and influences. Once again, it is useful to have an experienced professional to develop the research protocol. However in this, as in all the foregoing activities, it is vital that the architect be involved, for the data gathered serves little purpose if it cannot be put to use by the professional.

INTERACTION ORGANIZATION AND TECHNIQUES. Contemporary programming inevitably must involve very close client/user/architect collaboration, so much so that the traditional techniques of a series of short presentation-type meetings are generally inadequate. Among the methods which add intensity and interaction to the process are squatting, marathoning and interactive planning.

Squatting. Innovated by Caudill Rowlett Scott, the "squatter" technique is an on-the-spot, intensive work session involving clients, user groups, consultants, other concerned parties and the architectural team. Squatters are used in both the programming and schematic design phases. Concepts concerning spatial affinities and organization are tested, as is the space program against the project budget.

The use of graphic analysis cards and scaled squares for itemized space re-

EXHIBIT 11-1. INTERDEPARTMENTAL RELATIONSHIPS

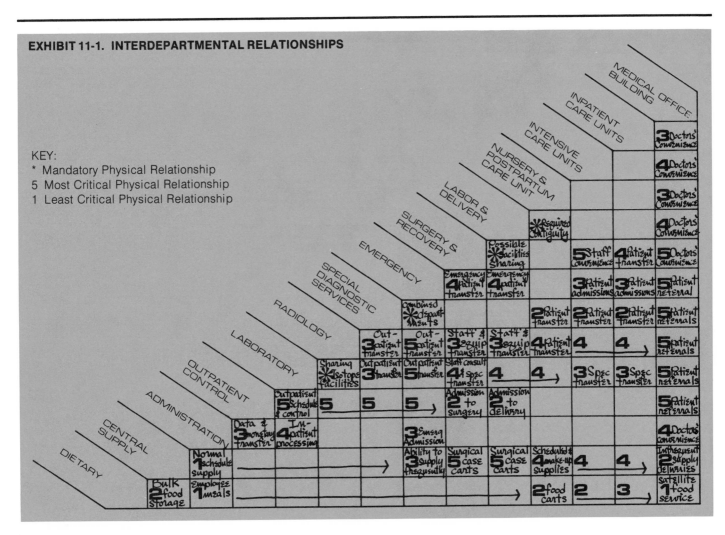

KEY:
* Mandatory Physical Relationship
5 Most Critical Physical Relationship
1 Least Critical Physical Relationship

quirements aids in the understanding of the scope of the project and the organization of groups of spaces.

Some firms in adopting this technique have found a danger in that all concerned can be swept along into a solution. The intensity and short duration of the process can inhibit second thoughts and reexamination. This is particularly true if, as is usually the case, the architect comes prepared wih more extensive knowledge of all aspects of the problem than anyone else, retains that position and overly dominates the process.

Under any circumstances, squatting requires education of all participants before it starts and, ideally, an outside group leader experienced in group psychology without a special interest in the project.

Squatting does dramatize the process. It is also usually structured with continuous open access to the working sessions so that a variety of individuals can participate or feel that they have done so, by "touching" or "looking in" on the process.

Marathoning. The same cautions about guarding against the typical intense

group dynamic reactions of rapidly seeking consensus apply to marathons, in which small groups meet for long and intense sessions—8 to 12 hours or longer, sometimes over a two- or three-day period. Advantages of this technique are that it focuses energies and through exposure (and sometimes fatigue) can break down preconceptions and status protection. This technique can be integrated into the squatting process which usually follows the short-meeting format of information gathering but compresses it into a continuous process.

It is recommended that such meetings occur at intervals with time between for review and reexamination, once a week for instance. Generally, if real innovation is sought, small groups are preferred. Usually, the process is structured so that there is the key decision-making group that meets regularly during the program and design process. Other groups, organized around specialized subissues can also use this technique to examine their particular area but need not meet regularly or for the duration of programming.

Interactive Planning. Representatives of the various users of the facility to be designed are assembled into groups, from the department head through maintenance and supply personnel, to make extensive use of visual communication. Group members are positioned at tables arranged in semicircular fashion facing a bare wall. Each group member is furnished with a stack of blank index cards and a quarter-inch felt marker.

The participant who has an idea felt to be important enough to be entered into group consideration prints out the essence of the idea on a card in letters large enough for all to see when the card is subsequently affixed on the wall. A Polaroid picture of the cards, as they are arranged on the wall, captures the essence of the agreed-upon essentials and serves as a record of the meeting in place of a written report. The technique essentially is a recording and interaction stimulus device in either a large- or small-group situation. It can be applied within the overall organizational concept of marathoning, squatting or more traditional techniques.

This technique is equally successful in using three-dimensional objects on a horizontal surface. Exhibits 11-2 and 11-3 illustrate the use of model blocks for determining and evaluating fundamental relationships in interactive planning sessions between client and architect. Ex-

EXHIBIT 11-2. A STUDY OF FUNDAMENTAL RELATIONSHIPS—LEVEL I

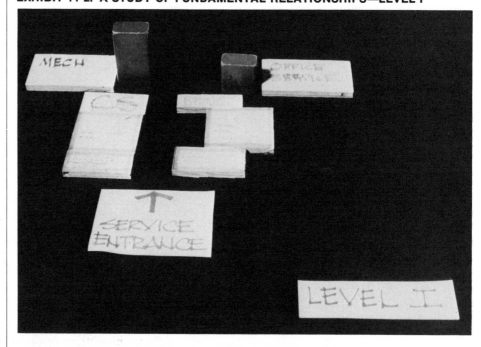

EXHIBIT 11-3. A STUDY OF FUNDAMENTAL RELATIONSHIPS—LEVEL II

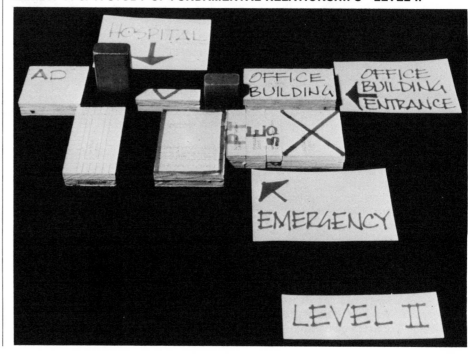

EXHIBIT 11-4. FORM AND FUNCTION EVALUATION

BUFFALO C.M.H.C.		SCHEME 5	
PERFORMANCE MANDATE	FORM EVALUATION	PERFORMANCE MANDATE	FUNCTION EVALUATION
CAMPUS FEEL	Good / Needs more horizontals	ELEVATOR CORES -2-	Yes!
VARIETY OF EXTER. SPACES	Fair / needs more level	COMPACT CIRCULATION	Fair
OPEN TO COMMUNITY	Masses too Large	HIGH % OF EXTERIOR WALLS	Good
IRREGULARITY	Good / add Towers	CLEAR SEPARATION OF CHILDREN'S SERV.	Good
LANDMARK ENTRANCES	Fair / add Towers / clarify pathways	EASE OF PEDESTRIAN CIRCULATION	Fair / add walkways
SKY PROFILE	Good / add Towers	INTER-RELATIONSHIP MATRICES	Excellent!
NON-MONUMENTALITY	Fair / Break masses up	CONSTRUCTION ECONOMY	Good
POTENTIAL VARIETY OF INTERIOR SPACES	Excellent!	EXPANSION	Good
IMPACT OF EXPANSION	Hard to Handle visually		

hibit 11-4 shows the results of an evaluation technique in which proposed forms and functions are compared with performance criteria.

COMPARATIVE RATING SYSTEMS.
This concept allows a planning group to evaluate complex alternatives system-atically. Exhibit 11-5 depicts a matrix for evaluating comparative nursing floor plans during design of a hospital. It allows the planning group to make judgments not only about which plan functions best in a particular area but also permits the group to assign a weighting factor to the importance of that function.

BROADSCALE COMMUNITY INTERACTION. Widespread community interaction is extremely difficult to achieve at any level beyond a simple yes or no on a general scope and organization of a project. The processes by which the community can be educated as to its roles and expectations for a real contribution to the

EXHIBIT 11-5. EVALUATION MATRIX

EXPANSION

TOTAL 21.5   VALUE 5   PERFORMANCE 4.3

		13	65.9

MAJOR ADDITION   PERF V → 37 153 4.1 5 20.5

	R	V	RV
Ability to expand vertical circulation core	5	5	25
Ability to expand by increments	4	5	20
Directions available for new growth	4	5	20
Ability to add various shapes	4	3	12
Accessibility of new space	3	5	15
Clarity of new circulation system	4	4	16
Separation of traffic in new system	5	4	20
Avoidance of demolition	5	2	10
Operational impairment of base block	5	4	20

MINOR ADDITIONS AND INFILLING   PERF V 37 139 3.8 3 11.4

	R	V	RV
Ability to expand vertical circulation core	5	5	25
Ability to expand by increments	3	5	15
Directions available for new growth	3	5	15
Ability to add various shapes	3	4	12
Net to gross area ratio of new space	3	4	12
Accessibility of new space	3	3	9
Clarity of new circulation system	4	4	16
Separation of traffic in new system	5	4	20
Operational impairment of base block	5	3	15

DEMOLITION AND RECONSTRUCTION   PERF V 33 159 4.8 5 24.0

	R	V	RV
Access for demolition and reconstruction	5	3	15
Shape and size of area cleared	5	4	20
Operational impairment during reconstruction	5	4	20
Operational impairment of base block	5	4	20
Accessibility of new space	5	5	25
Clarity of new circulation space	5	5	25
Per cent of floor available for renewal	5	5	25
Accommodation of new shapes aesthetically	3	3	9

FLEXIBILITY

TOTAL 4.8   VALUE 3   PERFORMANCE 1.6

		14	22.6

MAJOR CHANGE IN FUNCTION AND PLAN   PERF V 15 36 2.4 4 9.6

	R	V	RV
Prevalence of "fat" spaces	2	5	10
Flexibility of circulation system	2	4	8
Flexibility of mechanical system	3	3	9
Flexibility of structural system	3	3	9

MAJOR CHANGE WITHIN PORTION OF FLOOR   PERF V 27 48 1.8 5 9.0

	R	V	RV
Independence of areas subject to change	5	4	20
Accessibility of areas from vertical core	3	4	12
"Fatness" of areas subject to change	2	5	10
Breadth of access, or "touch", of each area	-5	4	-20
Flexibility of circulation system	2	4	8
Flexibility of mechanical system	3	3	9
Flexibility of structural system	3	3	9

MINOR CHANGE WITHIN PORTION OF FLOOR   PERF V 19 16 0.8 5 4.0

	R	V	RV
Breadth of access, or "touch"	-5	4	-20
"Fatness" of areas subject to change	2	5	10
Flexibility of circulation within each area	2	4	8
Flexibility of mechanical system	3	3	9
Flexibility of structural system	3	3	9

ORGANIZATION & CIRCULATION CHARACTERISTICS

TOTAL 16.   VALUE 5   PERFORMANCE 3.

		8	2

CLARITY OF SPATIAL ORGANIZATION   PERF V 30 113 3.8 5

	R	V	RV
Comprehensibility of major circulation	4	5	20
Perception of sub-areas from vertical core	3	4	12
Clarity of sub-area circulation systems	3	4	12
General hierarchy of forms and spaces	2	4	8
Landmarks for orientation	5	4	20
Separation of service areas at core	5	5	25
Provision for separate service circulation	4	4	16

SPATIAL CHARACTER   PERF V 26 65 2.5 3

	R	V	RV
Exterior views from public space	4	4	16
Interior views from public spaces	2	4	8
Exterior views from patient beds	3	4	12
Distinctiveness of design	1	4	4
Adequate privacy in staff work areas	4	4	16
Patient awareness of staff activity	2	3	6
Patient and Visitor Recreation and Waiting	1	3	3

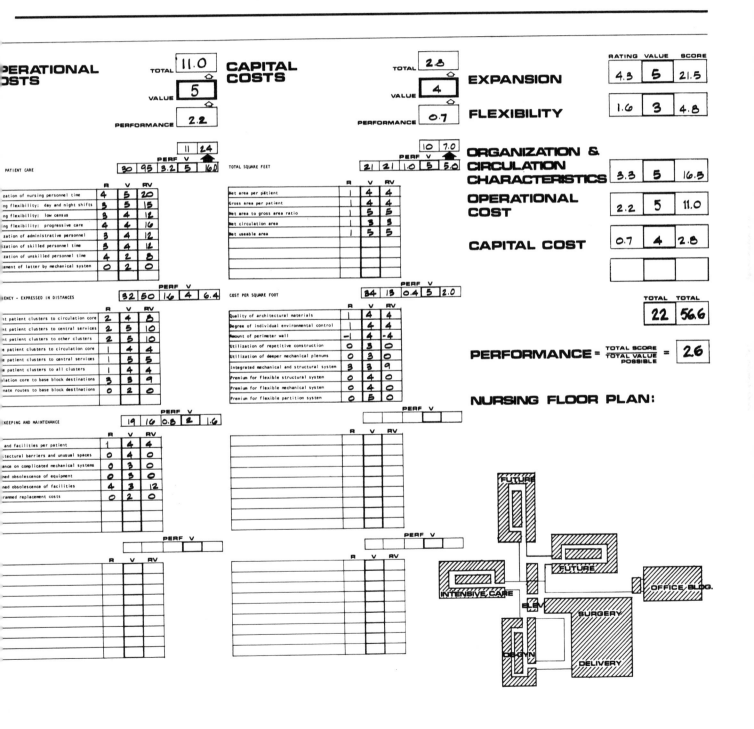

PERATIONAL **OSTS**

TOTAL: 11.0
VALUE: 5
PERFORMANCE: 2.2

CAPITAL COSTS

TOTAL: 2.8
VALUE: 4
PERFORMANCE: 0.7

	RATING	VALUE	SCORE
EXPANSION	4.3	5	21.5
FLEXIBILITY	1.6	3	4.8
ORGANIZATION & CIRCULATION CHARACTERISTICS	3.3	5	16.5
OPERATIONAL COST	2.2	5	11.0
CAPITAL COST	0.7	4	2.8

TOTAL: 22   TOTAL: 56.6

$$\text{PERFORMANCE} = \frac{\text{TOTAL SCORE}}{\text{TOTAL VALUE POSSIBLE}} = 2.6$$

NURSING FLOOR PLAN:

PERF: 11 V: 24

PATIENT CARE — 30 | 95 | 3.2 | 5 | 16.0

	R	V	RV
zation of nursing personnel time	4	5	20
ng flexibility: day and night shifts	3	5	15
ng flexibility: low census	3	4	12
ng flexibility: progressive care	4	4	16
zation of administrative personnel	3	4	12
ization of skilled personnel time	3	4	12
zation of unskilled personnel time	4	2	8
cement of latter by mechanical system	0	2	0

TOTAL SQUARE FEET — PERF: 10 V: 7.0 — 21 | 21 | 1.0 | 5 | 5.0

	R	V	RV
Net area per patient	1	4	4
Gross area per patient	1	4	4
Net area to gross area ratio	1	5	5
Net circulation area		3	3
Net useable area	1	5	5

ENCY - EXPRESSED IN DISTANCES — PERF: 16 V: 4 — 32 | 50 | 1.6 | 4 | 6.4

	R	V	RV
t patient clusters to circulation core	2	4	8
t patient clusters to central services	2	5	10
t patient clusters to other clusters	2	5	10
e patient clusters to circulation core	1	4	4
e patient clusters to central services	1	5	5
e patient clusters to all clusters	1	4	4
lation core to base block destinations	3	3	9
nate routes to base block destinations	0	2	0

COST PER SQUARE FOOT — PERF: V — 34 | 13 | 0.4 | 5 | 2.0

	R	V	RV
Quality of architectural materials	1	4	4
Degree of individual environmental control	1	4	4
Amount of perimeter wall	-1	4	-4
Utilization of repetitive construction	0	3	0
Utilization of deeper mechanical plenums	0	3	0
Integrated mechanical and structural system	3	3	9
Premium for flexible structural system	0	4	0
Premium for flexible mechanical system	0	4	0
Premium for flexible partition system	0	5	0

KEEPING AND MAINTENANCE — PERF: V — 19 | 16 | 0.8 | 2 | 1.6

	R	V	RV
and facilities per patient	1	4	4
tectural barriers and unusual spaces	0	4	0
ance on complicated mechanical systems	0	3	0
ned obsolescence of equipment	0	3	0
ned obsolescence of facilities	4	3	12
rammed replacement costs	0	2	0

EXHIBIT 11-6. DESIGN QUALITY PROFILE

An appraisal of a building or a building design is made possible by a list of performance criteria which can be used as a yardstick for measurement.

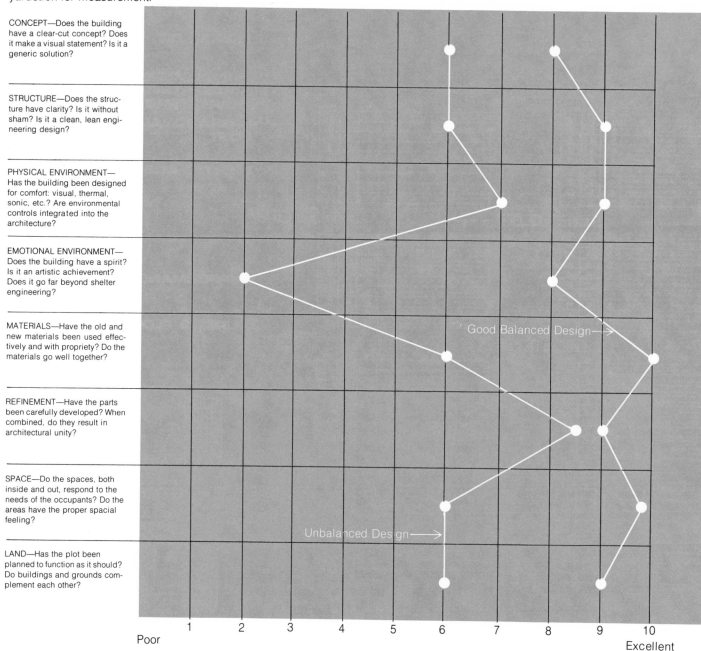

CONCEPT—Does the building have a clear-cut concept? Does it make a visual statement? Is it a generic solution?

STRUCTURE—Does the structure have clarity? Is it without sham? Is it a clean, lean engineering design?

PHYSICAL ENVIRONMENT—Has the building been designed for comfort: visual, thermal, sonic, etc.? Are environmental controls integrated into the architecture?

EMOTIONAL ENVIRONMENT—Does the building have a spirit? Is it an artistic achievement? Does it go far beyond shelter engineering?

MATERIALS—Have the old and new materials been used effectively and with propriety? Do the materials go well together?

REFINEMENT—Have the parts been carefully developed? When combined, do they result in architectural unity?

SPACE—Do the spaces, both inside and out, respond to the needs of the occupants? Do the areas have the proper spacial feeling?

LAND—Has the plot been planned to function as it should? Do buildings and grounds complement each other?

Good Balanced Design→

Unbalanced Design→

1   2   3   4   5   6   7   8   9   10
Poor   Excellent

Source: *Emerging Techniques of Architectural Practice*, AIA, 1966.

finer issues of programming are time consuming, expensive and frequently inconclusive. Input into detailed programming and planning decisions can result more meaningfully perhaps through questionnaires and structured interviews.

It is, of course, good public relations to make the community feel that it has access to the planning process. Citizens may not be able to contribute, but at least they may see interaction taking place rather than being passive recipients of presentations once the work has been done. However, even this access must be controlled if the process being used is particularly intense or dynamic such as marathoning. In this case, continuous broadscale community access can become extremely distracting.

EVALUATION. The profession needs more evaluation of its product, whether it be buildings or the documents and processes which create them. Programs should be evaluated while in process and when completed. The task is simple but only if clear guidelines and performance standards are set at the beginning of the process. A design quality profile as illustrated in Exhibit 11-6 may be used for such an evaluation either during design or after occupancy.

COMPENSATION. Government agencies and private-sector clients with ongoing building programs and construction administration departments are accustomed to paying for programming separately.

Many other clients are reluctant to pay separate compensation for programming, but this is changing with the increased use of cost-based compensation methods and precise definitions of professional services. Payment may also be justified as a part of a master planning study.

Not too long ago, architectural practice centered around styles and preconceptions. Today, the tendency is to seek solutions through an intelligent examination by all concerned, based on the concept of client/user/architect collaboration. Programming, when put to work in this fashion, stimulates the imagination and intuitive capability of the designer and at the same time strengthens the constructive involvement of the client.

BIBLIOGRAPHY

"Activity Data Method." Ministry of Public Building and Works, Great Britain. London: Her Majesty's Stationery Office, 1966.

Describes a method of recording user requirements.

"The Anatomy of Office Space Planning." William Leonard. *The Office,* June 1971.

Guide to the planning of an architectural program for office spaces.

Architect's Handbook of Professional Practice. Washington, D.C.: AIA, parts updated periodically.

Current compendium of practice information; section on programming in chapter on project procedures especially pertinent.

"Architectural Analysis—Prelude to Design." William M. Peña and William W. Caudill. *Architectural Record,* May 1959.

Illustrative 10-point outline of one firm's early approach to the programming process.

Architectural Design and the Social Sciences. Donald Conway, ed. Washington, D.C.: AIA, 1975.

A research report based on a design charette which developed a process model for architect and social scientist collaboration.

Architectural Determinants of Student Satisfaction in College Residence Halls. Mary C. Avery, Gerald Davis and Ronald Roizen. San Diego: University of California, 1971.

Study to determine user satisfaction in relation to environmental characteristics.

"Architectural Programming." William Peña and Leroy V. Good. *Junior College Journal,* October 1967.

Description of a step-by-step outline of an analytical procedure for programming new educational facilities.

"Architectural Programming, Environmental Design and Human Behavior." Raymond G. Studer and David Stea. *Journal of Social Issues,* October 1966.

Discussion of the need for environmental problem formulation in terms of behavioral systems.

"Back to the Office Design Drawing Boards and Work Some Intuition into the Science." Malcolm J. Brookes. *Contract,* March 1974.

Describes how one should resolve design errors through the appropriate use of both science and intuition.

Building Research. Washington, D.C.: Building Research Institute, April 1969.

Portion of magazine devoted to programming.

Comprehensive Architectural Services. William Dudley Hunt Jr., ed. New York: McGraw-Hill, 1965.

Chapters 32, 33 and 34 on various aspects of programming especially pertinent.

Council of Planning Librarians Exchange Bibliography. Mary Vance, ed. Monticello, Ill.: Council of Planning Librarians, issued irregularly.

Includes references to programming and related topics such as behavioral studies; accumulative indexes published sporadically.

Designing for Human Behavior: Architecture and the Behavioral Sciences. Jon Lang, et al., eds. Stroudsburg, Pa.: Dowden, Hutchinson, & Ross, Inc., 1974.

Explores environmental psychology and its place in today's architecture.

Emerging Techniques 2: Architectural Programming. Benjamin H. Evans and

C. Herbert Wheeler Jr. Washington, D.C.: AIA, 1969.

A basic reference on programming.

"Hard Choices in Double Time." *Building Design & Construction,* May 1974.

Description of a method of computer-aided hospital programming.

Hospital Outpatient and Emergency Activities: Functional Programming Guidelines. U.S. Dept. of Health, Education and Welfare. Washington, D.C.: Government Printing Office, DHEW Publication No. (HSM) 73-4002, 1972.

Covers the gamut of programming of health facilities.

Houses Generated by Patterns. Christopher Alexander, et al. Berkeley: Center for Environmental Structure, 1969.

Presentation of designs and principles based on a UN competition for a Peruvian community.

"How to Buy a Better Building: The Value of a Program." Gerald Davis. *Business Horizons,* February 1968.

Description of the role of programming in architecture as well as an illustration of client decision-making capability.

Introduction to Architectural Programming. Edward T. White. Tucson: Architectural Media, 1972.

A basic primer for students, architects and clients.

The Man-Made Object. Gyorgy Kepes, ed. New York: George Braziller, 1966.

Chapter on "From a Set of Forces to a Form" by Christopher Alexander especially pertinent.

Notes on the Synthesis of Form. Christopher Alexander. Cambridge: Harvard University Press, 1964.

Introduction to the thinking which gave rise to the area of design methodology, including a worked example.

"Office Space Programming." Jeffrey E. Clark. *The Office,* June 1971.

Description of the basic process necessary for architectural programming.

"Performance Concept in Buildings," Bruce E. Foster, ed. Washington, D.C.: National Bureau of Standards Special Publication 361, Vol. 1, 1972.

Explanation of the five-step programming process of Caudill Rowlett Scott in a paper titled "Performance Requirements of Buildings and the Whole Program" by William M. Peña and John W. Focke.

"Planning for Hospitals: A Systems Approach Using Computer-Aided Techniques." James J. Souder, Weldon E. Clark, Jerome T. Elking and Madison B. Proun. Chicago: American Hospital Association, 1964.

In-depth coverage of the use of computer-based models.

"Pre-Programming and Programming for the Live Performing Arts." William A. Briggs. *AIA Journal,* December 1964.
Brief look at the civic facility.

Problem Seeking: New Directions in Architectural Programming. William M. Peña and John W. Focke. Houston: Caudill Rowlett Scott, 1969.

Description of the approach to architectural programming employed by CRS.

The "Process" for Creating a Better Building Project. Gerald Davis and Geoff Shuttleworth. Vancouver, British Columbia: The Environmental Analysis Group, 1973.

Presentation of the "process" method of structuring information and ideas in programming.

"The Program's the Thing." Harold Horowitz. *AIA Journal,* May 1967.

Description of an architectural pro-

gram format and a discussion of behavioral science techniques in information collection and organization.

"A Simulation Model for Renewal Programming." Ira M. Robinson, Harry B. Wolfe and Robert L. Barringer. *American Institute of Planners Journal,* May 1965.

Details main elements and operations of the model as used in San Francisco.

"The Theory and Invention of Form." Christopher Alexander. *Architectural Record,* April 1965.

Discussion of the assumption that programmatic clarity is essential to the achievement of proper physical form.

"What Is New About Building Programming?" Gerald Davis. *The Construction Specifier,* October 1969.

Illustration of the systems analysis approach to the programming method.

"When Architects Consult People." C. M. Deasy. *Psychology Today,* March 1970.

Explanation of the need for use of consultation and planning prior to the design of buildings.

"Where Programming Is the Design." Bess Balchen. *AIA Journal,* April 1973.

Case study of how programming and research have become an integral part of the architectural process in the firm of Kaplan/McLaughlin.

Why Programming. Edward T. White and Richard L. Anderson. Tucson: William Wilde and Associates, Inc., 1972.

Description of the programming process used by the Wilde firm.

With Man in Mind: An Interdisciplinary Prospectus for Environmental Design. Constance Perin. Cambridge: MIT Press, 1970.

Outlines a new organizing principle for the conduct of work to be found in this area.

Chapter 12
Construction
Cost Control

JAMES Y. ROBINSON JR., AIA

Construction cost *estimating* requires some technique, some science and, at the right moment, an emotional decision. Construction cost *control* puts more emphasis on technique and science and should require less emotional involvement. Some refer to this as "cost management."

BASIC PROCESS TECHNIQUES

Several techniques for cost estimating and control have evolved. The most important of these are briefly reviewed.

OLD STANDBYS. Numerous techniques have been developed over the years. Most rely on extrapolation of cost from historical data, the basis of almost all systems. The variation is in the degree of refinement. The square foot method of projecting construction cost is perhaps the most widely utilized for early cost estimating and is used by many for final cost estimates. The process is relatively simple. Historical data is developed by dividing bid cost or award cost at the user's discretion by the gross building area to get cost per square foot for historical records. This information is used to estimate cost per square foot for future projects. This estimated cost per square foot times the number of gross square feet in the program yields the project budget.

This simple process is, at best, unreliable and is quite often grossly in error. A number of modifications of the basic technique have been developed which render it more reliable. And these, like the basic system, are in wide use. One of the simpler disciplines applied to the basic technique is to specialize the historical information by building type and apply the historical data base for the appropriate building type when estimating future projects. Breaking the square foot price into percentages for the major trade groupings, such as mechanical, elec-

trical, vertical transportation, equipment and general construction, helps to provide many budgets, each of which can be monitored as the project progresses. This development requires a larger overall data base and some care in accumulation of the data so that cost information is accurately applied to the proper category. In the large trade classifications mentioned above, the information is generally available on request or can be gleaned from the project documentation in the early phases of construction.

A further modification of the basic technique which improves the accuracy of the estimate is to develop historical information by cubic feet rather than square feet. This method has the advantage of accounting for the building's volume, as well as the square feet of planned area. It is most appropriately used for large-volume structures such as theaters, auditoriums, etc. Among the standard techniques for early cost estimating are those built around cost per use unit. Hospitals, for instance, are quite often priced on a per bed basis. Likewise, schools are sometimes priced on a per student basis. This method is extremely quick, but, like the basic square foot technique, is subject to gross error in the results since there is no account taken of building configuration or ancillary facilities which may be out of proportion to the average developed from the historical base.

BUILDING UNIT ESTIMATING. Building units are the pieces and parts which go together to make up a completed building, e.g., floors, walls, roofs, partitions and others. This technique is a cross between quantity surveying and elemental analysis, both of which are described later in this section. To implement this system, the estimator determines the number of building unit types and develops a cost for each building unit type. This cost is developed from either market or historical sources. The

unit cost is multiplied by the quantity for each unit type. After completion of each unit estimate, the respective subtotals are added, and the sum is modified by appropriate adjustment factors for inflation, market conditions, length of expected construction time, building complexity, building site accessibility, and the stage of planned development at the time the estimate is done. This system, though generally reliable, requires a great deal of discipline to develop unit cost, and the takeoff of unit types involves considerable work. The technique does not lend itself to quick estimates.

Unit cost information for the data base can be developed from historical information, from consultation with contractors and sales representatives and from direct solicitation of prices from local suppliers. This information can be collected for individual items and stored in the data base either as unit cost for materials and estimated hours of labor to put in place or it can be lumped as building units in place.

Another building unit estimating technique is the unit of enclosure method. This method and its implementation is detailed in the 1967 AIA book, *Creative Control of Building Costs,* edited by William Dudley Hunt Jr., FAIA, and in an article, "Preliminary Cost Estimating," by William E. Blurock, FAIA, which appeared in the July 1971 *AIA Journal.* The unit of enclosure technique is particularly adaptable for estimating at the late schematic stage and at the design development stage. The historical base for implementation of this system is developed by determining the square foot area of enclosure. Enclosure is defined as the surface of walls, roof, floors and interior partitions (measured one side only). These measurements do not make any allowance for site conditions, building finishes or special features such as elevators, escalators, dust collection systems, etc. This total enclosure area, a measure of complexity, is divided into the contract cost to provide a cost per unit of enclosure. Calculation of the unit of enclosure may be deceptively simple, but selection of the correct single unit rate is agonizingly difficult.

STATISTICAL TECHNIQUES. There are a number of statistical and analytical techniques which hold great promise for use in cost estimating. These include regression and correlation analysis, cost risk estimating, and exponent base technique. These techniques are touched on to indicate their potential use in cost management systems. To be employed efficiently, great quantities of source data will be needed.

Regression and Correlation Analysis. These are tools developed by mathematicians for solving problems involving uncertainty. Cost engineering, as those involved know, is complicated with a high degree of uncertainty.

As a statistical technique, *regression analysis* has been known for many years; however, the rigors of doing the necessary calculations for multidimensional problems made its application unfeasible. The advent of the electronic computer has made this technique a possibility. Most students of algebra have had occasion to apply the basic technique in its simplest form: plotting one variable against another on a graph, developing a curve which fits the generated data, and applying a formula so that new points on the curve can be predicted.

This system has been used extensively in the costs-in-use technique developed by the Department of the Environment, Property Services Agency, of Great Britain and is illustrated in Exhibit 12-1. Records of annual maintenance costs for 75 primary schools were analyzed to determine if there was any relationship of age to maintenance cost. The plots show a definite correlation. The resulting straight-line "curve" of the averages indicates a trend which may be used for projections for

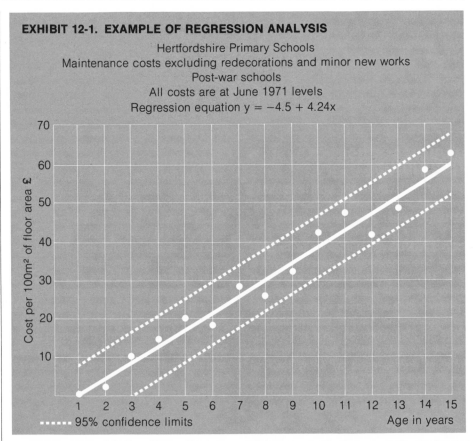

EXHIBIT 12-1. EXAMPLE OF REGRESSION ANALYSIS

Hertfordshire Primary Schools
Maintenance costs excluding redecorations and minor new works
Post-war schools
All costs are at June 1971 levels
Regression equation $y = -4.5 + 4.24x$

Cost per 100m² of floor area £

Age in years

- - - - - 95% confidence limits

Source: *Costs in Use: A Guide to Data and Techniques*, U.K. Department of the Environment, Property Services Agency. Crown copyright 1972. Reproduced with the permission of the Controller of Her Brittanic Majesty's Stationery Office.

similar buildings within the same time frame. This same technique can be used for forecasting costs for various building types and for extrapolating costs for building systems.

Application of the system requires a considerable quantity of cost and data performance which tends to limit the usefulness of this technique. However, firms wishing to use this procedure can develop it for special projects where the building type recurs within the practice or for particular systems within the building such as roof or wall systems, structural systems or other elements of the total package which repeat on a regular basis.

The exponent base technique discussed later is an illustration of the refinement of the regression analysis process.

Correlation analysis is a mathematical technique which tests the relationship between dependent and independent variables for particular situations. The figure 1.0 indicates a positive association; 0.0, on the other hand, signifies no association. For information, the square of the correlation coefficient is called the coefficient of determination and represents a portion of the dependent variable which is explained by the independent variable. The unexplained part of the dependent variable is determined by some other variable or by chance. Use of this technique allows the projection of the percent change of the range of true cost and enables the prediction of an estimated cost within a range. This is often described as a degree of confidence or range of confidence and is illustrated by the dotted lines in Exhibit 12-1, which designate a 95 percent confidence range.

Cost Risk Estimating. This technique is based on a business tool developed by Standard Oil of Indiana and adapted to construction of its buildings. The program has been applied by design professionals to other structures. It uses the cost estimator's full range of experience, plus computers to produce a simulation of the distribution curve for cost and quantity for each item in the building. The Monte Carlo Gaming technique used in this statistical routine is a tool for developing the limits for probability and is arrived at by computer experiments applied to construction costs. Costs for each building system and for the total building can be projected for a range with a low expected cost, a high expected cost and then a most likely expected cost. Cost risk estimating is based on a quantity survey type of estimate and lends itself readily to final project estimates. It has the advantage that it replaces the old-style single figure estimate with a high percentage probability cost range. This reasserts the fact that the estimate is simply an estimate and is only as good as the historical data being used and the judgment of those applying modifying factors to that data.

Exponent Base Technique. Simple and fast, this method can be reliable for making preliminary evaluations or for filling in missing data. To use this technique, modifying factors must be developed from historical sources, noting the difference in cost as a result of changes in size. The factor or factors can then be applied to known costs for equipment and materials in a known size and quantity and adjusted upward or downward to fit the specific conditions of the problem being estimated. The method is more reliable for some parts of the building than others. For instance, mechanical equipment lends itself well to this type of estimating. Preliminary costs for equipment to be installed can be determined with relative accuracy by multiplying the figure resulting from dividing the size of the first unit by the size of the second unit, times the cost of the first. Base cost can be developed from information which is immediately available. This method is particularly useful for developing partial estimates of building components. It could be generated for a total building system, but the developmental cost would be extremely large, and maintenance costs would likewise be burdensome.

QUANTITY SURVEY. Among the oldest cost estimating systems is the quantity survey, the name given to the technique of determining the quantity of materials and the hours of labor required for construction. In this technique, organization of the building materials and labor cost into building units is not necessary. Cost information can be obtained from suppliers, from consultation with contractors, and by direct solicitation of quotations on various bills of quantities, as well as from historical sources. This technique has proven itself over the years as a reliable system for final cost estimating; however, quantity surveying can be done at design development and even at schematic stages of design if enough information is known. Application at these early phases requires that decisions or simulations often be made concerning building components whose need has not yet been established. At the early stages, significant cost elements may be overlooked.

The technique at any stage of application is time consuming. A number of automated systems have been developed for processing this type of estimate. Computerization speeds the processing of the cost information and minimizes possible areas for human error. Nevertheless, the process of taking off the quantities of materials and determining the amount of labor to install each building component is still a time-consuming job.

The results, like other estimating techniques, are no better than the historical cost information on which the estimates are based and the care which is taken in the processing of the information.

Quantity surveying has been developed to the fullest extent in the United Kingdom and is part of the construction process in that country. There, cost responsibility is placed in the hands of a quantity surveyor, who prepares the bills of materials prior to bidding and monitors building work for quantity and cost during the construction period. With this wealth of cost information available, the British quantity surveyor should be well equipped to estimate building costs.

In the traditional linear method of project delivery in the United States, the cost control function in the design stages falls to the architect. The development of the bill of materials and the cost for that bill, as well as the labor required to install the items in the bill, is traditionally the responsibility of the contractor, construction manager or cost consultant. This dichotomy of the responsibility precludes the full development of the quantity surveying system in this country without major changes in the role of both the contractor and the architect. However, the nontraditional methods of project delivery discussed in Chapter 3 point out emerging changes in these roles.

ELEMENTAL ANALYSIS. This method of cost control seems the most responsive to architectural needs, particularly for early cost estimating. Cost control is one of the construction industry's most troublesome problems. Each new system may seem to be the panacea which will render all other systems obsolete, and yet, none of the systems can utilize fully the information generated within the industry because it is not generally available. For this reason, there is no really unlimited, substantial, comprehensive and dependable data base behind the systems for cost estimating in the conceptual stages of design. Some existing available systems and services are very good, but they must all suffer from the lack of a data base of sufficient scope, breadth and depth to make them truly responsive to architects' needs during this crucial period of decision making.

Consequently, in 1972, the AIA began work on a cost forecasting and cost control system that has come to be called "Mastercost." In the first phase, say its designers, Mastercost will be a "national building cost data file, for large-scale pooling and sharing of critical cost information." In an effort to provide budgetary road mapping early in the design process, Mastercost will "collect critical cost data continuously from a large variety of building projects around the country, convert the data into forms most useful at the concept state," and then distribute the data to subscribers.

Contractors' schedules of values, as required by AIA contract forms and normal industry practice, constitute the most widely available and most accurate source of cost data. Therefore, Mastercost would begin with these schedules and, in effect, translate them from the language of construction into the language of conceptual design.

Key to this translation, and to the potential usefulness of Mastercost, is a framework for organizing cost data into major building elements—essential functional parts, or chunks, of buildings (Exhibit 12-2). This is intended to more closely match the way in which an architect approaches a project in the early de-

EXHIBIT 12-2. MASTERCOST CONSTRUCTION ELEMENTS CATEGORIES

Group element (Level 2)	Element (Level 3)
01 Foundations	011 Standard foundation 012 Special foundations
02 Substructure	021 Slab on grade 022 Basement excavation 023 Basement walls
03 Superstructure	031 Floor construction 032 Roof construction 033 Stair construction
04 Exterior closure	041 Exterior walls 042 Fenestration
05 Roofing	
06 Interior construction	061 Partitions 062 Interior finishes 063 Specialties
07 Conveying systems	
08 Mechanical	081 Plumbing 082 HVAC 083 Fire protection 084 Special mechanical systems
09 Electrical	091 Service & distribution 092 Lighting & power 093 Special electrical systems
10 General conditions & profit	
11 Equipment	111 Fixed equipment 112 Furnishings 113 Special construction
12 Site work	121 Site preparation 122 Site utilities 123 Site improvements 124 Off-site work

Source: *AIA Journal*, November 1974.

sign stages. Level 1 categories, not shown, include construction, furniture and equipment supplied by owner, design and management, site acquisition, leasing/occupancy, financing and contingencies. The Level 1 category of " construction" is broken down into the Level 2 group element categories shown in Exhibit 12-2 and further broken down into Level 3 elements.

Unlike the specifier, the designer begins the work of putting together the jig-

saw puzzle of a building project by first thinking of the big pieces of the puzzle. As the designer does not conceptualize in terms of specific materials or assemblies, traditional craft and materials breakdowns are of little use at this point.

Essentially, Mastercost would take such breakdowns as found in the schedules of values and, through a system of cross referencing on the schedules, reorganize the data according to the list of building elements.

With the organization of cost data according to building elements, Mastercost would allow the architect to make early estimates independent of specific materials choice and reflect in conceptual estimates from the earliest stages the effects of height, site condition, building configurations, interior functional uses and other factors. It would permit the architect to set percentages of the budget for allocation to each building element.

The list of elements for Mastercost is not an arbitrary or whimsical arrangement of building components. It is the product of a great deal of cooperative effort, in which the AIA and its consultants have worked with a number of other groups, including nationally known construction cost consultants and the General Services Administration (GSA), the country's largest building client/owner.

As a system, Mastercost would be designed to assist the architect in several ways. By providing information by building type and size on an area and volume basis, it would simplify budget checking. Too many projects are well underway before a determination is made that the budget may be insufficient. As a result, designs may have to be substantially altered at an awkward time or contractors are required to bid on an unacceptable number of alternates.

Provided that the budget is adequate, the designer ideally should be able to allocate it for the best possible solution. Few architects enjoy the luxury of a client with unlimited resources, so the designer must balance budget requirements by allocation of the budget to wall, floors, roofs and other elements required by the architectural solution. There must be available sufficient information to intelligently alter plan configurations, details or specifications to meet budget requirements. This process starts before materials and methods of construction have been established.

Continued experience with many similar projects forms the backbone of most architect's cost estimating, and lessons are learned from a series of successes and failures to bring the building in within the budget. But even with a great deal of experience, results can be unreliable as the data changes over time. Mastercost, with its sizable and well-organized data base, would provide a sort of "instant" or "ready-made" experience for the subscribers, yielding current and dependable data.

Mastercost, however, is not intended to relieve the architect of the need for exercising judgment or fulfilling contractual responsibilities. It cannot be a cure-all for all cost problems. It is planned as a tool to allow the architect to make better judgments and better estimates, based on an increasing flow of accurate and useful information.

As the system develops, it could be well suited to computer use, with access to Mastercost files through computer terminals a possibility. But computer equipment can be costly if underutilized, and it is by no means universally used. The system as envisioned will not depend on automated data handling on the part of the subscriber. Access to the data could be in many modes depending on the needs of subscribers, from the smallest to the largest firms.

During the period of several years needed to bring the Mastercost system to the point of availability, architects can benefit from the preparatory work by using the basic formats for their own projects. Thus they can begin to build their own cost data base with the use of a standardized vocabulary. Then, when it comes time to share information with colleagues through the Mastercost system, all will be speaking the same language.

How Mastercost could work is suggested by the sample input forms shown here: the schedule of values (Exhibit 12-3) backed up by the building description form (Exhibit 12-4) for a specific project.

As the basic form of input, the schedule of values is designed to translate cost data from the language of construction to the language of conceptual design. Standardized for use by all participants for the sake of comparability, it is cross-referenced between the Uniform Construction Index categories on the left and the Mastercost construction element categories on the right. Both the list of elements and the specification section headings on the sample schedule are designed to be as comprehensive as possible and to be supplemented, augmented and changed as experience dictates. Headings are developed to reflect subcontract work or major parts of subcontracts. Some items are subdivided into pieces which can be made responsive to the list of elements, e.g., concrete, which may appear on the exteriors, in walls, roof or floor, etc.

The second essential mode of input, the building description form provides the context for the cost data. It identifies the building by type, size and location and synopsizes the materials and systems used in its construction. Planned to be as simple and concise as possible, the form has been completed in less than 20 minutes by those familiar with the project working from the contract documents.

One possible way that Mastercost output data may be organized and reported as derived from the schedule of values and building description forms for subscribers is illustrated in Exhibit 12-5. (This is an early design for the project sheet, and the categories vary slightly from those shown previously.) It represents a storehouse of cost information that does not now exist—and a uniquely valuable tool for a profession acutely, if not painfully, conscious of the need to know where each project dollar is going.

AVAILABLE SYSTEMS. Numerous commercial sources of building cost information are available. Most of the data is

EXHIBIT 12-3. MASTERCOST SCHEDULE OF VALUES

Project: Owner:			Architect: Contractor:		Project No. Date:	

Item description		Item amount	Item description		Item amount
1. GENERAL REQUIREMENTS			4. MASONRY		
a. Mobilization & initial expenses	(10)		a. Masonry foundations	(011)	
b. Site overhead & fee	(10)		b. Masonry basement walls	(023)	
			c. Masonry exterior walls	(041)	
2. SITE WORK			d. Masonry interior partitions	(061)	
a. Clearing & demolition	(121)		e. Interior paving & finish	(062)	
b. Grading & earthwork (site)	(121)		f. Exterior paving & masonry (site work)	(123)	
c. Excavation & backfill (foundations)	(011)				
d. Excavation & backfill (basement)	(022)		5. METALS		
e. Fill below grade slab	(021)		a. Structural steel in foundations	(012)	
f. Rock excavation	(012)		b. Structural steel framing	(03)	
g. Pile foundations & caissons	(012)		c. Metal joists & decking	(03)	
h. Shoring	(022)		d. Metal stairs	(03)	
i. Underpinning	(012)		e. Misc. & ornamental metal (building)	(063)	
j. Site drainage & utilities	(122)		f. Misc. & ornamental metal (site work)	(123)	
k. Foundation & underslab drainage	(021)				
l. Dewatering	(012)		6. WOOD & PLASTICS		
m. Paving, landscaping & site improvements	(123)		a. Rough carpentry (framing & decking)	(03)	
n. Off-site work	(124)		b. Rough carpentry (exterior wall)	(041)	
o. Railroad, marine work & tunnels	(124)		c. Rough carpentry (partitions)	(061)	
			d. Rough carpentry (roof, other than framing & decking)	(05)	
3. CONCRETE			e. Heavy timber & prefab. structural wood	(03)	
a. Conc., forms & reinf. (foundations)	(011)		f. Exterior wood siding & trim	(041)	
b. Conc., forms & reinf. (slab on grade)	(021)		g. Fin. carpentry, millwork & cabinet work	(063)	
c. Conc., forms & reinf. (basement walls)	(023)		h. Wood paneling	(062)	
d. Conc., forms & reinf. (superstructure)	(03)		i. Wood stairs	(03)	
e. Conc., forms & reinf. (exterior walls)	(041)		j. Plastic fabrications	(063)	
f. Conc., forms & reinf. (site work)	(123)				
g. Concrete finishes (exterior walls)	(041)				
h. Concrete finishes (interiors)	(062)				
i. Concrete finishes (site work)	(123)				
j. Precast concrete (exterior wall panels)	(041)				
k. Precast concrete (structural components)	(03)		7. THERMAL & MOISTURE PROTECTION		
l. Precast concrete (site work components)	(123)		a. Water & dampproofing (slab on grade)	(021)	
m. Cementitious decks	(03)		b. Water & dampproofing (basement walls)	(023)	
			c. Water & dampproofing (exterior walls)	(041)	

published in hard copy and can be put into five categories.

Unit Price Books. Estimated unit prices for various materials and operations are contained in these publications. Prices are fairly detailed, and the books are often marketed to contracting and subcontracting firms as well as to the design professions.

Among the best known of at least a dozen of these books produced annually is *Building Construction Cost Data,* pub-

lished by Robert Snow Means Company, Inc., of Duxbury, Mass. Another is the *Dodge Manual for Building Construction Pricing and Scheduling,* a publication of McGraw-Hill Information Systems Company of New York City, which is produced in cooperation with Wood & Tower Incorporated. A third is the *Building Cost File,* issued by Construction Publishing Company Inc. of New York City from data supplied by McKee-Berger-Mansueto Inc., with four regional editions being offered.

Such volumes provide a useful source of detailed construction cost information and can be helpful in preparing estimates once design documentation is developed to the point that an accurate quantity survey can be made.

Valuation/Appraisal Manuals. These are mainly published for the appraisal profession to assist in the preparation of replacement cost estimates for existing structures. They also achieve a steady sale within the construction industry as

EXHIBIT 12-3. MASTERCOST SCHEDULE OF VALUES (CONTINUED)

d. Thermal insulation (foundation & slab)	(021)		11. EQUIPMENT (specify:)	(111)	
e. Thermal insulation (exterior walls)	(041)				
f. Thermal insulation (roof)	(05)				
g. Roofing shingles & tiles	(05)				
h. Shingles on exterior walls	(041)		12. FURNISHINGS (specify:)	(112)	
i. Preformed siding & panels	(041)				
j. Preformed roofing	(05)				
k. Membrane roofing, traffic topping	(05)				
l. Sheet metal & roof accessories	(05)		13. SPECIAL CONSTRUCTION (specify:)	(113)	
m. Sealants & calking	(041)				
8. DOORS & WINDOWS					
a. Exterior doors & frames	(042)				
b. Exterior windows & curtain walls	(042)		14. CONVEYING SYSTEMS		
c. Interior doors & frames	(061)		a. Elevators, dumbwaiters & lifts	(07)	
d. Exterior glass & glazing	(042)		b. Moving stairs & walks	(07)	
e. Interior glass & glazing	(061)		c. Conveyors, hoists, etc.	(07)	
f. Hardware & specialties (exterior)	(042)		d. Pneumatic tube systems	(07)	
g. Hardware & specialties (interior)	(061)				
9. FINISHES			15. MECHANICAL		
a. Lath & plaster (exterior)	(041)		a. Exterior mechanical (to 5 ft. of bldg.)	(122)	
b. Lath & plaster (interior)	(062)		b. Water supply & treatment	(081)	
c. Gypsum wallboard	(062)		c. Waste water disposal & treatment	(081)	
d. Tile & terrazzo	(062)		d. Plumbing fixtures	(081)	
e. Acoustical ceilings & treatment	(062)		e. Fire protection systems & equipment	(083)	
f. Wood flooring	(062)		f. Heat generation equipment	(082)	
g. Resilient flooring	(062)		g. Refrigeration	(082)	
h. Carpeting	(062)		h. HVAC piping, ductwork & terminal units	(082)	
i. Exterior coatings	(041)		i. Controls & instrumentation	(082)	
j. Interior special flooring & coatings	(062)		j. Insulation (plumbing)	(081)	
k. Interior painting & wall covering	(062)		k. Insulation (HVAC)	(082)	
			l. Special mechanical systems	(084)	
10. SPECIALTIES			16. ELECTRICAL		
a. Chalkboards & tackboards	(063)		a. Utilities & serv. ent. to 5 ft. of bldg.	(122)	
b. Compartments & cubicles	(061)		b. Substations & transformers	(091)	
c. Signs & supergraphics	(063)		c. Distribution & panel boards	(091)	
d. Partitions	(061)		d. Lighting fixtures	(092)	
e. Lockers	(112)		e. Branch wiring & devices	(092)	
f. Toilet, bath, wardrobe accessories	(063)		f. Special electrical systems	(093)	
g. Sun control devices	(041)		g. Communications	(093)	
h. Access flooring	(063)		h. Electric heating	(093)	
i. Miscellaneous specialties	(063)				
j. Flagpoles	(123)		TOTAL		$

Source: *AIA Journal*, November 1974.

they offer possibilities for producing preliminary cost estimates from minimum details. All of them supply regional cost modifiers to adapt base costs to a specific locality, and some issue special residential building valuation manuals.

One of a number in common circulation is the *Marshall Valuation Service*, published by Marshall and Swift Publication Company of Los Angeles. Released in three volumes, *Boeckh Building Valuation Manual* is the work of the American Appraisal Company of Milwaukee, with a bi-monthly Building Cost Modifier available. McGraw-Hill also publishes a manual called *Dodge Building Cost Calculator & Valuation Guide*, with quarterly supplements.

Building Project Cost Manuals. The only extensive feedback of actual building costs marketed in the United States results from McGraw-Hill's Dodge Building Cost Services, as part of the Dodge construction contract reporting operation. As soon as a contract award becomes known, a questionnaire is mailed to the project architect in an attempt to collect basic data on the building as far as award cost, floor area, outline specifications and some other details are concerned. This approach produces information on a considerable number of buildings for which a rudimentary form of cost analysis can be prepared and is published in a manual called the *Dodge Digest of Building Costs and Specifications*, with semi-annual supplements. No evaluation of the data is made, but it provides a useful

EXHIBIT 12-4. MASTERCOST BUILDING DESCRIPTION FORM
(First page of a three-page input form)

(757)

① Building type: *ART CENTER (UNIVERSITY)* ⑥ Bid date: *OCT 71*
② Location: *COOK COUNTY, IL.* ⑦ Est. construction period: *24 MTHS*
③ Client: *PRIVATE INSTITUTION* ⑧ Market conditions: *COMPETITIVE*
④ Architect: *(e.)* ⑨ Number of bids: *11* (invited)
⑤ Type of contract: *STIPULATED SUM*

⑩ Brief description of building: *TWO STORY FACILITY SEPARATED IN TWO BLOCKS : ART GALLERY 126' x 134'; OFFICES + CLASSROOMS 60' x 134' WITH SCULPTURE COURTYARD IN BETWEEN . ART GALLERY COMPRISES EXHIBIT + SUPPORT AREAS WITH SOME OFFICES. OTHER BLOCK CONTAINS 4 CLASSROOMS AND STAFF OFFICES .*

⑪ Occupancy group: *F.2.* ⑫ Construction type: *II*

⑬ Number of stories - below grade: *1* - above grade: *2*

Level	Gross floor area		
⑭ Basements	*13,300* sf	㉔ Basement volume:	*142,750* cf
⑮ Ground floor	*24,010* sf	㉕ Vol. balance bldg.	*635,950* cf
⑯ Upper floors	*10,670* sf	㉖ Building volume	*778,700* cf
⑰ Penthouses etc.	*—* sf	㉗ Roof area:	*28,170* sf
⑱ Gross floor area:	*47,980* sf	㉘ Footprint area at grade:	*24,010* sf
⑲ Net floor area-assignable/~~rentable~~	*40,290* sf	㉙ Basement wall area:	*6,060* sf
		㉚ Exterior wall area:	*31,640* sf
㉑ Net finished area:	*34,680* sf	㉛ Fenestration area:	*4,130* sf
㉒ Plan type: *SIMPLE RECTANGULAR*		㉜ Exterior closure area:	*35,770* sf
		㉝ Partition length:	*2,593* lf
㉓ Use units: *N.A.*		㉞ Partition area:	*33,850* sf

㉟ CONSTRUCTION DESCRIPTORS:

Foundations (01)

011 Standard foundations : Reinf.conc. [✔] Masonry [ ] Other ....

Soil cond. ...*POOR - WET & SANDY*... Bearing cap. *1,500*lbs/SF

Slope of site : flat [✔] sloping [ ] ...... % slope av.

012 Special foundations : Unusual subsurf. cond. *DEWATERING NECESSARY*

Piling - Concrete [ ] Steel [ ] Wood [ ]

Shoring - Steel [✔] Wood [ ] Caissons [ ]

Substruct. (02)

021 Slab on grade : Structural [ ] Non-structural [✔]

022 Basement excavation : Water problems [✔] yes [ ] no

023 Basement walls : Reinf. conc. [✔] Masonry [ ] Other ....

Waterproofing [✔] Dampproofing [ ]

Source: *AIA Journal*, November 1974.

---

function as a rough check of early "square footage" estimates.

As an important part of Dodge Building Cost Services, McGraw-Hill, in conjunction with Wood & Tower, initiated publication in 1975 of an annual building cost and assembly manual which offers composite unit rates, suitable for use in preliminary estimating stages. Called *Dodge Construction Systems Costs,* it is based on an elemental method which varies somewhat from the Mastercost categories shown in Exhibit 12-2.

A manual similar in nature to the above is the *Design Cost File* issued by Construction Publishing Company, in association with McKee-Berger-Mansueto.

Miscellaneous Publications. There are a few sources of intermittent building cost information, including a series initiated by *Progressive Architecture* in 1973 under the heading "P/A Building Cost File."

Engineering News-Record for many years has published a parameter cost series giving trade cost analyses of several projects in its quarterly cost issue.

On the West Coast, the monthly *Architectural Design Cost & Data* produces anywhere from three to six building cost analyses on a trade basis, together with a building description, articles and advertisements. Some of the case studies are incorporated in the *Preliminary Cost Guide* published by Architectural Data Corporation of Pasadena, Calif.

Computerized Estimating Systems. Several firms of cost consultants offer computerized estimating systems, some of which are specifically designed to assist architects and owners with early cost estimates. They usually contain extensive cost data bases, but such information is infrequently marketed separately from the cost estimating services provided by cost consultants. One of the oldest is a system for estimating costs by building parameters (essentially the same as the building elements listed in the Mastercost elemental breakdown), and a considerable amount of development continues to be done in this area. All cost estimating must rely on historical data in one form or another, the maintenance of which is a costly but essential process.

ADMINISTRATIVE TECHNIQUES

To this point, techniques for estimating construction costs have been the primary consideration; indeed, many construction cost estimating services often are sold as cost control systems. While the architect's responsibility is to determine the fair market cost of the design, it is not the only one. To effectively control costs, the architect must be able to influence that cost effectively. Certainly, the ability to substitute materials and specifications is one of the key tools at hand. The elemental analysis system provides such a tool at the early stages.

It is the architect's goal to make sure that the client receives the best possible price for constructing the project, the final price of which is determined by the contractor's estimate of construction cost. But this estimate has several factors hidden within it which account for the differences between the contractors' bids on bid opening day. A number of these hidden factors result from unknowns within the contract documents such as prices for items which cannot be obtained prior to bid time. Costs assignable to restricted site conditions during the course of the project and escalation of material and labor costs are among the unknowns, and factors must be included for each of these. Alternates and addenda also introduce opportunities for errors, and many contractors include hidden factors for these potential errors. Unknown items must be covered in the contractor's estimate.

EXHIBIT 12-5. MASTERCOST CASE STUDY (PART 1)

Building type: ART CENTER

Location: Cook County, IL.   **Client:** Private institution

Bid date: Oct. 1971   **Market conditions:** Competitive

Est. const. period: 24 months   **Type of contract:** Stipulated sum

Building description: Two story facility in two blocks, art gallery 126' x 134', offices and classrooms 60' x 134' with sculpture courtyard in between. Art gallery comprises exhibit and support areas with some offices. Other block contains four classrooms and staff offices.

Statistics:

Gross floor area:	47,980 sf
Net floor area:	40,290 sf
Volume:	778,700 cf
Use units:	n.a.
No. of stories above grade:	2
No. of basement levels:	1

Ratios:

Net to gross floor area (GFA)	0.60	: 1
Volume to GFA	16.23	: 1
Ext. closure area to GFA	0.87	: 1
Roof area to GFA	0.59	: 1
GFA per	n.a.	sf
Complexity factor	3.164	EU : 1

OUTLINE SPECIFICATION:

011 Flat site, conc. fdns., wet and sandy soil. 150lb/sf bearing capacity.
012 Dewatering & steel shoring
021 Non-structural slab on grade
023 Reinf. conc. walls, waterproofed
03 50% reinf. conc. 50% steel. 100#/sf floor load, 30#/sf roof. Bay sizes: 20' x 25', 56' to gallery.
041 Stone finish; o.13 U factor
042 Alum. double glazed windows. 13% of ext. closure.
05 2" rigid insulation, built-up roofing, o.15 U factor.
061 Masonry 60%, stud 30%, demount. 10%, wood drs. 80%, glass 20%, metal frames. 0.054 lf per sf of GFA.
062 Floors: concrete 85%, resilient 13%, tile 2%. Ceilings: suspended 85%, applied 15%; plaster 42%, drywall 50%, acoustic rated 8%. Walls: paint 47%, plaster 30%, drywall 20%, tile 3%.

063 Washroom accessories, darkroom cabs.
07 Dumbwaiter
081 Copper piping. 1 fixt. per 1,499 sf.
082 100% air cond., double duct system: 240 sf per ton; 65 Btu/hr per sf; 1.02 cfm per sf. Remote heating source.
083 Standpipe
091 106.6 sf per kva, 120/208v primary and secondary distribution.
092 100 ft. candle lighting intensity
093 Fire alarm, clock, PA, telephone
10 50% performance bond, fire insurance by owner.
111 Nil
112 Kitchenette and chalkboard
113 Nil
121 Sculpture court
122 Water and sewer connections, steam line, exterior lighting
123 Nil

Cost Summary: Cost per sf: $40.08 **Cost per cf:** $2.47 **Cost per.......** $

Source: *AIA Journal*, November 1974.

EXHIBIT 12-5. MASTERCOST CASE STUDY (PART 2)

Elemental Category	Element cost		Element amount ($)		Cost per SF		%
	Quantity	Unit Rate	Sub	Group	Sub	Group	
01 FOUNDATIONS	24,010 sf	3.12		74,799		1.56	3.6
011 Standard foundations	24,010 sf	2.54	60,999		1.27		
012 Special foundations	–	–	13,800		0.29		
02 SUBSTRUCTURE	142,750 cf	1.07		152,300		3.17	7.4
021 Slab on grade	24,010 sf	1.68	40,390		0.84		
022 Basement excavation	142,750 cf	0.18	25,000		0.52		
023 Basement walls	6,060 sf	14.34	86,910		1.81		
03 SUPERSTRUCTURE	52,140 sf	5.21		271,794		5.66	13.3
04 EXTERIOR CLOSURE	35,770 sf	6.19		221,580		4.62	10.8
041 Exterior walls	31,640 sf	5.56	175,940		3.67		
042 Fenestration	4,130 sf	11.29	45,640		0.95		
05 ROOFING	28,170 sf	2.17		61,129		1.28	3.0
06 INTERIOR CONSTRUCTION	151,830 sf	1.91		289,264		6.03	14.0
061 Partitions	33,850 sf	2.42	82,018		1.71		
062 Interior finishes	34,680 sf	5.41	187,472		3.91		
063 Specialties	47,980 sf	0.41	19,774		0.41		
07 CONVEYING SYSTEMS	– No.	–		2,400		0.05	–
08 MECHANICAL	778,700 cf	0.54		421,688		8.79	20.6
081 Plumbing	32 No.	1,816	58,117		1.21		
082 HVAC	5,519 MBH	64.73	357,271		7.45		
083 Fire protection	47,980 sf	0.13	6,300		0.13		
084 Special mech. systems	–	–	–		–		
09 ELECTRICAL	450 kva	397		178,700		3.72	8.7
091 Distribution	450 kva	236	106,025		2.20		
092 Lighting and power	47,980 sf	1.18	56,525		1.18		
093 Special elec. systems	47,980 sf	0.34	16,150		0.34		
10 GEN. CONDITIONS & PROFIT				247,394		5.16	12.0
NET BUILDING COST:			$	1,921,048	$	40.04	93.4
11 EQUIPMENT	47,980 sf	0.04		1,892		0.04	0
111 Furnishings	– sf	–	–		–		
112 Fixed equipment	47,980 sf	0.04	1,892		0.04		
113 Special construction	– sf	–	–		–		
GROSS BUILDING COST:			$	1,922,940	$	40.08	93.4
12 SITEWORK (excl. 123)	49,120 sf	2.78		136,728		2.85	6.6
121 General sitework	49,120 sf	0.93	45,748		0.95		
122 Site utilities	49,120 sf	1.85	90,980		1.95		
123 Off-site work	–	–	–	–	–	–	–
CONSTRUCTION COST: (excluding 123)			$	2,059,668	$	42.93	100.0
NET STANDARD BUILDING COST: (net building cost less 012, 084, 093)			$	1,891,098	$	39.41	

Source: *AIA Journal*, November 1974.

In preparation for the bidding period, every effort should be made to improve the competitive climate by increasing the contractors' general awareness of the project and an understanding of its specific conditions. Just how these objectives to control costs will be accomplished varies from office to office. Exhibit 12-6 is a checklist of administrative cost control procedures which have the broadest base of application. Developed by the author, the checklist is an aid to any practitioner to ensure a cooperative yet competitive climate for projects, and items can be added to meet the needs of a particular architectural firm.

ANCILLARY TECHNIQUES

Associated with cost control are concerns which deal with construction cost and the evaluation of design decisions related to cost.

LIFE CYCLE COST ANALYSIS. One of the fastest developing adjuncts to construction cost control is life cycle cost analysis. A number of governmental agencies and private corporations are considering life cycle costs in evaluating projects. The requirements vary, but most deal with energy utilization, the other facets of the total cost being incorporated as the methodology and needs dictate. A total life cycle cost analysis system will require perhaps a dozen areas of analysis. As of this date, such a system is in the development stages, including these nine categories:
—Capital investment costs: first costs of construction
—Financing costs: costs of equity, short-term and long-term credit related to capital investment
—Use costs: costs of people and supplies to perform the program function
—Operations costs: costs of heating, cooling and utility services (people and supplies)

—Maintenance costs: costs of upkeep (people and supplies)
—Alteration and improvement costs: costs of changes to meet user needs which are not anticipated at the time of initial planning
—Repair and replacement costs: costs of restoration (people and supplies)
—Lost revenue: costs of not building
—Denial of use costs: costs of delays from establishment of need to occupancy of facilities

Projection of first costs is the estimate of capital costs. Capital cost estimating can be done by the elemental analysis or the quantity survey methods.

Financing costs, or the cost of money during construction, as well as tax information, are available from the client for inclusion in life cycle cost analysis.

The Building Research Division of the National Bureau of Standards found that for government office buildings over a 40-year period, the life cycle costs of the system are approximately 92 percent for people to process information (salaries); 6 percent for maintenance and operation of the facilities; and only 2 percent for capital costs of the building. A private study for a university complex showed considerably different percentages, indicating that different users produce widely varying results. Obviously, the life cycle time period selected will also produce wide variations. It becomes immediately apparent that an important consideration in life cycle cost analysis is the cost of personnel to use the facilities, a situation typical of most buildings. Life cycle cost control therefore must be very much a part of creative solutions of the building program requirements.

Operations cost analysis has become highly developed. With growing concern for energy conservation, this technique is being increasingly required in one form or another by various users. For years, design professionals have had the capability to do energy efficiency studies to

determine heating and cooling costs and to evaluate the economies of alternative systems for particular buildings. Several computer programs are available to relieve the tedium of calculation involved. Most programs require estimates of utility rates, which in recent periods of rapid change make accurate total cost forecasting difficult.

Maintenance cost information has been a subject of development by various manufacturers and suppliers over the years. Many of these studies have been self-serving. With only a few exceptions, there exists little maintenance cost data which can be accessed for use within the client's own organization, and generally this information is not available for public consumption. Unfortunately, most of the obtainable data cannot be related back to capital planning decisions.

In reference to alteration and improvement costs, phasing of construction incorporated in the initial planning process should be evaluated as capital costs, in adjusted dollars, in consideration of life cycle costs. However, many users consider that certain typical changes are inevitable and should be considered in determining total life costs. Changes of this type should be subject to specific life cycle cost analysis at the time the change is considered.

Repair and replacement costs are determined from obsolescence information provided from manufacturers, industry associations and occasionally from user experience. These costs may be regarded by some as maintenance costs but are definitely part of a total system. Costs include capital investment costs of restoring building components whose life cycle is shorter than the life cycle established for the particular analysis.

Since lost revenue is the comparative cost of management's decision not to build, this information must come from the user or the user's economic advisers. In terms of the life cycle cost, it is an included cost only if the other analytical areas are not relevant or are too costly.

Related to lost revenue but part of the building-related costs are the costs incurred due to denial of use. This denial can result from any delays which occur between the time the need for new facilities exists and the time the facilities are ready for use. These costs affect capital costs, financing costs and the costs for interim provisions for the user or lost efficiency due to functioning in inadequate facilities. Where the need is established at the time of analysis and an expected occupancy date can be established, then the impact of these costs can be determined from information available from the user. Where delays occur or are contemplated in the planning process, their impact on the analysis should be evaluated.

For an analysis of costs which relate to the components of a building, the 12 elements of the design which comprise a building (Exhibit 12-2) provide a useful reference and organizational tool for evaluating total life cycle costs.

The life expectancy is generally user-determined and is a judgmental decision, or one related to management parameters considered relevant by the building owner. Obviously, the length of the cycle greatly affects total costs and the relative value placed on capital costs and financing costs as opposed to operating, maintenance, repair and replacement, and other recurring costs.

In determining life cycle costs, the architect is responsible for some information and its accuracy; other pieces of data must evolve from those involved with the building over the life cycle period. Not all areas of life cycle cost will be required for every life cycle evaluation.

VALUE ANALYSIS. This process identifies the functional requirements of a building or facility, and evaluates design alternatives to satisfy those requirements

EXHIBIT 12-6. CHECKLIST OF ADMINISTRATIVE COST CONTROL TECHNIQUES

PRELIMINARY DESIGN PHASE

1. Have any contractors who showed any interest in the planning stage been asked to make comments? _____

CONSTRUCTION DOCUMENT PHASE

2. Have notices to bidders been placed in newspapers and trade magazines ahead of the release of bidding documents? _____

3. Have money-saving suggestions and comments from interested contractors been incorporated into the documents? _____

4. Has a value analysis review been made? _____

CONTRACT BIDDING PHASE

5. Have sets of the bidding documents been sent to local plan rooms? _____

6. Are documents available for inspection at the office of the designers and the owner, and is this information available to the contractor? _____

7. Has a date been established for the architect's project representative to visit the site during the bidding period to answer questions and provide information? _____

8. Will the bids be opened during the latter part of the week? (Thursdays are preferable and Fridays should be avoided.) _____

9. Has the bid opening date been checked so that it does not conflict with bid openings or contractors' conventions and vacations? _____

10. Are there any holidays during the week of the bid opening or the week following bid opening? (Holiday weeks should be avoided.) _____

11. Are there serious labor negotiations pending? (If so, the bid opening should be delayed.) _____

12. Have the contractors bidding the project been advised that the design engineers are available to answer bidders' questions? _____

13. Have addenda been issued to clarify the answers to all questions of all bidders? (No addenda should be issued less than a week prior to the opening. If the need for an addendum develops during the last week, then it should be sent out with a postponement of the bidding date.) _____

14. Does the bid proposal form have a place for bidders to acknowledge addenda? _____

BID OPENING

15. Prior to opening the bids, have the addenda been restated and has opportunity been given for bidders to correct discrepancies? _____

16. Have sufficient bidders been contacted to ensure a minimum of three and preferably five bids for each prime contract? _____

OTHER FACTORS

17. On large multimillion-dollar projects and on those of a unique nature, has the possibility of small packages rather than one large package been considered? (These packages might be site work, foundations, structural framing, mechanical, electrical and equipment.) _____

18. If the project is a collection of smaller separate projects, or as in the illustration above, has the possibility of optional individual or combination bids been considered? _____

on the basis of the initial construction cost of the structure and its anticipated maintenance and operational expense over its projected life span. By value analysis, savings in capital costs and various other life cycle costs can be determined. It deals with specific functional requirements of a building or facility and can be applied at almost any stage of the building process. The AIA has gone on record recommending application of value analysis, in the early stages of design and throughout the design process. The Corps of Engineers and GSA have developed techniques for value analysis after the construction contract has been awarded; therefore, value analysis can be applied at any step during the construction process.

The potential for greatest savings resulting from value analysis exists in the early phases of the planning process. At that time, the potential for savings is as great as 100 percent, decreasing quickly as the program is established and the design implemented. By the time documents are ready for bidding, the typical project savings are in the range of 10 percent and continue to decrease as construction proceeds.

Value analysis is in essence a second look at design decisions made by qualified personnel, requiring a combination of specific expertise with a general overview. Many times the most economical solution for one portion of the building or one system of the building will result in added cost to other parts of the building or other systems within the building. Since these added costs to other systems may result in an overall increase in the total project cost, it is necessary to keep a total picture of the project in mind as specific recommendations for cost savings are evaluated.

It is important that the value analysis responsibility be assigned to the highest level of management possible. Persons charged with the responsibility should meet these criteria: they should be able to move freely within the organization and should not be hampered by departmental lines; they should be able to get required guidance and administrative assistance from any and all consultants hired by the firm and by all personnel of the firm; they should have freedom of operation and be able to question items of administration as well as design. Value analysis from time to time requires expenditure of money for studies and tests, and this money should be available for utilization by the individual. The value analyst should be in a position to identify sources of new material and techniques of construction and should be able to make this information available to others within the organization.

The process of value analysis has several steps. First, it is important to get all the facts and determine the cost of proposals as they exist at the time process is begun. If possible, the functions should be defined, dollars placed on the specifications and requirements of the system, and the work of the system determined.

The second step is to creatively and innovatively evaluate alternatives to answer clearly the question: What else will perform the function?

Third, the basic function should be evaluated to see if there are other ways by which it can be accomplished. As ideas are developed, they should be priced. Refinement of an idea should not be delayed. Extensive investigation is quite often required. Consultants from suppliers and companies, as well as professional consultants, must be contacted and questioned. Many times, these individuals will have suggestions for other materials and methods which may do the job equally well. Contractors should be considered in this process as they often have a view of problems which may be overlooked by other members of the construction team.

Investigation should include analysis of standards. Quite often, the job is being done more effectively than is necessary. By the same token, some proposals might be rejected because, although they meet rules of thumb and accepted standards, the latter are not adequate. Costs reflect not only the cost for those functions which are changed, but should be inclusive to determine the effect on other functional units.

Finally, recommendations should be made, backed up and supported by exact data. The recommendations should be summarized and put into action, and those responsible should be motivated to take positive steps to ensure that beneficial changes result.

TAX CONSIDERATIONS. In the September 1973 *AIA Journal*, Kris R. Nielsen, who is a cost consultant, an engineer, an attorney and an officer in the firm of McKee-Berger-Mansueto, wrote an extended article on the effects of tax laws on cost and design decisions. Tax laws covering new physical facilities outline two basic depreciable property types.

The first basic property type is that which is eligible for short-term or rapid depreciation, and is known as "38/1245 property": Internal Revenue Code of 1954, Sections 38 and 1245 (a) (3). Such 38/1245 property must be depreciable and amortizable with a useful life of at least three years and includes tangible personal property such as production machinery, printing presses, transportation and office equipment, refrigerators, grocery counters, testing equipment, display racks and shelves, neon and other signs and most fixed and movable equipment which is attached to or contained in a building.

Other tangible property is also included but only if such other property is used as an integral part of manufacturing, production or extraction, or of furnishing transportation, communications, electrical energy, gas, water or sewage disposal services and does not include a building and its structural components. Such property would include machine foundations, environmental control systems, shipping and receiving docks, crane superstructure and foundations, and special industrial process cooling systems and piping. Also included are research facilities or storage facilities, provided that such facilities are integrally used with a manufacturing, production or extraction process. Finally, elevators and escalators installed after June 30, 1963, are included.

The second basic property type, which is eligible for long-term depreciation, is known as "1250 property": Internal Revenue Code of 1954, Section 1250 (c). Such 1250 property is that which is depreciated or amortizable and which is not 38/1245 property: the structure, permanent walls and partitions of a building.

The differences between these two types of property are important in light of recent Congressional action changing the Internal Revenue Code and in view of future action anticipated to curb inflation. Job development credit, commonly called investment tax credit, is available for certain types of property under specific circumstances. Current tax laws and rulings should be carefully checked to determine eligibility. The Internal Revenue Service publishes useful life depreciation guidelines for various types of property. Under the "asset depreciation range system," the taxpayer may adjust the useful life guidelines to reflect the impact of technological improvement, automation, foreign competition and other things on the useful life of equipment.

The cash flow due to tax credit is greater from 38/1245 property than from 1250 property. Therefore, the more of a new facility classified as 38/1245, the greater the return to the owner. Several judicial cases have established that components of real property may be designated as 38/1245 property. Through the component depreciation technique, a building is broken down into various substantive parts, a useful life and value are assigned to each part, and each part is depreciated separately.

In order to maximize tax advantages, the areas of the building which may be applicable to classification as 38/1245 property must be identified and useful lives assigned to these portions. The proper allocation of all direct and indirect construction costs are then assigned to those parts. This requires a team effort of the client, the client's legal and accounting counsel, and the architect and engineers. Accounting and tax personnel or consultants can establish property accounts for complete construction cost property allocation. The limits and extent of the accounts can then be included in the drawings and specifications, and the contractor can provide a schedule of values for each of these accounts. The assistance of the architect in setting up in the construction documents the limits and extents of various accounts for component depreciation purposes can be invaluable to the owner.

Architects and engineers are called on continuously to offer greater cost control services and information, and the degree of liability assumed in so doing cannot be underestimated. The use of elemental estimating techniques can expand the capabilities to deal with problems in this area and provide information for earlier decision making. The availability of a broad data base and improved cost control procedures for capital costs and other life cycle costs will have tremendous impact in the coming years.

BIBLIOGRAPHY

"Building Systems Unit Costs Guide to Estimator in Controlling Costs." *Engineering News-Record*, September 20, 1973.

Good background material on elemental or "systems" analysis.

Computer Applications in Architecture and Engineering. G. Neil Harper, ed. New York: McGraw-Hill, 1968.

Computerized detailed cost estimating covered in Chapter 5.

"Computerized Cost Estimating Is Ready Now—Almost." Bradford Perkins. *Architectural Record*, February 1970.

Possibilities and problems as seen through 1969.

"Cost Estimating, Tubular Design Refined in Standard Oil Building." *Building Design & Construction,* November 1971.

Cost control on technology working hand in hand with additional information on cost risk estimating.

"Cost Estimating by Use of Six-Tenths Factor." John D. Constance. *Consulting Engineer,* September 1973.

Information on the development of factors for estimating and exponent-base estimating.

"Cost Knowledge: Tool for Budget, Program and Design." Bradford Perkins. *Architectural Record,* June 1970.

Discussion of the familiar pitfall of early budget troubles discovered too late.

Creative Control of Building Costs. William Dudley Hunt Jr., ed. New York: McGraw-Hill, 1967.

Interesting thoughts on a wide range of cost-related concerns; Chapter 6 on enclosure method especially pertinent.

"Estimating with Recycled Cost Data." Brian Bowen. *Progressive Architecture,* October 1973.

Includes development of building classification code.

"Federal Agencies Shift to Value Engineering." Milton F. Lunch. *Professional Engineer,* May 1973.

Discussion of government requirements for value engineering; includes PBS guidelines for selecting an item for value engineering study.

"Getting the Lowest Bids . . . After Design Is Done." Thomas Lindtvit. *Consulting*

Engineer, February 1969.

How to make the most of the period between completion of design and opening of bids.

"Here You Have It: Life-Cycle Costing." Robert Ramsey and Robert Guthrie. *AIA Journal*, July 1973.

Discussion of the technique as tied to award of a government contract.

"Ingredients for Accurate Cost Estimating." Gerald M. Hollander. *Actual Specifying Engineer*, June 26, 1974.

Helpful review of cost estimating techniques and analysis of use at various stages of projects.

"It's a Wide Open Field: Construction Management." Philip J. Meathe. *AIA Journal*, March 1973.

Interesting sidelight on the potential possible with good cost estimating techniques and useful data.

"Management Firms: New Watchdog of Construction Costs." *Building Design & Construction*, July 1971.

Deals with money management before and during construction.

"New Data for Cost Estimating at the Conceptual Stage." James Y. Robinson Jr. *AIA Journal*, November 1974.

Commentary on the proposed AIA

Mastercost construction cost control system for budgeting and preliminary cost estimating.

"An Overview of Cost Management." Charles B. Thomsen. *Architectural Record*, September 1973.

Recap of what cost control encompasses on page 69.

"Planning of Capital Investments: Architectural Primer." Paul B. Farrell Jr. *AIA Journal*, April 1969.

Basic information on capital management; interesting reading list.

"Preliminary Cost Estimating." William E. Blurock. *AIA Journal*, July 1971.

Explanation of units of enclosure as an estimating technique; early elemental analysis development.

"The Price of the Schoolhouse." Earl R. Flansburgh. *Progressive Architecture*, February 1972.

Early work toward elemental analysis relating material selection and other design decisions to cost.

"A Scotsman Surveys Our Cost Control." Brian Drake. *AIA Journal*, December 1972.

Possible relevance of the quantity survey system in the U.S.

"Some Common Errors in Cost Control

Programs." Bradford Perkins. *Architectural Record*, January 1970.

Guidelines on where one can go astray told in three case studies.

"Tax Considerations in Building Design." Kris R. Nielsen. *AIA Journal*, September 1973.

Outstanding explanation of tax considerations related to building design and costing techniques.

"Using Functional Building Systems Costs for Preliminary Estimates and Cost Control." Howard W. Shaw. *Consulting Engineer*, April 1972.

Review of cost systems engineers efforts as of 1972; much good thought on system development.

"Value Analysis." Harold J. Rosen. *Progressive Architecture*, December 1971.

Cost control from the view of specifications.

Value Engineering in the Construction Industry, Alphonse J. Dell'Isola. New York: Construction Publishing Company Inc., 2nd ed., 1974.

Good guide for anyone interested in value analysis and its implementation; many pictures and charts which express clearly the process and why it is worth money to the client.

Chapter 13
Regulations Control

PEYTON E. KIRVEN, AIA

In today's complex age of technology, society in general and the design professions in particular must comply with an ever-increasing number of regulations, imposed by all levels of government. To properly fulfill responsibilities in this area, the architect must understand the regulatory process and its vehicles, along with means of compliance. Furthermore, the practitioner must participate in the process to effectuate its improvement.

REGULATIONS: THEIR EVOLUTION

By whom, when and why was building first regulated? How have building regulations evolved into such complicated constraints? Why are regulations so numerous?

HISTORICAL BACKGROUND. For centuries, governments have exercised the right to regulate how buildings are built—for the public's protection. In 1750 B.C., Babylonian King Hammurabi's Code prescribed, "In the case of collapse of a defective building, the architect is to be put to death if the owner is killed by the accident, and the architect's son if the son of the owner loses his life." In Julius Caesar's time, Roman laws regulated the height of buildings and the distances between them. During Queen Anne's reign, the English found it necessary to require noncombustible roofs. By the time of America's settlement, the legal concept of building codes was well established. In 1796, for example, the city of New Orleans, then a Spanish province, passed an ordinance prohibiting the use of wood roofs.

TODAY'S REGULATIONS. Though the historical background and public concern for building safety date back hundreds of years, the accelerated growth of the nation's cities and their problems after the turn of the 20th century have

prompted more universal development of building controls. Presently, more than 14,000 jurisdictions have such regulations, many differing in content and application.

Initially, fire-oriented building codes, generated by insurance interests, were widely utilized. However, since the late twenties, most local and state jurisdictions have adopted or based their regulations on one or another of several "model" codes that address the full range of safety and health concerns of modern building methods. The model codes are developed and maintained under the aegis of organizations of building code administrators with construction industry assistance.

The basic authority for building regulation resides with the states as a police power reserved to them under the 10th Amendment to the Constitution. Judicial interpretation has made such authority operative for municipalities as well but only as agents of a state. Exhibit 13-1 provides a listing of regulations typically determining building construction in a community.

REGULATORY VEHICLES

What are the vehicles of present-day building regulations? How, when and by whom are they developed and maintained? What are the involvements of the design professions, special interests and the federal government? How are building standards utilized in building codes? Why are the statutory building laws usually disadvantageous?

CATEGORIES. Today's building regulations and codes are promulgated in five major categories, as represented in Exhibit 13-2.

MODEL CODES. Much of the nation's code system—that of approximately two-thirds of the municipalities as well as

many states that regulate construction—is based on one or another of three model codes: the Basic Building Code (BBC), the Uniform Building Code (UBC) and the Standard Building Code (SBC). They are promulgated by general interest membership organizations controlled by building code administrators of local and state governments. These groups are the Building Officials & Code Administrators International (BOCA), the International Conference of Building Officials (ICBO) and the Southern Building Code Congress (SBCC), formed in 1915, 1922 and 1945, respectively.

Though independent in structure, these organizations seek unanimity in building code matters by their tripartite participation in the Model Codes Standardization Council (MCSC), the Council of American Building Officials (CABO) and the National Academy of Code Administration (NACA).

The model code organizations also provide building product evaluation and other special services for their membership. In addition to building codes, they promulgate supplementary specialty ones, including plumbing, mechanical and fire prevention codes.

The model codes are revised on an annual basis and published on a three- or four-year cycle with annual cumulative supplements. Revisions may be submitted by anyone, and participation at all stages of the process is afforded to all interested parties. Voting rights, however, are limited to building code administrators.

NATIONAL ASSOCIATION CODES. Besides the model codes produced by the organizations of building code administrators, two others are widely used nationally and are thus considered model codes, though produced by associations having focused or limited interests. These are the National Building Code (NBC) published by the American Insurance As-

EXHIBIT 13-1. LISTING OF REGULATIONS TYPICALLY DETERMINING BUILDING CONSTRUCTION IN A COMMUNITY

TYPICAL BUILDING TYPES	P.L. 90-480 as Amended; Federal Property Regulations	Federal GSA Construction Standards	Locally applicable building code**	Zoning ordinance	Health Code (State & Local)	Housing Code (1–2 family dwellings)	Housing Code (Multiple dwellings)	Fire Safety Code	Plumbing Code	Electrical Code	State Housing Construction Corp.	State Educational Construction Authority	Regional Hospital Planning Council	FEPM (HEW) Construction regulations	Veterans Administration Construction Standards	Subdivision regulations	FHA Property Standards	OSHA regulations	Regulations of private food, service, hotel, retail, theater, service station chains	Insurance companies
Federal Buildings	X	X		X														X		
Other Public Buildings	X		X	X	X			X	X	X								X		
Hospitals	X		X	X	X		X	X	X	X			X		X	X		X		X
Schools	X		X	X	X			X	X	X		X						X		
Colleges	X		X	X	X			X	X	X		X						X		
Churches			X	X	X			X	X	X								X		
Housing	X		X	X	X	X	X	X	X	X	X					X	X	X		
Theaters	X		X	X	X			X	X	X								X	X	
Industrial Plants			X	X	X			X	X	X								X		
Shopping Centers and Other Commercial Buildings			X	X	X			X	X	X								X	X	X

* Where Federally financed
** May incorporate State architectural barrier legislation

Source: *Into the Mainstream: A Syllabus for a Barrier-Free Environment*, AIA, 1975.

sociation (AInsurA—formerly the National Board of Fire Underwriters) and the Life Safety Code (NFPA 101) issued by the National Fire Protection Association (NFPA).

The AInsurA's voting membership is limited to insurance industry representatives, and its code is promulgated by the association without formal participation by the design professions or the construction industry. The NBC is revised and published on the basis of administrative convenience.

The NFPA has two kinds of members: organizational, such as trade associations and insurance rating bureaus, with voting privileges; and associate, including representatives of the design professions and the construction industry. The NFPA also produces the National Electrical Code (NEC) and the National Fire Codes which, as specialty codes, have been widely adopted nationally. NFPA documents are issued annually.

Other specialty or technical codes are produced by various national associations such as the American Society of Mechanical Engineers (ASME), the American Society of Heating, Refrigeration and Air Conditioning Engineers (ASHRAE),

EXHIBIT 13-2. CATEGORIES
OF BUILDING REGULATIONS[1]

MODEL CODES
Basic Building Code (BBC)—BOCA[2]
Uniform Building Code (UBC)—ICBO
Standard Building Code (SBC)—SBCC

NATIONAL ASSOCIATION CODES
National Building Code[3] and
Fire Prevention Code—AInsurA
Life Safety Code,
National Electrical Code and
National Fire Codes—NFPA
Housing Code—APHA
National Plumbing Code—PHCC
Boiler and Unfired Pressure
    Vessel Code—ASME
Mechanical Refrigeration Safety Code—
    ASHRAE

MUNICIPAL, STATE AND FEDERAL
    REGULATIONS

BUILDING STANDARDS[4]
Agency Standards (Engineering practice
    standards, materials standards, test
    standards)
    ASTM
    ANSI
    NFPA
Federal Standards
    Standards—NBS
    Minimum Property Standards—HUD
    Minimum Standards—HEW
    Product Standards—USDC
    Occupational Safety and Health Stan-
        dards—DOL
    Consumer Product Safety Standards—
        CPSC

STATUTORY BUILDING LAWS

1. Regulations listed are representative, not all inclusive.
2. Promulgating agency. For abbreviation identifica-
tions, refer to chapter text.
3. The National Building Code, promulgated by the
American Insurance Association (formerly NBFU), is
sometimes considered a "model" code.
4. Only those standards referenced in legal vehicles have the force of law.

the American Public Health Association
(APHA), and the National Association of
Plumbing, Heating & Cooling Contractors
(PHCC).

**MUNICIPAL, STATE AND FEDERAL
REGULATIONS.** Building regulations
have traditionally been a function of local
government, although instances do occur
of statewide regulation. A good many
municipalities have adopted a model
code, availing themselves of the technological updating and services provided
by the sponsor organization. Others, particularly the larger cities, maintain their
own codes as more responsive to their
own urban requirements—usually with the
penalty of some nonuniformity and conflict with the state and/or federal regulations. Most cities also regulate zoning
and property subdivision, noise insulation, noise abatement and building security by appropriate local ordinances.

In recent years, an increasing number
of states have chosen to exercise their
rights to adopt preemptive statewide
codes, frequently based on one of the
model codes. The National Conference of
States on Building Codes and Standards
(NCSBCS), an organization constituted of
appointees of the governors, is instru-
mental in this, in the interests of governmental efficiency, reciprocity, uniformity,
etc.

Numerous federal agencies such as the
Department of Housing and Urban Development (HUD), the Department of
Labor (DOL), and the General Services
Administration (GSA) also have promulgated regulations that address specific
aspects of building design and construction when federal funds or guarantees involve either the construction or the occupancy of the building. These regulations
are maintained by federal employees,
and little or no opportunity for formal participation is afforded the design professions or the construction industry. The
regulations are not updated on any spe-

cific schedule but primarily at administrative convenience.

The federal government, as well as
many of the states, is also imposing on the
construction industry a variety of building-
related regulations reflecting current concerns for environmental protection and
for problems relating to materials, energy,
and price and wage controls.

BUILDING STANDARDS. A vital component of the building regulatory system,
building standards generally specify the
performance that an engineering practice or material must meet under certain
test conditions, often achieving operative
legal status as referenced material in the
particular building code adopted by a
political jurisdiction.

Most nationally recognized standards
are prepared by trade, engineering and
professional organizations authoritative in
their particular field. The bulk of the standards widely used nationally are produced by the American Society for Testing and Materials (ASTM), the American
National Standards Institute (ANSI) and
the NFPA.

In addition to private agency standards,
an increasing flow of federal standards
is exerting significant influence on the
construction industry today. These include the Minimum Property Standards
(MPS) of HUD; the Minimum Standards
(for grant programs and social security
assistance) of the Department of Health,
Education and Welfare (HEW); the employee safety standards of the Occupational Safety and Health Administration
(OSHA) of the DOL; and the safety standards of the Consumer Product Safety
Commission (CPSC). Various standards
are issued by the National Bureau of
Standards (NBS), and product standards
are produced by the U.S. Department of
Commerce (USDC).

STATUTORY BUILDING LAWS. Another
regulatory vehicle is the statutory building

law, which is initiated and enacted by a political jurisdiction, usually in reaction to an alleged hazard of political concern. These laws, unlike codes and standards adopted after formalized development that includes a consensus of all interested or affected parties and possessing updating mechanisms, are frequently developed on a "crash" basis without benefit of comprehensive research or professional and industry input to insure utilization within a rational and orderly framework of existing regulations. Furthermore, being statutory, and therefore requiring legislative action for revision, such laws usually suffer rapid obsolescence and effectuate a difficult appellate process.

NONREGULATORY INFLUENCES ON THE DESIGN PROFESSIONS. Insurance, financing and public agency influences on the design process, though nonregulatory, have also evolved into major concerns for the design professions. Requirements of this sort are generally enforced by means of financial controls.

REGULATORY COMPLIANCE

How are applicable codes, standards and regulations affecting a project identified, obtained and maintained? How are they best used to insure compliance, and who should be responsible? Why and when should the jurisdiction's building official be involved? When and how are appeals best made?

IDENTIFYING AND OBTAINING CODES/STANDARDS/REGULATIONS. At the inception of a project, the architect must identify the legal, regulatory constraints of the jurisdictions involved and obtain up-to-date copies of the effective editions of all applicable codes, standards and regulations. Verification of the regulatory process, as well as the estab-

EXHIBIT 13-3. MAJOR MODEL BUILDING CODES AND STANDARDS

Category	Title	Source*
Building Codes	Basic Building Code	BOCA
	National Building Code	AInsurA
	Standard Building Code	SBCC
	Uniform Building Code	ICBO
	One- and Two-Family Dwelling Code	MCSC
	Life Safety Code	NFPA
Mechanical Codes	Basic Mechanical Code	BOCA
	Standard Mechanical Code	SBCC
	Uniform Mechanical Code	ICBO
Plumbing Codes	Basic Plumbing Code	BOCA
	Standard Plumbing Code	SBCC
	National Standard Plumbing Code	PHCC
	Uniform Plumbing Code	ICBO
Gas Codes	Standard Gas Code	SBCC
	National Fuel Gas Code	NFPA
Electrical Codes	National Electrical Code	NFPA
	National Electrical Code for One- and Two-Family Dwellings	NFPA
	Lightning Protection Code	NFPA
	Handbook of the National Electrical Code	NFPA
Housing Codes	Basic Industrialized Dwelling Code	BOCA
	Basic Housing-Property Maintenance Code	BOCA
	Standard Housing Code	SBCC
	Uniform Housing Code	ICBO
	Standard for Mobile Homes	NFPA
Sign Codes	Uniform Sign Code	ICBO
	Model Sign Control Ordinance	AIA
Fire Codes	Basic Fire Prevention Code	BOCA
	Uniform Fire Code	ICBO
	Standard Fire Prevention Code	SBCC
	Fire Prevention Code	AInsurA
	National Fire Prevention Code	NFPA
	National Fire Codes	NFPA
Standards	Uniform Building Code Standards	ICBO
	ASTM Standards in Building Codes	ASTM
	NBS Index of U.S. Voluntary Engineering Standards	NBS
	ANSI Standards Catalog	ANSI
	ASTM Standards Catalog	ASTM
	NFPA Standards Catalog	NFPA

EXHIBIT 13-3. MAJOR MODEL BUILDING CODES AND STANDARDS (CONT'D)

	Standard of the Design and Installation of the Fire Suppression System for Life Safety	BOCA
	Standard for the Installation of Sprinkler Systems	NFPA
	Standard for the Installation of Sprinkler Systems for One- and Two-Family Dwellings	NFPA
Miscellaneous	Minimum Property Standards	HUD
	MPS One- and Two-Family Dwellings	
	MPS for Multifamily Housing	
	MPS for Care-Type Housing	
	Manual of Acceptable Practices	
	Dwelling Construction Under the Uniform Building Code	ICBO
	Uniform Code for the Abatement of Dangerous Buildings	ICBO
	Plan Review Manual	ICBO
	ICBO Research Recommendations	ICBO
	Southern Standard Swimming Pool Code	SBCC
	BOCA Official Code Interpretations	BOCA
	SBCC Compliance Approval Reports	SBCC
	Fire Protection Handbook	NFPA
	Standard Types of Building Construction	NFPA

NOTE: Contact sources for latest edition of listings and for publications lists.

SOURCES OF BUILDING CODES AND STANDARDS LISTED

AIA
American Institute of Architects
1735 New York Ave. N.W.
Washington, DC 20006
202-785-7300

AInsurA
American Insurance Association
85 John St., New York, NY 10038
212-433-4400

ANSI
American National Standards Institute
1430 Broadway, New York, NY 10018
212-868-1220

ASTM
American Society for Testing and Materials
1916 Race St., Philadelphia, PA 19013
215-569-4200

BOCA
Building Officials & Code Administrators, International
1313 E. 60th St., Chicago, IL 60637
312-324-3400

HUD
Order standards from Superintendent of Documents, U.S. Government Printing Office
Washington, DC 20402

ICBO
International Conference of Building Officials
5360 S. Workman Mill Road
Whittier, CA 90601
213-699-0541

MCSC
Model Codes Standardization Council
Order documents from AInsurA, BOCA, ICBO or SBCC

NFPA
National Fire Protection Association
470 Atlantic Ave., Boston, MA 02210
617-482-8755

NBS
Order index from Superintendent of Documents
U.S. Government Printing Office
Washington, DC 20402

PHCC
National Association of Plumbing, Heating & Cooling Contractors
1016 20th St. N.W.
Washington, DC 20036
202-331-1675

SBCC
Southern Building Code Congress, International
3617 Eighth Ave. S.
Birmingham, AL 35222
205-252-8930

lishment of good working relations, is usually best accomplished by contacting the agencies empowered to issue a project's construction permit. Source availability of the model codes and various material standards is listed in Exhibit 13-3.

Projects within a municipal jurisdiction, for a private client with independent funding, are customarily regulated by local building and zoning ordinances. However, in the case of projects for a governmental client, or those involving public funding, municipal regulations are frequently preempted by state and/or federal regulations. Projects affecting occupant (employee) occupational safety and health, in the construction phase as well as the completed ultimate–use phase, are subject to federal and/or state requirements of the Occupational Safety and Health Act (OSHA). These initials are also used to designate the Occupational Safety and Health Administration of DOL. It should be noted that the contractor, not the architect, is responsible for compliance with OSHA project-site standards for construction workers. Environmental impact assessment/reporting is frequently required for projects of some magnitude.

MAINTAINING CODES/STANDARDS/ REGULATIONS. Once regulations are obtained, subscription revision services usually available from the sponsor organizations are recommended. In any event, updated materials must be obtained upon issue and promptly and methodically entered in the base publications. To facilitate timely availability and use, all regulatory documents most often are filed in the office library.

USING APPLICABLE CODES/STANDARDS/REGULATIONS. For an architect using or applying a code, there are several paramount premises to be recognized. First, building regulations are society's laws to be obeyed or changed by due process. They should not be considered as barriers or obstacles to be arbitrarily circumvented. Second, they must not be considered as optimum standards of good practice and certainly not as design or construction handbooks. Building regulations normally express only basic or legally acceptable minimum standards of construction to be satisfied for public safety, health and welfare.

The architect must understand the basic intent of the regulations for the protection of public safety, health and welfare performance, and not merely focus on the details of the requirements. Allowance can often be made by appeal boards for innovative designs which meet the basic intent or desired level of performance of the code but which technically may be noncompliant with code wording. In case of any question, again the construction permit issuing agency or building code administrator can be of assistance.

A systematic approach to code compliance is important. During a project's design development phase, integral with the creative process, execution of some form of comprehensive code analysis, or checklist, is advisable, not only for the applicable building code but also for zoning requirements. Exhibits 13-4, 13-5 and 13-6 are representative.

Equally important are periodic timely checks of the project's code compliance by the applicable jurisdictional agencies. Many building departments, in fact, encourage architects to bring in project design development documents, sufficiently finalized, for a preliminary review. Potential code violations identified can then be resolved before construction documents are produced.

Code analysis and compliance verification data should be incorporated into a project file since this information can serve as a guide to progress being achieved in meeting requirements. Responsibility for all such activity is nor-

mally a project management function; however, some offices have a code specialist who is charged with these duties.

PROJECT CHECKLIST. A valuable tool in reminding the architect of regulatory compliance checkpoints during development of the work is the Project Checklist, AIA Document D200, particularly tasks 34, 47, 69, 77, 110, 118 and 142.

APPEAL. The problem in keeping codes abreast of the times is accentuated by the prescriptive rather than performance wording found in many cases. Moreover, the rapid changes in the public lifestyle (open-plan schools, office landscaping, multiple-occupancy structures, etc.) make it difficult to accommodate regulations. As has already been indicated, the inability of an architect's innovative project solution to satisfy prescriptive or specification requirements may be justification for an appeal.

Though adaptable revisions of the basic code may be sought by proposals directed to the promulgating body, a more direct, immediate request may be made to the jurisdiction's appeals body. Virtually all jurisdictions have such an appeal avenue, frequently with one or more architect members.

When an appeal is filed, any mitigating hardships should be stated, and clear documentation must be provided to indicate that the project complies with the basic intent of code provisions and has a level of preference at least equivalent to pertinent requirements. Appeals so presented warrant, and ordinarily will receive, serious consideration. Time lags caused by the appeal process should be considered in project management.

REGULATORY IMPROVEMENT

How can the practicing architect influence the building regulatory process

and its improvement, locally and otherwise? What role is the AIA playing in the process? What will be the role assigned to the National Institute of Building Sciences?

ARCHITECT'S ROLE. If building regulations that have a minimum of variance and reflect today's technology and lifestyle are to come about, the architect's participation in the development and revision process is a must. Views have to be expressed, knowledgeably and consistently, to the building official, the building official's model code organizations, the standards promulgating bodies and to other design professionals—at all forums addressing building regulations.

The practitioner must further communicate with governmental jurisdictions responsible for enacting or acting on building regulations at municipal, state and federal levels. These include the executive, legislative and judicial entities and their respective agencies.

The architect's influence may also be indirectly exerted through public influence channels such as chambers of commerce, broadcast and printed media, and professional organizations, among them the AIA.

AIA'S ROLE. On the local and state scene, code committees of the AIA chapter and regional components address all of the influence avenues enumerated. The individual practitioner is urged to participate in those endeavors for regulatory improvement.

Nationally, the AIA, supplementing and coordinating chapter and regional component efforts, has undertaken to achieve its proper place in the building regulatory process—and its improvement—by the establishment of its Codes and Regulations Center (CRC) in 1971 within the Department of Professional Practice. The principal objective is to strengthen the collective voice and participation of the

EXHIBIT 13-4. CODE SEARCH CHECKLIST   Project _____ Job No. _____ Date _____

                                            Project Manager _____ Job Captain _____

1 APPLICABLE BUILDING CODE   **2 USE ZONE**   **3 FIRE ZONE** (Chapter 16)
   Los Angeles City _____ Los Angeles County _____ UBC _____

4 REGULATIONS OTHER THAN BUILDING CODE
   Zoning Ordinance_____Title 19_____Title 21_____Hospital_____Elevator_____Other_____

   State Housing_____Industrial Safety Orders_____

5 BUILDING OFFICIAL CONSULTED   **6 CONSTRUCTION TYPE(S)**
                                                      Refer to Chapters 17–22 and Chapters on Occupancy

   Name   Address   Phone   Exterior bearing walls _____
                                                      Interior bearing walls_____
                                                      Exterior nonbearing walls _____
7   Structural frame _____
                                                      Permanent partitions_____
EXITS AND OCCUPANT LOADS (Chapters 33 and 42)   Vertical openings_____
                                                      Floors _____
                                                      Roofs _____
   Occupancy   Sq. Ft.   Sq. Ft./Person   No. Persons   Exterior doors and windows_____
   _____   Inner court walls _____
   _____   Parapets required?_____
   _____   Attic area subdivision required?_____
   _____
   _____ **8 UNIT LIVE LOADS** For each occupancy (Chapter 23)
   _____
   _____
   _____
   _____

                  Total No. Persons_____
No. exits required each floor_____   **9 ZONING**
                                                         Classify zone according to use (see paragraph 2)
No. exits required total building _____   Offstreet parking required_____
                                                         Offstreet loading required_____spaces
Widths of exits_____   Yard requirements
                                                                        Front_____
Dead end corridor limit _____Ft.   Side_____
Smoke tower required? _____   Rear_____
Exit lights required? _____   Minimum lot area_____
Exit signs?_____   Maximum allowable height
Special hazard requirements_____   Stories_____
_____   Feet_____
_____   Special setback and/or height requirements
                                                         _____
                                                         _____

EXHIBIT 13-4. CODE SEARCH CHECKLIST (CONTINUED)

10 OCCUPANCY (Refer to Chapter 5 and subsequent applicable chapters)

Occupancy type(s)				
Basic allowable area				
Increase for Fire Zone 3 (for UBC and county)				
Increase for added stories				
Increase for separation (two, three or all sides)				
Increase for fire extinguishing system				
Total allowable areas				
Actual floor areas (see definition Chapter 4)				

Note: Consideration should be given to areas for future additions to project.

Maximum allowable building height

Increase for fire sprinklers (UBC and county for one story)

Total allowable height

Separations between occupancies
(Fire ratings and construction)

Fire resistive ratings of exterior walls

Protected openings in exterior walls (rating)

Enclosure of vertical openings (see also Chapters 17 and 30)

Location on property related to property lines, side yards and access to public space

Light

Ventilation

Sanitation

Fire extinguishing systems required?

Wet standpipes?

Dry standpipes?

Special hazards and requirements (see group occupancy)

Exceptions and deviations (see group occupancy)

11 LANDSCAPING (Special requirements)
(County Regional Planning Commission)

12 SPECIAL REQUIREMENTS FOR OTHER DEPARTMENTS

NOTE: Refer to paragraph numbers when attaching added information; chapter numbers refer to Uniform Building Code.

Source: *Emerging Techniques of Architectural Practice*, AIA, 1966.

EXHIBIT 13-5. CODE ANALYSIS FORMAT

A. Code Applicable, Standards
   Applicable
   (List, including date amended)
B. Occupancy Classification
   (Determine building use; If more
   than one use, note fire separation)
C. Type of Construction
   (Select type to suit or type governed
   by zoning)
D. Fire Zone
   (Establish zone from location)
E. Area Limitations
   (For occupancy group, type construc-
   tion, zoning)
   (Allowable area increases)
F. Height Limitations
   (Allowable number stories for occu-
   pancy group and type construction)
   (Allowable height increases)
G. Occupancy Requirements
   1. Exit requirements
      (Occupancy allowance, length of
      travel, number exits, exit widths)
   2. Stairs
      (Width, limitations of run, tread,
      riser, landing, handrail)
   3. Mechanical requirements
      (Sprinkler, alarms, standpipe,
      ventilation, plumbing, electrical,
      boilers, water supply, refrigera-
      tion)

4. Sanitation
   (Number of lavatories, water clos-
   ets, urinals, drinking fountains, service sinks)
H. Construction Requirements
   1. Structural
      (Columns, beams, girders, floors,
      roof, roof covering)
   2. Walls and partitions
      (Exterior, interior, shaft enclosures,
      stair enclosures)
   3. Door requirements
      (Exterior, interior, stairs, shafts)
   4. Fire protection
      (Standpipes, sprinklers, extin-
      guishers)
I. Location on Property
   (Relation to property lines,
   alleys, streets)
J. Special Requirements
   (Work on or under public ways, items
   extending over public property, front-
   age consents, permits, hazardous
   uses, existing buildings, use of public
   property, elevators, escalators)

EXHIBIT 13-6. ZONING ANALYSIS FORMAT

A. Ordinance and Regulations Appli-
   cable
   (List, including date amended)
B. Zone Location
   (Locate lot, establish zone)
C. Floor Area Ratio
   (Compute lot area, establish floor
   area ratio)
D. Use and Bulk
   (Check zone for occupancy per-
   mitted and bulk limitations)

E. Height and Area Limitations
   (Establish using floor area ratio and
   maximum floor area limitations)
F. Loading Berths
   (Establish offstreet loading berths
   required from building area)
G. Parking Berths
   (Establish offstreet parking berths
   required from building area)

design professions in the advancement of the building regulatory system. The CRC maintains a limited library of national codes, regulations and standards for reference (see Exhibit 13-7 for the CRC organization).

Established concurrently with CRC, the AIA Codes and Standards (CO/ST) Committee coordinates its activities with the Center and develops programs to insure AIA participation with major regulatory and standards agencies, to bring about the modernization of criteria governing design and construction, and to produce creative tools rather than constraints on professional practice. The CO/ST Committee is composed of practitioners who are knowledgeable and experienced in building regulations involvement and their counterparts from other design professions, the model code groups and related professional organizations.

A long-range proposal for improvement of the nation's building regulatory process has been put forward within a December 1974 report of the AIA Task Group on Building Regulation. The report is titled "One Code: A Program for Building Regulatory Reform."

NIBS. The National Institute of Building Sciences, authorized within the omnibus Housing and Community Development Act of 1974, will hopefully develop as another avenue for regulatory improvement. It has been initiated as a nonprofit, nongovernmental organization charged with shaping proposals and recommendations for uniformity in building regulations keyed to improving use of modern technology.

Overly numerous, complicated and constraining though they may be, regulations of our modern-day life are necessary for the public welfare. And when the built environment is involved, the architect must be involved, in all the standardization and regulatory processes, and their

EXHIBIT 13-7. STRUCTURE CHART—AIA CODES AND REGULATIONS CENTER

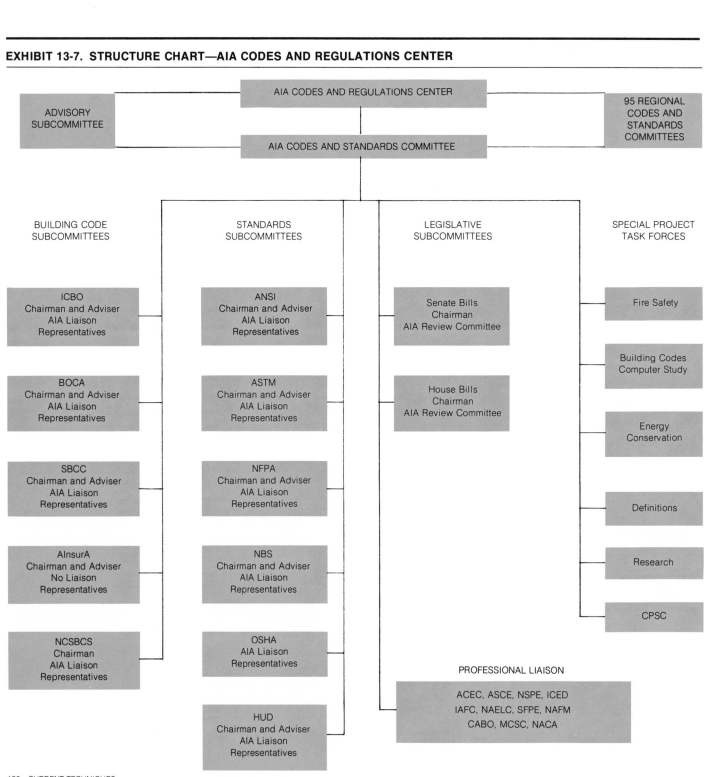

development, usage and improvement as creative vehicles.

BIBLIOGRAPHY

America Burning. Washington, D.C.: National Commission on Fire Prevention and Control, 1973.

Based on two year's work recommending solutions to fire safety problems in building and regulatory control.

Codes and Code Administration. Richard L. Sanderson. Chicago: Building Officials Conference of America, Inc., 1969.

Textbook covering the historical development and influences on codes and examining the responsibilities and activities of the building official in code administration and enforcement.

Fire Protection Through Modern Building Codes. New York: American Iron and Steel Institute, 1971.

Correlation of factual data and regulatory procedure, emphasizing the necessity for constant rationalization and modernization of fire protection techniques and regulations.

PART FOUR
MANAGEMENT
AND
PRODUCTION
TOOLS

Chapter 14
Information
Resources

HAROLD J. ROSEN, PE, FCSI
AND ROBERT ALLAN CLASS, AIA

The reference world of many architects is confined to subscriptions to several architectural magazines, some frequently used manuals and a collection of books, a few building codes, a set of Sweet's catalog files plus additional loose manufacturers' literature, a shelf of material samples, and several drawers of old drawings and specifications. If the alma mater's architectural school is nearby, its library can enlarge this world.

As the quantity of available information and the amount of needed quality data increase explosively, the inadequacies of this relatively narrow reference world become apparent. The time required to dig out succinct data from the flood of material in document form becomes burdensome and economically impractical. And the need to organize growing information resources into a system for logical storage and rapid search and retrieval is of paramount importance.

There is no utopian comprehensive information system for the architect to press a few inquiry buttons and get a quick answer in the form of dependable digested data. There are a few services which package information on selected subjects or which provide leads to such information.

Most sources of information needed by architects are scattered and are in many different forms. For maximum efficiency in an office, the most frequently used data should be available in-house and organized to permit quick access when needed. As relatively few firms can afford to maintain files of less frequently used data, knowledge of where to find such information outside is a reasonable substitute. A number of useful information sources and services in addition to those referenced in other chapters are cited here to aid in the task of identifying resources covering the major information needs of architects.

Architecture as well as other disciplines in the construction industry can benefit substantially from a comprehensive information system tailored to the needs of the industry. Exhibit 14-1 is a preliminary matrix identifying many of the disciplines and general categories of their information needs. The list is not complete, and each category requires detailed analysis prior to development of an operating format for the complete system, which lies in the future.

FORMS OF INFORMATION

Most information flowing to architects is in published form, textual or graphic. For greatest utility, the best of this material must be broken down into data form, some of which may be stored in data banks for recall when needed.

PUBLICATIONS. The majority of material worthy of retention is most frequently found in the form of books, periodicals and technical literature. Other information of interest to architects appears in such forms as office manuals and blank forms, printouts, papers and reports, of which some may not yet be published.

Books. The backbone of a good architectural library is a carefully selected collection of books which grows over time. Book reviews appearing in newspapers and magazines are good sources for learning of important new books, in addition to advertisements, announcements and publishers' lists.

There are also useful aids for those seeking specific books or listings by subject. Every book store, and nearly every library, has a copy of Books in Print, published annually by R. R. Bowker Company, New York. Indexed alphabetically by title and author, almost all books available in the U.S. are listed complete with bibliographic data. Names and addresses of all known U.S. book publishers are included.

Subject Guide to Books in Print is a companion set of volumes also published annually. Library of Congress subject headings are used, together with cross references. Books in Print Supplement is issued midyear to provide new entries for both and to list books which have gone out of print.

Periodicals. Architectural magazines and those on related environmental subjects are most frequently subscribed to by architects for keeping abreast of the latest trends in the design world. Periodicals relating to specific building types may also be found in many architectural offices.

Most magazines print an annual or semiannual index to articles appearing in previous issues. Among periodical indexes most useful to architects for locating magazine articles from a variety of sources are:

—Architectural Index, published annually in Boulder, Colo., with back issues available. Ten U.S. periodicals in the fields of architecture, landscape architecture, interior design and urban planning are indexed under subject headings. Many architectural firms subscribe to this index, which is relatively inexpensive.

—The Architectural Periodicals Index, published quarterly (with an annual cumulation in the fourth issue) by RIBA Publications Ltd., London. About 350 worldwide current periodicals are indexed under subject headings, covering the fields of architecture and allied arts, construction technology, design, environmental studies, landscape architecture, planning and relevant research.

—Art Index, published quarterly (with annual cumulations) by H. W. Wilson Co., Bronx, N.Y. About 180 American and foreign current periodicals are surveyed, with subject, title and author entries indexed in one alphabet. Covered fields include architecture, industrial design, interior design, landscape architecture and

EXHIBIT 14-1. PRELIMINARY MATRIX OF CONSTRUCTION INDUSTRY INFORMATION NEEDS

KEY:
- ● Potential Major Interest
- ◦ Minor Interest
- ☐ Little or No Interest

User Disciplines	Building Products									Costs			Activity				Other Resources											
	Catalogs	Condensed Data by Attributes	Product Selectors for Evaluation	Installed Cost Range	Specifications/Performance Data	Graphic Details	Samples	Installation/Maintenance Instructions	Lists: Manufacturers, Representatives, Suppliers	Capital Costs: By Building Type and Elements	Capital Costs: By Detailed Units	Life Cycle Costs: By Elements and Units	Contemplated Projects	Projects in Design/Construction	Project Groups: By Type and Location	Forecasting/Economic Indicators	Construction Technology	Site Tools/Techniques	Office Tools/Techniques	Regulatory Data	Building Standards	Consultant Resources	Design/Planning Information	Research Activity/Reports	Behavioral Data	Post-Occupancy Evaluation	Automation	Guides to Information Sources
Architecture	●	●	●	●	●	●	●	◦	●	●	●	●	●	◦	◦	●	●	◦	●	●	●	●	●	●	●	●	●	●
Engineering	●	●	●	●	●	●	●	◦	●	●	●	●	●	◦	◦	●	●	◦	●	●	●	●	●	●	◦	●	●	●
Interior Design	●	●	●	●	●	●	●	◦	●		◦	◦	●	●	◦	●	◦		●	●	◦	●	●	●	●	●	◦	●
Landscape/Planning													●	◦	◦	●		◦			●	●	●	●	◦	◦	◦	●
Cost Management	●	●	●	●	◦				●	●	●	●	●	◦	◦	●	●	●	◦	◦	●		◦			◦	●	●
Construction Management	●	●	●	●	◦			◦	●	●	●	●	●	◦	◦	●	●	●	●	●	●	●		◦			●	●
Contracting/Subcontracting	●	●	●	●	◦		◦	●	●	●	●	●	●	●	●	●	●	●	●	●	●	●		◦		◦	●	●
Labor								●										●										●
Manufacture												●		●	●	●	●	●	●	●	●	●		●			●	●
Assembly												●		●	●	●	●	●	●	●	●	●		●			●	●
Supply													●	●	●	●					●							●
Marketing													●	●	●	●												●
Finance										●		●	●	●	●	●												●
Real Estate/Development										●		●	●	●	●	●				●		●	●	●				●
Insurance/Bonding													●	●	◦	●				●								●
Statistics/Economics															●	●												●
Code Administration													●	●						●	●							●
Tax Administration													●	●														●
Testing													●	●														●
Moving																●												●
Building Management		●	●	●				●	●			●					◦	◦	●	●	◦	●				●	●	●
The Architect's Client			◦							◦		◦							◦			●				●	●	●
Information Handling	●	●	●	●	●	●	●	●	●	●	●	●	●	●	●	●	●	●	●	●	●	●	●	●	●	●	●	●

Source: Robert Allan Class, AIA.

urban planning, in addition to other art-related fields.

—*Avery Index to Architectural Periodicals*, now in its second edition with periodic supplements, published by G. K. Hall Co., Boston. About 385 American and foreign current and deceased periodicals are included in the single listing by author, title and subject; not all are indexed in their entirety. A photographic reproduction of the card file of Columbia University's Avery Memorial Architectural Library, the index includes the fields of architecture, urban planning, housing, landscape architecture and interior design.

—*Engineering Index*, published by Engineering Index Inc., New York, in various modes: annual and monthly hard copy issues, monthly computer tapes, 16 or 35mm positive or negative microfilm and weekly abstract cards. The international coverage is very broad both in subject area and in the forms of publications indexed. Several engineering professional and trade journals, which frequently contain articles of interest to architects, are included in the periodicals index.

—*Geodex System/A,* published by Geodex International Inc., Sonoma, Calif. More than a periodical index, it covers architecture and related disciplines; selected articles from about 50 American and foreign current periodicals are included. Available on annual subscription, it is a coordinate retrieval system accessed by punched keyword subject cards. One-page excerpts from articles of significance to architects are included in "digest volumes," together with bibliographies and keywords. Updates are furnished every few months.

Most librarians can supply addresses and subscription costs to these indexes. They can also provide information on articles of general interest appearing in inprint periodicals. One reference source used by librarians for this purpose is *Readers' Guide to Periodical Literature.*

For a listing of periodicals published throughout the world, *Ulrich's International Periodicals Directory* is a good source. By consulting "union lists of serials" found in public libraries, copies of periodicals containing articles of interest may be located at another library in the region if not available at the one where the initial inquiry is made.

Other Material. Reports, papers, etc., may be published by associations, foundations, universities, government agencies and other organizations. Occasionally they are published privately. Periodicals in general circulation may carry notices of availability of this type of material. However, such notification is more frequently found in various publications and lists of the publishing organizations.

Technical literature most usually is concerned with specific or generic building products. This subject is discussed in the section devoted to specialized information sources.

Abstracts and Digests. Subscriptions to abstracting services can save considerable time in short-cutting the formidable task of browsing through the endless mountain of published material forming the information resources of value to architects. Abstracts and digests summarize the meat of pieces and are useful for pinpointing those which may merit a full reading.

The recently initiated *Review of Architectural Periodicals* by AIA Continuing Education, Washington, D.C., is an example of an abstracting service. Culled from over 50 professional and business publications, RAP provides monthly several dozen digests of selected pieces and their sources.

Engineering Index's weekly *CARD-A-LERT* service provides printed cards with brief abstracts covering over 200 subject divisions in areas such as urban and regional planning, construction equipment

and methods, structural design, construction materials, material properties and testing, and transportation.

Published about five times a year in Montreal, *Industrialization Forum* contains tear-out abstract cards mainly relating to research projects on all phases of industrialized building. An alphabetical index to keywords is included in each issue.

Planned for launching in 1976 is a "Design Data Service" by the Cooper-Hewitt Museum of Design in New York. The service expects to have a design data bank of abstracts and bibliographies of design-related information drawn from periodicals, reports and news items, classified under 22 areas of study and indexed by keywords.

Additional sources of abstracts are identified in later sections on government and on building research. A local librarian can suggest further sources.

DATA BANKS. The future of information storage and retrieval systems centers around comprehensive data banks. A data bank may be as small as a manual listing and brief description of a dozen frequently specified pieces of laboratory equipment picked from a 500-page catalog. Or it may be as large as the labor and material cost spreads of 10,000 building components fed into a computer's memory for recall when preparing a cost estimate.

Only information that is needed more than once has a place in a data bank. The more that data is used, the more valuable it becomes. For example, salary and benefit rates of all personnel used for the biweekly payroll belong in a data bank. This information is also used in the firm's financial management system for such activities as producing project status reports, monitoring expenditures and estimating proposed compensation for new projects.

A master specification is a data bank. Information is drawn from it repetitively to prepare project specifications. Similarly, standard details used on construction documents may be selected from the firm's data bank of favorite details.

When a firm's storehouse of repetitively accessed data reaches a size where specifically sought pieces are hard to find or need to be used interactively for a number of purposes, then the establishment of a computer data bank should be considered. Some firms have computer programs to list interior furnishings for bidding purposes as well as to estimate their costs, prepare purchase orders and designate installation areas; the same basic data is used more than once (recycled) for different purposes. Others use computer-generated lists to identify and access their holdings of information resources, a basic step in establishing more comprehensive data banks for the architectural firm.

Many outside information sources use data banks. Examples are sources which provide data on construction costs, building activity, published material, product manufacturers, and application of building products.

GENERAL INFORMATION SOURCES

As most sources of information needed by architects are scattered, the most promising ones where a search may be initiated are listed here. Primary sources of general information include libraries, associations and other organizations, government and the news media.

LIBRARIES. As they concentrate on information which architects seek, architectural school libraries are excellent sources. The AIA Library in Washington, D.C., which has 19,000 cataloged volumes, is a valuable reference resource used by many AIA members. Accession lists are published bimonthly, and librarians will respond to information requests

and prepare short bibliographies.

Other national libraries located in Washington, D.C., of specific interest to the architectural profession include the National Referral Center of the Library of Congress and the Library and Information Division of the U.S. Department of Housing and Urban Development. The former serves as an intermediary, directing inquirers to organizations or individuals with specialized knowledge they are willing to share, including abstracting and indexing services, information and document centers, professional societies, and university research bureaus and institutes. The latter's library houses over half a million pieces which may be referenced there, and personnel provide many services, including consulting and reference services, literature searches, abstracting and indexing.

Often overlooked sources are public libraries. Virtually every town, no matter how small, has one, usually linked to a regional system for broader coverage. Librarians are knowledgeable people, willing to respond to any number of reasonable questions. In addition to zeroing in on locating published material and other resources, many will even look up addresses and telephone numbers in the larger cities for which directories are carried.

Some firms find it advantageous to have a handy reference to libraries in the office. *Subject Collections* by Lee Ash and Denis Lorenz, published by R. R. Bowker Company, covers university and college as well as public and special libraries in the U.S. and Canada. Most libraries have a copy of *Directory of Special Libraries and Information Centers*, published by Gale Research Company, Detroit. This lists nearly 14,000 libraries and centers in the U.S. and Canada, including those operated by the public and private sectors. Data on each includes location, subjects covered, special collections, publications and services.

ASSOCIATIONS AND OTHER ORGANIZATIONS. Many professional and trade associations provide design, detailing, specification and other literature pertinent to the materials, products, systems and services with which they are associated. Indexes and listings of their literature and other publications can be obtained by calling or writing them. Many associations, universities and similar organizations can provide guidance to locating additional sources of information.

Encyclopedia of Associations, published annually with periodic supplements by Gale Research Company, lists relevant data on over 14,500 trade associations, professional societies, labor unions and other nonprofit American organizations of national scope. Listings are grouped by general type.

National Trade and Professional Associations of the United States and Canada and Labor Unions, published annually by Columbia Books, Washington, D.C., covers the vital statistics of over 5,500 associations and unions with national memberships. Listings are alphabetical, with a subject index.

The above two works do not list foundations. Those interested in seeking grants or sources for identifying material published through grant programs may wish to consult *The Foundation Directory,* published every few years by The Foundation Center, New York. Over 2,500 major U.S. foundations are listed.

GOVERNMENT. The U.S. government is probably the largest information storehouse in the world and is an important generator in establishing automated information programs. The government's information resources are so vast that it requires considerable work on the architect's part to identify all areas of interest and sources, making selectivity of search essential.

A good source is *National Technical Information Service* (*NTIS*), Springfield, Va.

NTIS publishes an annual catalog of holdings, which include over 700,000 government-sponsored research, development and engineering reports and analyses prepared by federal agencies, their contractors and grantees. It also publishes an index to current abstracts in weekly journals. Services include on-line computer bibliographic searches and abstracts of current NTIS documents; reports on paper or in microform; and rush mail orders by certified mail.

A Directory of Information Resources in the United States contains in one volume the government's list of information services—automated and otherwise. The directory includes a number of references on architecture and related fields and covers all federal organizations, regardless of their areas of interest. A product of the National Referral Center of the Library of Congress, it is available from the U.S. Government Printing Office (GPO), Washington, D.C.

The GPO also publishes two lists which are useful in keeping track of government publications: *Selected U.S. Government Publications,* an annotated biweekly which covers all fields; and *Monthly Catalog of U.S. Government Publications,* a list arranged by issuing agency with subject, author and title indexes (the December issue cumulating the year's indexes).

NEWS MEDIA. Newspapers and news magazines, as general information sources, often print material of specific interest to architects. Firms may clip articles to add to their resources or subscribe to clipping services.

The New York Times Information Bank contains abstracts of articles from the *New York Times* and 60 other publications. *Times* input dates back to 1969, the other journals from 1972. Information from the *Times* is stored within three days. This on-line retrieval system with a reader/printer is especially useful for government announcements, statistics, etc. It is available in many large public libraries and at major universities.

SPECIALIZED INFORMATION SOURCES

Some sources in specialized areas of information are covered in other chapters, for example, construction costs in Chapter 12; building regulations in Chapter 13; computer applications in Chapter 15; networking in Chapter 17; specifications in Chapter 19. This section discusses specific sources in three areas: building activity; building products; building research.

BUILDING ACTIVITY. Numerous sources report on activity in building planning, design and construction in both the private and public sectors. Some, such as general circulation newspapers, carry sporadic reports, frequently in a weekly real estate section. Others, mainly commercial, are more highly organized in reporting building and other construction activity. The better organized and more complete data usually goes for a higher subscription price.

Architects are naturally interested in reports on planned projects for which an architect has not yet been selected. This subject is discussed in Chapter 5. While reports on projects in the design or construction stages may appear to be of peripheral interest to many architects, such information can in fact prove of benefit to them.

A general knowledge of increased or decreased activity in certain geographic areas can aid a decision to open or close an office or to adjust personnel levels. Volume of activity in various building types can affect a firm's emphasis in practice, and a study of trends in changing activity may aid a decision in this area. Wide dissemination of information on bid dates of a firm's projects may attract a wider field of bidders and sub-bidders and affect the potential of more attractive bids. And knowledge of what the competition is up to doesn't hurt.

Data derived from project reports is used to compile valuable statistics on past and current activity in the construction industry, which may in turn be used as a base for formulating forecasts of future activity. Such reports and forecasts are important to all in the industry as economic indicators of current and future demand.

Reports. Activity in building and other construction is reported either by individual projects or in the form of broader statistical data.

The best known nationwide reporting source is the F. W. Dodge Division of McGraw-Hill Information Systems Company, with corporate headquarters in New York plus some 125 offices throughout the continental United States and Canada. Current selective data on individual construction projects is available through subscription to daily *Dodge Reports,* available in innumerable combinations of specialized data and in up to 10 stages of project progress. If an architect needs information on special products going into a project, this fact will be noted in the report if so requested.

Dodge Bulletins contain nonselective compilations of *Dodge Reports* in major market areas. *Dodge Management Control Service* reports semimonthly or monthly on major construction projects, while a flexible custom version titled *Dodge Major Projects* provides data tailored to the needs of subscribers.

An ancillary service provides Dodge Plan Rooms, open to subscribers to *Dodge Reports* and *Bulletins* in approximately 115 cities to review drawings and specifications of local projects for bidding purposes. Another is the Dodge/SCAN Microfilm System for selective national distribution of bidding materials (the architect for the project getting a free copy). Other groups, such as contractors' and other construction industry associations, also have plan rooms in principal cities.

An example of a nationally circulated periodical reporting selected project and statistical information is *Engineering News-Record,* McGraw-Hill's construction weekly magazine. Its "Pulse" section lists a sampling from *Dodge Reports* of current U.S. and foreign significant jobs in planning, bidding and contract award phases. *ENR*'s "Construction Scoreboard" regularly features, in addition to its quarterly roundups, broad statistical data on bidding volume, new plans and new construction capital, as well as cost indexes. Its "Official Proposals" section carries detailed bid notices.

Numerous local and regional construction newspapers, periodicals and services report on specific projects in various phases from contemplated, through design/documentation, to bidding and contract award.

Statistical data for all types of construction is compiled on a national basis by Dodge and the U.S. Department of Commerce. Data on housing is compiled by the National Association of Home Builders (NAHB), based in Washington, D.C. Other organizations compile data suited to their specific areas of interest. The data is analyzed and arranged in various modes for reporting; some is of interest to architects.

In measuring the construction market, Dodge uses *construction contract value* or physical measurement at the time new construction is started. It does not include land values, post-contract changes, some small projects and minor alterations and additions, small force account work, farm/rural construction, mobile homes or design costs.

Commerce uses value of new *construction put in place* in measuring building activity, reporting on construction or parts thereof installed during a given period. It does not include land values or mobile homes, but it does include estimates of other items excluded by Dodge. Thus Commerce's figures may be as much as one-third higher than Dodge's. Lists of government publications containing Commerce's data may be obtained from the GPO.

Among the statistical information available to subscribers from NAHB's Economics Department are housing component cost reports, monthly reports on the economy and the construction industry, monthly tables and analysis of the most recent housing starts, and quarterly reports on union wage rates in over 100 areas.

Forecasts. Statistics derived from reports, together with analyses of trends, cycles, demand and economic health, are used in forecasting future building activity. Some architects recognize forecasts as general economic indicators in the construction industry, others as trends in activity in geographical areas where they practice and building types in which they have an interest.

McGraw-Hill Information Systems Company issues the Dodge/Sweet's *Construction Outlook* annually, with periodic updates. *Dodge Construction Potentials* and *Dodge Product Potentials,* as basic parts of *Construction Outlook,* are also tools for forecasting. On a custom basis, McGraw-Hill prepares economic forecasts and market research for individual manufacturers, industry groups and government bodies.

The NAHB has available to subscribers an econometric housing forecast service, by types of units and by metropolitan area, state and region. And the forecasts of government and other economists are quoted in the daily press and in periodicals.

BUILDING PRODUCTS. There is no substitute for personal contact with qualified manufacturers' representatives for help in solving specific problems on the proper selection and application of building products. Those well equipped with technical know-how can be of inestimable value to the architect. But such personal contact is not always necessary, sometimes not feasible, when conducting a broad search for information on the myriad products needed to put together a building.

Technical Literature. The numerous trade associations in the construction industry are frequently sources of generic design and application information on building products. They may be identified through the reference sources cited in a previous section. Some of the research sources cited later may provide leads to research papers on characteristics and applications of generic types of products.

The prime sources of information on technical design, selection, specification and detailing of specific products may be found in the wealth of individual manufacturers' catalogs or technical literature. Individual pieces of manufacturers' technical literature or binders containing several pieces must be obtained directly from the manufacturers or their representatives.

To locate specific manufacturers of many products (including building products), a good source is *Thomas Register of American Manufacturers and Thomas Register Catalog File,* published annually by Thomas Publishing Company, New York. This multivolume publication indexes manufacturers and suppliers by products and services, company names and brand names. It includes catalogs and advertisements of some companies appearing in the indexes.

The local public library may have additional directories arranged geographically or by type of business or industry. These may be of great help in finding the address of a manufacturer when only the name is known. Also, many trade periodicals have a directory issue. Pioneered by the Philadelphia Chapter AIA as part of its efforts to establish a regional information center, some AIA chapters regularly publish guides to locating local manufacturers' representatives who can in turn supply product literature as well as consulting services.

In addition to periodic convention exhibits and trade shows, a few major cities have commercially organized building products showrooms featuring samples of the latest offerings of participating manufacturers and are sources for obtaining technical literature.

For many years, a service has existed in southern California for stocking architects' libraries with the latest literature of participating manufacturers. This type of service has not yet caught on in other parts of the U.S., although it is prevalent in the United Kingdom.

Some manufacturers condense their technical information into data forms preferred by many architects and specifiers over those designed to be more eye-catching than informative. Progress is being made in this area by availability to manufacturers of such documents and programs as *Technical Literature for the Construction Industry,* AIA Document E101, and *Sweet's GuideLines.* The SPEC-DATA Technical Literature Program of the Construction Specifications Institute (CSI) produces SPEC-DATA sheets complementing conventional product literature. This program is based on using a compact standard 10-point format for evaluating, comparing, selecting and specifying products. The sheets are distributed to the CSI membership as part of the program and may be further distributed to others by the manufacturer.

Catalog Files. Acquisition and proper filing of huge numbers of individual pieces of manufacturers' and other product literature is a monumental task. To cope with this problem, the idea of a bound file of manufacturers' catalogs emerged around the turn of the century. Central catalog files are the most convenient means of having a broad range of product literature available. An occasional regional effort in this direction has been made, but few have survived.

The nationally distributed catalog files from Sweet's Division of McGraw-Hill Information Systems Company are no doubt the best known such files among architects and other users. Each bound volume is classified by a version of the *Uniform Construction Index* and indexed by firm and by product as well as by trade name. Each individual catalog is identified by a separate Sweet's UCI-related catalog code number.

Sweet's Catalog Files—the first was established in 1906—contain the most recent manufacturers' literature on construction products, interior furnishings and mechanical equipment. They are distributed annually to the most active offices designing, specifying and purchasing in the construction industry. Prequalification each year is necessary to obtain a set. Among Sweet's U.S. catalog files and services are:

—*Sweet's Architectural Catalog File:* commercial, institutional and high-rise residential construction; about 1,500 catalogs from 1,200 manufacturers.

—*Sweet's Industrial Construction & Renovation File with Plant Engineering Extension:* manufacturing plants, power plants and utilities; about 400 catalogs from 350 manufacturers.

—*Sweet's Light Construction Catalog File:* light nonresidential, single-family and low-rise multifamily construction; about 175 catalogs from 150 manufacturers.

—*Sweet's Interior Design File:* commercial and institutional interior design; samples and about 150 catalogs from 130 manufacturers.

—*Sweet's Engineering Catalog File:* mechanical/sanitary and related products; about 250 catalogs from 200 manufacturers (1976, first edition).

—*Sweet's Showroom:* annual photo compendium of interior commercial furnishings for interior design and architectural firms.

—*Sweet's Buyline:* nationwide, toll-free telephone service for recipients of a Sweet's file, giving the name and telephone number of the closest representative for any building product found in Sweet's.

Microfilm Libraries. Within the last few years, three major microfilm data banks have been introduced which provide information not only on manufacturers and their product literature but also on such subjects as specifications, standards, codes and regulations. Each offers somewhat differing services:

—*SPEC-DATA II,* developed for the Construction Specifications Institute and distributed by Information Handling Services, Englewood, Colo., is available on an annual subscription basis with quarterly updates. The library contains catalog data of approximately 4,500 manufacturers and 150 associations/institutes/societies, standards, test methods and applications data. The *CSI Manual of Practice,* specifications series and monograph series are included. Comparison of product performance and criteria are shown in grid structures. The service provides indexes, 16mm cartridge-loaded microfilm with reader/printer and 8mm cassette-loaded microfilm with reader. Other files of standards, military specifications and federal construction regulations are also available from Information Handling.

—*Showcase Microfilm Library for Construction,* Detroit, contains about 1.4 million pages of product data from over 5,000 manufacturers; building standards and specifications from American Society for Testing and Materials, National

Electrical Manufacturers Association and others, as well as from the military services and the General Services Administration. The library, on 16mm microfilm, can be leased with reader or reader/printer on a monthly or annual basis. A KWIC (keyword-in-context) index to the subject classification scheme used to arrange the catalogs is supplied. The service is updated every 45 days, with 15-day updates on military specifications and standards.

—Instant Data Access Control (IDAC), New York, includes products of about 5,000 manufacturers, as well as specifications, standards, codes, research related to design and construction, and design case histories. The user is provided with an abstract when there is doubt about the value of a specific report. Subscriptions are for microfilm or microfiche; reader/printers are offered on two-year leases. Research reports are published as additional data. Building Information Programs is a major service to help architects accelerate the design and documentation process of a project; each program is categorized in three major segments: project management, project programming, and information retrieval.

BUILDING RESEARCH. Although not always so, research today is an integral part of the practice of architecture and of educational endeavors. Ways are being sought for a technology transfer from research to practice. The AIA Research Corporation, an AIA subsidiary, is active in this field by the use of grant programs. Research programs are conducted by many manufacturers to improve the utility and marketability of their products.

Considerable building research activity and/or reporting is centered in Washington, D.C. Among the most prominent sources are Center for Building Technology of the National Bureau of Standards; Environmental Design Research Association, Inc.; Journal of Architectural

Research, an interdisciplinary forum for researchers, practitioners and educators; Building Research Advisory Board (BRAB) of the National Research Council.

In addition to administering several committees to study research needs (e.g., the Federal Construction Council), BRAB also provides the secretariat for the U.S. National Committee for the International Council for Building Research, Studies and Documentation (CIB). Information on reports of the many worldwide CIB working parties may be obtained from BRAB. The National Research Council of Canada in Ottawa provides Canadian Building Abstracts to subscribers, covering all aspects of building research published in Canadian technical journals.

The Research Division at AIA Headquarters in Washington, D.C., can provide further information on recent research activity as well as abstracts and bibliographic searches. It maintains the AIA Research Information Retrieval System, currently containing a data base of approximately 6,000 abstracts of which some 1,500 are unsolicited research reports. Accessed by keyword terms via optical coincidence cards, the system primarily covers the field of environmental psychology. Included are abstract cards from Industrialization Forum, referenced previously, and research abstracts and citations from such sources as the Smithsonian Science Information Exchange and the John Crerar Library in Chicago.

ORGANIZING INFORMATION

Information worth retaining for future reference becomes useless if it cannot be found again. It is thus essential to organize a workable and dependable system for filing and rapidly retrieving such information. Whether the collection is scattered among a library, a corner of the drafting room, and some assorted shelves and filing cabinets, or is organized into a

resource center (or better still, an information center), is a matter of each firm's decision. Organized information resources should include not only external but also internally generated material such as drawings, specifications, design notebooks, presentation material and feedback notations.

Several years ago a service was initiated to organize and update the information resources of a dozen large firms of design professionals. Although such a service may not be needed by many offices, a firm should consider retaining a trained librarian, information specialist or other consultant to help set up a system. As firms grow, many add such personnel to their staffs, full or part time, to operate the system. But however arranged, access to the material should be simple enough so that staff can find it unaided if necessary.

The relatively simple data filing format of the 16-division Uniform Construction Index is described in the November 1972 AIA Journal article by Robert Allan Class, AIA, titled "Today's Answer to Data Filing." If a classification system other than this is contemplated, a good review of several in common use may be found in the October 1974 Interim Report D-41, An Evaluation of Architectural Information Systems, prepared by N. D. Lane for the Army's Construction Engineering Research Laboratory of Champaign, Ill.; copies are available from NTIS. Some of the listings below on classification and indexing are selected and digested from this source.

CLASSIFICATION AND INDEXING. Classification is a systematic arrangement in groups or categories according to established criteria, or the segregation of like and unlike subjects. The act of classifying material is identifying it within a selected classification system and is primarily for designating a single home in which the material can be placed. Indexing, or cataloging in some cases, is a primary technique for identifying by single or multiple entries where the material may be found, or the organization of attributes of information. Simply expressed, classification serves for putting it in, indexing for getting it out.

Most firms use the *Uniform Construction Index* (UCI) for classifying and filing product literature and information relating to the use of building products. Many do not realize that the subject headings of the UCI's Division 1 are designed to provide comprehensive data filing capability on subjects relating to everything *not* incorporated into the construction. For example, the listed headings cover many subjects on administrative, design and technical aids of value to the architect. The system is sufficiently flexible that additional headings and subheadings may be included by users to suit their needs.

Developed by the AIA cooperatively with seven other construction industry associations and several consulting organizations in the U.S. and Canada, the UCI's Data Filing Format correlates with the 16-division formats for specifications and cost analysis. The format for data filing, replacing earlier AIA and Uniform System filing and classification systems, was developed specifically as a construction industry standard for information storage and retrieval on all subjects relating to the building process. It features 16 easily remembered division titles, under which are relational subject headings stated in words rather than numbers. The UCI also contains a project filing format arranged in four divisions related to project phases, with subjective subdivisions. An alphabetical keyword index is found in the UCI.

Architects practicing abroad may encounter the alpha-numeric SfB or CI/SfB classification systems, neither of which is used in the U.S. A few large U.S. architectural libraries use the primarily numeric hierarchical codes of the Library of Congress (LC) Classification System. Other numerical systems used by libraries include the Dewey Decimal Classification System and the Universal Decimal Classification System. None of these systems use simple words for codes as does the UCI, nor are the last three particularly construction oriented.

The key to locating and accessing stored information, whether in document or data form, lies in indexing procedures. An index in its simplest form is a list in alphabetical order which points the way to the information being sought, or a communications bridge. An equally simple form is the use of project identifiers employed in the architectural office.

As data is refined into smaller and more specific units, other indexing forms are needed. Among the most common is the subject heading index, used by *Architectural Index* and *Art Index*. In this technique, representative concepts of a document are labeled by descriptive terms from a standardized list of subject headings or from a thesaurus which indicates hierarchical relationships to other terms.

Most adaptable to automation are keyword-in-context (KWIC) and keyword-out-of-context (KWOC) indexes, in which significant words are selected from titles of documents for the former, from document content for the latter. Coordinate indexing for manual or automated retrieval is useful for many tasks, among them accessing abstracts and bibliographic citations. By using such manual devices as aperture, notched or optical coincidence cards, or computer technology, the field of search is narrowed by bringing into coordination terms designating the subject matter sought: the more specific the terms, the narrower the field.

Before adopting other than the simplest classification and indexing systems, a specialist should be consulted.

STORAGE AND RETRIEVAL. Storage methods are generally dictated by retrieval requirements, which are in turn tied back into classification and indexing methods.

Among the many forms of material requiring storage for later retrieval, hard copy is the most familiar and prevalent. The term designates any documentary material which can be read or viewed other than that in photographic or computer form. Books, periodicals, reports, catalogs and drawings are examples. Storage simply involves shelves, drawers and filing cabinets; the material is handled manually.

Photographic materials such as slides and microform require some form of projection to view their content. Microform, which is hard copy reduced on 8, 16 or 35mm film (or even on opaque media), is becoming more frequently used in architectural offices. It may be stored in drawers, in safes or simply in small boxes on top of a desk. The material can be retrieved either manually or automatically.

Microform techniques are used primarily to reduce the bulk of files or libraries and as a means of keeping records in a safe place. Transparent jackets are available for storage of microfilm rolls in a grid pattern. Aperture cards come with holes designed to hold a frame or frames of microfilm, and microfiche holds multiple micro-images in a grid pattern on transparent sheets.

Microfilm readers, produced in a range of sizes, are necessary since the film image is too small to read unaided. Reader/printers can be used to reproduce the negatives back into hard copy. A 35mm frame can be enlarged to drawing size; most equipment can produce prints up to 17×22 inches.

The *Yellow Pages* list dealers under the heading Microfilm Services, Equipment and Supplies. Just about every major publication is available on microfilm. Xerox University Microfilms, Ann Arbor, Mich., is a large center for microfilm copies of a number of periodicals, among them the *AIA Journal*.

Computer storage, always automated, may be on cards, discs or magnetic tape. To date, most generally available computer-stored information related to the architectural field is on cost estimating, planning, and behavioral and social science. More often than not, computer data banks are developed and run by federal or private agencies, although in-house systems are gradually being developed by professional design firms.

The almost unlimited capabilities of the computer for processing data will eventually lead to its much greater use as the basis for information storage and retrieval systems for architectural offices. The most up-to-date methods of storage, such as microform and computer, are worth little unless the information sought can be swiftly retrieved. The organization must be logical if it is to be of full benefit, and it must be used consistently.

ORGANIZATIONAL EXAMPLES. In setting up or revamping an architectural firm's library, resource center or information center, it may be worthwhile to first read the article titled "A Data Bank for a Small Architectural Office," by Donald P. Grant and Arthur J. Chapman. This was published in the July–September 1973 issue of *DMG-DRS Journal: Design Research and Methods*. The subjects of data systems, files/indexing, search/retrieval and automation are covered.

A discussion on architectural office libraries may be found in *Libraries for Professional Practice*, edited by Patricia Calderhead and published in 1972 by the London Architectural Press. A basic how-to article titled "'Launching' Your Own Library," by Jean Boucher, appeared in the August 1975 issue of *Consulting Engineer*.

As an organization grows and more people require access to information, it is to be expected that arrangements for storage and retrieval will grow in utility and sophistication. Three examples are briefed here to indicate how some of the larger architectural firms handle their information resources.

The Architects Collaborative, Inc. (TAC), headquartered in Cambridge, Mass., maintains a full-time library staff. In addition to TAC publications such as feasibility studies and master plan and design reports, the library houses the following: Sweet's catalog files and product literature cataloged according to the UCI; books classified by the LC system; periodicals shelved alphabetically by title, with articles identified through *Architectural Index* and *Art Index;* presentation and historical slides; material samples; photographic equipment; project histories; and either microfilm or half-size reproducibles of some project drawings. Original drawings and project files are in a remote storage vault, and some of the more frequently used material housed in the library is duplicated at various work locations. Computer-generated data is growing, encompassing such areas as project and office management information, building requirements, and interior furnishings and equipment.

Caudill Rowlett Scott (CRS), headquartered in Houston, has, in addition to a full-time library staff, an information storage and retrieval center. The library collection, indexed by author, title and subject, includes books, periodicals and research files on a broad range of architectural, engineering, planning and management subjects; general reference books; maps, codes and standards; indexes; and internal archival matter. Library services for personnel include reference, research, interlibrary loans and acquisitions. The retrieval center is a centralized bank of project-related information which includes drawings, "paperwork" (project files), slides and photographs, and program analysis cards. All drawings and paperwork are microfilmed in duplicate, with one set placed in a bank vault. The office set of drawing microfilms is on 35mm aperture cards coded by project number, phase, drawing type and sheet number, and is computer indexed. CRS also has considerable computer-generated data for such uses as programming and management information.

Hellmuth, Obata & Kassabaum, Inc. (HOK), headquartered in St. Louis, was somewhat set back by a recent fire in implementing its resource organizational plan. This plan is described in the article "'Small' Firm Gets Big Results" by Nancy D. Lane, former director of information services, published in the November 1970 issue of *Information and Records Management*. Drawings and specifications are microfilmed and filed by a four-digit project number (the first two digits representing contract year, the last two chronologically within that year) and indexed by computer. A computerized index and retrieval system which inventories and categorizes information from various sources (microfilm, slides, publications, etc.) is being formulated. The library collection uses the LC system for books; periodicals are arranged alphabetically by title using commercial indexes as aids; and slides, photographs, photostats and HOK publications are arranged by building type category. Library services for personnel include research, acquisitions, interlibrary loans, compilations of slide shows, and data collocation. A project information exchange between offices is in operation, with all data centralized at the main office.

Another example of the organization of an information center is that of the national Canadian *Construction Information System* (CIS), operated by the nonprofit Canadian Construction Information Corporation, Ottawa. Developed and recently launched in several key cities with considerable government support, the first thrust is on building products, with later planned additions in such areas as standards, codes, costs, office administration, accounting, statistical and project management information. Elements of the system for users are microfiche files, reader/printer, computer terminal, thesaurus, and indexes and directories. Search procedures are by parameters and criteria, using thesaurus keywords. Although search of the microfiche files is possible manually by using the indexes and directories, search procedures are enhanced by computer terminal connection to the corporation's data banks.

In setting up a basic library and information resource center, the smaller architectural firm should bear in mind that the system should be kept as simple as possible so that it can be used by anyone in the office. One person should be assigned the responsibility of maintaining it and recording borrowings, with clerical support as needed.

The first step is to list the categories and specifics of information needed, then identify and list the sources of this information. Collect that needed in-house for frequent reference, and begin the task of extracting frequently used data from the collected information.

Before accumulating too much material, decide on a classification system. If the UCI is selected, make a master list of the subject headings and subheadings to be used initially. Identify each piece by the appropriate heading (and subheading if used), both on the piece itself and on a file card. The file cards will become the basis of the index to the collection; each should contain the subject heading (and subheading) and identification of the piece as a minimum. As the collection grows, additional cards can be made for title and author, and a more sophisticated indexing system may ultimately be selected.

Organize documents and data for rapid retrieval, starting with material produced in-house. Pick a storage system that will permit browsing by subject without having to consult the index each time. Clearly label each portion of the storage area by subject heading, preferably arranged alphabetically. Leave room for expansion if possible as collections never decrease in size. As each piece is labeled, store it appropriately, ready for instant retrieval. Data culled from documents may be placed in adjacent binders.

The use of abstracting, bibliographic and indexing services should be considered an essential part of the firm's outside information resources.

For most architectural firms, acquisition and organization of information resources need not be a complex procedure, at least not until they start to grow. Firms that have gone through the expansion process re-

late steps to be taken to avoid growing pains in the information area:

—Organize early before material gets out of hand.

—Label and index all documents *worth* saving.

—Mark all drawings and other project-related material with a project identifier and a date.

—Weed out old material at least yearly.

—Acquire as much documentary material as possible in abstract form, as good abstracts can be a bridge between documents and data.

—Gear toward *data* acquisition as the crucial step in providing material for an ultimate data retrieval system.

BIBLIOGRAPHY

Major bibliographic references on information resources are cited in the text. The following additional reference is of interest to those studying the problems of a comprehensive information system.

An Information System for the Construction Industry. Department of the Environment. London: Her Majesty's Stationery Office, 1971.

Final report of the Working Party on Data Co-ordination examining proposals for the improvement of information flow in the British construction industry.

Chapter 15
Computing

ROBERT F. MATTOX, AIA

Computing can help in design and business to deal more effectively with major problems of communication and data management. As an information machine, the computer handles information in various forms: numeric, alphabetic, graphic. These elements are, of course, the means by which ideas are assembled and communicated at all levels.

Today, the question of whether the computer can be used in the design professions is no longer the central issue; rather, the problem is to select hardware and applications which are most appropriate and cost effective in each circumstance. Both large and small firms have demonstrated that computing, carefully applied, can expand and improve services and increase their knowledge about business. The early mysteries of computing are being put aside. Communication with machines becomes simpler as languages become better adapted to the user and as machines do more of the work of translating human commands into action.

Since most discussions on computing in the design professions have tended to isolate applications from the mainstream of practice, computer applications are described and illustrated elsewhere in this book, where they can be better understood in context as supporting tools to each area of practice. This overview of computing hardware, software, terminology and application areas is meant to provide a better understanding of how applications are developed and employed.

HARDWARE

Computing developments in recent years have been staggering. Technological advances in design have been so rapid and so profound that the term "generation" is applied to describe phases of computer evolution.

The first generation of computers was created but 30 years ago with the first electro-mechanical calculators. These early devices used binary arithmetic and had the basic elements of memory, arithmetic, control and input/output. Those first-generation machines were physically very large, used vacuum tubes and were very expensive.

A second generation was introduced by 1960 when development of discrete solid state components provided a basis for a computer design many times faster and cheaper.

By the mid-sixties, integrated circuits combined thousands of functional units on small chips. The cost of one chip was little more than the cost of any one of the previous components it now included. The third generation of computers had arrived before the second generation was fully employed.

Development of integrated circuit technology has permitted design and manufacture of small computers. Compared to physical sizes of computers built using predecessor technologies, these computers are much smaller; hence, they are called *mini-computers.*

Mini-computers pack into smaller dimensions the same computing power as found in earlier computers and for less cost. The demand for small computers has increased rapidly as prices have been reduced. Initially, the market for mini-computers consisted of new users who could suddenly afford a computer and could begin to program it with small-scale applications. Users of second- and third-generation computers have a large investment in programs which are error free and tailored to their machines, and initially cannot make ready use of mini-computers. However, large computer manufacturers have expanded their markets by using this technology to offer equal or greater computing power at lower prices.

A similar pattern is seen in the evolution of the *micro-computer* through large-scale integration (LSI) technology which further advanced the micro-miniaturization of electronic parts. Astonishing computing capabilities are packaged into small units with concomitant reductions in price.

The availability of micro-computers may have a significant impact on the design professions since cost and accessibility have been major deterrents to widespread use of computing. As more and more power is packaged into smaller and smaller units for less and less cost, inexpensive computing will become accessible to almost everyone.

There is a large body of literature today which explains in great detail the mechanics of computers. Rather than describe how computers are built and catalog devices offered by manufacturers, this section briefly describes why various components are required.

Computing brings unique capabilities to the professional design team which can complement and expand its abilities. A most dramatic feature is the speed of internal operation. Within seconds, a computer can perform more arithmetic than a person can do in a lifetime. Not only is it fast but also highly reliable and accurate, performing repeatedly without degeneration from boredom.

Computers cannot make best use of their impressive speeds if they must wait at each step for the slower human to provide the next piece of data or next instruction before continuing their work. Instead, all data and complete process descriptions must be available instantaneously to the machine. The highest speed device generally used to store current data and instructions is called magnetic core.

Since applications involving large quantities of data and large programs cannot all reside in core storage simultaneously, secondary storage units are used. Magnetic tape can store data sequentially, i.e., the tape must be read in the order in which it was recorded in

COMPUTING 175

order to find and access a piece of data. Discs, drums and storage cells are random access storage devices, permitting data thus stored and on-line to be accessed in any sequence and only slightly less rapidly than if it were stored in core.

The arithmetic unit performs addition, subtraction, multiplication and division on binary numbers. It also performs logical operations, making decisions for subsequent processing based on conditions or values of variables. This logical decision-making capability distinguishes the computer and elevates it above calculators.

The entire computing machinery is driven by a central processing unit (CPU) which controls the flow and processing of data. It acts on coded instructions provided by users, retrieving a piece of data, finding the next instruction, operating on the data, etc.

Input and output units (I/O) get the data and process instructions into and out of the computer. Input may be provided as a deck of punched cards, a magnetic tape, a typewriter-type keyboard, a display scope (cathode ray tube: CRT), light pen or a digitizer. Output can be provided by these devices (except pen and digitizer) and by means of line printers, plotters, electrostatic printers and photocopiers.

Computer graphics is a form of computing input/output which has a special appeal for the design professional. Graphic output can be produced as hard copy from plotters or photocopy equipment of images generated on scopes. Images can be constructed using lines or halftone images. Plotting and scopes can be in multicolor to add yet another dimension and aid in comprehension.

Virtually anything that can be done on a plotter can be done on a scope with the added advantage of interactive display change. The scope can be used to simulate movement around and through spatial configurations and to display, edit and manipulate textual and statistical data.

Computer-aided design systems consist of such interactive hardware components as a cathode ray tube, light pen, keyboard console and hard copy output. Photo courtesy Perry Dean Partners Inc. and Digital Equipment Corporation.

Intermediate-sized computing systems may include, left to right, a card read/punch, central processing unit, operator console and line printer. Photo courtesy International Business Machines Corporation.

Output can be produced in hard copy form (plotter, printer or photocopier) for permanent record. Light pens and special functional keyboards aid in using more fully the interactive features of the scope.

Conceptually, the use of computer-generated graphics to support design is impressive. Graphic languages now facilitate and encourage the use of sophisticated hardware. Historically, graphic systems have generally been costly for design firms to develop and use in day-to-day operations. However, a few firms and universities have developed graphic-aided systems for planning and design. With the advent of less expensive hardware, graphics may soon be feasible for many firms.

SOFTWARE

Where *hardware* consists of physical devices used in computing, *software* is the set of diagrammatic and printed data such as programs, flow charts and operating instructions required to employ the hardware. *Data* are the numbers, characters and symbols which form the body of material which the computer receives, processes and outputs. (Information, a term often used interchangeably with data, can be regarded as the set of data which is relevant to a user in a particular context.)

LANGUAGES. A *language* is a system of numbers, characters and symbols together with a set of rules for combination and arrangement. Languages form one component of communication and permit society to give expression to its view of the world. And there must be languages by which to communicate with computing machines. Since the binary language of computers is far removed from languages employed by humans, several translating steps break down the relatively high-level symbolism into increasingly finer steps until it is all represented by binary

Small computing systems can make use of a mini-computer central processing unit. Photo courtesy Digital Equipment Corporation.

digits. The machine performs its operation, reconstructs the resulting data into symbolism, and outputs it in printed or graphic form which can be understood by the user.

In order to write programs more easily, new languages are constantly being developed in forms closer to languages in which users think and communicate and farther from the structural requirements of the machine. Languages evolve, continually building new forms from old ones. Dialects develop in user groups, and soon many special-purpose languages are available to particular application areas.

Computers are built to operate internally on binary conditions, i.e., any system in which only two states are possible such as on/off. A binary number system uses only two numbers: zero (0) and one (1). Computer operations symbolize both data and instructions in binary form. On the other hand, humans think better in terms of decimal numbers, words and drawings than in binary numbers. Thus there can be problems in translations between human languages and computer languages.

In utilizing the earliest machines, the users made extensive efforts to accommodate the machine rather than themselves. Therefore, much time was spent in coding instructions in binary notation (machine language). In those days, ma-

chine cost was so great as to justify the assignment of large numbers of personnel to provide data and programs to keep a machine productive. However, this situation is now reversed: Personnel is the larger cost of computing as machines become less expensive.

As emphasis turned to making the machine do more of the tedious work and the user to applying talent at higher levels of application, the logical step was to have the computer perform more and more of the translation from human languages to machine binary language.

From machine languages, problem-oriented languages such as FORTRAN (Formula Translation) and COBOL (Common Business Oriented Language) were developed for scientific and business applications, respectively. As the range of applications has broadened, features of both languages have been merged into general-purpose languages such as IBM's PL/1 (Programming Language One) which combines such features as the scientific calculation notation of FORTRAN and the input/output formatting ease of COBOL.

New languages are being developed constantly which enable users of special applications such as graphics to construct personalized sets of high-level commands. The user creates commands and defines what they mean in an operating context. Application systems such as STRUDL (Structural Design Language), STRESS (Structural Engineering System Solver) and COGO (Civil Engineering Coordinate Geometry) are engineering examples of this language type.

PROGRAMS AND APPLICATION SYSTEMS. A *program* is a set of instructions specific to a task, written in a selected language, operating on particular hardware, performing specific functions on data input and yielding specific output. An *application system* is a set of such programs, instructions for their use and specifications for required data, all of which are directed toward achieving some useful end product.

The development of application programs or systems normally follows a life cycle. The discipline inherent in this life cycle often gives the user insight into the problem. Computing is a very demanding discipline since every step of logic must be explicitly laid out and specified in detail. Human communications frequently go astray when the use of specific words or phrases have totally different meanings to people trying to communicate. While a person can sometimes be less than precise in conversation, computers demand extreme precision, and one must be extremely careful in using languages and structuring problems.

The first step in the life of a program is to define the problem. As in any design situation, if the problem is set up incorrectly, the real one may not be identified, or the wrong problem may be solved elegantly but without purpose.

Second, alternative solutions are proposed and evaluated in terms of relevant criteria: availability of similar programs already developed, feasibility of achieving a solution within estimated time and cost of development, etc. Once an approach is selected, the program is designed in terms of language, machine, data required, logic, processing, user interaction, etc.

Coding refers to the actual writing of programs using a particular language. Once written, the program is put into the machine via punched cards, keyboard terminal, etc., to see if it works.

Getting the bugs out of the program involves two stages. First, the rules of the language must be followed properly so that the machine will execute the program and the output results can be examined. The output must then be carefully scrutinized to insure that the logic embodied in the program is, in fact, what the user intended. Avoiding this step of

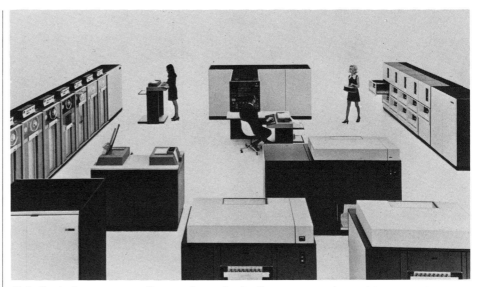

Relatively large computing systems typically use a variety of input and output units. In the center is a keyboard/printer operator console, attached to the central processing unit; at right are magnetic disc units; at right foreground are high-speed line printers; at far left are tape drives, in front of which is a card read/punch unit. Photo courtesy International Business Machines Corporation.

Operator consoles are checkpoints for information flowing through the system, often including a cathode ray tube display and a keyboard that allow the operator to communicate with the computer. Photo courtesy International Business Machines Corporation.

analysis may result in many faulty uses of computing since a computer can spew out incorrect or illogical data just as fast as it can produce correct output. Simply because the program operates does not insure its correctness. This discipline and the extensive time often required to trace sources of program logic errors are probably the biggest revelations and sources of irritation to new users of computing.

Concurrently with the program's being "debugged" and made operable, required data should be assembled and prepared; operating instructions are devised to direct the users and machine operators in the use of the application. Implementation then sees the program applied to real situations.

With time, programs are modified to update them, to expand capabilities and to alter formats. These modifications and alterations result from users becoming familiar with computing, gaining confidence in the operational programs and discovering new ways in which to apply computing.

Some programs exist indefinitely without modification. However, in the life of most programs, questions arise as to whether the program should be abandoned, be phased out in favor of rewriting the program as part of a larger or different system, or be integrated into larger systems with little modification. These questions are studied in terms of program capabilities, capacity to develop and maintain larger systems, available staff and computing power, costs of development and operation, and costs versus anticipated benefits.

DEVELOPMENT. Firms can access large computers through terminals or can have dedicated in-house systems. Programs can be developed by in-house staff, by consultants, or through user groups or through joint ventures.

In-house staff can range from the one-person office doing the programming and operation to the large offices having separate staffs for development (systems analysts and programmers) and for operations (keypunch, digitizer and machine operators).

Computing consultants are available from one-person specialists to large consulting firms, all offering a range of feasibility, development and operation services. Some firms specialize in fields such as management information, engineering, planning, graphics, etc. Obtaining services from independent consultants gives the user the ability to obtain expertise in particular areas as needed.

Many companies have invested in developing applications to meet particular markets. Most often these applications fall into one of two categories:

—An application may meet a particular need, in which case the procedure is well defined and is commonly accepted throughout the user market. Many applications in engineering and management fall into this category where there is a limited number of ways of performing given functions.

—A generalized application can be tailored to particular user needs and operating environments. These programs give the user latitude in defining terms; the manner in which data is entered, stored and retrieved; and specification of format and content of output. Data management and mapping applications are examples.

User groups exist for special interests and form either around application areas or around particular hardware. For instance, Automated Procedures for Engineering Consultants, Inc. (APEC) serves the engineering community; the 1130 Users Group serves those using the IBM 1130, a widely employed computing system. In each case, the common interest is in sharing development for a mutually accepted purpose.

Advantages in seeking software development companies or user groups that have developed applications are:

—Programs can be obtained for a fraction of the development cost, if one is willing to accede authorship to others.

—The application design has the benefit of more than one user's expertise, assuming it doesn't turn out as a camel.

—The application has probably undergone more extensive debugging than it normally would under a single user.

—Better user and operating documentation is provided, which is necessary if multiple users are involved and which frequently is never done properly in-house, due to lack of funds or time.

In a joint venture, two or more firms decide on a common need, draw up specifications for the application and develop it in any of the ways previously described. An obvious advantage is that each participating firm shares in only a portion of development costs. Data may be shared among the firms, or safeguards may be employed to insure security of data.

An impediment to joint ventures of this type is the inability of firms to agree on program specifications due either to real or imagined differences in operational needs and methods. An uncompromising position in such a situation leads to no application being developed, whereas investment in an application which is not totally designed in-house might provide a good return.

ACQUISITION. Programs can be acquired by purchase, lease or trade.

In purchasing, the user pays a one-time fixed fee and gains the right to use the application, usually with covenants not to resell or give away. Some features which may be included as services in the right of purchase are documentation, sample problems, assistance in installation and periodic improvements. Under these terms, a user normally obtains a set of programs which can be executed and used but cannot be altered to meet personal needs. Often the supplier will, for a fee, modify the programs, tailoring the operations to specific users.

Leasing gives the user the option of discontinuing the use of an application if, in the future, competing programs seem to be more appropriate or if the need for the application ceases. Services identified above in acquisition by purchase usually accompany leasing arrangements.

Trading of programs can be arranged in terms of services, consulting, data, machine time, etc. Trading probably occurs infrequently, due to:

—The difficulty in assigning relative values to the applications under consideration.

—The fact that the applications were not originally designed for others to use and, therefore, may be more user-specific and may be insufficiently documented.

—A general proprietary attitude toward applications.

As more accurate costs are assigned to applications and as user attitudes change, trading could become a means by which firms can increase their capabilities at greatly reduced development costs.

PEOPLE

Computing involves the client, the user, the development staff and the operating staff.

As in any design problem, the client may or may not be the user. Most often, the client pays the bills and sets policy, but the user implements the solution in a day-to-day operational environment. Whether developed by in-house staff or by contract, whether purchased, leased or traded, views of both policymaker and user must be considered in acquiring computing capabilities. Many applications have failed to be used effectively because the user was unconvinced of its value, not involved in its development, unclear on its proper use, etc. Computing

Terminals used in time-sharing operations provide capability for message preparation, message editing, on-line transmission and reception, and may consist of an operator console, display monitor and optional printer. Photo courtesy Teletype Corporation.

Drum plotters operate by rotating the paper on a drum in one direction and moving the pen on an axis at a right angle. Photo courtesy Gerber Scientific Instrument Company.

requires new attitudes and in some ways new approaches to thinking about problems on the part of the user.

The design, development and implementation of computing applications can be performed by a single individual or can be divided into tasks to be performed by many individuals, depending

on the scale and complexity of the project.

Systems analysts define problems and design solutions. They work with the user to establish objectives, to identify procedures and logic, and to design input/output. They design solutions in terms of program and data elements, their interrelationships and the procedures for implementation. Programmers construct programs and integrate them into the total system. Even when these functions are performed by different people, roles are not always clearly defined. A major constraint for analysts and programmers is that they must work within limitations imposed by available hardware and languages.

Operating staff prepare data for processing, perform the processing and assemble the output for distribution. Additionally, they maintain physical files of cards, discs, tapes, manuals, etc.

Design professionals initially may not understand computing. Computing professionals may not understand design problems and procedures. This has frequently led to difficulties in combining their efforts to achieve useful applications. Many design firms have become well versed through experience in computing and have developed useful applications. Additionally, a new generation of design graduates is emerging: those who have had some formal training in computing, who accept it as a useful tool and who are eager to put it to use. As more of these new professionals rise to positions of leadership, computing will find its way more easily and naturally into professional practice.

OPERATIONS

Location, access and processing mode affect the manner in which computing systems are used and must be considered in developing an operating environment.

Computers may be physically located

on the premises, i.e., on-site, in-house, on-desk or in-pocket. Conversely, the computer can be located at a remote site such as a service bureau or university.

In one manner of accessing computers, data is entered and received at the site of the main computer. At the opposite extreme is entry and receipt of data at remote sites through use of terminals. They can be teletype typewriters, small card-read/punch and line printer groups, display scopes or intelligent terminals. Where most terminals simply receive and transmit data over distances to the main computer, intelligent terminals perform a limited amount of computing prior to or following receipt or transmission of data.

Two modes in which applications can be processed are *batch processing* and *time-sharing.* In batch processing, all programs and data for an application are collected and processed in discrete passes through the computer. Time-sharing allows many users to use a computer simultaneously. Because a computer processes data so much faster than the user can respond, a computer can be set up to perform operations on several other programs while awaiting further instructions from any of the several users. Thus each user appears to have the full attention of the computer. This processing is useful for interactive applications in which the user "converses" with the machine, giving instructions and data and responding to the output of the machine with further input. Highly personalized, high-level languages are employed to facilitate this dialog.

TECHNIQUES

Within any functional area of practice there can be simple to very complex applications. For instance, there are applications for specifications text processing, ranging from simple listings of punched cards to systems which permit features

such as word indexing and building concordances, elaborate formatting, word search-and-replace, etc. A few suggested levels of computing techniques are discussed.

DATA PROCESSING. Frequently used to describe all computing applications, this term can be used to depict elementary applications not involving any of the more elaborate techniques. Data processing involves straightforward routine data collection and processing for record keeping, updating data files and displaying output. Applications such as basic project cost accounting, general accounting, mailing lists, elementary inventory systems and basic text printing are examples. Data processing is the level at which most firms begin to use computing and to realize their earliest returns.

NUMERICAL ANALYSIS. Basic data processing and extensive computation are both required for numerical analysis. Scientific approaches to analyzing and designing civil, structural, mechanical and electrical engineering problems most often fall into this category. Today, computing makes possible many engineering applications which before were only theoretically and conceptually possible due to the required computational complexity. Statistical methods for both analysis and prediction are widely employed.

INTERACTIVE APPLICATIONS. These are made feasible through advanced terminal equipment, expanded computing equipment and new high-level languages. A teletype can be used to type in data and commands and have the results displayed immediately. Based on those results, the user enters further commands and data. The user can choose part of a program to execute, recycle parts of the program to alter assumptions or data, or decide to sign off and think about the problem. Graphic devices have im-

mensely expanded the field of interactive programs. Text, numerical, vector and spatial data can be displayed and altered with the use of scopes, keyboards and light pens. Data is quickly displayed, changes made and the altered data displayed for immediate examination. Color displays add yet another dimension to this interaction.

DATA BASE MANAGEMENT. Data and programs are viewed in a highly modular fashion when applying this concept. Modules are combined to produce results, which can be end products or input to other modules. The user moves freely through data and programs at varying levels of detail. Graphic display terminals increase the dynamic aspects of this approach.

In the long run, data management systems are essential to the profitability and success of any computer-aided design system. The general objective is to create data bases which can, in whole or in part, be used repeatedly. Data management systems must be created to permit construction and maintenance of such data bases.

SIMULATION. At any level, simulation provides an abstraction (model) of a part of the real world for purposes of study. Constructing a model permits examination of the effects on some of its parts when others are altered. Thus the sensitivity or impact of decisions on certain system variables can be studied as other variables are changed. Simulations can be simple equations or complex data structures representing entire spatial schemes.

APPLICATIONS

Computer applications can be categorized by such factors as area of practice, function within an office, type of hardware used, type and complexity of mathematical or processing technique. This section examines types of applications in use organized around functional need. It is not a catalog of available applications. Such catalogs are necessarily voluminous, incomplete and quickly outdated, and descriptions would be insufficient to permit evaluation. Rather, *categories* of applications are identified to illustrate the breadth of development.

One long-term objective of professionals involved in computing is to create *total information systems*. Many programs have been created and much data collected in companies, institutions and agencies. Even within these organizations there is likely to have been little coordination among the applications and probably redundancy in the data collected. This somewhat inefficient process has been necessary as hardware developed and users gained experience through problems of application design and implementation.

There is now beginning to be a concern for coordinating these disparate efforts. Larger data bases are developed in which basic facts on many relevant topics can be organized. Modular programs are generated to perform specific functions. Users having different information needs which can be derived from common data elements can assemble the program modules, extract data elements needed and combine and use them for their specific purposes.

MANAGEMENT INFORMATION. This embraces all aspects of a firm's operations, permitting analysis, budgeting and control of resources in a timely manner. Computer-based systems support these functions by rapidly processing data of time, income, expense and schedule and by displaying the information in a variety of useful formats.

Project accounting and general company financial activities can be studied through a variety of reports: balance

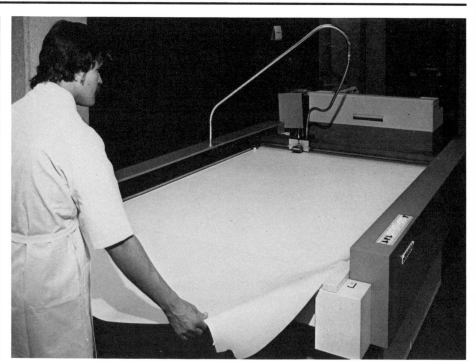

Large flatbed plotters work with the paper stationary and the pen moving incrementally on orthogonal axes. Photo courtesy California Computer Products, Inc.

Plotter/digitizers may include free-floating cursors for inputting drawing descriptions. Photo courtesy Gerber Scientific Instrument Company.

sheet, income and expense statement, office earnings, projected billings and income, cash flow projection, aged accounts receivable, etc. Such accounting and management systems have long been employed throughout the business world and have significant value to firms of all sizes. Specific applications to architectural offices are discussed in Chapter 6.

Project cost accounting tracks labor and direct and reimbursable expenses of projects; comparisons with budgets and income can be made for progress and performance evaluation. As project management techniques become more complex, computer-based systems are necessary to produce information faster and often in new forms. Control-oriented project budgeting and scheduling techniques with CPM and PERT characteristics (see Chapter 17) are useful in giving advance warnings so that design and construction problems can be anticipated and be more easily resolved. Chapter 10 provides additional discussion on the subject of budgeting and scheduling.

Cost estimating systems, among the earliest computer applications developed, require descriptions of buildings in terms of quantity and configuration of systems and materials. Components can be measured from plans manually, and the data entered through punched cards or magnetic tape; or plans can be digitized.

These cost estimating programs calculate lengths, areas and volumes of components and apply unit costs from files of building component data, kept current with market conditions. Factors for inflation, location and other variables are applied to each unit cost. Costs of the component are multiplied by the quantities taken off. The user can now have various detail and summary reports for analysis by building components, aggregated by construction trade category, by portion of the building or project, or by other categories discussed in Chapter 12.

Advantages of the application are similar to many such applications: It is conceptually simple, reduces tedious calculations, decreases arithmetic errors, permits easy substitution of interchangeable components to study alternate schemes, shortens time required to produce estimates giving more timely feedback to design, etc.

As in many applications, the output is only as good as the input quantities, costs and adjusting factors; and these inputs are all dependent on the user's judgment.

PLANNING. Computers have been widely used to reduce voluminous planning data into graphic and tabular formats. Plotters and scopes have been useful in summarizing, analyzing and displaying large amounts of data using perspective, graphing, mapping and contour-modeling techniques. Demographic data, land use data, land division geometry, engineering surveys and drawings, transportation models of people, vehicles and goods, and perspective views of land and structures are all well suited to analysis and graphic documentation with computers.

Economic analysis of proposed projects is often an interactive application because there are so many possible combinations of variables and so many ways to structure the problem such as what is the expected rate of return, how much building should be built, what is the required rent.

These programs can be deterministic, i.e., they give a solution to one of these questions using a given set of data; or they can be exploratory, i.e., given ranges on the variables, feasible solutions arising from the combination of variables can be reported for further investigation.

Programmable pocket calculators permit many of these analyses to be performed as project alternatives are considered. However, presently these computers do not permit permanent output records of data or results of computation, nor can they operate from extensive data bases. Applications requiring larger data files can be accessed with portable terminals using the nearest telephone.

PROJECT PROGRAMMING. Architectural and planning programming deals with resources in terms of numerical data and relationships of spaces, students, patients, faculty, areas, cars, costs, etc. Chapter 11 discusses these relationships. The computer is appropriate for areas such as statistical analysis, summaries of space requirements, preliminary cost estimating, plots of area requirements and functional relationships, feasibility studies and preliminary equipment scheduling.

Projects under design as well as completed projects can be analyzed regarding areas, functional relationships, project costs, equipment, etc., which often can provide input information into other design problems. Computer programs can assist these functions in varying degrees.

A project program can provide the beginning base to which a multitude of other data can be added as the project matures. For instance, an initial data base could be simply space identification and area; subsequently, data on dimensions, occupants, equipment, finishes, engineering performance criteria and enclosure construction could be added. Cost estimates, finish schedules, equipment schedules, perspectives and other information could be generated from the basic data.

DESIGN. In support of design efforts, many of the same approaches discussed above are continued in both printed and graphic form. There are also many applications for both analysis and design in environmental engineering disciplines such as civil, structural, mechanical, electrical and acoustical, and in transportation. Interior design programs can generate finish, color and furnishings schedules; study traffic and communication flows to find near-optimal solutions; draw perspectives of complex forms.

Designers can assemble standard components having predetermined design and engineering characteristics. Design decisions thus could be projected for costs and time of fabrication, shipment and erection.

Routines for space allocation have been the subject of considerable development effort. The problem is to develop two- and three-dimensional placement of spaces based on area, volume, adjacency, communication and other programmatic criteria. Inventories of existing or proposed spaces and equipment are developed and studied for misuse, multiple use, overuse or underuse.

DOCUMENTATION. There are currently available computer support systems for preparation of both textual and graphic documents as used in practice today.

Proposals, contracts and specifications—in fact, any written material used repetitively with modification—are adaptable to text processing. For successful application, there should be a master text which incorporates standard paragraphs and lists. The user selects those elements appropriate to immediate needs and edits for specific data (terms, location, materials, etc.). The computer prints out the edited copy by inserting, replacing and omitting text as necessary. The resulting document is tailored to the project; the master file remains intact. Of course, the master file can be updated in similar fashion. Review and editing can be performed by writing changes on printed pages and having the changes keypunched; or the user can directly interact with the material displayed on a scope through keyboards and light pens. Hard copy can reproduce exactly the final

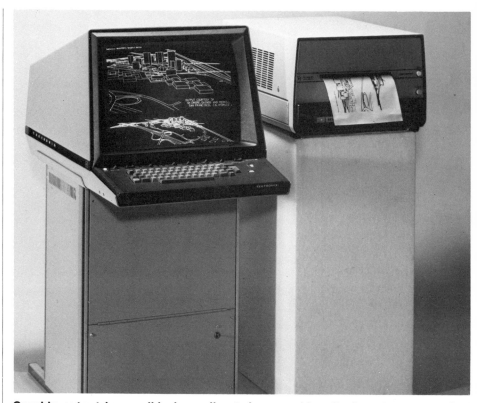

Graphic output is possible by a direct-view graphics display storage terminal and/or a hard copy device. Photo courtesy Tektronix, Inc., with display by Skidmore, Owings & Merrill, San Francisco.

acceptable copy displayed on the screen.

Plotters and scopes can be used in preparing site, architectural and engineering drawings. Building and site geometry can be depicted in terms that can be processed and drawn by the graphic hardware. Designs of entire rooms down to door details can be standardized and stored in the computer; the user can assemble these elements and have computing hardware draw them with appropriate coordination, dimensioning and notation. Plans, elevations, sections and perspectives (with or without hidden lines) can be generated, revised and regenerated. Finish hardware and color schedules can be produced, and checks performed for consistency, errors or omis-

sions. More accurate cost estimating and project scheduling can result from this kind of data base.

Some checking is possible for conflicts of building components, e.g., intersection of structural and mechanical elements. Similar checking is possible for compliance with codes, e.g., fire ratings of walls and doors used.

TOTAL INFORMATION SYSTEMS. One can imagine the types of applications mentioned, as well as many more not covered here, being coordinated and integrated into very comprehensive systems. Efforts thus far have produced fairly large-scale systems such as management and accounting as well as cost estimating and project scheduling. Much more work remains to be done before a management information system is possible which truly incorporates comprehensive planning, design, production and construction. But many of the basic elements are now available and extremely useful in themselves.

IMPLEMENTATION

Initial ventures with computing should be undertaken carefully and with reasonable planning. Small firms, lacking the need and resources to have a large investment in computing, can approach it in measured steps.

Time-sharing services are accessed through terminals placed in the office and use ordinary telephones. Users pay for monthly terminal rent plus time used on the computer and volume of data and programs stored. An alternative is to run in batch mode on computers at a local service bureau, university or company that makes excess time available.

Unless a firm has a staff person with computing experience, initial applica-

tions should probably be ones that are already developed and offered on a service basis by companies or by organizations. These programs will have been debugged and tested thoroughly so that the new user can concentrate on application rather than on problems with programs.

Where possible, cooperative ventures of two or more firms can share the cost of a terminal or of computer personnel. Assistance in analyzing needs and costs of applications can be obtained from consultants in industry or educational institutions.

An initial application should be one that is readily definable in terms of input, logic and output. Cost estimating, general accounting and simple structural design are common examples of first applications. Success breeds confidence. Therefore, one should undertake an application that has a high probability of success. Start with automating manual techniques that lend themselves to automation; further steps can lead to applications which are conceptually possible but impractical or impossible by manual means; in-

creased experience will foster new ideas and ways of approaching problems.

A few precautions in getting started:

—No computer application can be successful without support and involvement of the user.

—The largest expense in using computing is in personnel for analysis, programming, operations and education. In general, hardware and computing time are becoming a smaller share of the total cost.

—There are temptations to use the computer because it is available (but is it appropriate?); it can handle large volumes of data (but are they relevant?); and computer output is impressive (but is it relevant, right and readable?).

—Frustrations lead one to imbue the computer with personal characteristics and blame foul-ups on the machine. Most often, the mistakes are human, magnified by the speed and demanding logic of the machine.

—A willingness to share, to relinquish pride of total authorship and to cooperate with fellow practitioners will advance the

EXHIBIT 15-1. SELECTED ELEMENTS IN A POTENTIAL TOTAL INFORMATION SYSTEM

COMPANY	PROJECT	
Management information —Financial —Project —Personnel —Cost control —Schedule control —Contracts —Policies and procedures	Planning —Demographic —Land use —Facilities inventory —Site engineering —Landscape —Transportation —Economic Programming —Inventories and surveys —Economics —Functional relationships —Design criteria Design —Synthesis —Analysis —Visual representation	—Engineering —Building system and component selection Documentation —Drawings (visual) —Specifications (written) —Schedules Construction —Cost control —Schedule control Evaluation —Analysis

usefulness of computing as well as improve the practice.

The question of whether or not to commit to computing is not easy to answer. Approaching the problem by considering benefits and costs is the most rational way; yet it can be frustrating since not all benefits and costs can be reduced to objective statements and subjected to evaluation. In assessing benefits, one should be conservative; in assessing costs, one should be generous. It is easy to let enthusiasm replace realism.

Once applications are operational, there are potential benefits which can be somewhat objectively viewed:

—Time of professionals can be freed for other productive tasks, with the correlative impact of increased productivity.

—Professional services are improved through ability to analyze more alternative solutions in a given time period and through offering new services.

—Sale of computer-based services can help support R&D efforts.

Other benefits not so easily quantified:

—Information with fewer errors is available faster to decision makers.

—More strongly systemized approaches to structuring problems, organizing data and making decisions can lead to clearer decision making, to new approaches for problem solving and even to undertaking problems previously not considered possible.

—Interaction and cooperation can be enhanced among design disciplines.

Costs to be considered objectively:

—Personnel time must be devoted to developing, documenting, using and updating applications; machine operators must be available for data preparation, processing and maintenance.

—Hardware costs are items such as lease payments, data and program storage and use charges, maintenance costs and telephone lines (for teleprocessing).

—Overhead costs involve space, utilities, paper, computing supplies, etc.

Some costs are hard to define such as educating personnel to understand, accept and use computing.

At best, one can assign costs to items that are quantifiable; be aware of the subjective factors; and, on balance, decide if the venture is appropriate from business, technical and emotional viewpoints of the particular professional services firm.

Computing needs to be recognized for what it is, not for what it is not: It is a tool, not a panacea. It can be a very powerful tool when employed properly; it can be a demanding expensive taskmaster when used carelessly or frivolously. Without its use, many problems could not be identified, studied or solved.

The computer has moved from a prestige symbol, enclosed in glass and on display, to a diligent member of the professional team. Its faultless memory, accuracy and speed are good support functions to professional creativity, intuition and innovation.

Historical deterrents in using computing have been cost, difficulty of programming and lack of imagination in application. Cost is being met by less expensive hardware, although personnel cost is increasing. More powerful languages make programming easier. And, as the number of professionals involved in the science and art of computing grows, one can anticipate yet higher quality and more pervasive application. Used appropriately, computing can improve efficiency and effectiveness as the architectural profession seeks to deliver a fuller range of services in tighter economic and tougher market environments.

BIBLIOGRAPHY

Arcaid, The ARChitect's Computer Graphics AID. Robert Wehrli, Max J. Smith and Edward F. Smith. Salt Lake City: University of Utah Computer Science Division and the Advanced Research Projects Agency of Dept. of Defense, 1970.

Part 1 of a two-part research project; develops specifications for a computer-aided design system based on computer graphics for architects, engineers and other design professionals.

The Architect and the Computer. Boyd Auger. New York: Praeger, 1972.

Describes how computers may aid in reshaping architectural practice to be more responsive to client needs and to provide a more expert and coherent total design service; a specific automated drafting system comprehensively detailed.

"Architecture? Absolutely!" *Progressive Architecture,* April 1973.

Shows use of a computer model as an integral part of University of Louisville Urban Studies Center approach to the delivery of community services.

Bibliography of the Computer in Environmental Design. Kaiman Lee. 3 vols. Boston: Environmental Design & Research Center, 2nd ed., 1973.

Architecture, site planning, gaming, simulation, costing, office management, etc.; a data base with more than 2,000 entries.

"Can a 54-Year-Old Architectural Firm Find Romance and Happiness with an Interactive Computer System?" Clifford D. Stewart and Kaiman Lee. *Progressive Architecture,* July 1971.

Describes the development and capabilities of an interactive computer-based design system, ARK-2, involving graphic, text and numerical processing; well illustrated.

"Color Computer Graphics for Architecture." Donald P. Greenberg, S. Robert Hastings and David Simons. *Architectural Record,* September 1973.

Discusses research in developing perspectives using opaque color faces instead of lines.

Computer Applications in Architecture

and Engineering. G. Neil Harper, ed. New York: McGraw-Hill, 1968.

Emphasizes practical applications for professional offices and includes topics such as engineering, architectural production, accounting, specifications, etc.; organization and function of a computer in a design office.

"Computer Applications in Surveying and Land Development." Gary Neuwerth. *Consulting Engineer,* September 1973.

Describes use of the computer for calculating and plotting fully annotated subdivision plots.

"Computer-Based Financial Management." G. Neil Harper. *AIA Journal,* December 1972.

Operations and output of the AIA financial management system.

"Computer Basics: Hardware." Jerald L. Ripley and Jarrell C. Grout. *AIA Journal,* July 1974.

Discussion of fundamentals of computing hardware components.

"Computer Basics: Software." Jarrell C. Grout. *AIA Journal,* July 1974.

Describes flow charting, languages and programming.

Computer Programs in Environmental Design. Kaiman Lee. 5 vols. Boston: Environmental Design & Research Center, 1974.

Descriptions and abstracts of 335 computer programs in architecture and planning; outstanding reference source.

"Computer Specifications Programs." Harold J. Rosen. *Progressive Architecture,* September 1971.

Stresses features of computer-based text processing applications used for specifications.

"A Computerized Cost Estimating System." *Architectural Record,* November 1972.

Describes cost estimating system established by a construction and consulting firm to provide early pre-design stage estimates based on mathematical models of building types;

estimates refined and improved as design progresses.

Computers. Fred J. Steinberg. New York: Franklin Watts Inc., 1970.

Basic introduction to theory and technology of computers written in clear, concise language, removing much of the complexity and mystery from computing.

Computers and Society. Richard W. Hamming. New York: McGraw-Hill, 1972.

An excellent overview of the digital computer and its relation to society; very readable for people who wish to know about computers without learning to run them.

Design and Planning 2: Computers in Design and Communication. Martin Krampen and Peter Seitz, eds. New York: Hastings House, Visual Communication Books, 1967.

Technical papers presented at the 1966 International Conference on Design and Planning at the University of Waterloo (Ontario); some topics: computer-generated graphics, digital simulation, artificial intelligence and man-machine relations.

"Developing a Computerized Automatic Engineering Graphics System." Felix A. Anderson. *Consulting Engineer,* May 1969.

Describes and illustrates some uses of computer plotting for engineering applications: plans, profiles, structural drafting and some detailing.

"Earthwork and Rock Analysis Computer Program for Building Sites." Kami Targal. *Consulting Engineer,* February 1973.

Focuses on use of computer for calculation of earthwork and an economic analysis, given soil conditions and localized costs; and for plotting of such applications as elevations for roads and utilities, soil profiles, cut/fill images, perspectives of existing or proposed terrain, etc.

"Energy Guidelines for Schools." Edward

Stephan. *American School & University,* February 1975.

Discussion of study sponsored by Educational Facilities Laboratories and the Fairfax County, Va., school system, simulating alternative operational and construction modifications to existing schools and testing impact on energy requirements.

"The Engineering Discipline of Tent Structures." Horst Berger. *Architectural Record,* February 1975.

Describes mathematical procedure, programmed for a computer, that allows a designer to predict shapes that result from prestress forces of self-supporting tensile roofs and the stresses anywhere in the materials; excellent illustrations.

"First Steps in Computer Use for Small Firms." David Lorenzini. *AIA Journal,* July 1974.

Discusses how small firms can begin computing through use of time-shared facilities.

"From Pencil Points to Computer Graphics." Murray Milne. *Progressive Architecture,* June 1970.

Reviews development and state of art of computer-aided graphic systems in architecture and planning.

"Highrise Office Design: It Can Be Systematic." G. Neil Harper. *AIA Journal,* March 1971.

Describes input and output of the Building Optimization Program developed in the Chicago office of Skidmore, Owings & Merrill.

"Inventing the Systems for Planned Expansion of University of Minnesota Health Services Complex." *Architectural Record,* September 1973.

Examines a proprietary system, Facilities Planning Data Bank, used in planning large projects with many rooms and elaborate sets of attributes and equipment; generates tabular data such as cost estimates, room attribute lists, occupancy densities, related areas and furnishings inventories.

Management with Computers. James J. O'Brien. New York: Van Nostrand Reinhold, 1972.

General overview of hardware and software for managers who are not computer oriented; excellent glossary.

Planning for Hospitals, A Systems Approach Using Computer-Aided Techniques. James J. Souder, Welden E. Clark, Jerome I. Elkind and Madison B. Brown. Chicago: American Hospital Association, 1964.

Detailed description of systematic programming and planning for health delivery using computer-based models.

"A Project Scheduling System That Really Works." Garrett Thompson. *Architectural Record,* April 1975.

Explains step-by-step use of a project scheduling system as a monitoring and forward planning tool in Turner Construction Co., implemented on time-sharing and with graphic output; considers user input and implementation.

Reflections on Computer Aids to Design and Architecture. Nicholas Negroponte, ed. New York: Petrocelli/Charter, 1975.

Anthology of opposing views on the subject by 25 authors in research, in practice and abroad.

"Second Generation Computer Specifications." Mike Gilford. *Progressive Architecture,* May 1972.

Reviews a computer-based specifications system that employs decision lists which are completed by the user; lists are used by the computing program to decide which material of the master specification applies and which may be deleted.

Spatial Synthesis in Computer-Aided Building Design. Charles M. Eastman, ed. New York: Halsted Press, 1975.

Detailed survey of the state of the art in having the computer contribute to spatial synthesis problems.

"The Use of Computers Instead of Drawings in Building Design." Charles M. Eastman. *AIA Journal,* March 1975.

Reviews the research and development of "Building Description System," a partially implemented computer-based system which treats buildings as collections of three-dimensional elements arranged in space and which permits display and analysis.

"A User's View of Computer-Based Financial Management." Peter Piven. *AIA Journal,* July 1973.

Discusses the AIA financial management system as used by an architectural firm.

Chapter 16
Office
Machines

JACK D. TRAIN, FAIA

Aside from the computer and the calculator, virtually all office machines on the market which have proved useful in the architect's office deal with communication and reproduction which implements communication. These machines have been developed primarily to serve other enterprises and have been adopted by architectural offices to cope with the increasing complexity of practice.

ACQUISITION AND USE

No machine has a place in an office unless it will either improve the quality of service or increase the office profit, or both. Quality can generally be evaluated in terms of speed, accuracy, appearance, completeness and dependability. Office profit can generally be evaluated in terms of speed (profit per time interval), cost differential between machine capital and operating costs compared with manual costs, and improving people productivity. Both short- and long-term values should be considered, answering such questions as whether the machine is a gadget or a tool, and whether it is a luxury or a necessity. When an analytical evaluation appears to justify machine usage, it may be wise to lease the machine and test its value before undertaking the permanent obligation of purchase. Each firm consciously or unconsciously sets a policy on the use of machines. Such a policy must be related to office size, character of the work and availability of subcontracted services.

The work of large offices tends to break down into specialized tasks which sometimes justifies the use of machines that a small office cannot warrant. Also, the large office frequently requires more sophisticated machinery than the small one in order to deal with the greater volume of work. Fortunately, machines are available in a wide range of sizes and characteristics, enabling the smaller office to utilize the latest technology.

Firms located in metropolitan areas can frequently reduce costs and focus their attention on professional tasks by having some typing, accounting, reproduction and computer services performed by local subcontractors, thus reducing the need for some office machines. But when they are deemed desirable, an important factor in their selection is the availability and quality of maintenance service. The breakdown of a machine that has become indispensable and has no backup can cause serious problems.

Service contracts are available for almost all office machines sold by reputable firms. The cost of a service agreement should be considered an integral part of the overall investment. Because the services included in the contract vary considerably from company to company and from plan to plan, careful scrutiny of the agreement is essential. Some firms eliminate problems with contracts by leasing all machines from the vendor and including the cost of the service as a part of the lease. Nearly all equipment is available with this sort of arrangement. Leasing costs should be investigated as they are probably the most accurate indicators of the total expenditure if the machine is purchased.

It is desirable to standardize equipment wherever possible. Standardizing all typewriters within an office will allow everyone to work on the same project during a crash program. Backup is assured, and service costs should be less.

As office machines become more sophisticated, training personnel in their use is of increasing importance. Skills once expected to be learned in schools must be specifically adapted to the machines to be used. Office machines often have capabilities which are not understood by the operators and are, unfortunately, unteachable to many employees who are unsympathetic to changing procedures.

Training and continuing education, either by the machine supplier or a service agency, must be available in order to obtain proper and profitable operation of any machine. As an office utilizes new machines, it often becomes desirable to utilize several machines in a complex interaction program. The machine operator accustomed to only one machine cannot visualize how several can work together. Training programs that acquaint the entire office (technical and nontechnical personnel) with the capabilities of all machines available are essential to optimal usage. These training costs must also be considered in evaluating the economics of machine usage.

Unrecognized costs frequently result from the very convenience and capability for which the machine has been acquired. For example, many copying machines are paid for on a cost per copy basis. Rapid and convenient reproduction, therefore, increases the manufacturers' income per unit. The result is a tendency to make more copies than are necessary. In addition, easy availability and the simplicity of operation have frequently created abuse by employees using the equipment for personal rather than office-related tasks.

Compared to many products, modern office machines are most reliable. But all complex mechanisms are subject to malfunctioning. As machines become more complex, prompt and expert service increases in importance. Any single machine indispensable to office operation is especially vulnerable to maintenance problems. Often, two smaller machines will provide better service than a larger one. Organization of office work to provide optional ways of performing the task becomes essential.

Many promising office machines have not gained as much usage as they deserve because of theft and accountability problems. Pocket calculators, measuring wheels, improved inking pens, complicated stencils and the like are too expensive to be purchased by individual office employees. Because of relatively infrequent use, offices cannot supply them for everyone. Security and checkout systems designed to prevent pilferage become so complicated that the user finds the device more of a burden than a tool. In some areas, machines as large as typewriters are often stolen. Bolted-down devices and machines large enough to discourage easy removal become desirable.

Improvements in office machinery are introduced frequently. In making the selection of any machine, consideration must be given to new technological developments and what is likely to become available in the future.

WORD PROCESSING

As Datapro Research Corporation explains it, "Word processing has been used to define a class of automatic typewriters that speed typed document output. In the broadest sense, however, the phrase encompasses all aspects of word-oriented message input, output and communications." Thus it includes both the system and equipment used to transform verbal, written or recorded ideas to a typed or printed form. In word processing, the way machines are used is every bit as important as the machines themselves. Various types of dictating and typing machines are included in this general classification.

DICTATING MACHINES. There is a wide variety of recording and playback machines available which can be used for dictating. General-purpose tape recorders can be employed, but, for efficient use by both the originator and the transcriber, machines designed specifically for dictation and transcription are recommended. Practically all dictating machines now use magnetic tapes or belts. Belt-type machines feature instan-

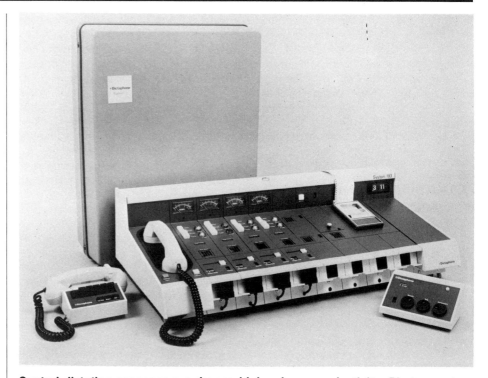

Central dictation processors enhance high-volume productivity. Photo courtesy Dictaphone Corporation.

taneous location of dictation on the belt but do not have as much capacity as most tape systems. Tape machines feature either the manufacturer's standard tape or commercial tape recorder cartridges.

Some tape machines enable the transcriber to work from the same tape soon after the originator begins dictation. Economical high-fidelity tape cartridges assure a readily available supply of recording medium for cartridge-type machines.

A dictating machine should have a sensitive microphone with convenient stop, start and rewind or reverse controls. A visible means for determining the length of recorded materials makes transcribing easier. A way of distinguishing between instructions and copy improves the transcriber's performance. Dictating machines range from hand-held battery-powered devices to desk models and can

be connected to telephone systems. The telephone instrument then becomes the machine's microphone.

A companion piece to any dictating machine is the secretary's transcribing unit. The transcribing unit and the dictating machine must be considered as an entity because the recording medium is often not interchangeable between units of different manufacturers.

TYPEWRITERS. Varying widely in cost, durability and features, nearly all machines suitable for office use are electric. Available features include a built-in erasing ribbon, changeable type styles and special-width carriages.

Some specialized typewriters are used in architects' offices. A parallel bar-mounted typewriter can be moved around a large drawing and notes can be typed directly onto the tracing. Machines with extra-large letters can be used for typing drawing titles.

Automatic or recording typewriters are those with a memory. They may also contain elements of a computer to help organize, search and retrieve information stored in the typewriter's memory. While often considered only as a device to rapidly retype form letters, specifications and other repetitive matter, these machines can greatly increase any typist's productivity. All original typing is done at draft speed. Corrections are easily made, and perfect final copy is produced at speeds up to 350 words per minute depending on the equipment used.

There are several dozen models of automatic typewriters being marketed. In the recording mode, whatever is typed on the machine is recorded on magnetic or punched paper tape or magnetic card. Errors are corrected by simply backspacing and typing over. The machine will play back what is recorded and can be set to stop at any point that the operator desires.

More complex machines enable the operator to "merge" old material with newly prepared copy and transfer it onto a new recording. Control symbols can be built into the recording to enable the machine to quickly locate specific parts of a recorded document. Some machines automatically respace words to provide copy justified or aligned on both right and left margins. Proportional spacing of individual letters is also a feature of some machines.

The control of storage and retrieval functions of an automatic typewriter is similar to that of a digital computer; and indeed some machines are designed to perform as the local terminal of a time-sharing computer system. New generations of the automatic typewriter are specialized mini-computers.

Automatic typewriters increase the productivity of the individual typist but per-

Automatic typewriters reduce time-consuming retyping of good material. Photo courtesy International Business Machines Corporation.

form best as a part of an integrated word-processing center. Properly utilized, typewriters offer a means of improving the status and responsibility of clerical workers.

CALCULATING

Of all the machines used in an architect's office, calculating devices show the most explosive growth both in availability and functions. In terms of calculating ability only, relatively inexpensive machines can perform as well as a large computer system. Some of the newer calculating machines feature programmable calculations and small memories. In applications where complete documentation of input and results is not required, these calculators can compete favorably with large computers.

Simple calculators are available as mechanical or electro-mechanical adding machines, and some provide a printed record tape. Machines calibrated to add feet, inches and fractions of an inch can be particularly helpful in the drafting room.

Most calculators are now electronic with integrated circuits. Hand-held battery-operated machines are economically competitive with a good slide rule. Such devices are capable of vast calculating power and are especially valuable for structural and civil engineers. For some operations, it is desirable to utilize a calculator that produces a printed record enabling the user to retrace calculations and verify the input. Programmable calculations enable the user to write simple calculating routines. Input to the calculator consists only of variables, thus simplifying the keyboard operation, reducing errors and speeding up the process.

DUPLICATING AND COPYING

There is no clear-cut distinction between duplicating and copying machines. Traditionally, duplicating has referred to the production of copies of legal- or letter-size documents prepared on a special master to permit reproduction. Copying has referred to the production of a copy of any previously written or printed material. The per page cost of a document produced by a duplicating operation is usually less than that of a document produced by a copying process. When many copies of a document are produced, the operation is called duplicating; when only a limited number are made, it is called copying.

SPIRIT DUPLICATORS. The simplest type of office duplicating equipment is the spirit duplicator, such as Ditto, which may have some application in the production of minor specifications. While low in cost, quality is poor and a limited number of copies can be obtained from one master.

STENCIL DUPLICATORS. These duplicators, among them mimeograph, have been the most common used by architects for specifications and reports. Copy must be typed on special stencils that permit ink to filter through the paper where the copy occurs. Masters are messy to handle especially after use on the duplicator. Corrections require special eradicator to patch the holes. A porous paper must be used which tends to be thicker than other papers.

Equipment is available to prepare stencils electronically from drawings or other camera-ready copy. Skilled operators using good equipment and paper can produce results similar to offset printing.

Hand-held calculators permit complex computations with user-written or pre-packaged programs. Photo courtesy Hewlett-Packard.

Pressure diazo printers produce rapid prints, requiring little power and no special ventilation. Photo courtesy Bruning Division, Addressograph Multigraph Corporation.

OFFSET DUPLICATORS. Using lithographic principles to produce copies, offset duplicators, such as Multilith, provide extremely high-quality reproduction at slightly higher cost than with stencil duplicators. Offset machines use metal, paper or acetate masters prepared either

photographically or by typing or drawing directly onto a special master. Typed masters are easy to prepare and relatively easy to correct.

Offset duplicators are somewhat more complicated than other types and require more operator care. Older machines tend to get ink on the operator and consequently are not popular with clerical workers. Larger offices or print shops with specially trained operators can afford machines with a built-in platemaker. Such machines automatically generate an offset master from camera-ready copy and feed it into the offset printer. High-quality copies are made at a high rate of speed.

COPYING MACHINES. In two decades, office copying machines have grown from a curiosity to a billion-dollar industry. While greatly improving communication, they are also partly responsible for the paperwork explosion that threatens to smother society in a blizzard of paper.

Office copiers operate by several different physical-chemical processes which are of only minor interest to users. Older technology required the use of coated or special papers. The feel, smell and appearance of the copy was much different from the original. Newer machines, whether reproducing on coated papers or not, produce copies which are sometimes superior in quality to the original. Bond paper copiers will copy on many materials in addition to paper. Mylar transparencies, card stock and adhesive-backed film can be processed.

There is a wide selection of copying machines designed to economically reproduce a few copies a month to several thousand a day. A wide variety of pricing plans, including purchase, various lease-purchase arrangements and many different lease plans based on copying volume, are available. Selecting the proper machine or combinations of machines requires considerable study of the office's copying needs.

Most copiers provide copies of standard letter- or legal-size documents. One way to reduce the physical volume of paper is to use a machine that produces copies at a reduced size. Machines are readily available to copy two legal documents onto one letter-size copy, thus lowering paper cost and filing space. Costs and the quantity of paper distributed can be further reduced by copying on both sides of the paper.

Various attachments increase the capabilities of copying machines. Automatic document feeders permit the reproduction of a number of documents without the assistance of an operator. Collating attachments automatically sort multipage reports into separate booklets. Devices which record the number of copies produced for different accounts enable the user to bill for copies or otherwise control the use of a copying machine.

Most copiers produce only black-and-white prints regardless of the color of the original. Machines have been developed to produce exact copies of multicolored documents. The machines are expensive, and the cost of copies is much greater than that of black and white.

Copying machines are being marketed as duplicators. By lowering the cost of multiple runs, copy machine manufacturers price their products to be competitive with offset duplicating for short- to medium-length runs. Since an office is likely to have a copying machine anyway, this pricing arrangement permits the elimination of a duplicating machine.

DRAWING REPRODUCTION

Because of the large size of most architectural and engineering drawings, the machines needed to duplicate or copy them differ greatly from those developed for general office reproductive needs.

BLUEPRINT MACHINES. The blueprint process used within the office is almost obsolete and has been largely replaced by the diazo process. However, blueprints obtainable from commercial reproduction houses are regularly used.

DIAZO EQUIPMENT. The most common system of drawing reproduction, diazo employs coated papers, a light source and an ammonia or chemical developing system. Machines vary from slow table models, suitable for making check prints in an office, to high-speed automatic-feed machines used in print shops. For best results, diazo processes require a translucent original.

In addition to copying drawings, the diazo machine can be used as an office copier. Because translucent originals are preferable for the diazo process, specialized office copiers have generally replaced diazo machines for copying and duplicating opaque original material.

Either ammonia solutions or ammonia gas machines are available. Many machines require ventilation systems to dispose of excess ammonia.

Flexibility in diazo machines is provided by the multitude of different kinds of papers available. Intermediate papers and films permit a new tracing to be produced from an old one. Papers producing dark backgrounds and white lines, papers with metallic finishes, and papers with black lines, blue lines or sepia lines on light backgrounds are all easily processed by diazo machines. Also available are those that, with the aid of special papers and dyes, produce multicolored prints from basically monochromatic originals.

OFFSET REPRODUCTION EQUIPMENT. An offset press of a size adequate to reproduce conventional size drawings is usually too expensive for most architects to own. Most offset-reproduced drawings are reduced to one-half the original drawing size. Even at one-half size, the machines designed for office use, rather than printer's use, are too small to print the large drawings that architects prefer. Consequently, most offset printing of drawings has been done as a result of drawing production techniques discussed in Chapter 18 or when the number of reproductions desired justifies the cost of the photomechanical service required to produce the offset master.

COPYING MACHINES. The same technology applied to office copiers can be used for reproducing drawings, provided the machines are made large enough. Because of the limited size of the market, manufacturers have not produced the low-cost, large platen machines required to make copies of architectural and engineering drawings. Most large platen office copier machines are so expensive that they can be used only by reproduction shops with a steady volume of work.

With office copier techniques, the architect is not limited to translucent originals. Pasted-up drawings can produce high quality prints without ghosting. Opaque decal tapes and preprinted details can be used as well as translucent materials.

PHOTOGRAPHIC REPRODUCTION EQUIPMENT. Most reproduction methods use some form of photography in the process, but the term, as mentioned here, means reproductions produced from a photograph of the original drawing. There are many processes and variations available from commercial print shops. In general, large optical systems are needed in order to prevent distortion in the reproductions. Cost for a limited number of copies is high in relation to other reproduction methods.

MICROFORM

As architectural offices get older and their volume of work increases, storage of records and filing for recall become major problems. To date, microform appears to offer the best solution to both. The miniaturizing of documents allows the storage requirements to be dramatically reduced. The convenience of storage also encourages appropriate reference to problems and details that have already been solved. One additional advantage to the use of microform is the fact that duplicate copies are extremely economical and thus will permit storage of records in two remote locations to eliminate the possibility of total destruction by fire or similar disaster.

Microform equipment is based on three more or less standard types of microform: roll film, microfiche and aperture card. Roll film is usually 16mm film wound on reels or mounted in self-feeding cartridges; 35mm and larger sizes are sometimes used. Microfiche is several individual pictures mounted or photographed onto a card. The usual configuration is 60 documents filmed on one 4×6-inch card. A variation uses strips of roll film inserted into a clear plastic holder. Aperture cards contain one frame per card and are usually 35mm or larger. Most viewing devices will accept any of the common types of microform. Even though an office may standardize on one type of microform, it is desirable to have machines capable of handling all three of the common types of microform because of the rapid expansion of information storage technology. Micropublishing of technical books and manufacturers' literature is increasing. Machinery should be flexible enough to accept microform from as many sources as possible.

There are two basic types of microform equipment: devices to produce the microform and to enlarge the images to usable size.

Microfilming is a photographic process. Producing film involves the use of cameras and film-developing chemicals. Machines roughly the size of a small office copier are available for producing microfilmed letter-size documents. While

Large-screen reader/printers combine viewing and copying of microform documents. Photo courtesy Eastman Kodak Company.

these machines can be operated by clerical personnel, most firms find it more economical to have the filming done by outside processors. Most processors will maintain a duplicate file of microfilmed works, providing document security through remote storage.

Drawings require rather large machines to produce a distortion-free photograph, and 35mm film is the smallest that will give reasonably accurate reproductions. While expensive, self-contained machines that photograph, process and produce an aperture card in a few seconds are used by some architects.

Machines used to view microformed documents are either readers or reader/printers. A reader consists of a film-holding device, light, lens and ground glass screen on which the microform

image is projected. A reader/printer adds a version of the office copier to the reading device in order to obtain a hard copy of the microformed document. The hard copy may be either the same size as the original or may be reduced or enlarged depending on the capabilities of the equipment. Naturally, the larger the print size, the more expensive the equipment becomes.

A major difference in various machines is the method used to locate individual documents. Roll- or cartridge-type films can be indexed by number of image or code symbols built into the film. Sophisticated systems can be designed which enable a user to locate a specific document in a very short time.

The selection of microform equipment must be carefully coordinated with the ways the microform will be used. An architect should utilize the service of a qualified specialist before embarking on a microform program.

GRAPHIC TRANSMISSION

While somewhat limited at the present time by the speed of the process, facsimile transmission may become a significant factor in the way architects perform their services. Present-day devices require four to six minutes to transmit an 8½×11-inch document over voice grade telephone lines (quite an improvement over mail service). Machines soon to be marketed will speed up transmission by skipping over all "blank" portions of the document. The big future of this equipment depends on the improvement of transmission facilities and equipment. Current uses include the transmission of sketches from office to office, office to field and office to consultant. Cost of equipment is low, but phone charges can be significant when toll calls are used.

Facsimile transmission and closed-circuit television have the potential of completely revolutionizing the operational procedures of architectural offices by permitting remote visual communication. This conceivably would permit a fairly large team practice to be carried on with each member working from home. The best consultant in the country can be utilized, regardless of remote location. Questions of construction in the field can be shown to architects in the office for consultation without taking the time to go to the field to see the problem firsthand.

ANCILLARY FUNCTIONS

There are several types of machines and equipment which are used in supportive roles in architectural offices.

COLLATING EQUIPMENT. Sorting reproduced materials into book form can be

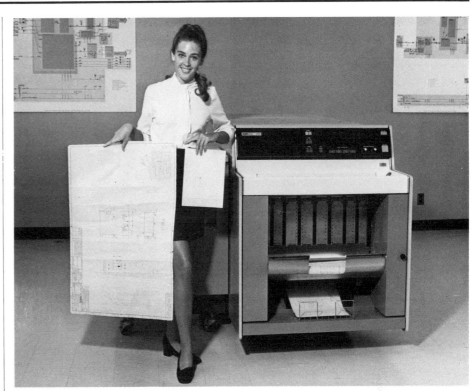

Engineering copying systems xerographically reproduce large-size drawings. Photo courtesy Xerox Corporation.

a time- and space-consuming procedure when done without the aid of a mechanical collating device. Some copying machines have built-in sorting bins which sort material as it is copied. The simplest sorting machine is a series of stacked boxes, similar to a bank of mailboxes, which provide a bin for each separate book. Mechanical gathering devices simultaneously strip the top sheet off several stacks of separate pages, allowing the operator to quickly gather the pages together into a booklet.

BINDING EQUIPMENT. Reports, specifications or brochures can be bound into a permanent form in several ways. Many systems use a paper punch and some type of mechanical fastener. The plastic spiral binder firmly binds together and allows the opened book to lie flat. Another type of plastic post-binder enables hard-bound books to be simply produced.

Adhesive bindings which glue the edges of pages together are a simple and effective way to provide permanently bound booklets. Some systems based on heat-softened adhesives enable pages to be removed or inserted after the initial binding.

Metal post and strip binders inserted in punched holes offer a convenient method of combining rapid assembly with easy insertion of new pages.

DRAFTING ROOM EQUIPMENT. Measuring wheels provide a convenient method of measuring and accumulating linear dimensions. These pocket watch-sized devices are very useful to estimators.

Planimeters are another mechanical device used for measuring areas, particularly the area of irregular shapes. They are frequently used in computing quantities of cut and fill.

The various types of drafting machines and other implements are beyond the scope of this discussion.

COMMUNICATIONS

While not thought of as office machines, communications equipment is a significant office cost and often performs work done by other machines.

TELEPHONES. The ubiquitous telephone instrument is so taken for granted that its full potential is seldom realized. Push-button "dialing," available in most areas, enables calls to be placed faster than by regular dialing. Automatic call-transferring devices, message and other recording devices, automatic dialing devices, amplified speaker systems and other accessories are available either as a part of the equipment supplied by the telephone company or purchased from commercial sources.

INTERCOMMUNICATION EQUIPMENT. Either competing with or as a supplement to telephone company equipment, intercom systems provide services similar to telephone equipment. The decision to use one or the other is usually based on economic and service considerations.

TELEPHONE DICTATING MACHINES. The telephone instrument can be used as the input device for dictating machines. Such equipment places a secretary as close as the nearest telephone.

AUDIOVISUAL

The most common machine used by architects to illustrate their accomplishments is the 35mm slide projector. Al-

Color copiers produce low-cost color copies of transparencies or full-color printed originals. Photo courtesy 3M Company.

though there are innumerable makes and models on the market, the Carousel model appears to be fast becoming the standard for the industry. It has these advantages: The standard Carousel tray will accommodate 80 to 140 paper-mounted slides, and a similar model called a universal Carousel slide tray up to 80 mix-mounted slides including thicker than paper; slides and trays are easy to install and change; the machine is light and easy to transport; the machine has become so widely used that it is frequently necessary to take only loaded tray(s) to the place of presentation since a suitable projector will be available there. Sales representatives can describe the merits of numerous lenses, but serious consideration should be given to the zoom lens, which greatly aids the set-up problem when all shapes and sizes of rooms are used for presentations.

All photographic buffs are aware of the vast visual superiority the 2¼-inch slide has over the 35mm. However, experience has proved that most offices which attempted to develop a 2¼-inch slide collection have changed over to 35mm for economy and convenience. Both development and equipment are considerably more expensive for the 2¼-inch slides.

Some offices have developed more sophisticated slide presentations using two slide projectors with a dissolve unit attachment that will alternate the projection of slides from each projector, fading one out as the alternate slide is faded in. This equipment can automatically time the slide changes, and a recorded sound device can be included to produce a

Self-contained camera processors make photographic reproductions of drawings, three-dimensional objects or microform on various types of film or paper. Photo courtesy Itek Graphic Products.

Facsimile copiers transmit graphic documents over ordinary telephone lines. Photo courtesy 3M Company.

Preloaded slide trays and projectors facilitate impromptu slide shows. Photo courtesy Eastman Kodak Company.

completely canned presentation. Even more complicated systems using three projectors simultaneously may be used.

Another type that has unique advantages is the overhead projector. This device permits the placement of a transparency of approximately 10×10 inches on an illuminated horizontal surface and, by a series of mirrors, project a large image on a vertical screen. Advantages, unique to this system, result from the possibility of pointing to areas of the transparency and even drawing on it while it is being presented. Certain copying machines permit quick and inexpensive acetate prints to be made of any opaque printed material either in black and white or color. Early models were large and unwieldy, but current ones can be folded into a manageable size for portability.

Opaque projectors are available which can project ordinary opaque printed documents. As the image projected is considerably weaker than other kinds of projectors, a darkened room is usually necessary.

The movie camera has been making inroads into architectural offices as a presentation tool. The stop-frame camera provides an inexpensive way of developing a concept before a client's eyes. By utilizing cameras designed for medical use, it is possible to conduct a people's-eye tour through a model, which is very enlightening for the client and useful to the architect.

While the more extensive use of machines offers hope of reducing the architect's personnel costs, most machines tend to improve performance rather than decrease the relative cost of personnel. The increasing complexity of professional services requires more machines to cope with current problems. But machines which will substantially decrease the architect's labor do not exist.

BIBLIOGRAPHY

Datapro Reports on Office Systems. Delran, N.J.: Datapro Research Corporation, updated monthly.

Provides information on the spectrum of office products and systems.

"Office Machines That Do More Than Type." James Swackhamer. *AIA Journal,* January 1970.

Discusses machines used for general office work and specifications as well as working drawings.

The Office: Magazine of Management, Equipment, Automation. Stamford, Conn.: Office Publications Co., monthly.

Office Product News. Garden City, N.Y.: United Technical Publications, Inc., 10 issues a year.

Above periodicals offer current information on office machines and systems.

Chapter 17 Network Scheduling

JAMES J. O'BRIEN, PE

The traditional method of representing scheduling factors in the construction industry has been the bar graph. Used extensively in the construction phase, it has also been the principal device used by designers to plan their own work. As a planning tool, the bar graph leaves much to be desired, particularly since it does not show sequence of operation. Activity spans are plotted, and sequences are thought out. As illustrated in Exhibit 17-1, if at a later time an arbitrary reduction in schedule is required, the bar graph is easily, but illogically, compressed.

In 1956, The Du Pont Company decided to study ways to utilize its new computers for construction scheduling. A combined team of mathematicians, operations research specialists and constructors worked together for more than a year. This team was joined by James E. Kelley Jr. of UNIVAC, a mathematician. The problem yet to be solved was a method of organizing scheduling planning intentions so that the computer could accept the information. Kelley recommended the use of a logical network to define the sequence of steps required during design and construction. This was rapidly developed, and computer software algorithms were prepared. The system developed by the Du Pont team was very sophisticated and received field testing in 1958.

At about the same time, the Navy Polaris special project office developed a network-based system called Program Evaluation and Review Technique (PERT). Calculation of the network in both systems defined a controlling or longest connected path through the network, which was called the critical path. The construction-based system which grew out of the Du Pont work was called the Critical Path Method (CPM). Initially, the two methods were different in at least 11 key ways, but today the difference is limited to one or, in some cases, no difference.

Through usage, both systems have be-come more simplified and less sophisticated. Perhaps the sophisticated applications are yet to come. Many computerized extensions of the basic network scheduling approach have been developed and are available. The basic important discovery in the process was not the computerization of the information but a common sense, self-disciplined method of expressing planning sequence. The development of a network simulates the human thinking process, permitting the scheduler to focus intensively on each area of activity in the present and then in the future. As the information is introduced into the network, the focus moves forward. The mind is not encumbered by having to recall details and reasons for interconnection because these have all been included in the network.

TRADITIONAL PROJECT PHASES

Exhibit 17-2 schematically describes the seven major phases of a project. All parties in the process tend to think of their portion as the major segment, which is only human nature. Many would describe this as a 2½-year construction project but that represents less than one-third of the actual time consumed. The architect is entering an active role after three years, and would tend to see the 1½ years of the design effort as 30 percent in terms of time, and the construction as 50 percent.

It is important that a perspective be maintained, as the major players tend to forgive their own roles. Accordingly, the owner will conveniently forget the investment of possibly three years of time prior to bringing an architect on board, yet will expend as much as a full year in arranging the funding and pursuing the bidding process for award. (This long time frame is typical for public work, more so than private.)

Each one of these areas could, and should, be carefully planned and scheduled. Detailed planning and scheduling does not necessarily shorten the time required. In fact, when full consideration is given to all the ingredients, the initial network plan generally projects a very pessimistic picture. This, in turn, brings the proper managerial forces to bear, and appropriate phasing can be instituted. Network planning applied early enough will help to provide the proper time context in which all parties have an appropriate time frame within which to work.

The owner is usually responsible for five of the seven phases. In the first three, the architect could add substantial input,

EXHIBIT 17-1. TYPICAL BAR CHARTS

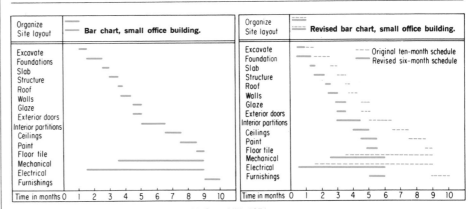

Source: *CPM in Construction Management*, McGraw-Hill, 1971.

EXHIBIT 17-2. TYPICAL PROJECT PHASES

RESPONSIBILITY

Owner	Concept/Budget							
Owner		Site						
Owner		Program						
Designer			Design					
Owner				Funding Bid and Award				
Contractor					Construction			
Owner								Move-In

| TIME (YEARS) | 1 | 2 | 3 | 4 | 5 | 6 | 7 | 8 |

EXHIBIT 17-3. PROJECT COMPONENTS SHOWN AS NETWORK (Time in Months)

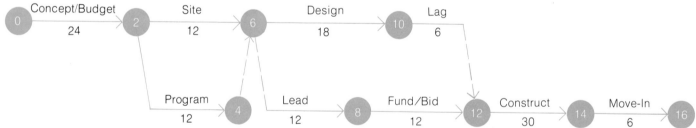

NETWORKING RULES: 1.) An activity is shown as a nonscalar line, with the direction of completion indicated by arrow. 2.) Figures in circles are event numbers, for identification of activities only. Assignment of numbers is abstract. Events have no time value. 3.) Activity 4-6 is added only to show definition between 2-6 "site" and 2-4 "program." It is sometimes called a dummy because it adds no logic. 4.) Activity 6-8 is a lead activity which indicates that "fund/bid" follows start of "design" by 12 months. 5.) Activity 10-12 is a lag activity which indicates that construction lags behind design by six months.

EXHIBIT 17-4. NETWORK TO TIME SCALE (Time in Months)

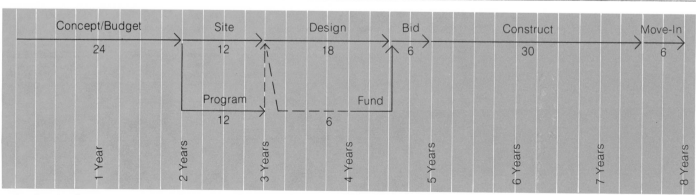

Note: Event numbers have been omitted because they interfere with the time scale. Activity "fund/bid" was broken into two more logical components: "fund" and "bid."

but in most cases has not even been selected. In an optimum situation, the design team could be preselected or function on a consulting basis to participate in the site selection, program preparation and even prebudgeting studies. Where this occurs, the design team can often institute overlapping or phased activity, which can shorten the overall process.

Any substantial shortening of the process saves in ultimate construction cost escalation so that consulting fees are paid back several-fold. In the public sector, even with scheduling improvements, the budgetary phase is often keyed to an annual cycle. If a project is not fully studied and included at an early enough point, the delay will not be a matter of weeks but a full year. To a degree, this occurs in corporate situations where the annual budget must be approved by owners or stockholders. However, in the private sector, there is usually more flexibility to accommodate special situations or problems. Exhibit 17-3 shows the project phases in network form. This is essentially a flow chart. Exhibit 17-4 illustrates the same network drawn to a time scale. Neither of these forms shows any information in addition to the basic block diagram of Exhibit 17-2. However, one advantage of networking is its ability to expand the detail at any required phase of the project.

Exhibit 17-5 is a NASA illustration showing a combined project network made up of several interconnected functional networks (fragnets). Two of these fragnets—one for R&D and one for construction—are expanded into more detail for actual performance.

PREDESIGN ACTIVITIES. In Exhibit 17-6, an example is given of the level of detail which can clearly spell out the stages in the preparation of an annual school budget. This is an actual example from the Philadelphia School District, and describes a series of steps to be taken by the School District Facilities Department,

EXHIBIT 17-5. NASA PERT NETWORK RELATIONSHIPS

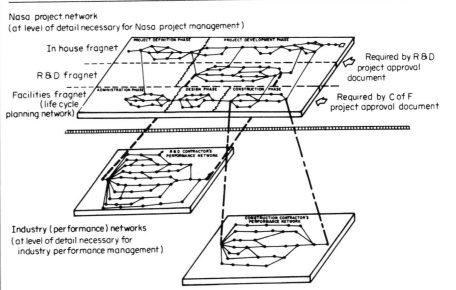

Source: CPM in Construction Management, McGraw-Hill, 1971.

EXHIBIT 17-6. CPM FOR PHASE 1 OF ACTUAL SCHOOL BUDGET PREPARATION

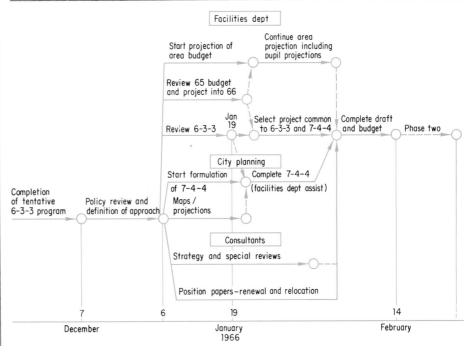

Source: Scheduling Handbook, McGraw-Hill, 1969.

EXHIBIT 17-7. CPM COMPARISONS OF FINAL BUDGET PREPARATION (Four-week public advertisement versus six-week)

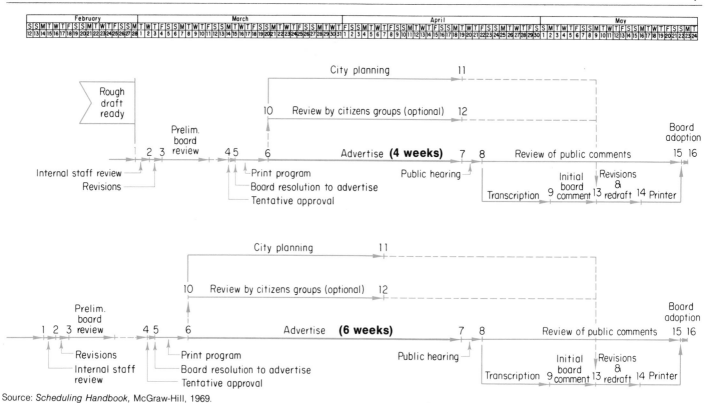

Source: *Scheduling Handbook*, McGraw-Hill, 1969.

the City Planning Commission and consultants over a three-month period to prepare a draft of the budget. The school district, as part of the budgeting process, was making a citywide decision in regard to the 6-3-3 grade system versus 7-4-4. However, completion of the draft budget did not mean completion of the final one.

Exhibit 17-7 shows the remaining three months of work anticipated before the board could adopt the draft budget. A number of these steps were legislative and mandated such as the period of advertisement (one month), public hearings and a one-month review of public comments. Accordingly, the actual preliminary board review constituted the only review which the school board had prior to public viewing of the documents, and was

projected as somewhat less than two weeks.

In Exhibit 17-8, an illustration is seen of the time required for development of a corporate budget in the private sector. Time is in weeks, and the total network adds up to just slightly more than six months. Other activities which are in progress following the acceptance of a budget include feasibility studies (economic and functional); programming (functional and architectural); site studies, selection and acquisition; funding evaluations; and other important predesign steps.

Not the least important of the design areas is the selection of the architect. Often a tentative selection will be made either during the budget or the pro-

gramming process, and the practitioner may be called on to participate as an interested party in the finalization of a number of stages. Use of a time grid or time-scaled network can be effective in bringing home to the decision makers the time (and cost) impact of delayed decisions. Also, it is possible to point out to management the value of reducing the time-cost risk by starting certain activities on a consulting basis prior to actual award or assignment of the final design contract.

If the design team does not have the opportunity to be a part of the predesign activities, it should still be interested in the scope and level of definition of these activities. A project for which comprehensive economic studies, property information and surveys, and functional and architectural programs are available can start into the design phase in high gear. The predesign network information, if available, should give a good indication of the accessibility of this data.

Exhibit 17-9 is a network which was prepared to describe the scope required for a design of campus site development. The campus was a medium-sized teacher's college which had been growing incrementally over a period of 100 years. However, the campus had doubled in size in less than 10 years, and the college was looking forward to a number of additional major structures. The director of campus facilities was well aware that patch-on additions to the existing utility system could no longer be depended on. In fact, the study was designed to evaluate necessary improvements in utilities for the existing building as well. The first portion of the campus design development would be assembling and plotting information on existing systems. This would be followed by design calculations and development of a proposed comprehensive site development. The network was a key to scoping the design, and became a monitoring device to plot progress.

DESIGN PHASE. The following three subdivisions describe network elements within the three major design phases: schematic design, design development, and construction documents. The networks shown would be suitable for planning and monitoring of a medium-sized design project. The elements would doubtlessly be rearranged to suit the specifics of the situation. Some activities might be deleted as unnecessary, while others would be added to suit the special situation of the design problem.

In these network examples, no times have been assigned. Assignment of the time dimension is an important element and reflects either the relative scope of effort or the relative priority of the individual activity.

EXHIBIT 17-8. CPM PLAN FOR PREPARATION OF BUDGET (CORPORATE)

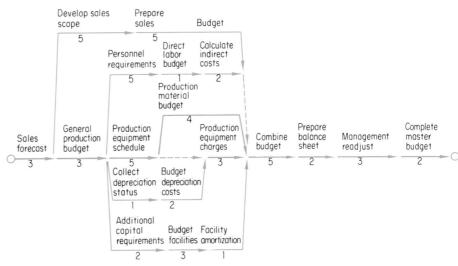

Source: *Scheduling Handbook,* McGraw-Hill, 1969.

EXHIBIT 17-9. CPM MASTER PLAN FOR CAMPUS DEVELOPMENT

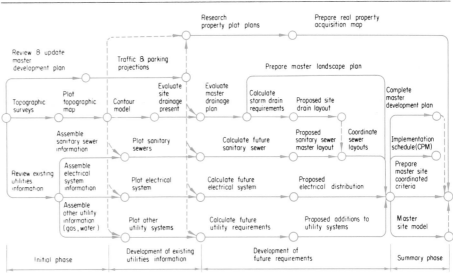

Source: *CPM in Construction Management,* McGraw-Hill, 1971.

Space limitations here preclude illustrating large networks. In an actual application, expansion of the individual activities into more levels of detail can add clarity. However, the continual daily liaison between the professional disciplines cannot be readily shown on a network presentation. The result would be almost a bewildering maze of activities.

During the design phase, personnel

scheduling is principally the concern of the design team. The networks developed generally anticipate a balanced work force, with a minimum of swings up or down. One of the most important personnel scheduling aspects is the projection of any hiatus in the design effort. This particularly tends to occur during design reviews. Since the design team can hardly be reassigned, it is not unusual for the architect to carry forward certain areas of the concept which have the least risk of change.

Schematic Design Phase. Exhibit 17-10 shows the basic network elements for a typical schematic design phase. Starting at Event 100, there is an organization of available information and review of prior predesign work. Time assignments would reflect the amount of preparation which the owner has accomplished. If the programmatic information is well organized and definitive, then the times for Activity 100–105 and 105–115 would be minimal. Activity 100–120 (assemble site plans and soil borings) could be a matter

EXHIBIT 17-10. BASIC NETWORK ELEMENTS, TYPICAL SCHEMATIC DESIGN PHASE

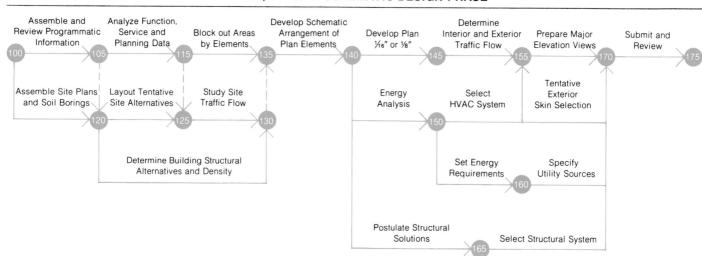

EXHIBIT 17-11. BASIC NETWORK ELEMENTS, PRELIMINARY/DESIGN DEVELOPMENT PHASE

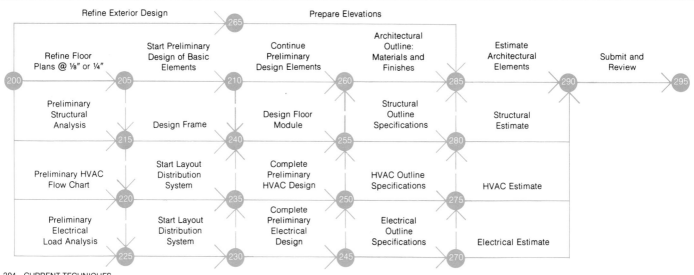

EXHIBIT 17-12. BASIC NETWORK ELEMENTS, CONSTRUCTION DOCUMENTS PHASE

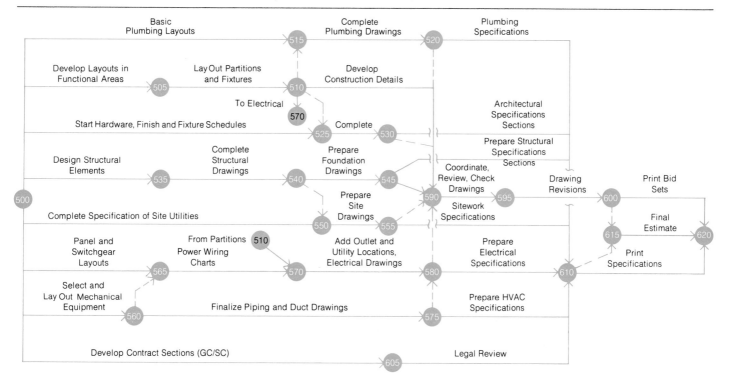

of picking up information in a day, or might require the assignment of field crews and several months.

The seven activities between 100 and 135 are the initial conceptual thought processes and organization of information. The key result is Activity 135–140 in which the schematic arrangement of plan elements is developed. This is the heart of the schematic design phase. Here, too, the engineering disciplines can begin to work with the initial spatial scheme.

Activity 170–175 (submit and review) is routine but very important. There should have been prearranged with the owner an agreement whether the work has to go into hiatus during review periods, or whether a tentative approval can be given so the work can go forward. In the schematic design phase, in particular, it is mutually advantageous to have an early owner's

review. Approval to proceed can be given on a conditional basis. The alternative is either for the design team to proceed at its own risk or for temporary demobilization which is expensive and impractical.

Preliminary/Design Development Phase. Exhibit 17-11 illustrates the basic network elements for the design development phase. Work starts after approval of the schematic design concept, at Event 200. The pattern here shows four parallel flows of activity. The architectural flow is on two lines, while each of the engineering disciplines starts with preliminary analyses, preliminary layouts and then more definitive design detail. The result of this phase is a set of design development documents fixing and describing the size and character of the project, and showing general distribution schemes, outline

specifications and a statement of probable construction cost.

Construction Documents Phase. Exhibit 17-12 has the basic network elements for the final or contract documents phase of design for a typical conventional project. Based on approval of the design development documents, work proceeds on preparation of the final construction documents. At this stage, the design concept is fixed, and the effort is now to generate a set of drawings, specifications and other necessary bidding information which can clearly define the work required by the contractors. The level of detail should be directly related to the type of contractual arrangement anticipated. A negotiated contract with flexibility for changes demands much less rigid contract documents. Similarly, the

EXHIBIT 17-13. CONSTRUCTION TIME ANALYSIS (DESIGN PHASE)

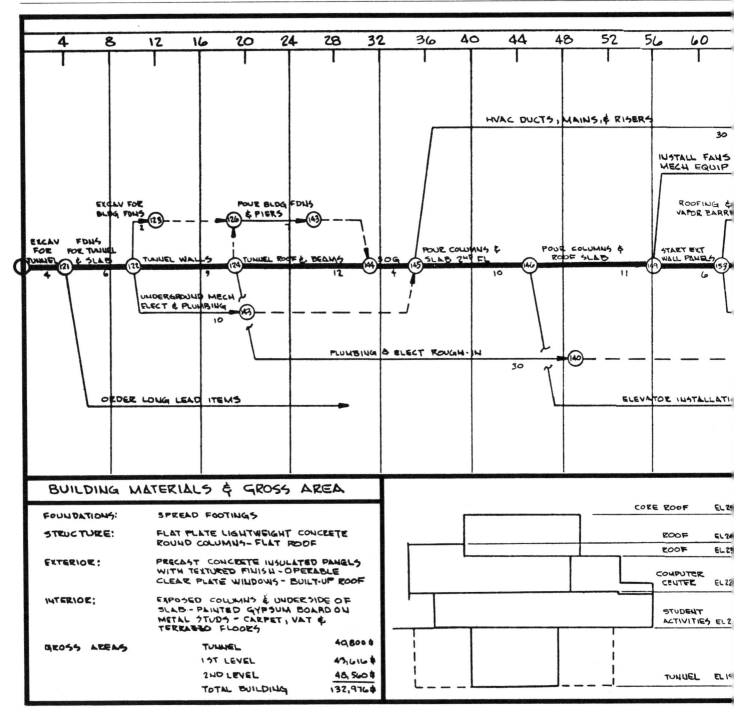

Source: Max O. Urbahn Associates Inc. and City University of New York.

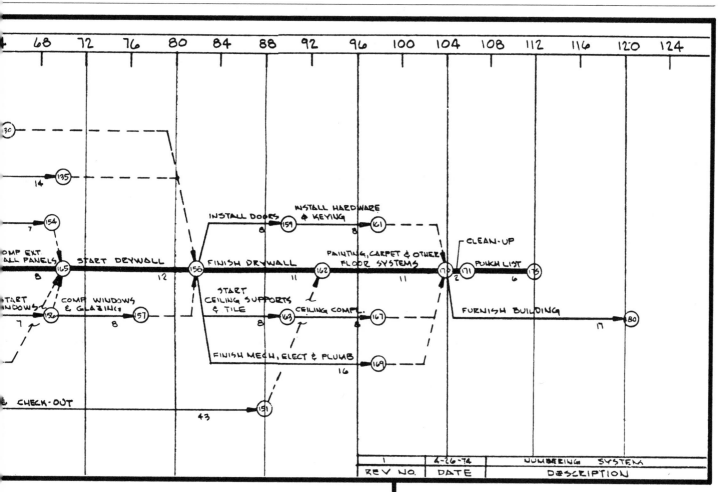

THE CITY UNIVERSITY OF NEW YORK

COMPUTER & STUDENT CENTER

MAX O. URBAHN ASSOCIATES INC.

LOGICAL SEQUENCE SCHEDULE (CONSTRUCTION)
JAMES J. O'BRIEN, P.E., CONSTRUCTION MANAGER

MARCH 4, 1974

EXHIBIT 17-14. MASTER SCHEDULE FOR NORMAL DESIGN AND CONSTRUCTION

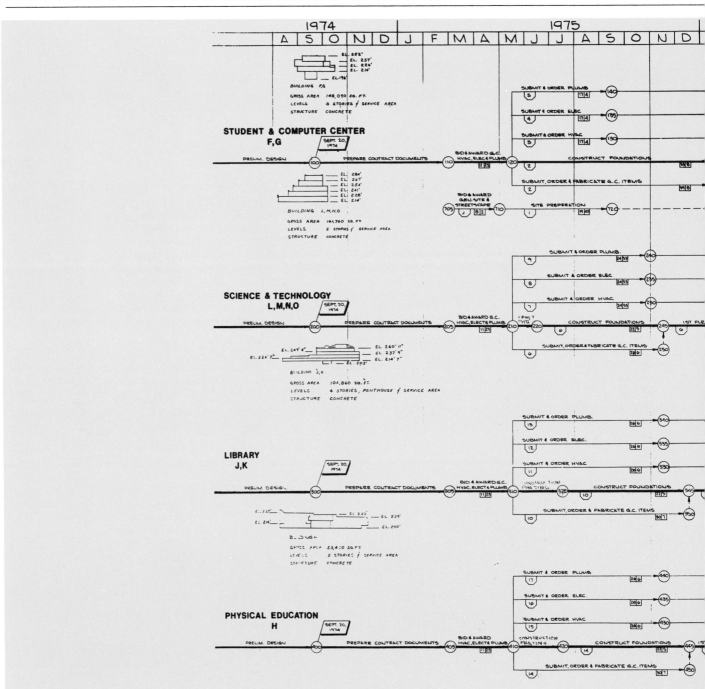

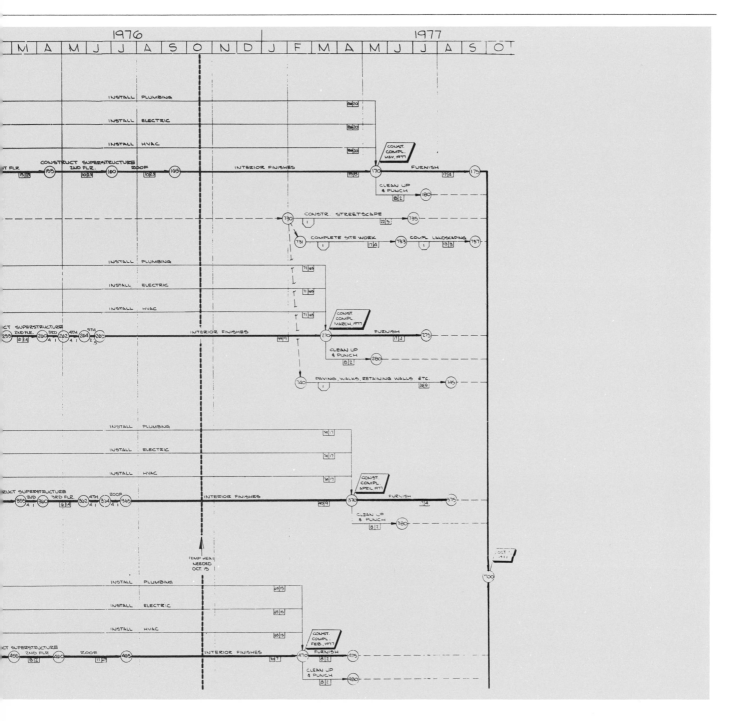

EXHIBIT 17-15. TIME-COST CURVE, ELEMENTARY SCHOOL

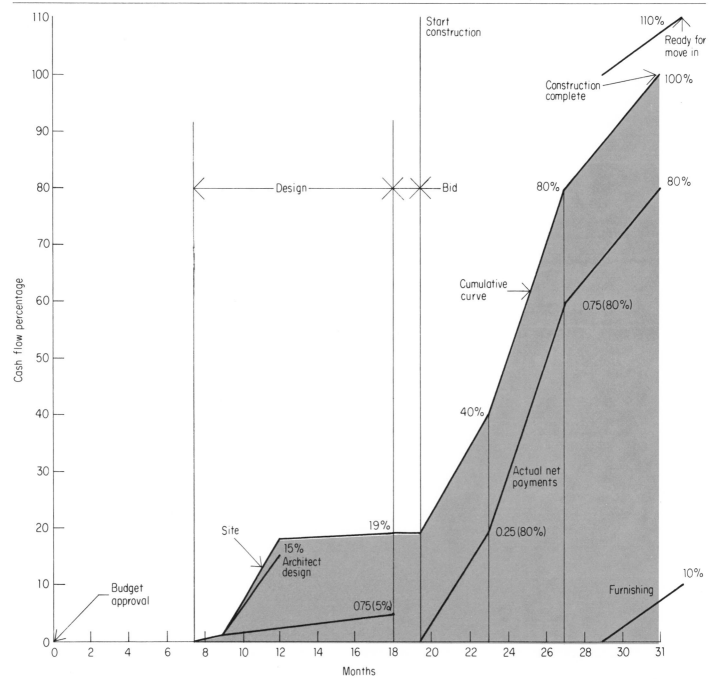

Cash flow, typical elementary school

Source: *CPM in Construction Management*, McGraw-Hill, 1971.

EXHIBIT 17-16. SUMMARY LEVEL DESIGN NETWORK

LINE A—PARALLEL REVIEW
Design Period (15 Months)

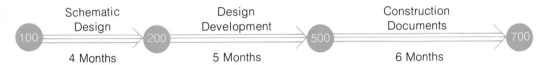

LINE B—SEQUENTIAL REVIEW
Sequential Design Review (21 Months)

EXHIBIT 17-17. NETWORK PLAN FOR SCHOOL DESIGN, INITIAL PHASE

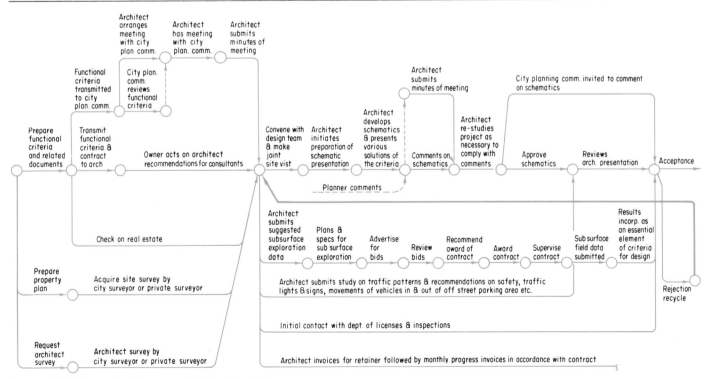

Source: *CPM in Construction Management*, McGraw-Hill, 1971.

EXHIBIT 17-18. NETWORK PLAN FOR SCHOOL DESIGN, FINAL PHASE

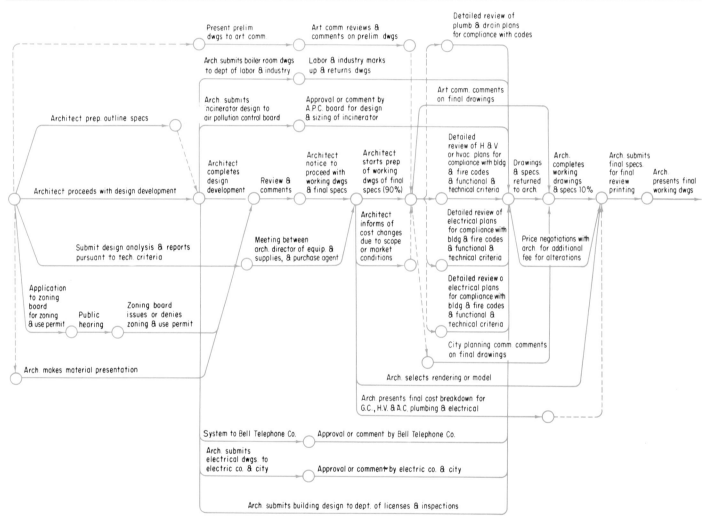

Source: *CPM in Construction Management,* McGraw-Hill, 1971.

time frame for preparation of these documents should be much less.

PREBID ANALYSIS. During the design phase, good results have been obtained by a prebid analysis of the construction phase. Using a network approach, the project is evaluated for a reasonable construction schedule. Using this as a basis, milestones and the overall sched-

ule are established on a rational basis rather than a hopeful one. Exhibit 17-13 is an example of one such analysis in summary form and to a time scale.

Exhibit 17-14 shows the combination, in summary form, of the design and prebid construction information for this building and several others. Using the time grid format, cash flow and encumbrance projections can be made. Exhibit 17-15 is a

time-cost curve developed for an elementary school project in Philadelphia. This project was one of several hundred ranging from renovations to construction of new high schools. The cash flow projection indicates the earliest possible time at which monies would be spent, showing a tremendous gap between the encumbrance of funds and their actual distribution.

CONSTRUCTION PHASE. A great majority of CPM applications in construction projects occur during the actual construction phase. Networks range in size from a few hundred to many thousand activities. In most cases they are not constructed to a time scale because the drafting costs would be prohibitive. (Computer programs do exist which can convert network output directly into time grid networks using X-Y plotters.)

PHASE COMBINATIONS. Exhibit 17-16 is a summary of the three fragnets for the main design phases. In Line A, the schematic design, design development and construction document phases are connected to show an overall 15-month time frame. This would be a fairly typical time frame for a medium-sized building. In Line B, the impact of adding sequential design reviews is demonstrated. If the owner requires a two-month design review cycle after each main phase, the time impact would be a six-month or 40 percent time extension. As ridiculous as this appears in network form, it is not an unusual real life situation. The time scale summary network could be used to describe to the owner an impaction of six months' cost escalation, which could conceivably be an amount almost equal to the cost of the design itself.

Exhibit 17-17 is a network flow chart of activities for the programming and schematic design phases which had to be accomplished for a typical project in the Philadelphia School District. These activities spanned between budget approval through completion of preliminary design. This is a CPM chart in all aspects, except one: the inclusion of a rejection cycle. The activity which spans from presentation to the school board backward to convening of the design team indicates schematically that in the case of rejection, nine major activities had to be repeated for resubmission of the scheme. Schematic information of this type is useful in a manually calculated network.

If this network were computerized, as it could be if event numbers and activity times were added, then the activity from rejection cycle backward would become a loop. The loop is in the logic which shows recycling of a string of activities. The computer would plod its way down through presentation to the school board, then follow the rejection cycle back, and become caught in the loop from which it could not escape. In an actual situation, if a design were rejected, the procedure would be to insert a similar string of activities following the rejection and prior to subsequent work. (This is what is meant by the schematic rejection recycle activity, but the computer is quite literal in its processing and cannot utilize judgment.)

Exhibit 17-18 shows the balance of activities which a typical project in the school district had to traverse following acceptance of the concept by the school board. Activities to the left are involved with design development, and to the right in the preparation of contract documents.

This stereotype design network was adjusted for each of the several hundred activities in a huge program on revitalization of capital facilities conducted by Philadelphia. The network was used to manually monitor progress and estimate percentage completion. Percentage complete was then evaluated and presented to the school district on all active projects on a monthly basis. In this network, each activity is not necessarily at the same level of importance or duration. However, each activity did have to be done.

The network plan shown in Exhibit 17-19 illustrates the many steps an architect should consider in developing a project from programming through construction documents.

FAST-TRACK

The overlapping of design and construction on a fast-track or phased construction basis has received substantial popularity in an effort to minimize time delays.

Exhibit 17-20 is a design CPM prepared by Max O. Urbahn Associates Inc. At that time (June 1974), scheduling had been completed for the project, and design development started. The center line showing targets summarizes the activities to be accomplished, looking forward to development of plans, review by the City University of New York, complete preliminaries, CUNY review, and approvals to the beginning of construction documents in December 1974. The detailed activities above and below the target line list the specific work activities.

The format is interesting in that the weekly time grid used to the beginning of 1975 is compressed for 1975. Following the approval of preliminary design, there are a number of alternatives suggested. On the lower line, at the end of September 1974, is a latest start date in order for conventional construction documents to be completed in March 1975. There are two alternatives open to CUNY on this basis. First, the construction documents could be started prior to approvals on a risk basis. An alternative would be the decision to go fast-track, wherein the schedule line must start in August (8/16/74) and would result in foundation construction documents being available in December 1974. This would provide additional time for developing the balance of construction documents after complete approvals of preliminaries.

This particular CPM report is an updating report as of 7/24/74. The project was on time. There was one notation that the design team was awaiting approval of the boring subcontractor.

CONSTRUCTING THE NETWORK

Before the network is constructed, calculations must be made and a time element assigned to critical activities.

EXHIBIT 17-19. NETWORK PLAN

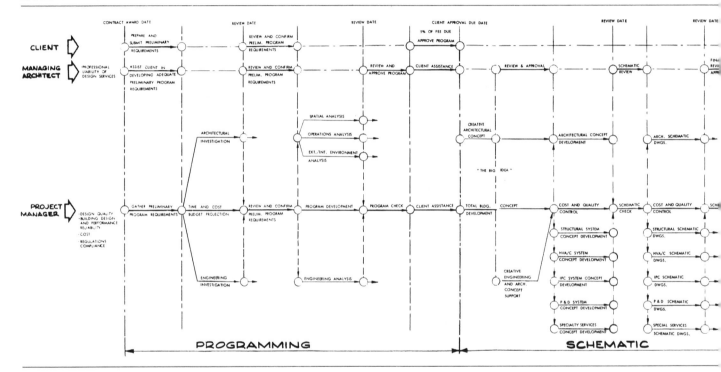

Source: *Emerging Techniques of Architectural Practice*, AIA, 1966.

EXHIBIT 17-20. DESIGN CPM: PRELIMINARY THROUGH BIDDING

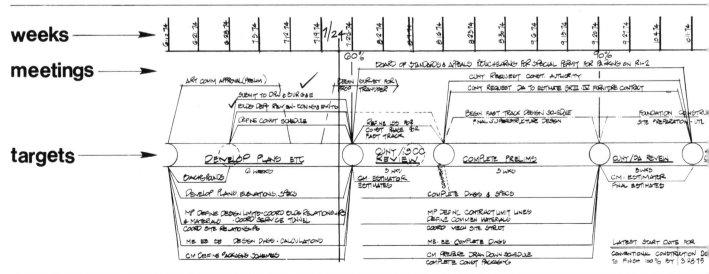

Source: Max O. Urbahn Associates Inc. and City University of New York.

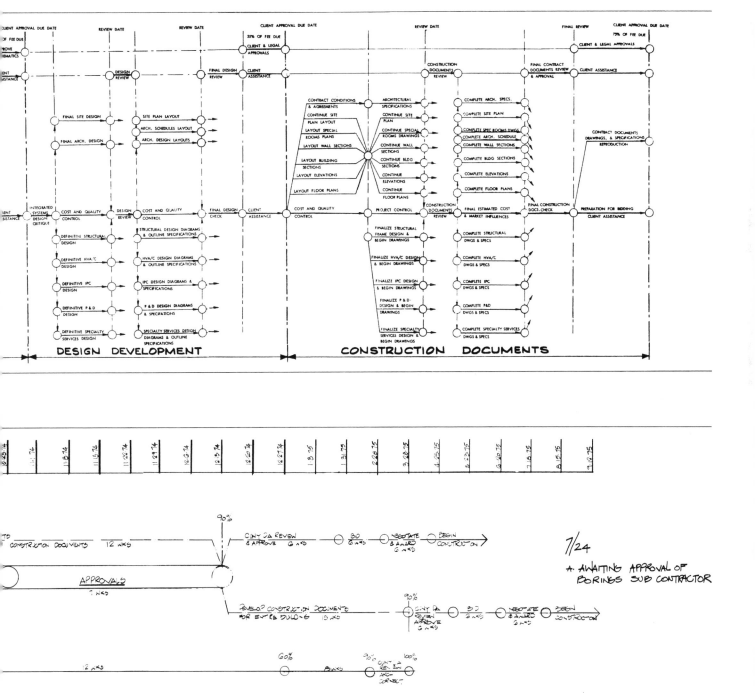

DESIGN DEVELOPMENT

CONSTRUCTION DOCUMENTS

NETWORK CALCULATIONS. Exhibit 17-21 is a small construction network. It represents the site work for a development in an industrial park environment. The site is in a low area, overgrown with scrub, timber and bushes; the soil is a sand and gravel mixture overlaid by clay. Cast-in-place piles will be driven to about 30 feet for the plant and warehouse foundations. The office building will be on spread footings. As there is no water supply available, a well and 50,000-gallon elevated water tank will be installed. Sewage and power trunk lines are about 2,000 feet away. Power connections will be by overhead pole line up to 200 feet from the building; from that point in, the power line will run underground. The sewer will pass under part of the power line. The activities (unsorted) representing the site work prior to the start of piling and footings will be:

—Survey and layout
—Clear site
—Rough grade
—Drill well
—Install well pump
—Install electrical manholes
—Install underground water supply
—Excavate for sewer
—Install sewer
—Install power feeder
—Set pole line
—Excavate for electrical manholes
—Energize power feeder

On the basis that site preparation and utilities work will be put out as a separate package to be accomplished as soon as possible, a single site preparation contractor is selected and directed to prepare a plan of work.

Exhibit 17-21 shows the network in basic flow chart form. The activities are not drawn to time scale. The start and completion of each activity have been assigned an event number for purposes of identification only. The number has no value or significance in the calculation of the network. The number at the start of the

EXHIBIT 17-21. CPM NETWORK, SITE PREPARATION AND UTILITIES

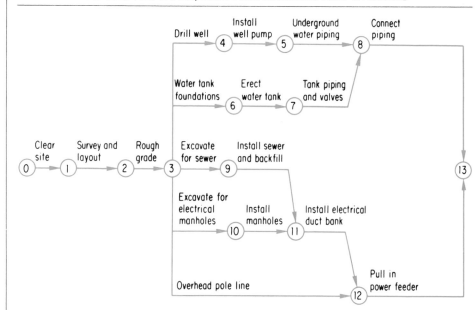

Source: *CPM in Construction Management*, McGraw-Hill, 1971.

EXHIBIT 17-22. EARLY EVENT TIMES, SITE PREPARATION

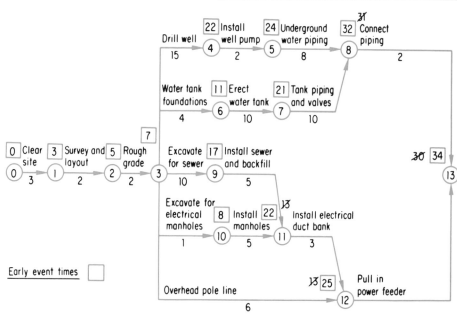

Source: *CPM in Construction Management*, McGraw-Hill, 1971.

arrow is the small **i** and at the head, small **j**; the number identification of an activity thus is known as the **i-j** number. In the example, activity 3–4 would be "drill well." It, of course, implies a subset of other activities which would be: move drilling rig on site; set up drilling rig; drill well; case; withdraw casing; insert screens; and test well.

Time estimates in working days have been added below each activity in Exhibit 17-22. In addition, an early event time calculation has been made. In this calculation, the objective is to determine the earliest time at which each event in the network can be started; this, in the cumulative, determines the time in which the last event can be completed. The calculation is addition of the times along each path, until two paths join. The rule of calculation at a juncture of arrowheads (an event) is that the event cannot be completed or reached until all paths into it have been completed. Accordingly, the early event time (EET) equals the longest of the paths coming in. Using this approach, the end of this network is calculated as 34 working days, or approximately seven weeks.

In Exhibit 17-23, the late event times have been calculated. These figures are placed in a circle over the event number. The late event time and its calculation are somewhat more subtle than the basic information offered by the EET. The late event time is that latest time at which an event can be started without delaying the EET of the last event. Accordingly, the event time of the last event is used as a point of departure for the calculation. In this case, the time sequence strings are subtracted from the starting point, and where the tails of two or more arrows come into an event, a comparison must be made. In this comparison, the information required is the latest time at which activities originating at the event must be able to start. That latest time is the earliest of the possible selections.

ACTIVITY TIMES. The source of activity time information is the event time calculation. Each activity is bounded by two events. The starting event is shown in the box over the event number in Exhibit 17-22. It is known as the early start (ES). Knowing the early start, the early finish (EF) is calculated by adding the duration of the activity to arrive at the earliest time at which the activity can finish.

The late event time at any event is the figure shown in the circle in Exhibit 17-23. As noted previously, it is calculated by working backward from the concluding event, subtracting durations and selecting the latest allowable time at any event. When this latest event time has been calculated, it establishes the late finish time for an activity (LF). Knowing the late finish, the late start can be calculated by subtracting the activity duration.

Thus, when the basic event times have been calculated on the network, certain information can be developed and tabulated. From Exhibit 17-22, the first nine activities offer this information:

Activity	Duration	Description
0–1	3	Clear site
1–2	2	Survey and layout
2–3	2	Rough grade
3–4	15	Drill well
3–6	4	Water tank foundations
3–9	10	Excavate sewer
3–10	1	Excavate electrical manholes
3–12	6	Pole line
4–5	2	Well pump

After the event times are computed, the following additional information from Exhibit 17-23 can be listed:

Activity	Duration	Description	ES	LF
0–1	3	Clear site	0	3
1–2	2	Survey and layout	3	5
2–3	2	Rough grade	5	7
3–4	15	Drill well	7	22
3–6	4	Water tank foundations	7	12
3–9	10	Excavate sewer	7	21
3–10	1	Excavate electrical manholes	7	21
3–12	6	Pole line	7	29
4–5	2	Well pump	22	24

Now, adding duration to the ES column and subtracting it from the LF provides the following:

Activity	Duration	Description	ES	EF	LS	LF
0–1	3	Clear site	0	3	0	3
1–2	2	Survey and layout	3	5	3	5
2–3	2	Rough grade	5	7	5	7
3–4	15	Drill well	7	22	7	22
3–6	4	Water tank foundations	7	11	8	12
3–9	10	Excavate sewer	7	17	11	21
3–10	1	Excavate manholes	7	8	20	21
3–12	6	Pole line	7	13	23	29
4–5	2	Well pump	22	24	22	24

CRITICAL ACTIVITIES. Exhibit 17-24 is a plot of this activity information on a time scale. Note that the activities 0–1, 1–2, 2–3, 3–4 and 4–5 show a solid connection. These activities are on the path of critical events (0–1–2–3–4–5, etc.). Look at the activity times for activity 4–5. The ES is 22 and the LF is 24. The time span between is 24–22, or 2. Since the time span available equals the duration for activity 4–5, this activity must start on its ES and finish on its EF if the site preparation is to finish by time 34 (indicated in Exhibit 17-22). Note that for these critical activities, early start equals late start; early finish equals late finish.

There are three conditions which a critical activity must meet:

—Early and late start times must be equal or the same.

—Early and late completion times must be equal or the same.

—The difference between LF and ES figures must equal the duration.

The subtle implication of these rules is that an activity standing between two critical events is not necessarily critical itself. That is, there need be only one critical path between critical events. Other paths spanning between critical events may have scheduling flexibility.

Conversely, there can be any number of critical paths through a network. A perfectly time-balanced network may have all paths critical. One critical path can spread out into a number of paths. However, the critical path or paths must be continuous chains of activities. They cannot be intermittent. Also, each network must have at least one critical path from the first to the last event.

The critical path approach is focused toward identifying those activities which control the progress of the project. During the design phase, there is a tendency for the work to be accomplished to be personnel-balanced; therefore, most paths are critical. Examination will usually indicate those paths which cannot be short-

EXHIBIT 17-23. LATE EVENT TIMES, SITE PREPARATION

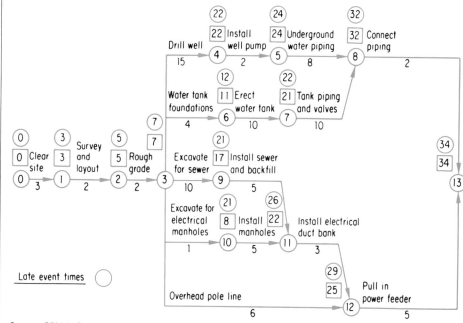

Source: *CPM in Construction Management*, McGraw-Hill, 1971.

EXHIBIT 17-24. PLOT OF ACTIVITY TIMES TO TIME SCALE

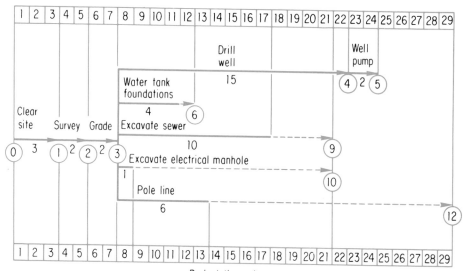

Project time, days

Source: *CPM in Construction Management*, McGraw-Hill, 1971.

ened by the addition of personnel. These are the truly critical areas.

During construction, usually 10 to 25 percent of the network may be critical, depending on the complexity of the work, the nature of the project and the availability of time.

The measure of the amount of time flexibility available is called "float." Initially, there were a number of types of float identified, but the principal measure is easily calculated as a difference between a late and early start, or the difference between the late and early finish. For a single activity, this difference will be the same, whichever calculation is used.

Float is a shared commodity, so that a chain of activities showing 10 days of float lose that float if the first activity is delayed 10 days in its start.

If more float is utilized than is available, the chain of activities actually becomes negative. In a chain of negative float, the early start dates which are projections become later than the late start dates. This apparent paradox has resulted because now the CPM is projecting the early dates as the earliest point at which something can start, based on progress and prior estimates. The late dates are still calculated from the desired end date (if it has been locked in to a calendar date). Negative float occurs only when the end date has been locked into a specific date.

MATERIALS

The design team carries a vital interest in materials from the design into the construction phase, including review of the procurement cycle.

In addition to time required for delivery of materials and the determination of the delivery time, which should be specified on the order, there are a number of other steps in material procurement which are time consuming and must not be neglected. These include shop drawing approval, architect's review of shop draw-

EXHIBIT 17-25. TYPICAL MATERIAL PROCUREMENT CYCLE

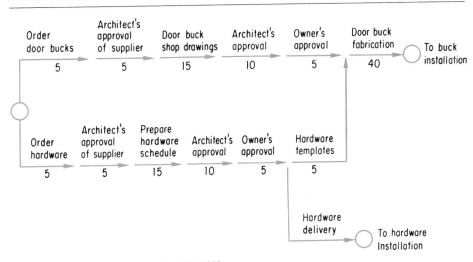

Source: *Scheduling Handbook*, McGraw-Hill, 1969.

EXHIBIT 17-26. DELIVERIES FOR JOHN DOE SITE PREPARATION, ZERO DELIVERY

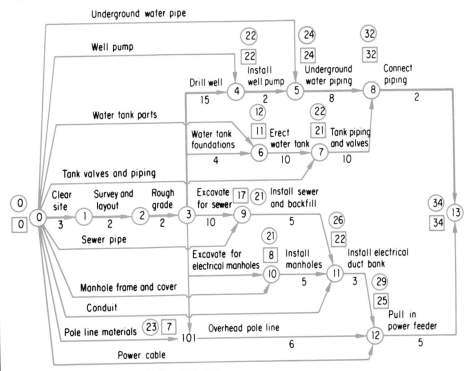

Source: *Scheduling Handbook*, McGraw-Hill, 1969.

ings, resubmittal time for shop drawing corrections and review by controlling agencies. These steps can sometimes be accelerated for critical activities (when they are, in fact, identified as critical). However, there is a tendency to minimize the impact of these routine steps, which require care to reflect them properly on the CPM diagram. Exhibit 17-25 shows the interrelation between two material orders (hardware and door bucks) before either reaches the project site. Note that in this example the door buck delivery has five days' float because of the additional time required to prepare hardware templates. Larger equipment may require additional time for the submission of formal bids.

Materials are involved throughout a construction project. Usually early delivery of materials cannot speed up an activity because the progress of other activities controls the early start time. However, failure to deliver the material for an activity can delay it indefinitely. Thus, unfortunately, the project purchasing agent or materials coordinator has a difficult problem. Late deliveries, of course, delay the project, and early deliveries result in extra handling and storage of materials. The problem reaches its most acute stage in urban areas where the project supervisor would like to lift materials from truck or rail car right to final location.

Just as subcontractors complain that the general contractor neglects their situation, most purchasing agents complain that their own company fails to keep them informed about material needs. Obviously, this is a need which can be satisfied with CPM information. One method is to locate those activities which require key materials. Since almost every activity requires materials, every activity would have to be reviewed to control all materials.

A practical method is to separate materials into two classes. Those materials which can be ordered out of stock for delivery in a week or less can be classified as commodities. The schedule for the first shipment of any type of commodity is useful. Key materials are those with long delivery times, or those which are custom orders. Review of the network computer run can furnish all the necessary material information, particularly the order in which key material orders should be placed. However, by adding an arrow to the diagram for each key delivery, the material information is generated as part of the computer run. Exhibit 17-26 is the site preparation network for the John Doe project with delivery arrows added.

Well pump and water tank would definitely be key deliveries. The others could be commodities or custom items depending on the specification to be met. If it is assumed that all materials are on hand (for instance, if the owner is furnishing them), the time duration for these activities would be zero. The computed information for the deliveries would be:

i–j	Duration	Description	ES	EF	LS	LF	Float
0–4	0	Well pump	0	0	22	22	22
0–5	0	Underground pipe	0	0	24	24	24
0–6	0	Water tank	0	0	12	12	12
0–7	0	Tank valves	0	0	22	22	22
0–9	0	Sewer pipe	0	0	21	21	21
0–10	0	Manhole frame and cover	0	0	21	21	21
0–11	0	Conduit	0	0	26	26	26
0–12	0	Power feeder	0	0	29	29	29
0–101	0	Pole line materials	0	0	23	23	23

Since materials would not usually be available at the start of the project, reasonable delivery time estimates are assigned to these delivery activities as follows:

Activity	Assume	Duration
Well pump	Stock delivery, 4 weeks	20
Underground water pipe	Mechanical joint, 6 weeks	30
Water tank parts	Standard size, 6 weeks	30
Tank valves	Standard gate valves, 4 weeks	20
Sewer pipe	Terra cotta, 1 week	5
Manhole cover	Stock, 1 week	5
Conduit	Stock, 1 week	5
Power feeder	Special order, 8 weeks	40
Pole material	Stock order, 2 weeks	10

These durations were added to Exhibit 17-27. Event times are computed on the diagram. The activity times for the deliveries are:

i–j	Duration	Description	ES	EF	LS	LF	Float
0–4	20	Well pump	0	20	20	40	20
0–5	30	Underground water pipe	0	30	12	42	12
0–6	30	Water tank	0	30	0	30	0
0–7	20	Tank valves	0	20	20	40	20
0–9	5	Sewer pipe	0	5	34	39	34
0–10	5	Manhole cover	0	5	34	39	34
0–11	5	Conduit	0	5	39	44	39
0–12	40	Power feeder	0	40	7	47	7
0–101	10	Pole material	0	10	31	41	31

The introduction of delivery times has increased this portion of the project from 34 to 52 days. The critical path has shifted and is now through events 0–6–7–8–13.

In preparing a shop drawing schedule, both contractor and designer should be aware of the relative priorities of review. In order of highest five priorities, these would be:

Shop Drawings	Float
Water tank	0
Power feeder	7
Underground water pipe	12
Well pump	20
Tank valves	20

COMPUTER APPLICATIONS

The basic networking techniques previously discussed may be adapted to computer applications.

CPM. To perform the CPM calculation, the computer needs only the starting event **(i)**, concluding event **(j)** and duration for each activity. From this information, the computer can mathematically reconstruct the network, just as a person could do so manually from an activity list. The activity descriptions are inserted for convenience. The computer merely stores them and puts them back into the output.

The data takeoff is a chore but an important one. It is relatively easy to forget an activity or to transcribe an incorrect event number. By reversing the **i** and the **j**, a logical loop can be created. This will not occur if the classical rule—**j** is greater than **i**—is used in assigning event numbers. In transferring data from the network to the input sheets, working in the order of consecutive event numbers will reduce the chance of omissions.

The next step is to transfer the CPM input from the data sheets to punched cards (the most common), tape or disk. The vertical columns on the data sheet represent the specific card column in

EXHIBIT 17-27. DELIVERIES FOR JOHN DOE SITE PREPARATION, WITH DELIVERY TIMES

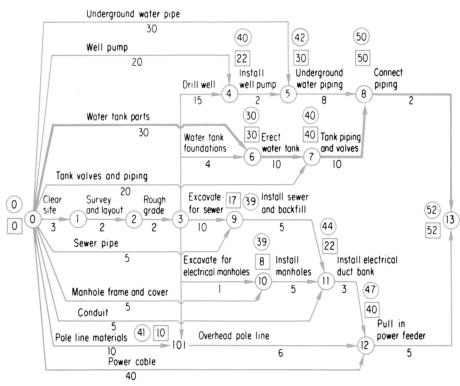

Source: *Scheduling Handbook*, McGraw-Hill, 1969.

which the **i–j** duration or description is to be placed. These specific assignments will vary with the program to be used.

The input is always placed as far to the right as possible. To keypunch, the operator places one horizontal line of data in the appropriate spaces on one IBM card. This is another area where errors are easily introduced. To avoid errors, the keypunch operator checks the cards on a verifier. On this machine, which is similar to the keypunch, the operator repunches the same input information in the same order. If a difference is noted, a signal lights up and the card is checked against the input. An experienced operator can keypunch and verify about 150 cards per hour. The verifying process is similar for

key-to-tape (keypunched directly to magnetic tape).

There are more than 20 digital machines which can process CPM or PERT information. How about the programs? The computer manufacturers usually furnish CPM or PERT programs through their users' share groups. Companies offering CPM-PERT computer services have their own proprietary programs. The cost of computation is a function of computer size and running time; the running time in large part depends on the program. To avoid confusion, one can evaluate the relative advantages of the various machines and programs by comparing costs. The output of each CPM or PERT computation should be similar.

One item not necessarily included in the CPM or PERT program (or in the cost quoted) is an efficient routine for checking errors. This first step in the computation of the CPM input will stop the computation before it starts working on incorrect data. This can save the cost of many dry runs. An error check looks for dangling activities (either an **i** or **j** end unconnected), duplicate activities or loops. The first two are not difficult to locate, but loops are another matter. One method of checking for the presence of a loop is to watch for a project duration greater than the total of all the project activities. This does not indicate the location of the loop, but can indicate its presence. This check falls down when the loop is made of dummy activities with zero time duration. In this case, computer running time in excess of the estimated time is an indication of a loop.

When the error check has been completed, the actual CPM computation commences. The CPM program is input from punched cards, tape or disk. Next, the CPM input is read in and the computation starts. The computation time varies with the computer and the size of the network; between 5 and 30 minutes is an average range. When the computer completes its computation, the results are automatically placed on punched cards, tape, disk, typewritten or printed list. These can be sorted in various orders.

The most common output is an **i–j**; in this output, the activities are arranged in consecutive order of the **i** or starting events. The **i–j** list is most useful in working with the CPM networks. If information is desired on a specific activity, it is easily found in the listing. The **i–j** list functions as an index or dictionary of activities. Exhibit 17-28 shows the **i–j** listing (partial).

The computer output should be checked for errors. This is quite important since the CPM data is susceptible to error in its transfer from network to data sheet to punched card.

EXHIBIT 17-28. JOHN DOE OUTPUT I-J SORT, COMPUTER CPM OUTPUT

| I | J | Dura-tion | | | Description | Start | | Finish | | Total Float |
						Ear	Lat	Ear	Lat	
0	1	3	1	1	Clear Site			3	3	0
1	2	2	1	2	Survey and Layout	3	3	5	5	0
2	3	2	1	1	Rough Grade	5	5	7	7	0
3	4	15	1	7	Drill Well	7	7	22	22	0
3	6	4	1	3	Water Tank Foundations	7	8	11	12	1
3	9	10	1	1	Excavate for Sewer	7	11	17	21	4
3	10	1	1	1	Excavate Electrical Manholes	7	20	8	21	13
3	12	6	1	4	Overhead Pole Line	7	23	13	29	16
4	5	2	1	5	Install Well Pump	22	22	24	24	0
5	8	8	1	5	Underground Water Piping	24	24	32	32	0
6	7	10	1	6	Erect Water Tower	11	12	21	22	1
7	8	10	1	5	Tank Piping and Valves	21	22	31	32	1
8	13	2	1	5	Connect Water Piping	32	32	34	34	0
9	11	5	1	5	Install Sewer and Backfill	17	21	22	26	4
10	11	5	1	4	Install Electrical Manholes	8	21	13	26	13
11	12	3	1	4	Electrical Duct Bank	22	26	25	29	4
12	13	5	1	4	Pull in Power Feeder	25	29	30	34	4
13	14	1	2	2	Building Layout	34	34	35	35	0
14	15	10	2	7	Drive and Pour Piles	35	35	45	45	0
14	23	3	2	1	Excavate for Office Building	35	65	38	68	30
15	16	5	2	1	Excavate for Plant Warehouse	45	45	50	50	0
16	17	5	2	3	Pour Pile Caps Plant-Warehse	50	50	55	55	0
17	18	10	2	3	Form + Pour Grade Beams P-W	55	55	65	65	0
18	19	3	2	1	Backfill and Compact P-W	65	65	68	68	0
18	21	5	2	3	Form + Pour RR Load Dock P-W	65	73	70	78	8
18	22	5	2	3	Form+Pour TK Load Dock P-W	65	73	70	78	8
19	20	5	2	5	Underslab Plumbing P-W	68	68	73	73	0

Source: *CPM in Construction Management*, McGraw-Hill, 1971.

One quick check of the computer output is to trace the critical path on the CPM network. To assist in this, a listing of activities in order of total float is useful. The critical activities are listed first and then float in ascending order. This listing is also useful for a fast review of the project by management. Exhibit 17-29 is the sort by total float for the John Doe project.

PERT. There are other recognized variations on the network approach. All should produce essentially the same results. As mentioned previously, the Navy PERT approach was developed as part of the Polaris program. To avoid confusion, in 1962, the Department of Defense adopted PERT as its single network approach. The basic sophisticated differences in the two approaches have gradually been reduced to the single-time estimate (CPM) versus the three-time estimates for PERT (most likely, optimistic, pessimistic). However, before the PERT calculation proceeds, each activity is converted into a single activity by applying the formula

$$\text{Time} = \frac{a + 4m + b}{6}$$

Where **m** is the most likely, **a** is optimistic and **b** is pessimistic. Exhibit 17-30 is an event-oriented PERT network which is the earlier version. In these networks, milestones were emphasized, so that although the calculation was performed on the activities between events, the output was in terms of events. PERT has been converted to activity-oriented descriptions, increasing the similarity to CPM.

PDM. The Precedence Diagramming Method, too, was developed in the construction industry, and is also an activity package approach. Instead of an arrow, the work to be accomplished is shown in a box. Exhibit 17-31 is the project network of Exhibit 17-21 diagrammed in precedence form.

Precedence networks are slightly less

EXHIBIT 17-29. JOHN DOE OUTPUT TOTAL-FLOAT SORT (PARTIAL)

I	J	Dura-tion			Description	Start Ear	Start Lat	Finish Ear	Finish Lat	Total Float
0	1	3	1	1	Clear Site			3	3	0
1	2	2	1	2	Survey and Layout	3	3	5	5	0
2	3	2	1	1	Rough Grade	5	5	7	7	0
3	4	15	1	7	Drill Well	7	7	22	22	0
4	5	2	1	5	Install Well Pump	22	22	24	24	0
5	8	8	1	5	Underground Water Piping	24	24	32	32	0
8	13	2	1	5	Connect Water Piping	32	32	34	34	0
13	14	1	2	2	Building Layout	34	34	35	35	0
14	15	10	2	7	Drive and Pour Piles	35	35	45	45	0
15	16	5	2	1	Excavate for Plant Warehouse	45	45	50	50	0
16	17	5	2	3	Pour Pile Caps Plant-Warehse	50	50	55	55	0
17	18	10	2	3	Form + Pour Grade Beams P-W	55	55	65	65	0
18	19	3	2	1	Backfill and Compact P-W	65	65	68	68	0
19	20	5	2	5	Underslab Plumbing P-W	68	68	73	73	0
20	22	5	2	4	Underslab Conduit P-W	73	73	78	78	0
22	29	10	2	3	Form + Pour Slabs P-W	78	78	88	88	0
29	30	10	3	6	Erect Struct Steel P-W	88	88	98	98	0
30	31	5	3	6	Plumb Steel and Bolt P-W	98	98	103	103	0
31	32	5	3	6	Erect Crane Way and Crane P-W	103	103	108	108	0
32	33	0			Dummy	108	108	108	108	0
33	34	3	3	6	Erect Bar Joists P-W	108	108	111	111	0
34	35	3	3	6	Erect Roof Planks P-W	111	111	114	114	0
35	36	10	3	7	Erect Siding P-W	114	114	124	124	0
36	37	0			Dummy	124	124	124	124	0
37	38	2	3	4	Set Electrical Load Center P-W	124	124	126	126	0
38	43	20	3	4	Install Power Conduit P-W	126	126	146	146	0
43	49	15	3	4	Install Branch Conduit P-W	146	146	161	161	0

Source: *CPM in Construction Management,* McGraw-Hill, 1971.

complicated in appearance than CPM, but the correlation between the computer output and the network is fairly complex because precedence permits the use of lead and lag notations to indicate overlapping of work packages. In CPM, this overlapping must be shown by breaking the work down into two or more arrows (Exhibit 17-3). While the CPM approach produced a more complex appearing network, there is a direct 1-to-1 correlation between the network and the computerized output.

Networking can be a powerful aid in the organization, planning and monitoring of the design process. In the fast-track approach to construction, this level of planning and control becomes even more important.

During the design stages, the design network can be reasonably small and still be useful. This permits drawing of the network to a time scale which is readily interpreted by the client as well as the team involved in design and construction.

The network should be monitored and reviewed on a monthly basis. Use of color coding can provide rapid visibility of the progress. The design network can also be utilized to game or exercise various alternative approaches. Time is money, and the design phase is the principal area where time can be gained at minimal risk. However, as the major beneficiary of these time gains, the owner also should pay for the risk. A graphical network presentation can often bring forward this approach.

Since the beginning of networking, architects have encouraged the utilization of better methods of planning and coordination during construction. CPM should be used as a basis for reviewing progress monthly. This review should include a narrative report. To gain the advantages of the time-scaled presentation, a summarized version of the CPM is often prepared showing only milestones, with

EXHIBIT 17-30. JOHN DOE EVENT-ORIENTED PERT NETWORK, SITE PREPARATION AND UTILITIES

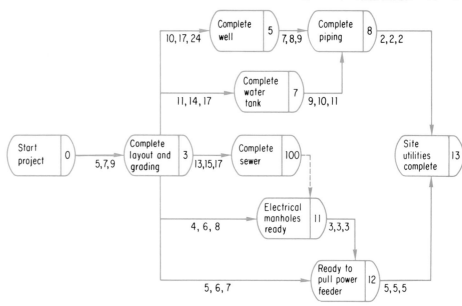

Source: *CPM in Construction Management*, McGraw-Hill, 1971.

EXHIBIT 17-31. JOHN DOE PRECEDENCE NETWORK

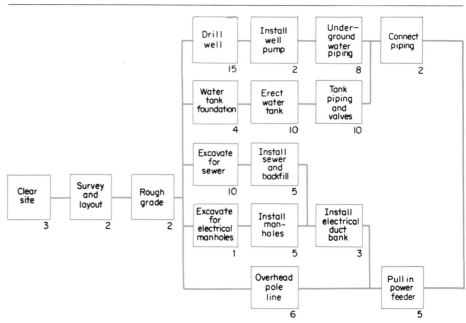

Source: *CPM in Construction Management*, McGraw-Hill, 1971.

these drawn to a time grid. Often, an entire project can be shown on one or two sheets to a time grid, representing 20 or more detailed network sheets.

During the construction, the network information can be utilized to identify relative priority of areas. These priorities, in turn, can be used to establish the order of review of shop drawings.

The accepted CPM schedule and its regular reviews and narrative reports form a documentation of the progress and problems for the whole project. If the architect indeed has insisted on a comprehensive documentation, many postproject problems and claims can be avoided. CPM has figured in many recent litigation cases involving construction delay claims.

Networking, whether it be CPM, PERT or PDM, is like any good tool. Used well, it serves well; used poorly, it fails.

BIBLIOGRAPHY

Construction Scheduling and Control. George E. Deatherage. New York: McGraw-Hill, 1965.

Part of a series on construction by an experienced construction specialist; the CPM section is one chapter.

Cost Control and CPM in Construction. Washington, D.C.: Associated General Contractors, 1968.

Adds cost aspects of CPM; introduces the AGC uniform numbering system based on the CSI numbering; includes case study project.

CPM in Construction. Washington, D.C.: Associated General Contractors, 1965.

Concise presentation of CPM of considerable importance since it has been broadly utilized by members of AGC; textbook portion of the manual prepared by Glenn L. White.

CPM in Construction Management. James J. O'Brien. New York: McGraw-Hill, 2nd ed., 1971.

Presented in a case history format.

Critical Path Method. Byron M. Radcliffe, Donald E. Kawal and Ralph J. Stephenson. Chicago: Cahners, 1967.

Comprehensive presentation of networking, including detailed network examples.

Critical Path Method. L. R. Shaffer, J. B. Ritter and W. L. Meyer. New York: McGraw-Hill, 1965.

Well oriented to teaching of network techniques.

Critical Path Methods in Construction Practice. James M. Antill and Ronald W. Woodhead. New York: Wiley, 2nd ed., 1970.

In-depth approach to networking, with some sophisticated extensions.

Critical Path Networks. R. L. Martino. New York: McGraw-Hill, 1970.

Presents information on networks in very dynamic fashion.

Critical Path Scheduling. Joseph Horowitz. New York: Ronald Press, 1967.

Reflects a basic approach to use of networking in construction projects; treatment is comprehensive and includes resource, least cost, project control and reporting procedures.

Network-Based Management Systems. Russell D. Archibald and Richard L. Villoria. New York: Wiley, 1967.

Comprehensive text presents networks as a special class of management information systems developed primarily for project management.

Planning and Control with PERT/CPM. Richard I. Levin and Charles A. Kirkpatrick. New York: McGraw-Hill, 1966.

Concise treatment of basic networking; orientation toward business, operations research and PERT.

Precedence Networks for Project Planning and Control. P. J. Burnam. New York: McGraw-Hill, 1973.

By a project management consultant from South Africa, one of the most complete presentations of precedence diagramming.

Project Management with CPM and PERT. Joseph J. Moder and Cecil R. Phillips. New York: Reinhold, 2nd ed., 1970.

One of the network classics; presents networking with an industrial engineering organization and slant.

Resources Management. R. L. Martino. New York: McGraw-Hill, 1970.

Information on resource allocation offered in a dynamic manner.

Scheduling Handbook. James J. O'Brien. New York: McGraw-Hill, 1969.

Contains many of the basic references and credits in the evolution of network systems.

Systems Management Techniques for Building and Contractors. Paul G. Gill. New York: McGraw-Hill, 1968.

CPM applied in unique ways; very construction-oriented; although small construction examples are used, information applies to large building projects as well, as seen by an independent consultant.

Theory of Scheduling. Richard W. Conway, William L. Maxwell and Louis W. Miller. New York: Addison-Wesley, 1967.

Presents the mathematical basis for scheduling systems.

Chapter 18
Drawings

NED H. ABRAMS, AIA

Drawings ideally present those aspects of a project most easily explained graphically, and specifications those aspects most easily described by language. While they complement each other, their respective functions should not be interchanged or duplicated under normal circumstances.

Drawings, then, show what is involved, where it is located, and what the physical dimensions are. Specifications state what the materials are, how they are to function and from where they can be obtained.

The number of options available to architects for the graphic delineation of information is constantly growing, and at a rapid pace. Having an understanding of these options will allow the practitioner to use all, or parts, of any method described.

The customary hand process is still very much in evidence during the early design stages. Use of some of the described options could change this. With the application of more advanced techniques during the documentation phase, the task should become less laborious and more mechanical and economical. Trends affecting decisions to move toward systematization and greater efficiency are:

—The approach to interdisciplinary matters, such as environmental and behavioral aspects previously not a part of architecture, which increase the complexity of design problems and demand that the architect have more time to use primary talents for designing, planning and coordinating the total design effort.

—The economic necessity to find a means of offsetting costs of services, which are rising more rapidly than the rate of compensation within outmoded fee schedule recommendations.

—The need to compete both with sophisticated independent disciplines seeking to supplant the architect and with practitioners who have already embraced more sophisticated methods.

—The necessity to serve clients who have come to expect competence in architectural services which requires modern methods and techniques capable of conserving the client's time and money.

—The requirement to produce better, more detailed construction documents for contractors and subcontractors, requiring greater numbers of sets of these documents for better bids.

—The common-sense judgment to stay abreast of the latest developments in any profession and make a qualitative choice of acceptance or rejection based on reasonable understanding of the available options.

CONVENTIONAL DRAWING MEDIUMS

Fundamentally, most architects rely on some means of translucent material to prepare the design, usually a thin sketch paper, either white or canary. When defined, the design is committed to a final drawing surface, one of several mediums generally used on one side:

—Tracing paper or vellum. These basic drawing materials are used extensively.

—Tracing linen or cloth, used by some offices, particularly for official work, with either ink or pencil. For many years, this was the only material approved for permanent record drawings required by public clients.

—Drafting film (usually acetate or Mylar), generally replacing tracing linen. This has great dimensional stability and unsurpassed transparency over any other present drawing material.

Drawings are still made with pencil or pen, but the ruling pen of old has been generally replaced by reservoir pens with nibs of fixed dimension to produce uniform line character. Pencils vary in hardness to the degree of precision desired. There are many other drawing aids, such as templates, used with either pencil or pen, and wax-based transparent overlays

to transfer preprinted information of lettering, symbols and architectural elements. Many offices use special stamps for landscaping effects, but the design so done is permanent and cannot be removed easily.

ORGANIZATION AND STANDARDS

The architect must decide on the size and shape of the drawing medium. The final document size may determine this, but it must be resolved in advance of doing any work if the end result is to be uniform. The architect may elect to use a stock precut size (expressed here in inches), such as 18×24, 24×36 or 30×42, or may prefer those sizes compatible with commercial printing: multiples of the familiar 8½× 11(A) such as 11×17(B), 17×22(C), 22× 34(D) or 34×44(E).

Along with selection of sheet size, a manner must be determined giving each sheet a means of individual recognition. The numbering system can be strictly numerical, or can be a combination of numbers and letters, with the latter used for the discipline such as "E" for electrical, "S" for structural, etc. In this case, each subdivision under a separate letter would be numbered consecutively within the discipline, and a list or index is required to tabulate all the drawings in a set of documents, as described later on.

Drawings can be subdivided into multiples of 8½×11 (for that group of sizes, for example) with partial information provided in smaller format, and these sheets can be assembled to make a composite drawing sheet. Modular coordination, based on a 4-inch or 100mm module prepared on preprinted, gridded drawing surfaces, has been used by architects, as have systems using a grid of arbitrary size to identify cross-referencing from one drawing to another, much like a road map system of letters in one direction and numbers in another.

DRAWINGS 227

Examples of abbreviations, legend and symbols are shown in Exhibit 18-5A and schedule formats in Exhibit 18-5B, as used by Stone, Marraccini and Patterson. Recommended standards proposed by a task force of the AIA Office Practice Committee are covered in an article titled "A Uniform System for Working Drawings" in the January 1974 *AIA Journal.* Similar information appears in Recommended Standards on Production Procedure issued by the Northern California Chapter AIA. Most offices have developed their own standards, some recorded in office manuals. There are sufficient differences between these various standards that can cause confusion; a single national standard would eliminate this kind of problem.

An article titled "Bidding Document Microfilming" by James W. Robertson in the November 1971 *AIA Journal* discusses a microfilm system and some of the precautions which should be adhered to in the preparation of drawings for microfilming.

No matter what format, drawing size or numbering system is used, one practice should always be followed: the creation of a small mockup (about 5½×8) of every drawing before final documents are started. Each mockup should have a freehand sketch, as closely to scale as possible, to determine that:

—All of the required information will be included.

—Repetition of the same information in more than one place, on the other hand, will be prevented.

Use of drawing mockups will aid in making the decision as to the scale of each drawing and/or detail, and will assist in the preparation of the design since the overall comprehension of the work required is in hand at the start of the effort. Such use also makes it possible to determine at the outset personnel needed for the drafting effort and its probable cost, to organize the work in the drafting room

efficiently, and to assist in controlling production step by step.

ADVANCED DRAFTING TECHNIQUES

In addition to the production of drawings solely by hand, there is another approach. Objectively examined, the usual set of working drawings will reveal a tremendous amount of redundancy in repetition of similar rooms in structures such as hospitals, schools, office buildings, hotels and apartments—kept similar for economy in both construction and flexibility of use. Elevations and sections repeat many of the same elements on all sides of the structures. It is here that an opportunity exists to reallocate much of the usual time devoted to the routine design and drafting to methods whereby much more time can be spent on design and exploration of design alternatives, and much less time on the production of the finished drawing.

These techniques may rely to a great part on copiers which make an exact 100 percent reproduction without distortion. A copier which does not make such an exact reproduction has only limited use in this accelerated technique. It should be noted that most copiers used to reproduce letter-size material are set to produce slightly oversize copy.

Experience and exposure to these methods can progress from the simple office copier to the professionally staffed photographic and lithographic capabilities of progressive reproduction firms in nearly every large city. Areas not having access to these reproduction shops, or so-called blueprinters, invariably have printing shops with untapped photographic and lithographic facilities. These are untapped because many printers do not realize that a market exists, and many architects in turn do not understand the potentiality.

Some architectural offices have in-house equipment, which is surely a con-

venience, but all the work can be done by specialists outside the architect's office, provided working habits can be adjusted to accommodate somewhat different schedules. If the mockup principal is followed, the architect can usually schedule the release of portions of the work for reproduction or photographic assistance without interfering with the office routine in any way. A careful study of available options to simplify the design effort and drafting requirements will lead to greater efficiency and increased time for design itself and very likely to more profit.

The techniques are means of transmitting information and have no intrinsic or professional advantage except to transmit information in a clearer and more economical manner.

COMPOSITE DRAFTING. Components of composite drafting include photo-drafting, appliqué drafting, scissors drafting and registration drafting. Of these, the most familiar method is photo-drafting. Simply put, this method uses photographically prepared paper or Mylar working surfaces and, mainly, previously produced drawings and information as some component of the photo-drafting application.

This is particularly applicable for the incorporation of previously prepared plans for a project where alterations and additions are to be made. If, instead of an existing structure, previously prepared preliminary drawings or schematics were used, they could be incorporated into a final set of plans, provided this procedure was contemplated when they were prepared. This foresight eliminates the need of redrafting and, more importantly, preserves the design concept from its inception through the construction documents phase.

One of the reasons for the popularity of photo-drafting is the dissemination of clearly understood information about this process. (In fact, all of the advanced techniques are especially well illustrated and documented in manufacturers' literature and trade publications.) The February 1972 *Architectural Record* article titled "Photo-Drafting: Time-Saving Aid to Quality" succinctly presents 16 steps in organizing and planning the process as used by Gruzen & Partners.

Three articles published in the *AIA Journal* are among the photo-drafting references. One by the author, "A Design System That Produces Contract Drawings," appearing in March 1970 utilizes techniques familiar to all commercial reproduction establishments. Illustrations of later extensions of these techniques accompany this text. Another by Donald E. Jarvis, FAIA, in the March 1974 issue titled "Integraphs: An Experiment in Production" spells out the working of the system and the reasoning behind its adoption, based on an available publication which carries a similar name. He says in the original document, "But a truly efficient system should do more than recover wasted hours . . . it should assist us in the creation of architecture. By its nature it should help us produce the buildings we conceive—and produce them on time and in the money." The search for a better direction led to subdivision of documentation by Jarvis Putty Jarvis, Inc., into these 11 categories:

—Chapter 1. Site Improvements
—Chapter 2. Demolition
—Chapter 3. Structural
—Chapter 4. Envelope
—Chapter 5. Space Dividers
—Chapter 6. Ceilings
—Chapter 7. Fixtures and Fittings
—Chapter 8. Conveying Systems
—Chapter 9. Air Conditioning
—Chapter 10. Plumbing
—Chapter 11. Electrical

Segregating the work in this fashion allows, among other things, the development of concurrent activities without the necessity of awaiting the completion of other parts. The firm utilizes overlays for

better design effort as well as automatic capability of multicolor printing of the final construction documents. The drawings are identified with two sets of numbers, both large, in blocks, one over the other. The uppermost is the chapter number with the title of the chapter. Below this is the drawing number of the consecutively numbered complete set of drawings.

Jerry Quebe, AIA, of Hansen Lind Meyer, clearly outlines the characteristics and tools for registration drafting in "A Comprehensive Approach to Improving the Quality of Contract Documents" in the February 1975 issue. This firm organizes its documents into an integrated format in the following 12 categories:

—Section 1. General Information
—Section 2. Site Development
—Section 3. Structural
—Section 4. Building Enclosure
—Section 5. Building Division
—Section 6. Ceiling Construction
—Section 7. Fixtures and Furnishings
—Section 8. Plumbing
—Section 9. Piping
—Section 10. HVAC
—Section 11. Electrical Power
—Section 12. Communications

Additional subjects may be included in sections identified by further numbers in the series.

All sheets of each section are numbered with the number of the section as a digit, and each sheet as a decimal, e.g., 4.23 is the 23rd sheet in Section 4. There is no attempt to number the sheets consecutively throughout the set, and the complete drawing list is in the Index to Drawings in Section 1.

While a full discussion of all of the possible systems is not intended here, two offices—one very large and one medium size—use a tool known as an Itek Positive Printer to produce many of their contract documents. This piece of equipment, costing in the neighborhood of $20,000 if purchased outright, and leasing for about

$20 per day, has the capability of producing black copies on white background from original copy, or in the words of the reproduction people, positive to positive. The machine comes in two sizes, and the larger (which is what these offices are using) accommodates drawings up to 36×48 on the copy board. The size of the finished copy is limited to 18×24. There is no original tracing of any of the sheets, and when a large drawing is needed, the printed small sheet is sent out, a film negative of 105mm size is made, then a film positive at 36×48 size, and from this Ozalid prints can be made.

The Itek Positive Printer has mechanisms for producing halftones. Renderings, pencil drawings, etc., can be reproduced with the line quality and gradation intact, as well as making halftone positives of photographs for brochures and published material. As drawings are prepared, an 18×24 positive print is made, and if additional information, such as numbering, becomes necessary, it is either added to the print or a new portion is added where applicable. The positive print is sent to a commercial printer who makes a paper plate and prints the copies, usually 100 to 300 of each sheet.

The basic philosophy of Stone, Marraccini and Patterson (SMP) in producing contract drawings is, simply put, to convey the design requirements concisely in the most economical way, both in the amount of drafting and in labor cost. To accomplish this end, the firm incorporates two techniques: systems and photo-paste-up drafting.

Whenever possible, SMP sets up systems in documenting the design requirements. The majority of the firm's current systems are based on simple standard masters for all projects such as door, modular casework and finish hardware schedules. All masters are used completely for every project with only small additions for specific requirements. A certain code from the standard master for a door, casework or hardware item will always have the same requirements. The advantage is very clear when everyone involved in the project, including the plan checker and estimator, knows what each code represents. The time saved in not having to work out schedules for every job is substantial.

SMP's system of using codes to indicate room materials and standard indications for various items such as partitions and equipment on the floor plans also is a time saver. Some of the SMP systems have been referenced in the Northern California Chapter AIA publication.

Photo-paste-up drafting involves using equipment as well as setting up production systems to facilitate the work. SMP has set up the tracing sheets in modules from one-quarter of the standard sheet size down to 8½×11 sheets. The firm has also developed banks for standard details and special details, all on one module or multiple modules and typed instead of hand lettered. Each detail drawn is a potential detail for future projects, and details can be added to or changed in part to become the final detail. For photography, SMP uses in-house equipment or commercial printing services. In-house equipment includes the Itek 18.24 Positive Printer, Headliner 820, VariTyper 1360 engineering typewriter and Xerox 7000.

The Itek 18.24 is a camera assembly which can produce a positive print in two minutes without a negative. It can reduce in one operation to 33½ percent or enlarge to 300 percent. Besides being used for other artwork, it will produce all scale changes in drawings and compositing of available drawings and details.

The Headliner is a machine with typemasters and works like a giant Dymo which composes words on adhesive-backed transparent or opaque films. This machine greatly reduces the use of press-on lettering.

The VariTyper typewriter has an open end carriage and a selection of different letter type fonts. Typing is used for details and key plans.

The Xerox 7000 is used for reproducing and reducing drawings for paste-ups when accuracy is not of importance. A typical SMP project may have some or all of the following techniques used:

—The index-legend sheet is composed of paste-ups of standard legends, symbols, abbreviations and typed drawing index.

—The site plan may be drawn directly on a halftone survey Mylar reproduction.

—Key plans are actually mosaics of all photo-reduced large-scale plans.

—Exterior elevations may be paste-ups of preliminary drawings or paste-ups of repeated bays to form complete elevations.

—Building sections may be paste-ups of hard-line final study sections.

—Any detail sheets may be composed of final study details and final details.

—Room material schedule and details are paste-ups of standard details and special details which may be drawn or retrieved from the special detail bank.

—Door schedule and details, casework schedule and details, food service equipment details and miscellaneous details are similarly handled.

—Reflected ceiling plans may be drawn on reduced-size halftone floor plans.

To make everyone aware of all the standards and procedures, SMP has issued to all production personnel an Office Drafting Standards Book which outlines in detail the do's and don'ts of each type of drawing sheet. This book is updated with changes and additional standards as new ones are developed.

There is constant review of the firm's details with field feedback. Each detail is separate and independent and not tied to others on the same drawing. Detail sheets are filed in a letter file with a set of masters for reference. The tendency is to use stan-

dard details known to have been successful, rather than to create new details continuously, most of which are hardly distinguishable from those previously produced. Because there is system in the organization of work, efficiency results in its execution.

On the other hand, Lucas and Stubbs Associates Ltd. uses a different approach. Speaking of a particular project, Frank Lucas says, "Our prime use was to draw at large scales, piece the buildings together by using Itek photography, paste them on large sheets and have a Mylar or autopositive made for the final sheet. We found the Itek Printmaker to be just as valuable to us in our early presentation process. We make large sketches which are very rough and freehand. We then reduce these and have them applied or use them, of course, mounted and framed. The camera is invaluable to us, and we constantly find new uses for it. We have practically prepared our entire brochure by having a camera-ready master to be reproduced by a local printing company. This, of course, results in a substantial savings in our printing."

COMPUTER DRAFTING. When using computer drafting techniques, original software (computer programs) must, of course, be developed by an experienced programmer. Data entry and manipulation can usually be performed by the architect, designer, draftsman or technician. Where there is a great deal of repetition of the kinds of elements and a great variety as to their interfacing and juxtapositioning, computer applications are very useful. The programmed input can be a mathematical model, or it can be developed by means of an illuminated console and a light stylus, which effects modifications to the input material.

The stylus method has electrical mechanisms which will straighten lines, round circles, square corners and change scale on command. Thus actual drafting skill is much less critical than for a drawing. When so commanded, the display will show the corrected format and will also permit the movement of previously displayed material in different configuration, arrangement, sizes and shapes. At the same time, it will keep track of all sorts of other input data such as area, perimeter, scanning for minimum sizes, orientation and estimating for materials. To date, however, it is expensive and can generally only be used conveniently by the larger offices which can support a programmer as a part of their work force. There are a few program packages available on the market that can be easily used by practitioners who do not have prior computer experience.

If the visual qualities of a project must be displayed in many aspects to the client or approving body, the computer is capable of producing any number of perspectives from a plan and elevation. It can draw eye-level, worm's-eye, bird's-eye, close-up or distant perspectives from every conceivable location in a full half sphere of space around the building. It can eliminate hidden lines or can even draw scenes from inside the structure looking outward, revealing elements of the design as seen from the interior. Very few of these are full drawings, most being well-defined armatures for the delineator, but it is possible to have a full perspective produced, as is seen in the example by Richardson Associates (Exhibit 18-9B).

PRINTING TECHNIQUES

The most common approaches to printing are described here, although progress is being made in such developments as four-color process printing.

DIAZO AND PHOTOCOPY PROCESSES.

In conjunction with both conventional and photographic techniques, selection must be made of the medium by which the information will be transmitted to the user. For conventionally drawn documents, where no intermediate level of information is required, the choices are limited, and the most generally used process is the diazo, or ammonia-developed, print. This can be produced in black, blue or even a deep maroon paper. These copies are almost invariably made at the same size as the drawings, and the costs are computed by the square foot.

It is possible, however, to have the original drawing reduced to a smaller size, usually half size, by a xerographic process by using a machine such as the Xerox 1860. This will make both opaque and transparent copies at smaller size. The transparency (either a paper or polyester base material) can be used to produce half-size diazo prints. While the initial Xerox copy is more expensive per drawing, once it has been reduced, subsequent copies made by diazo will be considerably less costly. As they are but one-quarter of the size of the original, the per square foot costs are proportionately less. The reproduction quality of later machines has improved over that of the original models, but care must be taken in storage of the reduced transparencies: There is a possibility of image transference from the face of one sheet to the back of another stored above it in a drawer. The photocopy process is indeed the first step toward photographic reproduction when the machine used is a type of camera with a lens system but with an electrostatic negative carrier and transferral process.

Depending on the size of the data to be transmitted, office copiers are highly useful for the preparation of information for drawings as well as their distribution to the ultimate user. The author has used the office copier extensively in the preparation of final architectural documents to reduce and eliminate much of what would be a full photographic effort. It is important to determine in advance what information will be required and then to use the most effective or economical means of producing this information in final form.

OFFSET PRINTING. This is most often used for the reproduction of sets of bidding documents, the majority of which are made in the range of 17×22. Some prints are produced up to 28 inches in length, but this requires a larger printing press which is not always available. Most printers have 17×22 presses and are quite competitive. If a set of documents has been prepared with reasonably large lettering, it can be reduced to one-half size quite easily for a substantial reduction in printing costs. A much larger quantity of these reduced size sets can be produced for the same price as the old-time "20 sets" by standard diazo process. Since the Standard Form of Agreement Between Owner and Architect, AIA Document B141, calls for the former to pay for reproduction, it is to the owner's advantage to secure sufficient bidding documents so that each subcontractor has access to the entire set for bidding purposes. This tends to reduce contingency factors in subcontractors' bids.

Offset printing also has uses in the production of the drawings before final printing of bidding sets. If there is a predetermined desire to use either half-sized photocopy or offset printing of the final documents, many standard details can be prepared by offset printing on 8½×11 sheets which are affixed to the base drawing in lieu of redrawing the same information over and over.

One word of warning at this point: No set of drawings should ever be marked or stamped "This is a reduced set of plans." Every drawing should be capable of being scaled at the exact scale indicated. If it is contemplated that the drawings be produced on reduced-size sheets, the scale stated on the drawings should be that at which they are shown. If there are two sizes of drawings, then each size should be shown with the proper scale indicated. Under these conditions, no confusion exists in the mind of the bidder as to whether or not the information shown is at the correct scale.

COLOR LITHOGRAPHY. There is no difference between offset printing and color lithography insofar as the printing is concerned. Both are done on an offset press, the principal dissimilarity being in the preparation of the information to be printed. Generally, color lithography is made from a series of individually prepared documents, one for each color, and these must be registered by matching marks or holes, etc., so they can be kept in exact alignment with each other. When printing, the printer matches only the registration marks and is not concerned with the information contained on the plates and cannot make corrections at that stage of the work. Each color is printed separately and may be in several intensities of the same color, or in different colors, each carrying a different level of information. Difference in intensity is accomplished by "screening" (the use of a Benday screen which has an intensity value and a fineness value), enabling the user to determine the degree of contrast between the levels of information.

The degree of clarity of work printed in several colors is totally dependent on the preparation of the original information and the constant awareness of the need to check continually for any interference of one level of information with that in a different color. Usually the beginner will believe that if everything is shown on one sheet, it will be crystal clear. What happens is that very little is legible, and the proponent must start again to simplify levels of information. This will produce an understanding of the importance of pre-planning each step of the way, the basic approach of producing contract documents, whether they are produced conventionally or unconventionally.

APPLICATION OF ADVANCED TECHNIQUES
The most satisfactory means of examination and comparison of the methods of the various offices is to investigate and explore in some depth of detail the work done by some of these architects throughout the United States in their particular practice of architecture. Some of these firms are large and some are small, but the acceptance of advanced methods of practice shows no correlation with their

size. Essentially, each office has arrived at its own solution, and analyses are made from actual working documents, produced in their normal operation by the following firms:
—Jarvis Putty Jarvis, Inc., Dallas, using "Integraphs."
—Hansen Lind Meyer, Iowa City, using photography, lithography and multicolor format, with a system of production related to a division of the work similar to "Integraphs."
—Richardson Associates, Seattle, using photography and lithography, with solid and shaded single-color black-line methods of producing final documents.
—Lucas and Stubbs Associates Ltd., Charleston, S.C., a medium-sized office using in-house photographic equipment to prepare and present preliminary and final documents.
—Stone, Marraccini and Patterson, San Francisco, a very large office using the same type of equipment with a very different end result.
—Ned H. Abrams – Architect, Sunnyvale, Calif., whose office has used all of these techniques for more than 20 years, and who has supplied the photographs for the accompanying exhibits which illustrate these techniques.

EXHIBIT 18-1. NED H. ABRAMS—ARCHITECT: PRESENTATION DRAWINGS (Demonstration of use of photographic equipment to create rendered tones automatically, without necessity of a delineator creating such tones)

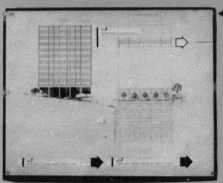

18-1A. a) Rough sketch of front and rear elevations; **b)** tracing paper strip elevation of one floor, upper right.

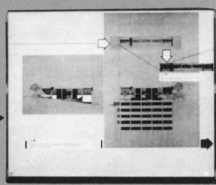

18-1B. a) Ozalid print strip elevation plus colored Zip-a-Tone; **b)** positive print of Ozalid of strip elevations, center right; **c)** Zip-a-Tone over openings on Ozalid print of elevations.

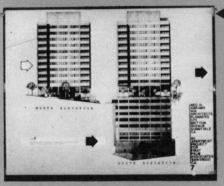

18-1C. Assembled elevation of positive print strips and positive print of front and rear elevations from 18-1B. All reproduction to this point is at same size and same scale.

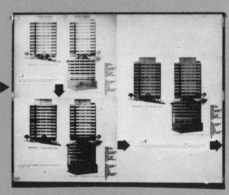

18-1D. a) Under- and overexposed prints, left, of drawing of sheet in 18-1C, which can be adjusted for tonal range desired; **b)** properly exposed positive print of same sheet cut out and pasted on plain background, right.

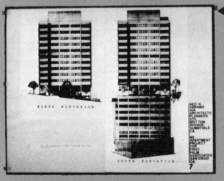

18-1E. Reenlargement of completed drawing in 18-1D(b) back to original size, producing drawing essentially the same as 18-1C from finished assembly.

18-1F. Final presentation cover with site plan and location plan, together with portion of final elevation used for final submission.

EXHIBIT 18-2. NED H. ABRAMS – ARCHITECT: PRELIMINARY DRAWINGS (Illustration of development of a project from preliminary studies, based on economic and site criteria, through unit design and elevations and finally to printed preliminary presentation copies)

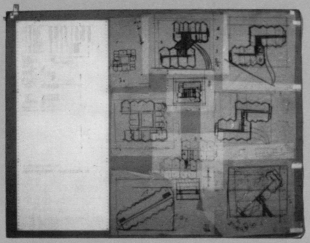

18-2A. Design starting with computer printout of economic analysis, left, followed by freehand felt brush studies of building configuration on site.

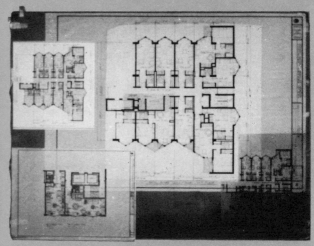

18-2B. a) Original drawing of apartment unit used for model, lower left; **b)** partial plan of ½ typical floor at larger scale; **c)** clear Mylar positive 50% reduction of ½ typical floor, lower right; **d)** portion of final printed preliminary.

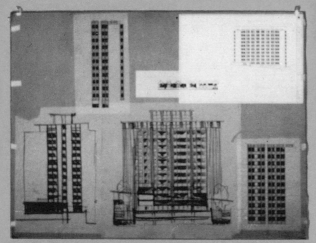

18-2C. a) Rough sketch of elevation; **b)** partial elevation component, lower right and upper center; **c)** print of final preliminary.

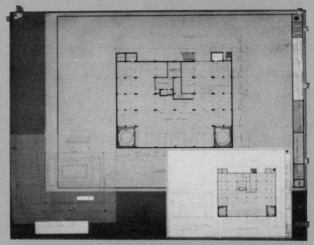

18-2D. a) Basement/garage plan drawn on vellum; **b)** site plan inadvertently omitted, lower left; **c)** print of final preliminary showing rearrangement of garage plan and addition of superimposed site plan, lower right.

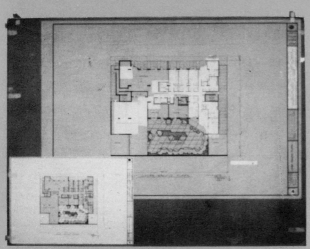

18-2E. a) Lowest level floor plan, with office copier reproduction of small Mylar in 18-2B(c), modified and cut out for appropriate location; **b)** reduced print of final drawing, lower left.

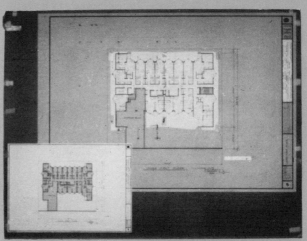

18-2F. a) Next higher level floor showing reuse of both right and reverse reading of office copier prints of reduced Mylar in 18-2B(c); **b)** cutouts for special conditions, darker tone; **c)** reduced print of final drawing, lower left.

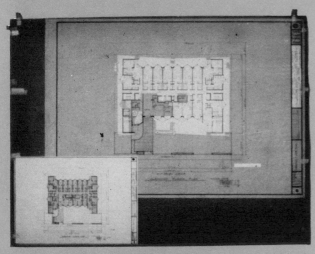

18-2G. a) Next higher level floor showing reuse of both right and reverse reading of reduced Mylar in 18-2B(c); **b)** cutouts for special conditions, darker tone; **c)** reduced print of final drawing, lower left.

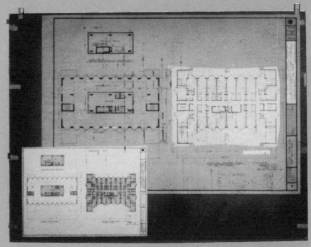

18-2H. a) Typical floor showing reuse of reduced Mylar used in 18-2B(c), with right and reverse reading office copier prints to delineate typical floor; **b)** roof and penthouse plans drawn separately on sheet of vellum, left; **c)** reduced print of final drawing, lower left.

EXHIBIT 18-3. NED H. ABRAMS – ARCHITECT: WORKING DRAWINGS

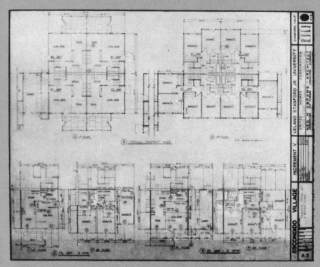

18-3A. Typical unit plan of first and second floors at ¼″ scale. Portion of fire wall indication at lower area of photo added for particular emphasis on specific call-out.

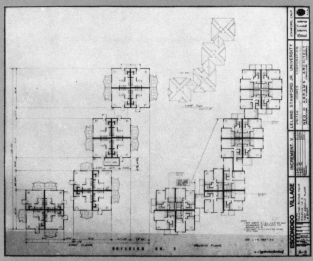

18-3B. ¹⁄₁₆″ scale assembly of unit plans into building arrangement.

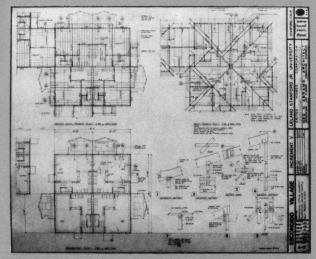

18-3C. ¼″ scale unit plans with structural engineering overlay.

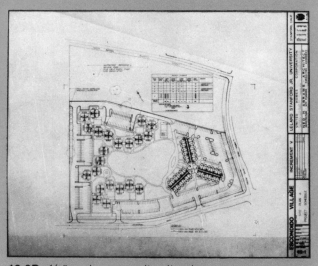

18-3D. ¹⁄₄₀″ scale composite site plan.

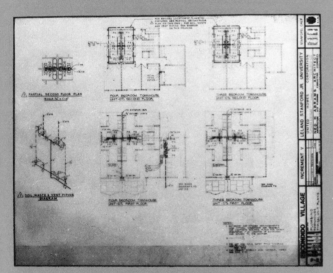

18-3E. ¼″ scale mechanical engineering overlay.

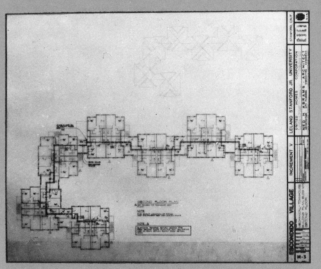

18-3F. ⅟₁₆″ scale mechanical overlay.

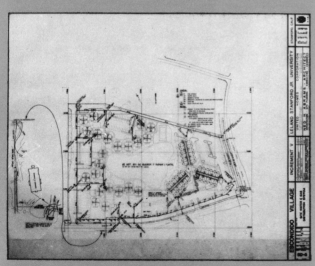

18-3G. ⅟₄₀″ scale mechanical overlay.

18-3H. Enlargement of portion of site plan at ⅟₂₀″ scale for landscaping drawing. Building in same orientation as in 18-3G. ▶

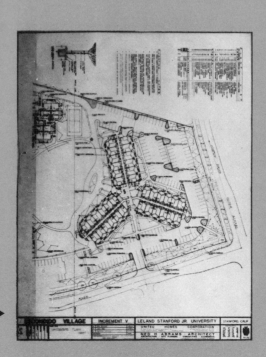

EXHIBIT 18-4. NED H. ABRAMS—ARCHITECT: SITE PLANS

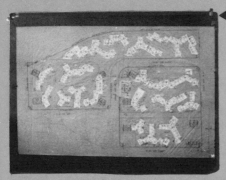

◄**18-4A.** ¼₀″ scale unit plans pasted on rough layout of site plan.

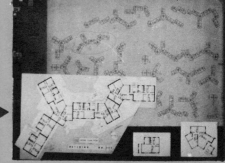

18-4B. ⅛″ scale unit plans pasted► to 18-4A building configurations and reduced to create a positive at ¼₀″ scale.

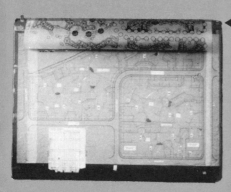

◄**18-4C.** Film positive with landscaping added, superimposed over drafted site plan with pasted-on notes.

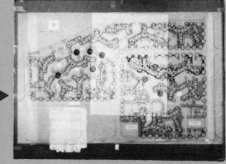

18-4D. Composite of buildings and► landscaping over site plan. Light rectangle in center is intended to separate buildings and site plan by blocking out a portion of the latter.

18-4E. Composite finished draw-► ing with revised schedule.

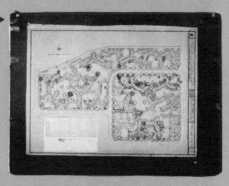

EXHIBIT 18-5. STONE, MARRACCINI AND PATTERSON: LEGENDS AND SCHEDULES

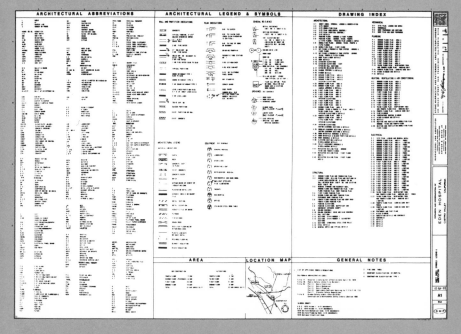

18-5A. Abbreviations legend, index and general notes, with applicable codes and regulations under general notes.

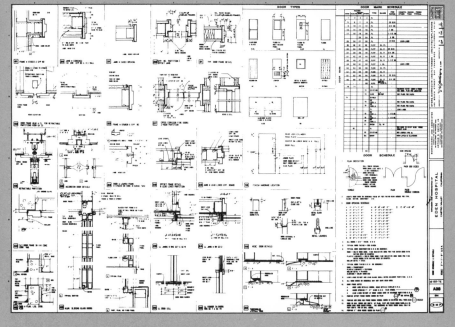

18-5B. Door schedule and details. Door types are covered with 10 typicals and door marks are numbered consecutively, a constant standard. Numbers in each type are increased by 4 for each fire rating (0–20 minute, ¾-hour, 1-hour, 1½-hour, 3-hour).

EXHIBIT 18-6. LUCAS AND STUBBS ASSOCIATES LTD.: PRELIMINARY AND WORKING DRAWINGS

18-6A. Positive print of rendered preliminary drawing showing quality reproduction.

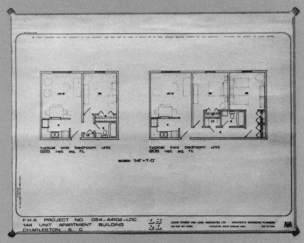

18-6B. Typical unit plans for apartment development.

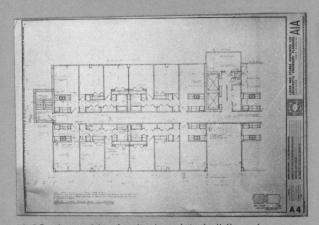

18-6C. Assembly of unit plans into building plan.

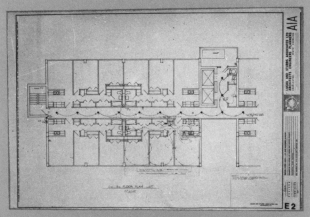

18-6D. Electrical overlay on screened background.

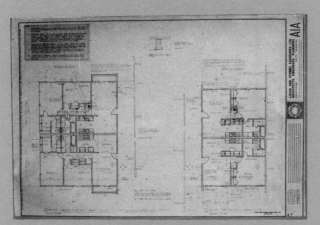

18-6E. Typical unit plans for apartment project.

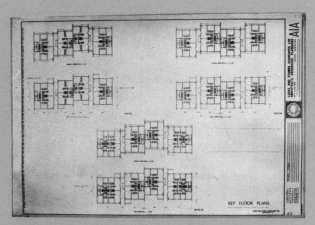

18-6F. Unit plans assembled into buildings.

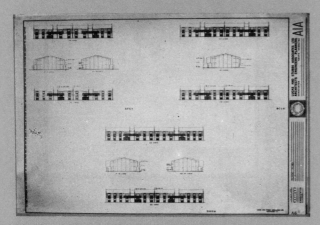

18-6G. Assembly of elevations from unit elements.

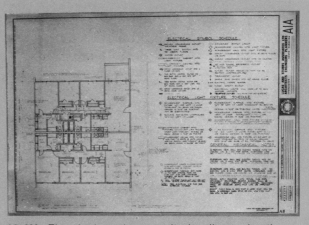

18-6H. Electrical overlay on unit plan (base sheet).

EXHIBIT 18-7. JARVIS PUTTY JARVIS, INC.: INTEGRAPHS (System of producing architectural contract documents)

18-7A. Cover sheet showing division of work into Integraph chapters.

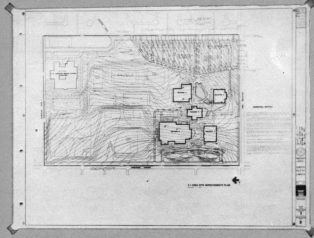

18-7B. Small-scale site plan, with numbering system as described in text.

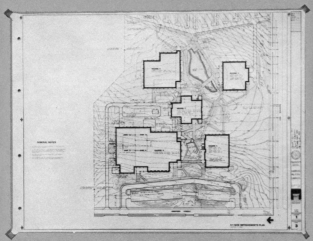

18-7C. Enlarged site plan photographically reproduced.

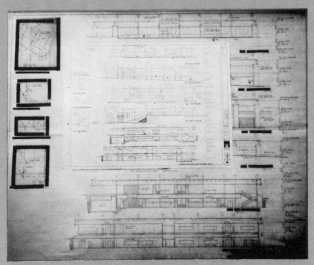

18-7D. Drawing of building elevations and sections superimposed over paste-up from which it was made.

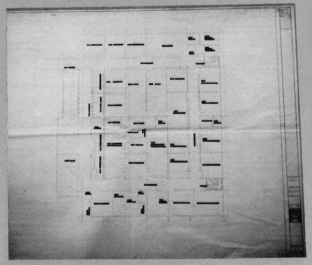

18-7E. Print of paste-up for a floor plan.

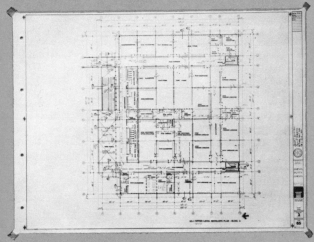

18-7F. Final plan document from paste-up shown in 18-7E.

EXHIBIT 18-7. JARVIS PUTTY JARVIS, INC.: INTEGRAPHS (CONTINUED)

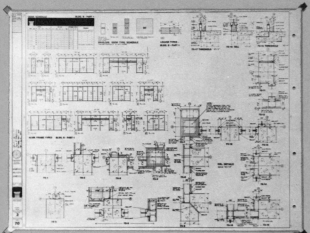

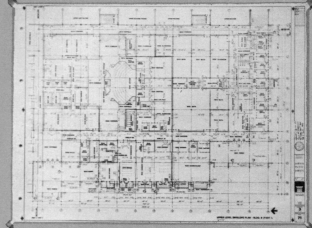

18-7G. Both sides of sheet are used for classification of data. Details shown on sheet at left are related to plan on sheet at right; both are visible simultaneously in bound set.

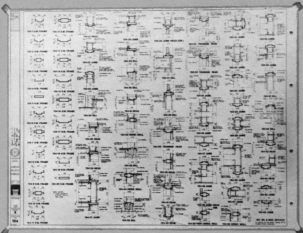

18-7H. Assembly of standard details drawn freehand and reduced to a smaller size.

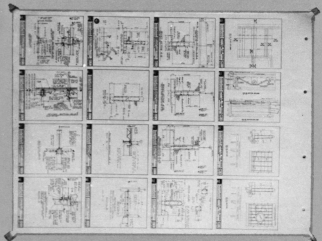

18-7I. Method of preparing addenda on 8½×11″ sheets, reduced 50% and printed in a block of 16.

EXHIBIT 18-8. HANSEN LIND MEYER: ANOTHER APPROACH TO WORKING DRAWINGS

18-8A. Cover sheet showing photo of model of building.

18-8B. Drawing symbols and Index to Drawings in various divisions as described in text.

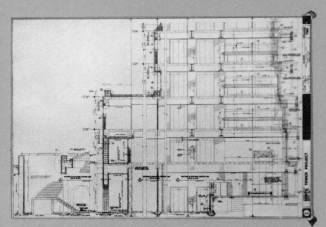

18-8C. Cross section of existing and new work printed in multicolor.

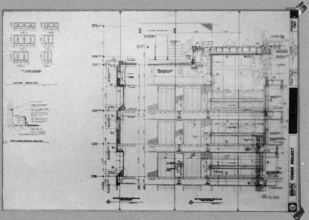

18-8D. Additional sections and details printed in multicolor.

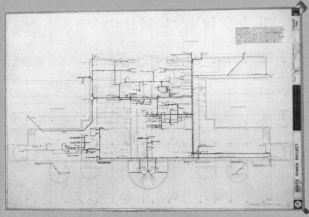

18-8E. Multicolor-printed overlay prepared for mechanical system.

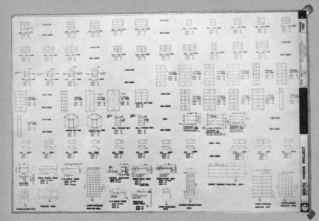

18-8F. Standardized cabinet details.

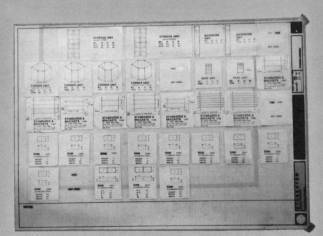

18-8G. Paste-up of prints of standardized cabinet details for a different project showing method of assembling sheets.

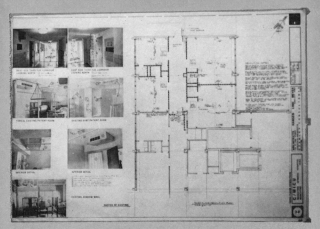

18-8H. Final drawing showing use of annotated photos for remodeling work to clarify extent and location of work to be done.

EXHIBIT 18-9. RICHARDSON ASSOCIATES: STUDIES AND WORKING DRAWINGS

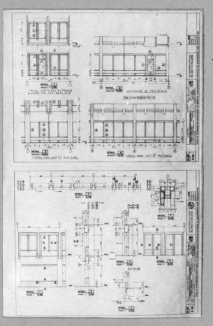

18-9A. Studies of precast structural panels in plan, elevation and section at large scale. Shading around one window is produced by use of 100% rag paper.

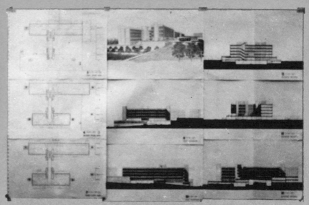

18-9B. Assembly of preliminary drawings into a brochure incorporating rendered window in 18-9A. Perspective is computer-drafted.

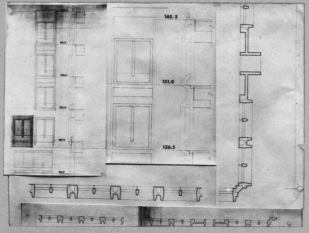

18-9C. Final drawings of wall ◀ panels delineating final use of studies in 18-9A.

18-9D. Base assembly of elements developed in 18-9A, shown in 18-9C, with structural reinforcing ▶ added to identical drawing base sheet.

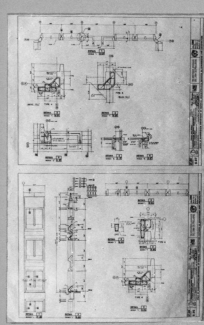

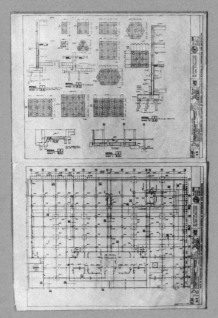

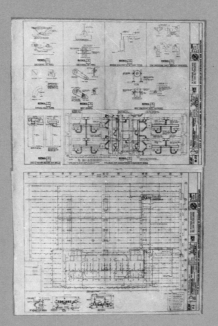

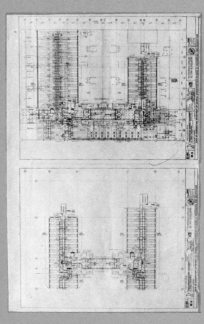

18-9E. Structural drawing of pile configurations drawn without reinforcement, reduced and placed on site plan. Reinforcement then added to typical details when no longer needed for foundation plans.

18-9F. Typical mechanical bay with details of air conditioning and lighting floor plan showing overlay of mechanical work over base plan.

18-9G. Reduced reproduction of typical air conditioning, lighting bay superimposed on overlay of building plans.

Why should an architect change a present method of operation to one of the design "systems" described here? If not for financial reasons or time saved, then it should be altered to provide a better set of contract documents and better service—the aim of all professional efforts.

Primarily, the objective of contract documents is to convey the greatest amount of required information in the clearest possible manner, with sufficient copies that every bidder and subbidder has access to every sheet of the set of drawings. Any bidder having only partial information must allow for a contingency which cannot be seen on the drawings at hand. If the method of producing bidding documents is one which permits multiple copies at nominal cost, the client will receive favorable bids to the credit of the architect. If the bidding sets are to be prepared for offset printing, then the preparation of the entire working drawing effort must be directed from the beginning to the end product. All of the documents must be made with this in mind.

The decision to use offset printing for reproduction of bidding documents can result in additional benefits. As the drawing medium may be opaque as well as translucent, the choice of subject matter to be applied is broadened considerably. For example, details from catalogs, books and other sources may be used in their opaque form. Thus the benefits of flexibility and the opportunities to save time and increase efficiency may be realized by all size firms. To stay competitive, the use of advanced drawing and reproduction techniques will be increasingly employed by the architectural profession.

BIBLIOGRAPHY

Architect's Handbook of Professional Practice. Washington, D.C.: AIA, parts updated periodically.

Current compendium of practice information; chapter on drawings especially pertinent.

Architectural Graphic Standards. Joseph N. Boaz, ed. Washington, D.C.: AIA, 6th ed., 1970.

Invaluable reference book in the drafting room.

"Bidding Document Microfilming." James W. Robertson. *AIA Journal,* November 1971.

How to make drawings acceptable to the camera.

"A Comprehensive Approach to Improving the Quality of Contract Documents." Jerry Quebe. *AIA Journal,* February 1975.

Presents registration drafting and organizational formats.

"A 'Design System' That Produces Contract Drawings." Ned H. Abrams. *AIA Journal,* March 1970.

Describes photo-drafting techniques.

"A Drawing Method for Fast Perspectives." Cliff Phillips. *AIA Journal,* February 1971.

Useful presentation for architects.

"Integraphs: An Experiment in Production." Donald E. Jarvis. *AIA Journal,* March 1974.

Means of interpreting written and graphic instructions to speed up the making of contract documents.

Integraphs–An Experiment in Architectural Communication. Dallas: Jarvis Putty Jarvis, Inc., 1973.

Valuable guide that should be in every architect's library and drafting room.

"Photo-Drafting: Time-Saving Aid to Quality." *Architectural Record,* February 1972.

Outlines 16 steps in using the process.

"A Uniform System for Working Drawings." AIA Committee on Office Practice. *AIA Journal,* January 1974.

Describes recommended standards for architects' working drawing abbreviations, material designations, graphic symbols, schedule formats, standard drawing sizes.

Working Drawings in Use. C. D. Daltry and D. T. Crawshaw. Watford, England: Building Research Establishment, June 1973.

A study of British practices in working drawings and recommendations for improvement.

For bibliographic references on computer-aided drafting, see Chapter 15.

Chapter 19
Specifications

PAUL HEINEMAN, FCSI

Communication of the architect's design decisions is accomplished fundamentally through the medium of drawings and specifications. The function of the latter is less well known than that of the former. Even less well known are the innovations taking place in the art of preparing specifications.

In their basic form, specifications set forth those project requirements most readily expressed in words: quality of materials and equipment, installation methods and techniques, and results to be achieved. Drawings show the requirements best represented in graphic form: size, shape, scope and location of the various building elements and the manner in which they relate to each other in the overall design.

The complementary functions and purposes of these two mediums, generally speaking, should not be interchanged or duplicated. Notes on the drawings for identifying materials should be made in broad, general terms, leaving more specific identification to the specifications. The simplified use of the same standardized terminology and other communication elements in both drawings and specifications will aid the coordination and integration of the contract documents.

APPROACHES

Two major approaches to the preparation of specifications are performance specifying and prescriptive specifying. Each has variants. Whatever the approach, the architect's intent should be communicated clearly and completely.

PERFORMANCE SPECIFYING. Specifications have traditionally been written in the prescriptive manner, as were those for the Market House in Annapolis in 1752: "A Market House . . . the Posts and Rafters to be of yellow Poplar, and the Weather Boarding to be of Feather-edged yellow Poplar Plank; a Roof of Galloping Rafters, with a small Turrett for a Bell, in the Middle of it, the Roof and Turrett to be shingled with good Cypress Shingles; and the Weather Boarding to be painted with Oil Colour . . ."

In today's competitive building economy and legalistic atmosphere, the prescriptive specification just for the weather boarding may require several pages of technical language. With the number of components of a market house multiplied a hundredfold since 1752, the writing of prescriptive specifications has become burdensome.

Architects and engineers have asked, and building contractors and owners have also queried, why not specify the result desired rather than prescribing every step to the result? Why not write performance specifications rather than prescriptive ones?

Since the early 1960's, the all-out performance approach has been applied in several construction projects, notably in aggregated programs of school construction, industrial structures, housing and government office buildings. Most of the projects have involved building systems for building skeleton, diaphragms and energy distribution.

Is the performance approach simpler than the prescriptive? The answer is no, except in rare instances. The performance of each major part of a building is complex. By the time durability, safety and resistance to water, cold, heat and movement have been specified, and by the time other factors such as availability, repairability, economy and the comfort of the occupants have been considered, the specification may become complicated.

Performance in use is better described at the level of building systems rather than at the level of materials, and systems are most effectively employed in repetitive mass housing or in aggregated markets such as multiple school building programs. The exclusive use of performance criteria has scarcely penetrated to the level of simple building-block products used in conventional one-of-a-kind construction specifications.

Some difficulties in employing performance criteria are:

—The need to be complete and exhaustive in selecting criteria is paramount. (It is crucial to specify in detail that the roof not deteriorate in a polluted atmosphere nor crack under winter foot traffic.)

—Tests must be devised to evaluate responses to a performance specification. (Many tests, such as for the brittleness of roofing or the accessibility of a ceiling system, have not been formulated, much less tried and documented. The time required for evaluation of test results may be considerable.)

—Contractor and manufacturer response must be generated. (The cost of responding to a performance specification that requires change in manufacturing or site erection procedures, with time-consuming engineering, submittal, mock-up, costing, testing and warranty procedures, can be high.)

—Many visually sensitive items must be specified prescriptively, "out-of-system." (Control of appearance is difficult in performance specifying.)

—Expert designers and specifiers must be employed to write performance specifications. (And design procedures must be altered to seek and respond to manufacturer input from the earliest stages.)

—It is not easy to find aggregated building markets which will economically justify the performance approach.

The last item needs interpretation. Performance specifications are usually advocated because they may, among other things, foster innovation. In prescriptive specifying, only two routes to innovation are possible: The architect takes a chance by specifying a product untested on an actual project (or only tested in a laboratory), or the builder requests substitution of a product that will purportedly do the job just as well. Both routes carry dangers to architect and owner. Therefore, the impetus to employ performance specifying is, in large part, that it will invite innovation with less risk to the architect and less cost to the owner. Unfortunately, the verification that must accompany the introduction of new materials or assemblies is expensive. Usually it takes a sizable building project to provide the economic climate in which performance specifying will pay off for all concerned.

The total use of performance criteria is a revolutionary approach in experimental stages for a few government-sponsored projects. Total performance-specified buildings will not likely be encountered in the near future, save for a few firms specializing in this approach.

However, the insertion of some performance concepts and language within prescriptively specified, conventionally delivered project specifications is definitely an opportunity in current practice. The art of easing the prescriptive approach toward expected results, with properly stated criteria, tests and evaluation procedures, is not casually accomplished. Today's architect should not let the buzz word "performance" lead to liability problems: The utmost in competence and completeness is needed here.

PRESCRIPTIVE SPECIFYING. The bulk of specifying is done prescriptively: describing each material and method. An understanding of how everything fits and functions rests in the mind of the architect and must be communicated. Three approaches to prescriptive specifying are in common use. In practice, two or three are frequently combined to more fully prescribe what is expected.

Descriptive Method. The descriptive way of specifying attempts to spell out the qualities of a product or workmanship without reference to standards or pro-

prietary names. For a simple product like natural stone, the method is ideal. It is the easiest way to communicate the expected attributes. But in the case of a manufactured product, the method can be tedious, presumptive and even questionable. It is wasteful to devote a page of text to the manufacturing processes that result in an acceptable locker. It is imprudent to specify what may be only one manufacturer's process when another's may produce just as serviceable a product. Many specifications for government projects are unnaturally limited by law to this one method except where a published standard providentially exists.

Reference Method. For many simple materials and material tests, and for some more complex assemblies of materials and techniques of fabrication, standards exist. The citing of a standard can cut many lines of descriptive text from a specification. The quality of many U.S. standards, sponsored by government as well as industry, is often adequate to the needs of good building. Standards should be used carefully. Many cover a range of qualities from which the specifier must choose; some are not effective in all regions and climates; some set the standard for a class of products too low and must be upgraded for better quality construction. A good specifier acquires a library of published standards for reference, employing them for their obvious advantages but only when the material is readily understood.

Proprietary Method. Along with citing a standard, naming a manufacturer's product is the most concise way to specify. In a free-market economy, there are usually several producers competing, so it has become customary and sensible to name three products. Many government agencies, in recognizing descriptive and reference specifying, permit and benefit from the inclusion of three proprietary

product names in the specifications.

Among the advantages of proprietary specifying are its directness and its shortening of estimating and review time. Trade names are frequently recognized by estimators and reviewers. Their use leaves less doubt as to what is wanted—a blessing in a complex building climate with short bidding and building times.

The use of proprietary references requires caution. The specifier must know what is being specified, must trust in the maker's quality control, must be prepared to make the tough decision of whether to accept as equal a product that differs in minor respects, and must know how to ferret out an unworthy substitution. In the hands of the experienced specifier, trade names are a powerful tool with which to set a standard of quality.

Combined Method. In practice, descriptive, reference and proprietary methods are often combined. Since, in a given specifying task, the three rarely match, the specifier should state in the supplementary conditions that the description of specific qualities needed for the project takes precedence over the more broadly written standards, and that the description of qualities and the reference standards together take precedence over the cited proprietary product. Then, if the producer reduces quality or if a doubtful substitution is proposed, the specifier is not put in the position of trying to defend a product over which there is no control. An example of the combined method:

2.10 ROOFING FASTENERS
  A. Qualities: Spread head type, noncorroding, with a withdrawal resistance of at least 40 lbs. each in gypsum concrete.
  B. Standard: ASTM A5000.
  C. Source:
    Lockdown A-5, by Ace, Inc.
    Duo-Prong, by Deucie Co.
    Gryptite 40, by Trey Corp.

By stratifying the specification information in this manner, priority of interpretation is made explicit. Flexibility also is given to a master specification since by adding "or approved equal" or by dropping the sources entirely, the text is quickly edited to the differing requirements of various government clients.

Not all text need combine the three specifying methods. For hot-rolled miscellaneous steel angle fabrications, the following is sufficient:

2.1 STEEL
A. Standard: ASTM A36.

Other Approaches. No major product reaches the project site directly as a result of being specified. There is always review before final approval. Whether the descriptive, the reference or the proprietary method is used, or all three, the specification is but the first step. The second—review and approval—can influence the selection process if one of the following approaches is employed:

—*Prebid substitution or approval.* If the bidding requirements are set up to accept pre-bid review of products, the range of products that may later be furnished can be controlled. To do this, ample bid preparation time must be allowed, the architect must review submittals promptly, and acceptable products should be listed by pre-bid addendum.

—*Post-bid substitution or approval.* The supplementary conditions may include a procedure for the post-bid review and approval of substitutions. This frequently is a disruptive and time-consuming process and may not be the best method of evaluating and approving substitute products.

—*Allowances.* A realistic allowance, well defined as to what is to be provided by its use, affords considerable latitude for deferred product selection by the architect. It is not cost efficient to use this method for large portions of the building budget since the existence of an allowance reduces market competition and defers decision in a time of escalating prices.

—*Performance written sections.* Applied to individual components of the building, this method may encourage the presenting of unimagined products to the architect for approval. The process can be expensive to the owner if the architect must make extensive studies or if testing or mockups are required. However, the owner, if fully briefed on the possible benefits of obtaining less expensive materials that will do the same job, may agree to the tradeoff in cost. It must be spelled out who is paying for what. For the fully competent—and the brave—this approach holds happy possibilities. It deserves serious attention.

MULTICONTRACT SPECIFYING. The traditional specification is frequently written for a single construction contract. When multiple prime contracts, bid at the same time, are used, division of the work must be clearly spelled out. This approach may require a different configuration of the project manual as compared with that required for a single contract.

The advent of fast-track contracts, two-step procurement procedures and design-build approaches may require radical surgery on the method of handling the project manual. The introduction of construction management and project administration often reflects these new directions in methods of project delivery. Organization of the specifications and the remainder of the project manual must be carefully studied in order to respond positively to requirements of these delivery methods.

ORGANIZATION

Just as the drawings require organization and packaging, all the remaining material comprising the bid package requires organization. The specifications form the bulk of this material.

PROJECT MANUAL. This is the book in one or more volumes which includes, as one of its parts, the specifications. The book is known as the project manual and usually incorporates the bidding requirements, the proposed owner-contractor agreement form, the conditions of the contract and its specifications, together with their accompanying forms, schedules, drawings list and even page-size drawings. The project manual concept divides the volume or volumes into two primary functional parts: bidding requirements and contract documents.

BIDDING REQUIREMENTS. Activities that take place prior to execution of the agreement are governed by bidding requirements. They do not become a part of the contract and are normally kept separate from the contract documents. Noncontractual information such as project summaries, bidding procedures, preliminary schedules and soils investigation reports may be included in the project manual but not as part of the contract documents identified in the owner-contractor agreement. Relevant portions of the bidding documents which are to be incorporated into the contract should be specifically referenced in the owner-contractor agreement at the time of execution of the contract.

CONTRACT DOCUMENTS. Everything that is needed to direct the construction of the project is collected in the contract documents. The contract documents part of the project manual incorporates, both by reference and physical inclusion, the agreement form, the conditions of the contract and the specifications. These should be bound in the project manual, with the separately bound drawings included by reference. Addenda, schedules, page-size details and sample forms may be

EXHIBIT 19-1. EXAMPLE OF ATTRIBUTES FOR PERFORMANCE SPECIFYING

Safety	Functional	Sensible	Practical

Life
   flammability
   smoke production
   toxicity
   radiation
   hazardousness
 	
Property
   fire endurance
   theft security
   vandalism security
   resistance to misuse
 	
Specific Code Restrictions
	Strength
	   static
	   dynamic
	   wind
	   seismic
	   thermal
	   internal
	Durability
	   impact resistance
	   moisture resistance
	   thermal resistance
	   corrosion resistance
	   chemical resistance
	   weather resistance
	   surface stability
	     (crack-, spall-, craze-,
	     blister-, delamination-,
	     chalk-, fade-resistance)
	   stain resistance
	   absorbency
	   cleanability
	   friability/frangibility
	   abrasion resistance
	   dimensional stability
	   cohesiveness
	   adhesiveness
	Transmission
	   conductivity
	   transparency
	   permeability
	     (to light, sound, heat, air,
	     radiation)
	Byproduct Emission
	   wastes
	   odors
	   dust
	   energy
	     (sound, light, heat, static
	     electricity, radiation,
	     vibration)
	Dynamic
	   force required to operate
	   speed of operation
	   cycle time
	   vibration
		Esthetic
		   arrangement
		   composition
		   texture
		   gloss
		   odor
		   color
		   uniformity
		
		Environmental
		   audibility
		   frequency reverberation
		   quality of illumination
		   color rendition
		   lack of glare, shadow,
		     reflection
		   air cleanness
		   air velocity, distribution
		   air temperature, moisture
		   touch
		
		Measurable
		   levelness
		   plumbness
		   dimensions
		   volume
		   flatness
		   shape
		   weight
		
		Physical
		   hardness
		   ductility
		   malleability
		   resilience
		   elasticity
		   reflectance
		   toughness
		   brittleness
		   density
		   viscosity
		   creep
		   coefficient of friction
		   coefficient of expansion
			Cost
			   initial
			   operation
			   maintenance
			   salvage value
			   replacement
			   depreciation
			
			Interface
			   fit
			   attachment
			   tolerances
			   modularity
			   relocatability
			   rotatability
			   sequence of erection
			
			Service
			   repairability
			   interchangeability
			   accessibility
			   replaceability
			   disturbance to other systems
			     and occupants
			   future extendability
			   modifiable in place
			   adaptability at interface with
			     other components
			   replacement sequence
			   frequency of service
			
			Source
			   multiple source
			   guaranteed source
			   stability of producers
			   dependability of energy
			     source
			
			Personnel
			   availability of maintenance
			     and repair personnel
			     and facilities
			   required education,
			     trainability of
			     maintenance and repair
			     personnel
			   labor restrictions

Notes

An outline of the Attributes that will most frequently be cited by the specifier in developing performance requirements.

Depending on the subject, some will drop out unused; others will have to be added. Note that many levels of scope exist side by side: some Attributes are very broad, some are very fundamental or detailed. Some Attributes are indeed subsumed under other Attributes on the list, as, 'hardness' will generally be one sub-attribute of 'vandalism security.' This is in recognition of the fact that various building components will require specification in greater or less detail, depending on the function of each and the magnitude of the assembly in which it is to be procured.

A checklist of attributes is desirable when preparing performance specifications.
The specifier should not omit any needed attribute, no matter how obvious, for a fully satisfying result.

Source: *CSI Manual of Practice*, Vol. 2, 1975.

EXHIBIT 19-2. EXAMPLE OF SPECIFYING BY ATTRIBUTES

REQUIREMENT (from List of Attributes)

Chemical Resistance

CRITERIA

.1   Weight loss: Not more than 1% after immersion in dilute hydrochloric acid.
.2   Surface condition: No discoloration, chalking, blistering or crazing after sodium hydroxide watch glass test.
.3   Staining: No stains or color change after application of bleach and vinegar.

TEST METHODS

.1   Immerse item for 30 minutes in 0.1N HCI at 20°K.
     Rinse, air dry and weigh.
.2   Apply 1ml of 1.0N NaOH to surface for 24 hours, with watch glass sealed in place over test area.
     Keep at 20°K.
     Rinse, air dry, examine visually at 400 mm under 750-800 lumens/sq. meter illumination.
.3   ASTM D 2299, using food-store grade sodium hypochlorite bleach and cider vinegar.

EVALAUTION

A slight loss of gloss in either test 1. or test 2. above, but not both, will not be cause for rejecting the item.
In Laboratory areas the Architect/Engineer will compare the performance of this item as tested above against the cost of providing borosilicate glass items. The cost of providing the latter, in laboratory areas only, if judged necessary, will be entered in the weighted overall cost calculation at the conclusion of the Prototype Stage.

Source: *CSI Manual of Practice*, Vol. 2, 1975.

bound in or referenced. If AIA standard documents are to be used, all should be the latest edition; modifications should be coordinated with other documents, including the owner-architect agreement.

CONDITIONS OF THE CONTRACT. The owner-contractor agreement form should incorporate, by specific reference, all of the contract documents. The conditions of the contract (general and supplementary) spell out the basic relationship between the owner and the contractor. The architect's status is also defined.

The general conditions, typically the time-tested AIA Document A201, form the core of the conditions of the contract. These are modified or added to by supplementary conditions and, in some government work, by equal employment regulations and prescribed wage rates.

DIVISION 1. As the 16-division format for specifications has gained acceptance in the decade following its introduction in 1963, Division 1 (general requirements) has become a useful vehicle for numerous administrative and work-related subjects. Because these provisions must be highly detailed to answer the needs of today's building process, they have long been too cumbersome to include fully in the conditions of the contract. Also, portions change from project to project, which would make these specific requirements, if they were included in the general conditions, highly subject to change.

The 1976 edition of AIA Document A201 establishes only the basic contractual responsibilities for such procedural, administrative and technical work-related subjects. Details and specific procedures related to these subjects are covered by the specifier in the Division 1 text. This change from former editions of A201 reduces the need to write supplementary conditions on these matters before preparing Division 1.

SECTIONS. An advantage of the method described thus far is that each section of the specifications may then be cross-referenced to the general requirements of Division 1, reducing space devoted to repetitious prescriptions for submittals, testing, work temperatures, protection, cleanup and records.

The sections, organized in broad categories called divisions, are designed to reduce the text to discrete topics, one or more of which may be the basis of a bid by each trade or specialty, frequently by subcontractors. The scope of sections permits the specifier to write and reuse the text in easily manipulated building-block units. Ideally, the sections are set up in such a way that subcontractors can bid and execute integral units of work, without the need to divide or share the work of a section.

SCHEDULES AND DETAIL DRAWINGS. Because door and finish schedules fall somewhere between drawings and specifications, both tabulations are often found in the project manual on larger projects, where hundreds of door openings and spaces make extensive hand lettering on the drawings inefficient.

Some detail drawings, because they are repetitive or because they are more easily handled on page-size format, have found their way into project manuals in recent years.

The traditional division of information

between drawings and specifications must occasionally yield, however, to the dictates of efficient production. Fortunately, the project manual concept provides an alternative framework for assembly of schedules and drawings within the volumes. Page-size drawings and schedules sprinkled throughout the project manual can be a production problem, but when organized separately—in a separate volume, for instance—efficiency can be gained.

More and more schedules are needed in today's projects. To the traditional door, finish, hardware, paint, food service equipment, plumbing fixture and light fixture schedules, many building projects require schedules of cabinets, sealants, glass types, shelving, toilet accessories, elevators, medical equipment, pipe color codes, piping types, etc.

In alteration work, there is a tendency to strip the specifications to generalities, while specification-like notes at the many variant conditions on the drawings multiply.

The traditional general rule for division of information remains: Draw or schedule what is best drawn or tabulated; specify what is most easily described in words and figures. Be flexible but consistent within a project. Judicious use of text on the drawings, and use of drawings within the project manual, can ease a sticky problem of how to say it in complex work.

SCOPE PARAGRAPHS. "The work of this section includes . . . ," commonly known as a scope paragraph, is unnecessary and dangerous. The main reasons are:

—Something may be inadvertently omitted by the specifier.

—The drawings indicate quantities and extent of work.

—Division of work among subcontractors and labor groups may be thereby complicated.

—The contractor's customary job of as-

signing, coordinating and ultimately bearing the responsibility for all work may be undercut.

Though the practice of starting specification sections with scope paragraphs has tended to disappear among prudent practitioners, two practices similar to scope writing have gained acceptance.

The first is use of the title "Related Work Specified Elsewhere." This is simply a short list of items, purposely not all-inclusive, that may be sought or overlooked by the user of the specifications. Use of this title is a help in organizing the specification sections. The list of related work need not be exhaustive. It need only assist the user in locating specifications for elusive items such as loose lintels, lock cylinders, sealants and elevator hoist beams. Some specifiers claim it aids in organizing their work and in keeping track of checklist items.

The second, "Extent Notes," or a similar heading, may be needed in the specifying of certain products, particularly some coatings which cannot be adequately shown on the drawings or scheduled. The waterproofing of pits and retaining walls, the painting of pipes and ducts, the finishing of the insides of cabinets, and the tiling of floors under casework may be most efficiently described in extent notes.

OTHER EXPRESSIONS OF SCOPE. The schedules within the project manual deal in quantities, scope and location of work, the functions normally left to the drawings. Schedules also imply completeness. For this reason, it is therefore wise to specify what is to be provided in cases not covered by the schedule. Since the use of schedules in the project manual is likely to increase, some safety provisions are well kept in mind.

Short schedules are made universal by use of the "residual legatee" technique: "Concrete in footings shall be 2500 psi, in columns 4000 psi; *all other concrete shall be 3000 psi.*"

Where examples must be given for clarity, the "general statement + such as" approach will hold arguments to a minimum: "Provide 0.015 in. stainless steel throughout, except at freestanding work, *such as gutters and downspouts*," stands as an example, not an expression of extent. "Freestanding" is hard to define, but at least the "such as" construction does not limit the definition.

WRITING PRINCIPLES

The individual who writes specifications must follow specification-writing principles, be aware of legal considerations, and be consistent, fair, grammatical, natural and fully in touch with reality. The specifier who is all of these things will produce the desired results—a clear communication of design intent that can be enforced. Put in terms of a formula:

Specifying = Information + Control

FOLLOW PRINCIPLES. The contract is first and foremost, and the contractor carries it out. This is the basic principle. There is no need to say "The Contractor shall do this and that"; the simple imperative "Do this" and "Do that" is sufficient. All instructions should be addressed to the contractor. Other principles to be followed are the leaving of quantity and location to the drawings, spelling out precisely what is to be guaranteed, and giving each instruction once, without overlap or repetition.

BE AWARE OF LEGAL CONSIDERATIONS. The specifier must be cognizant of liability implications and the proper division of responsibility. The contractor cannot be made responsible for design, code violations inherent in the design, undersized members or dimensional errors on the drawings. Likewise, the architect should not be put in a position of making detailed inspections, certifying workmanship or enforcing safety.

EXHIBIT 19-3. EXCERPT FROM A PERFORMANCE SPECIFICATION

9. PLUMBING

a. Location: All plumbing shall be concealed except valve controls and water spouts. Cleanouts and control stop valves shall be concealed but readily accessible and oriented for convenience of use. Each fitting shall have an accessible set of simple connections to the plumbing for ease of replacement. Plumbing runs shall be coordinated with all other services, such as HVC and electricity, to preclude mutual interference. Branch plumbing layout shall facilitate back-to-back configurations and stacked bathrooms of different plan options. Assume that plumbing chases will always be vertically stacked, although the bathrooms themselves may not necessarily be stacked.

b. Pressure and Temperature Control: Supply and install all pressure and temperature control devices necessary to maintain criteria defined by these specifications, or required by governing regulations. The simultaneous operation of all valves on a branch line, including flush valves at peak flow shall not reduce pressure on that line by more than 10%.

c. Noise and Vibration Control: Plumbing arrangement, attachments, and devices shall provide positive control of water hammer, valve chatter, and other sources of noise and vibration in the water supply system. The hot water branch line and the cold water branch line shall each have a water hammer arrestor tested and certified in accordance with PDI-WH 201. Normal and unavoidable noises generated in the supply, drainage, and vent systems shall be isolated within plumbing walls and chases. Sound transmitted from room to room via the plumbing system shall not exceed that permitted by the Partitions and Structure-Ceiling: STC 40. See Article F.14.

d. Special Devices, Materials, and Methods: The University may consider the possibility of using certain plumbing devices, materials, and methods not currently in general use in this country, including items not explicitly permitted by the governing regulations. Suggestions from manufacturers and contractors concerning such concepts will be welcome. The criterion for selecting items for study will be their potential for meeting the performance specifications more conveniently, efficiently, or economically than would be possible by conventional means, without jeopardizing health or safety. Suggestions shall be submitted not later than the Preliminary Design Proposal.

10. TOLERANCES

a. Joint and connection details and assembly procedures shall allow for variations in floor and ceiling elevations. The vertical construction tolerance from floor to ceiling dimensions is plus or minus 1/2 inch from datum. The maximum slope will be less than 1/8 inch in 10 feet for floors, 1/4 inch in 10 feet for ceilings.

b. The vertical live load deflection tolerance for floor and ceiling elevation is plus 0, minus 3/8 inch from datum.

c. If smaller tolerances are required for a particular bathroom design, the design will be considered coordinated only with Structure-Ceilings capable of meeting such tolerances.

d. The tolerance for surface irregularities, including such characteristics as warp, camber, and oilcanning, shall be plus or minus 1/16 inch with a maximum slope of 0.1%. This restriction does not apply to details of surface textures which are part of the bathroom design.

e. The tolerance for the straightness of all joints and exposed edges is a maximum slope of 0.1%.

f. The Tolerance for the space between parallel lines or edges is plus or minus 5% of the space.

g. The minimum cove radius shall be 1/8 inch, unless otherwise specified.

11. SURFACE CRITERIA

a. Inspection

(1) All plumbing fixtures shall pass the inspection described in Article 17. For the purposes of this test, the floor shall be considered a fixture, with the overflow line at the top of the room threshold. All other exposed surfaces of all bathroom elements shall be inspected in the same manner, and shall exhibit the same degree of freedom from imperfections as the fixtures above their overflow lines.

(2) All surfaces shall pass reinspection after certain tests, as noted in the descriptions of those tests.

b. Abrasion

(1) All plumbing fixtures, and the floor, shall pass the abrasion test described in Article 18.

(2) Wall, ceiling, and cabinet specimens shall show no change in gloss as measured by a Gardner 60-degree Glossmeter after 250 cycles of dry rub on a Gardner Model 105 Straight Line Washability and Abrasion Machine using a cheesecloth over a felt pad.

c. Washability

(1) The Bathroom Component Category shall be designed with special attention paid to ease of maintenance. Designs submitted by bidders shall be evaluated by the University in part on a judgment of the degree of ease with which the bathroom can be cleaned.

(2) The configuration of all elements and assemblies shall allow inspection and easy reach, with standard residential cleaning equipment, of all functional surfaces, from safe and reasonably comfortable postures. Cracks, crevices, small concavities and hidden surfaces capable of collecting dirt and moisture will not be permitted.

(3) All specimens from plumbing fixtures and floor subjected to the abrasion test described in Article 18 shall subsequently pass the washability test described in Article 19.

(4) Wall, ceiling, and cabinet surface specimens shall show no softening, color change, or more than slight abrading of the surface after 100,000 brush strokes while continuously wetted by a 5% solution of trisodium phosphate in a Gardner Model 5 Straight Line Washability and Abrasion Machine. This test shall be performed over joints between surface materials.

BATHROOMS

Source: University Residential Building Systems (URBS), University of California, 1967.

BE CONSISTENT. Write submittal, test and guarantee requirements according to a pattern regardless of where they appear in the project manual. Do not rephrase general conditions and Division 1 provisions within the text of the sections. Use standard terminology. Use a commonly accepted format. Address the contractor only. Work out procedures as to what goes on the drawings and what in the specifications.

BE FAIR. Avoid murder clauses, grandfather clauses and requirements that are not meant to be enforced. Don't specify performance and then say how to build it. If several sources of a product are acceptable, set a level of quality and write to that common denominator, not the peculiarities of one manufacturer. Do not specify one task in two places in hope of assuring that it will be done.

BE GRAMMATICAL. Use correct language, being careful of pronoun references, commas and the difference between "and" and "or." If "as required" is to be enforced, state the requirements. "Any" is a troublemaker; "all" is usually superfluous. Avoid complex, convoluted sentence structure. Avoid structuring sentences which depend on punctuation marks (so easily lost) for their meaning.

BE NATURAL. Legalese is lost on the reader. Verbosity, obscure words and inflated language interfere with communication. Say what is meant, and say it once. Any sentence requiring underlining or an exclamation mark is poorly composed and should be rewritten.

KEEP IN TOUCH WITH REALITY. Remember the economic implication of every choice made. Is the most expensive what is needed? Is it really necessary to modify a production item? Be aware of the structure of the building trades without being tyrannized by it,

and organize the text broadly along the lines of who normally sets a roof drain or who flashes a vent. What is available? What is subject to long delivery, price fluctuations, strikes and lack of craftsman installers? Where a product is not locally known, give a manufacturer's address and telephone number. What can go wrong with the product? Has each eventuality been covered? What accessories must be specified? Are tolerances realistic? Is the sequence of erection possible?

PROCESS STANDARDS

The principal generally accepted standards used in the process of preparing specifications are those relating to formats and terminology.

The contract documents are defined in AIA Document A201 (subparagraph 1.1.1), but the specific identification of all documents bound in the project manual, and the drawings bound separately, should be made in the owner-contractor agreement in explicit detail. No contract documents should be referenced or identified without being physically incorporated in the drawings or project manual.

FORMATS. The project manual concept provides the overall organization. The specifications, which are organized mainly by product or function, usually follow the arrangement of the *Uniform Construction Index* (UCI). The UCI's specifications format, listing types of products and likely units of work along the lines of the Construction Specifications Institute (CSI) 16-division format, is agreed on by all of the major architectural, engineering and construction bodies in the U.S.

The CSI has, over the years, developed and gained a large measure of acceptance of formats that deal with the detailed aspects of organization of specifications. By dividing the typical specification section into three parts—general, products and execution—administrative and pro-

cedural requirements are first listed, followed by the identification and fabrication of materials, and then the work to be performed on site. Typical article headings under each of the three parts are suggested to guide the specifier. Though by no means mandatory, many specifiers find the article titles such as description, quality assurance, submittals and job conditions a helpful device.

To serve as a benchmark in reducing the widely variant page layouts found in specifications, CSI now publishes a suggested page format for typists.

Most unrevolutionary in nature, the three-part section and page formats for specifications seem familiar to those who investigate them. They are indeed drawn from common practice.

Standardized formats for presenting information on building products have been used for years in CSI's Spec-Data program and more recently in the Sweet's GuideLines program. Product data arranged according to these formats aids the specifier in selecting materials to be included in the specifications.

TERMINOLOGY. The need for uniform symbols and abbreviations is being pursued independently by AIA and CSI committees. The effort is overdue. American National Standards Institute (ANSI) Z32.13 and Z10.1 provide little or no guidance to the architect in abbreviating words. Likewise, the symbols put forth in ANSI Z32.2.2, Z32.2.3, Z32.2.5 and Y32.9 are for mechanical and electrical work only, and are not in accord with many conventions in use in building construction. The work of the AIA committee is discussed in an article titled "A Uniform System for Working Drawings" in the January 1974 *AIA Journal*.

The most convenient source for uniform generic names of building products is the UCI. Though it is not detailed enough to standardize terminology for minor products such as joint filler (also called "backer rod" or "sponge rope"), the UCI has helped settle many office arguments by moving toward "gypsum wallboard" and "asbestos-cement," for instance. Not being a dictionary, it does nothing to define or differentiate such terms as "sealant" and "calking" or "acoustical panel."

APPLICATION STANDARDS

Several standards exist to aid the specifier in particular applications. These include those related to products and their tests and to fire safety.

PRODUCTS AND TEST STANDARDS. The prime source of solidly researched standards is the American Society for Testing and Materials (ASTM). Though a few ASTM standards have been set too low for quality construction, by and large they form the floor which each architect places under product quality. The way ASTM standards are published and updated does not subject the user to much fear of error or omission. As with most standards, the specifier must check to see that the desired type or class of material within the overall ASTM standard is correctly identified. It should be stated in the specifications that the latest edition current at the time of project bidding governs the work of the project, unless the specifier has taken care to affix the desired edition date to each ASTM reference. The specifier should make a point of knowing what is in the latest edition.

The American National Standards Institute (ANSI—formerly USASI and ASA) serves as a national collection point for ASTM and other standards. Some standards, such as those for elevators, steel doors, metal windows, plastering, gypsum wallboard installation, limestone and marble, are not easily purchased except through ANSI. Since ASTM standards are not promulgated by ANSI until at least a year after issue by ASTM, the specifier

EXHIBIT 19-4. COMPARISON OF APPROACHES TO SPECIFYING

> Initial Weather Resistance: It is required that the roofing and associated work be durable in normal weather exposure and not leak water during heavy rain storms. After completion of the roofing and associated work, and either during or immediately after a rain storm, (and before final acceptance of the work) the Installer shall meet with the Contractor at the project and inspect the building for evidence of leaks in the roofing and associated work. Prepare a written report without delay (by Contractor), covering the inspection, and submit to Owner (with copy to Architect).

PERFORMANCE SPECIFYING: Statement of performance requirements (without test methods and evaluation).

> Asphalt Quality (All Types): Provide only virgin residual petroleum-process asphalt, which has not been modified by the addition of softening oils or other compounds to modify the softening point, and which has been accurately air-blown (oxidized) to establish the required softening point.
>
> BUR Surfacing Aggregate:
>
> Slag: Crushed, air-cooled, blast furnace slag, complying with ASTM D 1863.
>
> Gravel: Clean, hard, durable, water-worn gravel of 3/8" nominal size (not more than 5% retained on 5/8" sieve, nor more than 5% passing #8 sieve), nominally dry at time of use.
>
>   Comply with ASTM D 1863.

PRESCRIPTIVE SPECIFYING: Generic Descriptive.

> Asphalt BUR on Nailable Substrates: Provide manufacturer's standard roofing and composition flashing, one of the following:
>
>   W-BB-3-15R or W-AB-2-15A; Bird & Son, Inc.
>   320-W or 420-W; Celotex Corp.
>   203-AN or 212-N; GAF Corp.
>   No. 800/900, or 600/3000; J-M Corp.

PRESCRIPTIVE SPECIFYING: Proprietary.

Source: *PSAE MASTERSPEC.*

will be more assured of being up to date if the ASTM designation is cited rather than its companion ANSI number.

Product Standards (PS) and the old Commercial Standards (CS) and Simplified Practice Recommendations (SPR) are the responsibility of the Department of Commerce's National Bureau of Standards (NBS). Most of the CS and SPR standards are undergoing revision for eventual reissue as Product Standards. Many are out of print in the meantime (see NBS 53, List of Publications, for titles which are available).

Federal Specifications (FS) are disseminated by GSA. Due to frequent revisions, it is necessary to subscribe to the monthly *Index of Federal Specifications and Standards* to keep abreast of the latest titles and revision numbers. With systematic effort, a file of these standards can be acquired and kept reasonably up to date. Since FS are rife with types and classes of materials under each heading, it is always advisable to have a specification in hand when citing it, as should be the case in all reference standards. FS SS-S-118a, "Acoustical Tiles and Panels, Prefabricated," lists no fewer than 9 types, 8 patterns, 3 classes and 26 grades. Though FS may seem troublesome and redundant in nonfederal work, they do form the only, or the critical, standard for some products, such as asphalt tile.

A good list of industry associations which publish meaningful standards can be found in Chapter 3 of the *Architect's Handbook of Professional Practice,* AIA Catalog No. M104. Some industrywide standards avoid setting levels of quality. Others have carefully detailed quality levels, with reasonable suggestions for their appropriate use. One test of the worth of an industry standard is to check the building code to see if the organization is recognized by the authorities. Also, a credible trade association will include a list of its member companies. The intent of a good standard is to establish

more than one level of quality or end use for its products, rather than to dive directly for the lowest common denominator or to present all products as suitable for all occasions.

FIRE SAFETY STANDARDS. ASTM and manufacturers have been jarred by the evidence of fire hazard presented by many products bearing ratings that seemed safe under the E84 surface burning test and the similar E119 and E162 tests. The public press, consumer advocates and government have made dependence on these tests uncomfortable. Many fire protection officials, engineers and architects have criticized the tests and the false security they engender.

ASTM has reacted sensibly by mounting a long-term study and review of tests and standards and, in the short term, by pulling back on the questionable aspects of E84. The short-term policy is easily summarized: Tests such as E84 should be recognized as laboratory tests. Their results under controlled conditions may not accurately predict performance in buildings, where placement of material, drafts and other factors may cause different performance in an actual fire. The controversy during the past half-dozen years over the unpredictable performance of cellular plastics (used primarily for insulation) remains unresolved. The problem has been highlighted by the failure of standard tests to disclose basic characteristics. Tests such as E84 should therefore be used with caution in areas of recognized unpredictability. Hopefully, new test methods will soon be developed and accepted to simulate actual fire performance in buildings more accurately.

Since ASTM recommends that laboratory type standards carry a warning (caveat) when they are cited to meet today's code requirements, it is this author's recommendation that a caution likewise be given in writing to the owner who insists on an unpredictable exposure of ma-

terials. The caveat should convey something to the effect that standards such as ASTM E84 should be used solely to measure and describe the comparative properties of materials in response to specific heat and flame under controlled laboratory conditions, and that they not be relied on for the description or appraisal of the fire hazard of materials, products or systems under actual fire conditions.

SOURCES

There are many sources from which the specifier may draw material for preparing specifications. The most comprehensive are master texts.

MASTER TEXTS. Though not new in concept, master specifications are being written and used more extensively. Several reasons for this can be cited:

—The drudgery and inefficiency of traditional specifying methods are no longer acceptable to highly skilled technical personnel nor to office managers.

—The professional's exposure to liability, which is frequently related directly to the skill with which a project is documented, has increased substantially, making accuracy and defensibility essential for contract documents.

—An explosion in new building products makes it necessary to systematize the decision-making procedure in order to optimize and coordinate the set of choices for each product.

—Nationally distributed building products, nationwide building procedures and widely accepted standards of format, language and documenting techniques call out for the devising of uniform specifications texts.

—The growth of automated text-handling systems provides an efficient means of storing and utilizing the text of a master.

—Manufacturers have wakened to the fact that, in addition to product data, there is a demand for ready-made specification text written around their products.

Cutting and pasting from former projects, though it has met deadlines in the past at some human expense, has not been a satisfactory way of maintaining quality and currentness. With the evolution of some specifiers toward the position of materials analyst, it has occurred to many offices that it is worth the investment to collect the best of previous experience, along with current information, into a master specification.

Various types of master specifications, written to include likely choices of materials, are in use in many architectural offices. They are also issued by many large building clients, especially government agencies with ongoing construction programs. In addition, there are commercial sources of master texts. One of these, MASTERSPEC, is produced by Production Systems for Architects & Engineers, Inc., and sponsored by the AIA to serve as a benchmark in accuracy and completeness and as a compendium of commonly accepted good practice. It is a national automated master specification system, with emphasis on content. MASTERSPEC may be used in many modes, manual or automated, with the content arranged in a format organized for project decision making, including editing reminders, product evaluation comments, drawing coordination notes and other instructions. The text is expanded and updated at frequent intervals.

TYPES OF MASTERS. The term "master specification" covers a number of types. To appreciate their range, some elementary distinctions must be made:

—A *full master* is made up of sections which describe each unit of work in detail. It attempts to offer the widest practicable choice among materials and methods of execution. A full master contains background technical information and specific editing notes.

EXHIBIT 19-5. COMPARISON OF MASTER AND GUIDE SPECIFICATIONS

NOTE: AS WITH ALL THE PRODUCTS OF THIS SECTION, DELETE ASTM COMPLIANCES FOR LOWEST COST, WHICH MAY THEN LEAD TO EXTENSIVE PRODUCT QUALITY VARIATIONS, AND THE POSSIBILITY OF UNUSUAL AND UNEXPECTED RESULTS IN THE ROOFING, INCLUDING EARLY FAILURE OR HIGH MAINTENANCE COSTS (CHECK REGIONAL PRACTICE STDS. BEFORE DELETING). SWITCH EACH PRODUCT COMPLIANCE TO A FEDERAL SPEC WHERE DESIRED OR REQUIRED BY OWNER.

No. 15 Coal-Tar Felt: Coal-tar pitch saturated organic fiber roofing felt, without perforations unless recommended by Installer for particular application, weighing approximately 13 lbs. per 100 sq. ft.

Comply with ASTM D 227, and label each roll to show compliance.

No. 15 Asphalt-Asbestos Felt: Asphalt saturated asbestos fiber roofing felt, without perforations unless recommended by Installer for particular application, weighing approximately 13 lbs. per 100 sq. ft.

Comply with ASTM D 250, and label each roll to show compliance.

Asphalt-Glass Fiber Mat: Asphalt impregnated mat of resin-bound glass fiber, weighing not less than an average of 7.5 lbs. per 100 sq. ft.

Comply with ASTM D 2178, and label each roll to show compliance.

MASTER SPECIFICATION: Inapplicable material is deleted.

3. *Felts:*

   a. Asphalt-Saturated Roofing Felt:—ASTM D 226-.... —......—.

   b. Asphalt-Saturated Asbestos Felt:—ASTM D 250-.... — ....—.

   c. Coal-Tar Saturated Roofing Felt:—ASTM D 227-.... — .....—.

   d. Base Sheet:..

   e. Cap Sheet: ....

   f. Prepared Roll Roofing:—ASTM .....—, — with .... inch

   salvage — ....

   g. ....

4. *Fabric:*

   a. ....

   b. ....

GUIDE SPECIFICATION: Applicable material is added.

—A *standard* or stock specification reduces the choices to a minimum, often to one selection. It is built for speed of editing. It offers few editing notes, if any, and, because it is written in more narrow-scope fashion, it tends to have less background technical information appended.

—*Abbreviated* specifications, sometimes called short-language or express or outline specifications, are terse versions of full or standard master specifications. By concentrating in specific sections on products rather than general or execution aspects, abbreviated specifications provide a short, to-the-point text which is particularly valuable in small projects, alteration work and owner-builder situations.

—*Guide* specifications are generally less comprehensive than full masters. They provide blanks for the filling in of limited choices. Additions are discouraged in guides, since guides are usually set up to steer the specifier through a limited range of products and methods. The notes appended to guides are more often warnings than general discussion.

—*Reference* specifications are based on a fixed text, which is referred to, with exceptions and additions noted in a separate project volume. Though once proposed as the style for architectural masters, the reference specification technique today is largely limited to highway construction and certain heavy engineering work.

All types of master specifications, unless issued by government bodies with limiting procurement regulations, use all of the classic means of specifying products: description of desired qualities, listing of standards, and citing of source using proprietary names. Also, in any master specification, appropriate parts can be written on a performance basis (result desired) rather than a prescriptive one (means required). Though some admixture of prescriptive requirements is essential in performance-based specifications, good performance masters hold prescriptive requirements to a minimum in such cases.

MASTER TEXT SOURCES. Among the principal sources of master texts are:

—*Producers.* Building product manufacturers produce standard specification sections in hope that they will be copied and used by architects. Some are technically competent and fair; some contain limiting language favoring the proprietary product.

—*Industry associations.* Similar to producer-originated text but admitting to more range and variety, association specification sections are often of high technical competence and fairness.

—*Technical studies.* The CSI Green Sheets are master technical outlines and monographs from which specifiers may develop their own project text or master text.

—*Commercial.* Frequently written by professional specification consultants, commercial texts vary in quality according to the size of the writing and updating budget. Some are one-shot efforts to sell books or automation services; some, like MASTERSPEC, maintain a permanent staff and a periodic update schedule.

—*Government.* These are usually in the form of guide specifications, although full masters and standards specifications are not uncommon. Government masters are not updated as systematically as would be desirable.

—*Owner or agency guides.* Like technical studies, these are not, strictly speaking, specifications. They are master compendiums of the owner's experience and preferences, from which the consulting architect constructs the project specification or modifies the standard text.

—*In-house.* Old dog-eared specs in many offices are cut and pasted in part or in their entirety to form an office standard. Or, by virtue of the items of practical experience they contribute, they flesh out master text acquired from other sources.

REFERENCE MATERIAL. Infrequently is a specification section freshly composed by the specifier. Caught up in the rush of contract documents production, project specifications traditionally rely more on cutting and pasting from previous office projects. For the experienced specifier in an office dealing in a limited range of repetitive building types, a shelf of well-worn project manuals and a good book copier are still an efficient basis for production. It should be emphasized that any specifier must have the experience and the time budget to do an assemble-and-edit job properly and must be able to discern changed conditions, to thoroughly update material, and to depart from old text in researching and writing new specifications.

Aside from text sources, much reference material is necessary in the job of specifying. The serious specifier builds a library which can be consulted for the many decisions which are needed in the writing or editing of both projects and master specifications. A minimal library will include ASTM standards, *CSI Manual of Practice* and Green Sheets, A Sweet's Architectural Catalog File and manufacturers' brochures for major products.

According to the needs of the specifier, the library will grow to include such items as a current set of Federal Specifications, Spec-Data sheets filed in notebooks, a drawer file of loose technical literature organized according to the UCI, old specifications from within and without the office, a bookcase full of manufacturers' literature in binders, bound reference texts and studies, a subscription microfilm reference system and an ample shelf for samples and swatches.

PRODUCTION

The tools used to produce the final specification text vary from simple manual ones to those involving varying degrees of automation.

MANUAL PROCESSES. A great number, perhaps a majority, of specifications still depend on manual typing. The office copier has done much to facilitate the task of the traditional specifier in assembling easily edited facsimile text, whether from old jobs, master texts or the office standard. With light editing, a neatly cut and pasted page can be given proper page headings and numbers. In some cases, it can be enhanced by skillful use of xerography to pass for freshly typed copy. These and other manual processes merge by small incremental improvements into what are virtually automated systems. Some specifiers have set up their favorite bits of text on typed cards for assembly into sections by copier.

Where a painstaking, reasonably fast, proofreading typist is available within the office for extended specifications typing efforts, there is little reason to change the system. But when other duties divide the typist's time, where the specifying professional becomes enmeshed in the details of formatting or proofreading, or when there are many missed deadlines, it pays to consider automation.

AUTOMATED PROCESSES. Automation has not taken the drudgery out of specifying, nor can it take over the specifying task completely. Yet, automation is on the increase every year. Architectural firms of all sizes have experimented with automatic typewriters. A small number, large in value of work designed, have used computers to aid in product selection, decision making and automatic text editing.

Automatic Typewriters. These store stock text on paper tape, magnetic tape, magnetic cards or magnetic discs. Automatic typing goes hand in hand with use of a master specification. In addition to text developed in-house or acquired from an outside source, then manually entered onto cards or tapes, it is possible to ob-

tain reference copy of master specifications ready for use.

Batch Computers. Some offices have small computers in-house, or have access to the computer in a neighboring firm or a nearby service bureau. If a batch-printing computer program can be loaded on such a computer, and if a properly formatted master text is developed, a fast, inexpensive printout of specifications can be obtained. Batch processing is par-

EXHIBIT 19-6.
PROJECT MANUAL CONCEPT

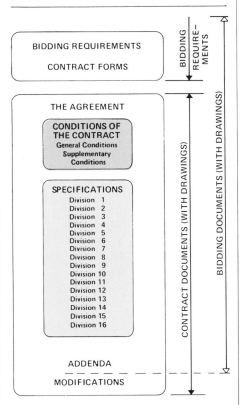

NOTE: Though they may be bound in the same volume, the bidding requirements are distinctly separated from the contract documents in following the organization of the project manual. All of the contract documents are bound or referenced in the project manual, which may be in one or more volumes.

Source: *The Construction Specifier,* April 1974.

ticularly efficient when a basic text is employed with little editing. If the master is organized to the point that stable edit copy is available, mail processing can be employed: The specifier marks up changes, keyboarding is done at the computer center, and the printout is returned by mail or courier. Turnaround times of four days to a week are common when batch processing is done by mail, one or two days when in-house processing is available. The batch mode of operation can be effective when good, tried-and-true master text is stored, when a limited number of building types is involved, and when the specifier can count on one-draft production. Second edits are a problem unless the system stores text as edited in earlier drafts for reworking.

Time-Shared Computers. Several companies offer specification processing systems which allow the typist to communicate with the computer, accessing stored documents, making corrections with immediate replay for proofreading, and transmitting messages and printout commands directly to the computer. These systems, termed "time-shared," "on-line" or "administrative terminal systems" (ATS), operate in the same way as batch mode systems when it is time to print. They offer the same high speed, faithful rendition and automatic laying out of the page. They can be commanded to hold a document in its edited form, ready for further changes, days or months later if needed.

Though in-house systems of the ATS variety are in common use within government, law, advertising and publishing offices, they are not always the answer for smaller architectural practices. Large offices with heavy production schedules, skilled specifiers and a good master specification can make efficient use of the systems in spite of added overhead cost in terminal and dedicated phone lines. For small offices, the ATS type systems may be better utilized as outside services, taking advantage of someone else's ability to serve as batch processor of edited master copy. A number of service bureaus are available to offices of every size in many locations.

The evolution of specifications work into a highly specialized discipline within architectural practice is not without its effect on the architects who do the work.

With a larger share of design commissions being executed by medium and large offices, a full-time specifier is now often found on the typical office staff. With products multiplying, with correctness essential, and with the need to systematize the learning from past mistakes, the full-time specifier has become a specialist. The small office lacking a skilled person, and even the large office with a production problem, frequently engages an independent specifications consultant, of which there is now at least one in most large urban areas.

Accreditation of specifiers to standards of training and competence is under study by CSI and is already a fact in the Canadian design professions, with pressure from the government bodies to see that the reviewers of specifications are also qualified. Just as various U.S. medical specialty boards identify practitioners with demonstrated competence, the Canadian architectural and engineering professions jointly accredit specifiers on the basis of experience and examination.

The education of tomorrow's specifiers, as well as the continuing education of those now in practice, is receiving increased attention from schools of architecture. The popularity of master specifications has in no way diminished the need for competent specifiers. If anything, the editing of a master requires heightened technical competence and judgment if the neatly packaged information and wealth of choices are not to lead the unwary astray.

Another direction in which specifying is moving in a few offices is its integration with such disciplines as construction cost control and value analysis. Clearly, education to a broader range of skills is needed if the professional is to see the larger problems of construction economics, information and control. The most productive advances in specifications are concerned with these areas and with logical techniques of organization as applied to the various steps of the design process.

EXHIBIT 19-7. PROJECT MANUAL ORGANIZATION

INTRODUCTORY PAGES
Cover Page
Title Page
Certifications and Seals Page
Signature Page
Table of Contents Page

BIDDING REQUIREMENTS
Instructions to Bidders
Information Available to Bidders
—Preliminary Construction Schedule
Preliminary Network
Preliminary Phasing Network
—Soils Investigation Data
Owner's Disclaimer
Soil Boring Data
Soil Consultant's Report
—Existing Conditions
Description of Existing Site
Description of Existing Buildings
Forms for Bidding
—Bid Form
—Bid Bond Form
—Subcontractor Listing
—Voluntary Substitution Listing
—Noncollusion Affidavit

CONTRACT DOCUMENTS
Contract Forms, Bonds and Certificates
—Agreement Forms
—Performance Bond
—Labor and Material Payment Bond
—Certification of Compliance with Applicable Laws and Regulations
—Certificates of Insurance
—Payment Forms
Application for Payment
Affidavit of Subcontractor Payment

Conditions of the Contract
—General Conditions
—Supplementary Conditions
Modifications to General Conditions
Additional Articles
Certification of Equal Employment Opportunity
Certification of Wage Rates
Certification of Nonsegregated Facilities
Specific Project Requirements
Drawings Index
—Drawings
—Schedules and Tables
—Standard Details
Addenda and Modifications
Specifications
Division 1—General Requirements
Division 2—Site Work
Division 3—Concrete
Division 4—Masonry
Division 5—Metals
Division 6—Wood & Plastics
Division 7—Thermal & Moisture Protection
Division 8—Doors & Windows
Division 9—Finishes
Division 10—Specialties
Division 11—Equipment
Division 12—Furnishings
Division 13—Special Construction
Division 14—Conveying Systems
Division 15—Mechanical
Division 16—Electrical

Source: Adapted from *CSI Manual of Practice*, Vol. 1, 1975.

BIBLIOGRAPHY

Architect's Handbook of Professional Practice. Washington, D.C.: AIA, parts updated periodically.

Current compendium of practice information; chapters on specifications and conditions of the contract especially pertinent; contains samples of all AIA documents.

Construction Dictionary. Phoenix: Phoenix Chapter, National Association of Women in Construction, 1973.

Deals with many troublesome terms current in construction.

Construction Materials and Processes. Donald A. Watson. New York: McGraw-Hill, 1972.

Covers data on basic materials and their use of interest to specifiers; typical of many good books on the subject.

Construction Specifications. Jack R. Lewis. Englewood Cliffs, N.J.: Prentice-Hall, 1975.

Inclusive why and how book.

Construction Specifications Handbook. Hans W. Meier. Englewood Cliffs, N.J.: Prentice-Hall, 1975.

Comprehensive textbook on specification writing, designed with an eye to office and classroom use; contains sample project manual.

Construction Specifications Writing: Principles and Procedures. Harold J. Rosen. New York: Wiley, 1974.

In-depth current treatment of the whys and hows of specifying.

CSI Manual of Practice. 2 vols. Washington, D.C.: Construction Specifications Institute, 1975, updated periodically.

Basic reference work for specifiers; covers formatting, techniques and presentation.

Dictionary of Architecture and Construction. Cyril M. Harris, ed. New York: McGraw-Hill, 1975.

Compilation of traditional and contemporary terms.

Handbook of Mechanical Specifications for Buildings and Plants. Robert H. Emerick. New York: McGraw-Hill, 1966.

Good supplement to specifier's library.

Manual of Built-up Roof Systems. C. W. Griffin Jr. Washington, D.C.: AIA, 1970.

Thorough and well-researched treatment of a technical subject; typical of many good technical books of interest to specifiers.

MASTERSPEC Reference Catalog. Washington, D.C.: Production Systems for Architects & Engineers, Inc., updated periodically.

Quarterly updating of sets in use included in service; nearly 400 sections of well-researched specification text, ready for editing into either office masters or text for specific projects (also stored on paper tape and computer for automated processing).

Principles of Specification Writing. Harold J. Rosen. New York: Reinhold, 1967.

A primary reference work for many years.

"Specifications Documents Series." Washington, D.C.: Construction Specifications Institute, updated periodically.

Basic reference work and guide specifications.

Specifications Writing for Architects and Engineers. Donald A. Watson. New York: McGraw-Hill, 1964.

An earlier reference volume for specifiers.

The Specifier and Building Science. Mervyn W. A. Jones, ed. Toronto: Construction Specifications Canada, 1974.

Good supplement to specifier's library.

Uniform Construction Index: A System of Formats for Specifications, Data Filing, Cost Analysis and Project Filing. Washington, D.C.: AIA, et al, 1972.

Framework on which North American construction materials and components are organized.

Chapter 20
Trends in
Architectural
Practice

ROBERT ALLAN CLASS, AIA

The face, form and character of the architectural profession are constantly changing. The profession's response to transforming influences requires a continuing and accurate evaluation of primary social, economic and other forces which affect everyone. It also demands a reaction to specific forces identified with the building process as well as effective utilization of and concern for physical, economic and human resources.

It has been observed by many in the business community that new opportunities are opened with every change, tending to more than offset those that are closed. Rather than succumbing to the "future shock" of overwhelming change, a period of economic slowdown and recovery is the perfect time for the architectural profession to prepare for anticipated evolutionary and revolutionary shifts in concepts, applications and vistas.

The trends examined in this closing chapter are neither predictions nor forecasts of the future of architectural practice, but rather they should be viewed as barometers of change on which to build new opportunities.

ORGANIZATION AND DELIVERY

Emerging methods of project delivery and their effects on the professional organization are having a major impact on architectural practice. Although the ability to respond to the increasingly complex demands of large and sophisticated corporate, institutional and governmental clients tends to favor the larger and frequently more sophisticated architectural organization, many clients continue to prefer the more personal relationship which is the hallmark of the smaller office.

Size is not a criterion of high-quality professional service; ability is. Some offices prefer to stay small and render only those services for which they are best equipped or which they favor. Others that plan to grow frequently organize to permit modular expansion with the least disruption, where staff may be increased as additional talents are needed or joint arrangements made with other organizations to provide further talents for total team expertise.

Some architects with the temerity to predict the future feel that offices of all sizes will probably continue to exist but with fewer small ones and more intermediate and larger ones. Regardless of size, all will be better organized and managed to answer the questioning attitudes of clients and the forces of the times.

Rapid and fluid changes in methods of project delivery are primarily concerned with cost and time. More clients are seeking a single source to coordinate their projects and balance the sometimes conflicting elements of quality, cost and time. Others want a single source to assume full responsibility for both design and construction or even financing and/or operation of the facility after construction.

To meet the needs of new approaches, services such as those of construction management and project administration are coming to the fore. The offerings of complete design/construction/operation packages by nontraditional teams are appearing in many forms. Government agencies are experimenting with delivery systems where the concepts and complexities go far beyond the traditional methods of project delivery.

The emergence of these new approaches affects the architectural profession and its concerns in areas such as ethics, liability exposure and professional competence. The architect's survival depends on a creative response and participatory leadership in these areas of changes in project delivery. Professional societies and many individual firms are continuing to examine these issues and to develop innovative solutions on a high-priority basis.

BUSINESS MANAGEMENT

The architect's ability to manage a business is another crucial aspect affecting practice. This subject was put in focus in a recent speech by Philip J. Meathe, FAIA. He said, "In every sense of the word, we are a profession, but we are also a business. Profit and loss determine our continuation in the arena, and we must become more businesslike and efficient. We must use all of the management tools that other businesses use, including automation of every possible operation, modern personnel policies, effective money management techniques, and knowledgeable sales and promotional methods. But more important than anything else, we will need a higher and higher capital investment in our profession. It is the only way to compensate for the squeeze between rising costs and relatively static fees."

He went on to say, "A cloud on the horizon is our increasing vulnerability to lawsuits based on claims of faulty professional services. We can't assume that clients will bear the cost of errors or omissions or delays or wrong decisions. It may well be the professional, instead. It is the professional's responsibility to provide first-class performance of services as the one sure way to stay out of that trouble."

This vulnerability to lawsuits is not restricted to the architectural and engineering professions. Other disciplines that similarly provide personal services, such as those of law and medicine, are experiencing the same problems. Premiums for professional liability insurance are increasing explosively to the point that some firms walking an economic tightrope can no longer survive, and availability of such insurance is tighter for some disciplines. Whether the concept of no-fault insurance to relieve this situation can ever become a reality remains to be seen.

Some wag has said that the way to avoid malpractice suits is to stop malpracticing. This is more truth than fiction. To avoid the pitfalls of inadvertent errors of omission and commission, alert architects are recognizing the need for substantially increased professional competence to cope with the greater complexities of practice. Although some architectural schools are gradually responding to the need for comprehensive instruction in business management and tight quality control, this is of little use to those already in practice. The AIA, through its professional practice and continuing education programs, is providing increasing management and production aids to the practitioner. Loss prevention programs of insurance carriers have similar objectives. And "classes for bosses," offering graduate business school courses, are gaining in popularity.

The professional business manager is now a rarity in architectural firms. As offices grow and become more specialized, the tendency is to employ a manager to look after the business aspects of the practice under the direction of a business-oriented principal. Smaller firms unable to engage the services of such a full-time person will require more business competence on the part of the principals.

Skill in developing new markets and interacting with clients is increasingly important to successful practice. In addition to the ability to cope with problems of liability exposure, the successful architect requires greater business orientation to add to design skills. This architect is inclined to master the special talents of the businessperson, including skill in fiscal planning and control, personnel management, quality control, legal problems, civic responsibilities and a host of others. Better capitalization to

survive financially is another growing consideration.

PROJECT MANAGEMENT

The generally accepted role of the architect is the design, documentation and administration of specific projects for clients. Management of these projects through their various phases from inception to completion is thus the architect's major responsibility. The central effort here is found in project management.

Some observers believe that there are major changes underway that are bringing the design and construction process closer together. An example is seen in accelerated and overlapping methods of project delivery, where the architect is becoming more deeply involved in basic construction decisions. The parallel tendency of marketplace forces pushing for integration of design and construction, with definite commitments to time and cost, seemingly portends a return to the concept of the master builder. Whatever the specific directions, a requisite is the architect's better understanding of the construction end of the business coupled with improved project management techniques creatively applied.

Control of design quality is a top-priority concern in project management. So is competent administration of budgets: energy budgets, construction cost budgets, internal time and cost budgets. With depletion of nonrenewable natural resources—especially energy— conservation and creative utilization of these resources is mandatory. The resulting constraints impact the statement of the design problem (the program), the design solution, the choice of materials and equipment, and the long-term costs of operating and using the facility.

The dearth of dependable and accurate construction cost data stated in terms most useful to the design professional, as well as training in proper use of the

data, has frequently hampered the architect's design decisions relative to the project budget. Even the ability to assess the cost impact of regulatory constraints has been difficult. The need is surfacing for good life cycle cost data and techniques to evaluate the impact of design decisions on the lifetime costs of a facility as well as on the initial costs. The effects of tax and economic laws on the potential return of a project must also be evaluated. It is in the best private interests of both client and architect, as well as in the public interest, that an effective construction cost control system be devised to make the wisest use of the nation's resources.

Emergence of more sophisticated facility programming techniques is all to the good. The better the program, the better the chance for a good design solution. Working with an interdisciplinary team and using such techniques as encounter-type programming, community interaction, user needs studies and feedback evaluation, new methods of problem stating combine art and science. Problem solving thus may become much more responsive to the real needs of the project. A problem well stated is half its solution, smoothing the way to more effective project management.

Not the least of the responsibilities of the project manager is the ability to control internal cost and time through techniques of budgeting and scheduling. Success in applying these techniques centers on the quality of the firm's financial management system. The movement toward automation of these systems enhances the project management function. But just looking at the cold, hard facts is not enough. The real key lies in good personnel relations: opportunities for professional development and advancement, a good benefits program, a flexible attitude on working hours, an understanding of employees' personal problems, and, above all, motivation and development of loyalty. After all, the architectural firm's principal asset is people, and proper handling of assets is a primary business principle.

MANAGEMENT AND PRODUCTION TOOLS

Rather than a threat, automation offers the hope of enhancement of the architectural process and relief from drudgery. This does not mean that the computer will take over and do away with the need for the architect—far from it. There are many ways to use the benefits of automation, and the computer is only one of the tools.

The architectural process uses both intuition and logic. The objective is to quantify the results of intuitive thinking and combine them in a logical pattern. Most architects are adept at this, and many have found ways to grow from manual approaches to various degrees of automated approaches for improved accuracy and efficiency.

A project's documentation phase is usually the most costly in personnel time but is also the one most susceptible to automated techniques. The task is mainly one of production of construction documents which detail earlier decisions on design, quality and cost. The documents are primarily drawings and specifications, with the drawings requiring the lion's share of working time. The search for means to improve the documentation process continues, with the goal of absolutely correct, clear and unambiguous documents.

A consistent glossary of terms and indicators can help both drawings and specifications. Production of the latter is aided by master texts, automatic typewriters and computer printouts, as well as by standardized formats and conditions of the contract. Should the concept of aggregated systems projects become popular or practical, full performance specifying could come into its own, together with required evaluation and test meth-ods. On the other hand, an upsurge of design-build projects would result in less precise specifications. And there are some indications of the possibility of allowing reasonable bidding alternatives on specified materials by prior approval during the bidding period of bidder-suggested substitutions, always the subject of debate between architects and contractors.

Drawing techniques such as composite drafting, photo-drafting and overlay drafting are gaining ground as a viable alternative to manual drafting. Use of multi-color process printing and other reproduction techniques is progressing but affects the way drawings are prepared. Standardized preprinted material symbols, abbreviations, schedule formats, etc., will improve the efficiency of the drawing process as will the use of typewritten textual material. But the major breakthroughs in documentation technology lie ahead. A very few use the computer for a complete graphic programming/design/documentation device. This approach may well be the forerunner of an integrated and interactive design communication system serving the programmer, designer, estimator, draftsperson, specifier, consultant, builder, subcontractor and supplier. Just now it's a dream.

As production techniques change, so will networking techniques. Development of a planning network simulates the human thinking process as a common sense and self-disciplined method of expressing planning sequence. Computerization is secondary to this basic process and may be useful for recalling relationships and details as the network is adjusted to suit changed conditions. Creative use of networking techniques can be of benefit to many aspects of practice.

Facsimile transmission holds promise for the architect. As networks and techniques are developed, instantaneous transmission of graphic information becomes a reality. The day may come when this process becomes a major asset, to the point where the geographic location of an architect's office may be of minor importance.

The use of computer technology as a management aid for architectural firms is common today, particularly for the management of internal cost and time. Frequent periodic readouts of project profitability and personnel utilization are tools for economic survival. As an automated financial management system is built up to handle more and more chores, its use becomes less expensive and more efficient than manual methods.

Mini-computers and micro-computers are evolving to perform similar tasks to those of their larger forerunners. With the advent of less expensive hardware, graphic systems should become more accessible to more architectural offices. On the other hand, design problems are becoming more complex faster than the computer is being developed to handle them. Through the programs of some architectural schools and other educational centers, new professionals are appearing to deal more intimately with challenges of designing and implementing computer-aided design application systems. Perhaps total information systems, permitting descriptions of projects and thorough evaluation of such implications as function and cost, will enable design professionals to work in an environment entirely supported by the computer without requiring the conventional design tools. This will require new techniques of structuring problems and a large variety of data bases for support.

The missing ingredient, not only in automated applications but in every facet of practice, is a comprehensive information system—a workable system to keep the profession from drowning in a flood of undigested information.

Trends affecting the future of architectural practice are often interrelated. Involvement in a design-build scheme, for example, may entail substantial differences in the balance between organizational structure, equity capitalization, financial risk, tax consequences, liability exposure, insurance coverage, ethics, staffing, design approaches, documentation methods and contract administration. Many of these considerations come into play in the architect's contact with construction management and accelerated and overlapping methods of project delivery. Energy shortages also have a domino effect.

Government intervention in methods of contracting for professional services may at first have seemed traumatic but, to the profession's credit, the response was innovative and an asset to both client and architect. One result is the movement toward cost-based compensation approaches to replace sometimes arbitrary standards. Services are better defined, professional compensation tends to be more equitable to both, the real costs are identified, the benefits of a good financial management system become more apparent, and the total result is greater business proficiency for the professional. Continuing government intervention in such areas as ethical standards and professional licensing can be met with equal creativity.

Efforts toward unionization of architectural employees have so far been confined to small pockets of unrest. So long as employers continue to recognize that the intellectual and creative capacities of trained professionals are more important than the mere productive capacity of warm bodies, there will be little need for union activity. Sensitivity to the precepts of good personnel relations is a must for a healthy practice.

The day of the 6B pencil and yellow bumwad will probably never end for most architects. These rather primitive tools have no equal for recording the first gleams of intuitive architectural creations. But they have no place beyond that point. Aside from changes engendered by external forces such as those of the marketplace and resource shortages, probably the most significant shifts lying ahead for architects involve the business and tools of architecture. Business acumen will be brought into balance with professional acumen. And a more businesslike approach will demand that stone-age tools be set aside for those space-age tools best adapted to the architectural process.

Index